Mary Sumner

Mission, Education and Motherhood

Thinking a Life with Bourdieu

Sue Anderson-Faithful

The Lutterworth Press

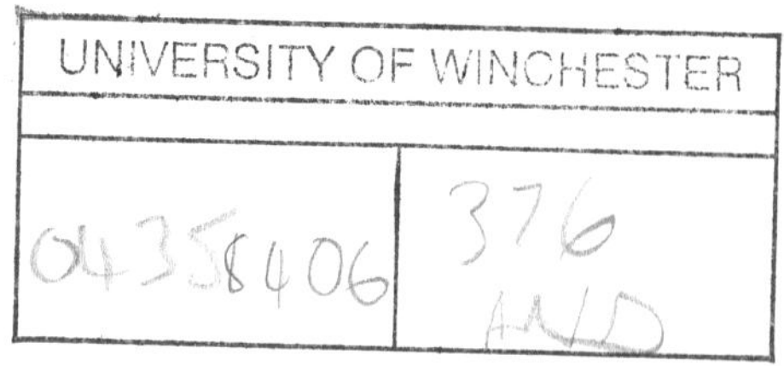

The Lutterworth Press
P.O. Box 60
Cambridge
CB1 2NT
United Kingdom

www.lutterworth.com
publishing@lutterworth.com

ISBN: 978 0 7188 9495 5

British Library Cataloguing in Publication Data
A record is available from the British Library

First Published, 2018

For my father Roy Newling Anderson
January 21st 1924-April 15th 2015

Profound thanks are offered to the members of the Centre for the History of Women's Education at the University of Winchester, a nurturing intellectual community without whom this book would never have been written. I am also very grateful to all the colleagues and friends who offered encouragement along the way. I would also like to offer thanks to the archivists and librarians of Lambeth Palace Library, The Church of England Record Centre, The Hampshire Record Office, The Armitt Library and the Maugham Library at King's College London.

Contents

Abbreviations *x*
Illustrations *xi*
Author's Note *xii*
Timeline *xiii*
Objects of the Mothers' Union *xix*

Introduction: Mary Sumner: Her Life and Work, Perspectives, Sources, Interpretations *1*

Chapter 1: Thinking Mary Sumner with Bourdieu: Habitus, Field, Capital, Pedagogic Authority, Symbolic Violence and Reproduction *12*

Part 1: Religion

Chapter 2: A Family Affair: Mary Sumner, Religious Habitus, Evangelical Enthusiasm and Anglican Advocacy *31*
2.1. Family life, living religion, capital assets and symbolic gifts
2.2 Anglican advocacy and contested authority in the field of religion
2.3 Synopsis: religious habitus and capital

Chapter 3: Anglican Motherhood for Church and Country: Mary Sumner, Religious Networks and the Mothers' Union *53*
3.1 Introduction
3.2 Mary Sumner's wider habitus, networking to establish the Mothers' Union
3.3 The Mothers' Union as an Anglican organisation: women in the Church, capital and field
3.4 The province of women: morality, motherhood, marriage, the symbolic capital of purity
3.5 The patriotic Mothers' Union: Church, state and claims to territory in the field of power
3.6 Synopsis: wider habitus, transactions of capital, entering the field

Part 2: Mission

Chapter 4: Home and Abroad: Mary Sumner and Traditions of Philanthropy, Evangelical Religion and Civilising Mission *89*
4.1 Introduction
4.2 Philanthropy and mission in family life; parochial philanthropy via organisations 1851 to 1886
4.3 Travels in the 'East': Mary Sumner in the 'contact zone', the habituated gaze, religious and cultural capital
4.4 Mary Sumner: habitus, wider network, and mission via the Girls' Friendly Society
4.5 Synopsis: capital assets and 'missionary' habitus

Chapter 5: Mary Sumner, Missionary Mothers and Imperial Aspirations *121*
5.1 Introduction
5.2 Mary Sumner: women's mission, the Mothers' Union, and the field of philanthropy
5.3 Mary Sumner and the Mothers' Union: missionary identities at home and overseas, missionary organisations, colonies and contact zones, and attitudes to indigenous members
5.4 Mary Sumner, the Mothers' Union, empire and the Church overseas
5.5 Synopsis: pedagogic authority and symbolic violence and field manoeuvres

Part 3: Education

Chapter 6: 'Education Begins at Home': Educational Habitus, Childhood and Childrearing *149*
6.1 Introduction
6.2 Mary Sumner's experience of childhood, educational capital, attitudes to women and education, educational activism in her kinship network.
6.3 Educational context, parochial work and initiatives relating to educational habitus and Mary Sumner's horizons of possibility
6.4 Mary Sumner's notions of childhood and child rearing
6.5 Synopsis: educational habitus and capital values

Chapter 7: Spreading the Word: Educating the Populace *173*
7.1 Mary Sumner, a popular educator
7.2 Leading by example: education in mothering for all classes

7.3 The power of reading: education through the Mothers' Union magazines
7.4 Education matters in the Mothers' Union: networking with other agents and resistance to secular education
7.5 Synopsis: Mary Sumner's manoeuvres in the field of education

Chapter 8: Mary Sumner: Agency and Constraint, Reproduction, Symbolic Violence and Changes in the Doxa *201*

Tables *214*
Table 1: Activists in the Mothers' Union and GFS
Table 2: Episcopal Contacts of George and Mary Sumner
Table 3: Wording of Mothers' Union Cards

Appendices
Appendix 1: Mary Sumner's Speech to the Portsmouth Church Congress *225*
Appendix 2: Biographical Notes on Women Activists *228*

Primary Sources *235*
Bibliography *239*
Index *251*

Abbreviations

BWEA – British Women's Emigration Society
CETS – Church of England Temperance Society
CEZMS – Church of England Zenana Mission Society
CMS – Church Mission Society
GFS – Girls' Friendly Society
LEA – Local Education Authority
MIC – *Mothers in Council*
MU – Mothers' Union
MUJ – *Mothers' Union Journal*
NUWW – National Union of Women Workers
PNEU – Parents' National Education Union
SACS – South African Colonisation Society
SPCK – Society for Promoting Christian Knowledge
SPG – Society for the Propagation of the Gospel

Illustrations

The Mothers' Union logo *xii*

Mary Sumner soon after her marriage c. 1848 *xx*

Mary Sumner, Margaret Lady Heywood, Heywood Sumner, 'Loulie' Louisa Gore Browne and George Sumner Golden Wedding, 1898 *30*

Old Alresford Rectory c. 1900 *30*

Original members of the MU being entertained at Upton House c. 1898 *86*

The title page of *Our Holiday in the East* by Mary Sumner *88*

The Honourable Ellen Joyce *120*

Mary Sumner with her daughter Louisa Gore Browne, Diocesan GFS president, and granddaughter Margaret Evans (with son Harold), GFS Diocesan President, 1911 *148*

Charlotte Yonge at Elderfield, 1898 *172*

Mary Sumner with a portrait of her husband George c. 1915 *200*

Author's Note

In the majority of instances I refer to Mary Sumner although there are occasions where, in the interests of euphony, only Mary is used. I also refer to the Mothers' Union in the introduction section, in titles, headings and at the start of paragraphs; thereafter MU is used.

The Mothers' Union logo

Timeline

1823 Charlotte Yonge born at Otterbourne House.

1824 George Henry Sumner born July 3rd.

1827 Charles Richard Sumner becomes Bishop of Winchester

1828 Mary Elizabeth Heywood born December 31st at Swinton, Manchester.

1833 Thomas Heywood moves to Hope End, Herefordshire. Publication of *Tracts for the Times.*

1839 First Custody of Infants Act allows divorced women of unblemished character the right to see their children.

1842 The Mines Act bans women and children from working underground.

1844 Charlotte Yonge publishes Abbey Church.

1846 Mary Heywood meets George Sumner in Rome.

1848 Mary marries George Sumner at Hope End July 26th.

1849 Mary and George move to Farnham Castle where George serves as his father's chaplain. Margaret Effie Sumner born. Laura Elizabeth Palmer (later Ridding) daughter of Roundell Palmer, first Earl of Selborne and Lady Laura Waldegrave born March 26th.

1850 Louisa Mary Alice Sumner born. Factory Act stipulates ten and a half hour days and no night work for women workers. Establishment of Roman Catholic hierarchy in England.

1851 George and Mary Sumner move to Old Alresford Rectory near Winchester.

1853 (George) Heywood Manoir Sumner born.

1854 Publication of figures from 1851 Census figures for religious worship show numerical challenge to Church of England represented by numbers of adherents to other denominations.

1857 Matrimonial Causes Act makes divorce possible without a private Act of Parliament and allows adultery as grounds for divorce to men but not women.

1866 Death of Thomas Heywood, Mrs Heywood moves to Old Alresford Rectory. Death of Tractarian John Keble, George Sumner attends the funeral. Dr George Ridding becomes Headmaster of Winchester College.

1869 Samuel Wilberforce translated to see of Winchester. Girton College become the first university college for women. The Endowed Schools Act provides funding for Grammar Schools for girls. Municipal Franchise Act allows unmarried women rate payers to vote in municipal elections.

1870 Death of Mrs Heywood. First Married Women's Property Act allows £200 of earnings to be retained by women. Elementary Education Act permits Women rate payers to vote and serve on new school boards.

1871 Louisa Mary Hubbard publishes *Anglican Deaconesses: Is There No Place for Women in the System?*

1872 Margaret Effie Sumner marries Arthur Percival Heywood. Girls Public Day School Trust established.

1873 Edward Harold Browne translated to see of Winchester.

1875 Mary Sumner is a 'Founding Associate' of the Girls' Friendly Society in Winchester. Starts parochial GFS Branch. The GFS becomes an officially sanctioned Anglican organisation.

1876 Parish mothers' meeting is distinguished by cards for mothers. This date is marked as the founding of the MU. Mary Sumner's sister Margaret converts to Roman Catholicism.

1882 Louisa Mary Alice Sumner marries Rev. Barrington Gore Browne.

1883 Heywood Sumner marries Agnes Benson.

1883-4 Mary Sumner's friend Mrs Augusta Maclagan starts a parish Mothers' Union in Lichfield.

1885 Mary Sumner speaks at the Portsmouth Church Conference on her vision of a religious society for mothers and canvasses support through correspondence. Winchester Diocese adopts MU as official organisation.

1887 Mary Sumner presides over the Winchester Diocesan Conference of the MU as President. First Diocesan Conference held in November. There are 57 MU branches, 11 of which are just starting.

1888-9 *The MUJ*, edited by Mrs. Jenkyns, is conceived as a newsletter from Mary Sumner. Circulation has risen to 46,000 by 1889. MU branches initiated in Ontario, Canada and Christchurch, NZ.

1890 Mary Sumner addresses a meeting to instigate the London Diocesan MU and continues correspondence and writing articles for *The MUJ*. Reads paper at Hull Church Conference. Lady Horatia Erskine and the Hon. Evelyn Hubbard start London Diocesan MU.

1891 Charlotte Yonge is asked to edit the new publication MIC for 'educated mothers'.

1892 Winchester Diocesan MU under the presidency of Mary Sumner considers central organisation. Conference of Diocesan Presidents to discuss centralisation in London. MU is organised in 28 dioceses in 1,550 branches with 60,000 members.

1895 Mary Sumner's collected addresses from *The MUJ* published as *Home Life*.

1896 Mary Sumner is Central President of the MU. First Central Council, meeting constitution adopted. Office space in Church House Westminster, London.

1897 Royal patronage begins. The 'Bracket Clause' exempts Scottish and New Zealand branches from the requirement for officials to be communicants of Anglican Church. Feast of the Annunciation March 25th adopted as Annual Day of Prayer and Thanksgiving.

1898 Mary Sumner continues as Central and Winchester Diocesan President. Charlotte Yonge and Mrs Jenkyns are made members of Central Council in recognition of their editorial work on MU journals.

1900 Annual Service in St Paul's Cathedral initiated.

1901 Death of Charlotte Yonge. George Sumner takes over as editor of *MIC* until 1908. Year of National Mourning for Queen Victoria.

1902 Empire substituted for England in Second Object in MU cards. MU protests against Parliamentary Bill to allow marriage to deceased wife's sister. Finance Committee instigated. Branches in China, Japan, Persia, Madagascar and other overseas locations.

1903 MU pledges to resist attacks on marriage.

1904-5 Mission of Help to South Africa following South African War.

1906 Literature Committee established.

1907 Religious education book scheme. A representative of Central Council tours Australia, New Zealand and Ceylon (Sri Lanka).

1908 Mary Sumner chairs, speaks at, and receives a standing ovation at the first MU Mass Meeting at Albert Hall addressed by her friends Archbishop Maclagan of York and Bishop Lang of Stepney. The Pan-Anglican Congress MU hosts reception for overseas delegate bishops and their wives. Mary Sumner insists on infant baptism and protests at alteration of card wording by Australian Baptists not in favour of this.

1909 Mary Sumner resigns as Central President; continues as Winchester Diocesan President. Diamond Wedding celebrations are marked by MU and royal patrons. Death of George Sumner. Mary writes for advice concerning an anti-divorce petition to Archbishop Lang of York. She signs letter of protest against legislative relaxation of grounds for divorce addressed to Lord Gorell as chairman of the Divorce Commission. MU supports a missionary worker in India, Miss Rix of the Society for the Propagation of the Gospel (SPG).

1910 Mary Sumner deemed Honorary President of the MU. Continues as Winchester Diocesan President. Corresponds with Lady Chichester the new MU Central President. Lady Horatia Erskine visits Mary Sumner to keep her in touch with the anti-divorce campaign. Evidence presented to Divorce Commission. Mrs Hubbard speaks for 'educated mothers' and Mrs Steinthal and Mrs Church present evidence against divorce representing working classes. MU becomes an Incorporated Society to legally protect the use of the name Mothers' Union. Support for 'Morality Bill' to increase the age of consent to 16.

1911 Corresponds with Mrs Maude Central Secretary of the MU and others on MU matters' Continues to write journal articles and pamphlets. Representatives sent to Central Councils of Women's Church Work and Parents' National Educational Union (PNEU). Literature Committee issues Coronation cards. George Sumner's memorial Buttress Fund started. Meeting to warn against dangers of Mormonism. Committee to oppose disestablishment of Welsh Church, Mrs Gell and Mrs Wilberforce preside.

1912 Mary Sumner yields to pressure to revise wording of membership cards. Laura Ridding initiates 'Watch Committee' 'to give information and to advise on desirable action with regard to legislative proposals in Parliament concerning matters affecting the welfare of the mothers of the nation.' MU invited to discussion of minority report of

Divorce commission. Scottish MU opts for affiliate status to avoid the requirement for official workers to be Anglican Communicants. Church Mission Society (CMS) worker Miss Davis supported in Southern India.

1913 Mary Sumner undertakes her Great Northern speaking tour to Newark, Sunderland, Durham and York where the annual MU conference is hosted by invitation of Mary Sumner's friend Archbishop Lang. MU resolution against birth control. The Bishops are asked for a ruling, but their response is indecisive.

1914 Launch of Workers Paper Magazine, as well as the Mothers' Union Religious Education Scheme

1915 Mary Sumner donates Winchester Cathedral Buttress Fund surplus to promote overseas work. First Official Handbook issued. MU joint conference on Religious Education with the Headmistresses' Association.

1916 Mary Sumner resigns as Winchester Diocesan President. MU sends patriotic message of sympathy to women of France. Fund established for building 'The Mary Sumner House'. Mrs Wilberforce becomes Central President.

1917 Mary Sumner attends opening of temporary Mary Sumner House opened by Princess Christian and the Bishop of London. Miss Lucy Soulsby attends the International Congress of the World's Purity Federation Kentucky, USA as MU representative. Mrs Russell Walker daughter of Mrs Wilberforce becomes Central Correspondent for Temperance Work. Marriage Defence Committee formed to oppose Matrimonial Causes Bill which made three years of separation grounds for divorce – this was withdrawn but issue remained topical. Mothers' Union in Australia launched.

1918 Inauguration of Naval Division of MU. Church of England Zenana Mission Society worker for Punjab Miss Gibson adopted. Evidence collected on declining birth rate.

1919 Queen and Princess Mary visit Mary Sumner House. MU anti-birth control resolution.

1920 Mass meeting at Albert Hall. 10,000 women sign anti-divorce petition. Conference of Overseas Workers – over 100 – many bishops' wives from Lambeth Conference at same time. 80 Overseas Dioceses, 800 branches, 10,000 members. Mrs Hubert Barclay elected as Central President.

1921 Death of Mary Sumner August 10th. Her funeral in Winchester Cathedral is attended by 4,000 mourners. Worldwide membership 391,409. Publication of *Mary Sumner: Her Life and Work and A Short History of the Mothers' Union.*

1925 Opening of purpose-built Mary Sumner House by Princess Mary, Archbishop of Canterbury and Bishop of Southwark. Guests of Honour include Princess Beatrice as well as Mary Sumner's daughter, Louisa Gore Browne.

1926 Jubilee pageant takes place June 21st at the Royal Albert Hall and a service is held in Westminster Abbey. 490,000 members worldwide. Publication of MU's history, *Fifty Years.*

Objects of the Mothers' Union 1896

I. To uphold the sanctity of marriage.

II. To awaken in mothers a sense of their great responsibility as mothers in the training of their boys and girls (the future fathers and mothers of England).

III. To organise in every place a band of mothers who will unite in prayer, and seek by their own example to lead their families in purity and holiness of life.

Mary Sumner soon after her marriage
c. 1848

Introduction
Mary Sumner: Her Life and Work, Perspectives, Sources, Interpretations

'What a wonderful life it has been!' exclaimed the Archbishop of Canterbury Dr Randall Davidson in his foreword to *Mary Sumner: Her Life and Work*. Published in 1921 as a combined edition with *A Short History of The Mothers' Union* shortly after Mary Sumner's death, the book served as a eulogy and memorial to the woman who, for over forty years, had personified the organisation that she founded. The Archbishop's congratulatory tone was understandable given that the Mothers' Union had at that point attracted a transnational membership of nearly four hundred thousand. The Mothers' Union commemorates its origin as 1876, the year in which Mary Sumner issued membership cards to attendees at her parish mothers' meeting. However, it was her extemporised speech at the 1885 Portsmouth Church Congress that was the catalyst for the adoption of the Mothers' Union as an official organisation by the Diocese of Winchester.[1] The biblical motto 'train up a child in the way he should go' encapsulated Mary Sumner's intention that the Mothers' Union should promote the role of mothers in the religious education of their children. By leading their families in 'purity and holiness of life', mothers would contribute to the improvement of national morality and hence redress social ills.[2]

The Mothers' Union followed the Girls' Friendly Society (GFS), established in 1875, as the second religious organisation to be established for women run by women to be sanctioned by the Church

1. Mary Porter, Mary Woodward, and Horatia Erskine, *Mary Sumner: Her Life and Work and a Short History of the Mothers' Union* (Winchester: Warren and Sons, 1921), 21-24.
2. Mary Sumner, *Home Life* (Winchester: Warren and Sons, 1895), 10. MU aims were expressed as 'Objects'. Object 2: 'To awaken in mothers a sense of their great responsibility as mothers in the training of their boys and girls (the future fathers and mothers of England).'

of England.[1] Drawing on traditions of class patronage and against a context of a proliferation of women's engagement in philanthropy, the Mothers' Union grew rapidly in numbers and geographical reach over the following decades. By 1892 membership had reached 60,000. In 1896 the Mothers' Union became centrally organised. Mary Sumner served as its Central President until 1909 and continued in office as Winchester Diocesan President until 1915.[2] She died in 1921, having lived to see the Mothers' Union become the dominant organisation for women in the Church. Her achievement merited an obituary in *The Times,* which reported that her funeral in Winchester Cathedral attracted 4,000 mourners.[3] The Mothers' Union today claims four million members drawn from eighty-three countries in the worldwide Anglican Communion. Mary Sumner's grave, which attracts visits from Mothers' Union members who find spiritual inspiration in her story, is behind the eastern end of the cathedral. She and her husband George, who served the diocese as Archdeacon and later Bishop of Guildford, are also commemorated by plaques on the cathedral buttresses and in Old Alresford Church.

Mary Sumner was the author of three full length books and a short volume, *To Mothers of the Higher Classes,* published in 1888. *Home Life* (1895) was a collection of material reprinted from journal articles concerned with promoting the Mothers' Union.[4] *Our Holiday in the East* (1881) and *George Henry Sumner, D.D., Bishop of Guildford* (1910) were respectively a travel diary and a memoir.[5] *Our Holiday* presents an account of an extended family tour of the Holy Land. The memoir, written when Mary was recently widowed, describes George's career as a clergyman and, although very much a eulogy, it gives attention to married life and the MU, and like other perspectival sources signals the possession of attributes considered by the author to be desirable.

---

1. Mary Heath-Stubbs, *Friendship's Highway; Being the History of the Girls' Friendly Society* (London: Girls' Friendly Society, 1926); Agnes Louisa Money, *History of the Girls' Friendly Society* (London: Wells Gardner, Darton, 1902).The GFS intended to protect the chastity of girls and young working women by educating them in Christian values and behaviour.
2. Porter, Woodward, and Erskine, *Mary Sumner.*
3. *The Times,* 'Obituary of Mary Sumner', *The Times,* August 12th, 1921.
4. Sumner, *Home Life.*
5. Mary Elizabeth Sumner, *Our Holiday in the East* (London: Hurst & Blackett, 1881); Mary Sumner, *Memoir of George Henry Sumner, D.D., Bishop of Guildford: Published for His Friends by Special Request* (Winchester: Warren and Son, 1910).

Mary Sumner was also the author of pamphlets, speeches and articles intended for publication in *The Mothers' Union Journal* and *Mothers in Council*. The absence of personal papers, which were destroyed on her death in 1921, leaves a gap in her archive. Despite some material relating to Mary Sumner in family memoirs, this means that remaining sources, including correspondence, largely represent documentation collected in the construction of official archives or materials produced with the intention of promoting the Mothers' Union. *Mary Sumner: Her Life and Work and a Short History of the Mothers' Union* (1921) and *Fifty Years* (1926) all fit into this category and valorise Mary Sumner as the 'foundress' of the society.[1] Early histories of the GFS such as *The Girls' Friendly Society*, first published in 1902, and *Friendship's Highway* (1926), which pertain to Mary Sumner in her network of philanthropic Anglican activists, were produced with a similar promotional agenda.[2] These perspectival sources illuminate the key messages that Mary Sumner and Mothers' Union officials wished to present in their preferred version of archive. Through drawing upon material produced by, or relating to, members of Mary Sumner's networks beyond official Mothers' Union sources, this book seeks to give contextual location to this material and to align the sources as representative (or not) of the social and religious category to which Mary Sumner belonged.[3]

A sympathetic narrative of Mary Sumner and her husband was published in 1965 by Joyce Coombs, a former London Diocesan President of the MU. *George and Mary Sumner: Their Life and Times* locates the careers, religious views and family life of George's relatives, his uncle, John Bird Sumner, Archbishop of Canterbury, and father, Charles Sumner, the Bishop of Winchester, in a historical context. Coombs includes Bishop Samuel Wilberforce, the distant kinsman of the Sumner family, and identifies the links of patronage between them. Coombs does not attribute her sources, some of which are anecdotes from anonymous eyewitnesses.[4]

1. Porter, Woodward, and Erskine, *Mary Sumner*; Lady Horatia Erskine, 'A History of the Mothers' Union' in *Mothers' Union* (Lambeth Palace Library, 1919); *Fifty Years* (Westminster: The Mothers' Union, 1926).
2. Money, *History of the Girls' Friendly Society*; Heath-Stubbs, *Friendship's Highway*.
3. June Purvis, 'Using Primary Sources When Researching Women's History from a Feminist Perspective', *Women's History Review* 1, no. 2 (1992): 276. See also Maria Tamboukou, *Sewing, Fighting and Writing: Radical Practices in Work, Politics and Culture* (Lanham: Rowman Littlefield International, 2015).
4. Joyce Coombs, *George and Mary Sumner: Their Life and Times* (Westminster: Sumner Press, 1965), 88. Coombs notes the contribution of Mrs Carlyon Evans, the daughter of Mary Sumner's daughter Louisa Gore Browne.

Mary Sumner's significance has been marked by Brian Heeney and Sean Gill in their work on *Women and the Church of England from the Eighteenth Century to the Present* and *The Women's Movement in the Church of England 1850-1930* respectively, and her participation in the Girls Friendly Society has been noted by Brian Harrison.[1] The most substantial scholarly reference to Mary Sumner to date is in Cordelia Moyse's *A History of the Mothers' Union: Women, Anglicanism and Globalisation 1876-2008* which is highly authoritative in its reference to official archival sources. However, in this officially authorised work, Moyse's primary interest is in the development of the corporate Mothers' Union and her focus is on the spiritual empowerment of MU members worldwide within the Anglican Communion.[2]

The significance of religion as a mediating factor in the negotiation of constraint and agency has formed a rich strand in scholarship concerned with understanding women's lives in the period concurrent with Mary Sumner's life trajectory and activism.[3] Religious institutions are a socio-cultural construct, related to sites of power and informing assumptions of value and contingent understandings of, and hierarchies of, knowledge. In this book I explore how religion mediates authority, identity and opportunity and how religion relates to education, gender, class, race and nation. I put Mary Sumner at the centre and offer a new perspective on her life and work by drawing on the ideas of Pierre Bourdieu, who understands social reality as a relational interplay between agents [persons] and social structures [family, institutions] to analyse the cultural forces, notably, religion and education, nuanced by class and gender that framed and informed Mary Sumner's identity, values, horizons of possibility and claims to authority. The book deploys Bourdieu's analytical thinking tools of habitus, capital and field to situate Mary Sumner in her informal and formal networks and explore her activism in relation to the values and practices of dominant social, gender and religious categories. Bourdieu's theory of reproduction, which sees dominant groups seeking to maintain their position through

---

1. Brian Harrison, 'For Church Queen and Family; the Girls' Friendly Society 1874-1920', *Past and Present* 61 (1973).
2. Cordelia Moyse, *A History of the Mothers' Union: Women Anglicanism and Globalisation, 1876-2008* (Woodbridge: Boydell Press, 2009), 28, 29, 32.
3. See, for example, Gail Malmgreen, *Religion in the Lives of English Women, 1760-1930* (London: Croom Helm, 1986); Sue Morgan, *Women, Religion, and Feminism in Britain, 1750-1900* (Basingstoke: Palgrave Macmillan, 2002); Sue Morgan and Jacqueline de Vries, *Women, Gender and Religious Cultures in Britain, 1800-1940*, 1st ed. (London: Routledge, 2010).

the assertion of their preferred values as legitimate, is deployed to locate Mary Sumner as an agent of, or recipient of, domination and position her in relation to the reproduction or negotiation of power.

Mary Sumner's life trajectory, her activism through the Anglican Girls' Friendly Society and the discourse of motherhood she promoted through the Mothers' Union were framed against a background of evangelical religious revival, stimulated by evangelical enthusiasm across denominations. In the field of religion there was a sustained contest over matters of doctrinal authority as the privileged position of the Established Anglican Church was pressurised by the demands of other Christian denominations for more equitable treatment.[1] The 'ownership of the goods of salvation' was also contested by factions within Anglicanism which placed different emphases on the interpretation of doctrine and forms of worship.[2] Mary Sumner's activism occurred against this contested context in which a defensive Anglican Church sought to maintain its status and authority.

The Established Church was patriarchal in excluding women from positions of power and in asserting biblical authority to legitimise their subordinate position.[3] Religion was significant in informing gendered female identities and was drawn on to legitimise activism in philanthropy.[4] The civil, legal and financial status accorded to women (despite some amendments) throughout much of Mary Sumner's lifetime also involved exclusion, constraint and prohibition. Yet as a woman from a dominant class, personally connected to high-status clergy and socially advantaged women, who exercised patronage over others and agency towards self-realisation, she cannot be categorised exclusively as an oppressed victim of her biological sex.[5]

---

1. Owen Chadwick, *The Victorian Church Part I 1827-1859* (A&C Black, 1966); *The Victorian Church Part 2 1860-1901*, 2nd ed. (London: A&C Black, 1972).
2. Terry Rey, 'Marketing the Goods of Salvation: Bourdieu on Religion', *Religion* 34, no. 4 (2004).
3. Sean Gill, *Women and the Church of England: From the Eighteenth Century to the Present* (London: Society for Promoting Christian Knowledge, 1994), 11-38, 76-89.
4. Frank Prochaska, *The Angel out of the House: Philanthropy and Gender in Nineteenth-Century England* (Charlottesville and London: University of Virginia Press, 2002); Prochaska, *Women and Philanthropy in Nineteenth Century England* (Oxford: Clarendon Press, 1980); Susan Mumm, 'Women and Philanthropic Cultures' in *Women, Gender and Religious Cultures in Britain, 1800-1940*, ed. Sue Morgan and Jacqueline de Vries (London: Routledge, 2010).
5. Sue Morgan, ed. *The Feminist History Reader* (London: Routledge, 2006), 3. I interpret Mary Sumner's social status as upper-middle class and use upper and/or middle class to refer to the diverse positions amongst the

Mary Sumner's activism also played out against, and engaged with, the growth of the British Empire. Religious preference was a significant element in legitimising imperial rule, codifying hierarchies of race and mediating the relationship between metropole and periphery. This book is distinctive in exploring Mary Sumner's experience as a traveller in the Middle East in relation to informing her response to race and religion, and contextualising her activism with regard to empire and transnationally. I use the concept of mission to position Mary Sumner in relation to varieties of religiously inspired activism 'at home' and overseas. Mission concerns missionaries and missionary societies seeking converts overseas which invites consideration of identities (racial and gendered), relations and transactions of meaning and power between 'home' and overseas, in diverse spaces and contact zones.[1] The term mission, evocative of valorous spiritual endeavour, was drawn on to sanctify by association women's performance of gendered roles within the home. It also applied to philanthropic activity beyond the home legitimised by religious authority, much of which was educational in that it sought to modify behaviour.[2] The expression 'women's mission' was used in both these senses by Mary Sumner, her network associates, and other contemporaries, to refer to the performance of home duties and philanthropic and to religious outreach 'at home'.[3] The notion of a

---

social milieu to which she claimed allegiance. See David Cannadine, *Class in Britain* (New Haven; London: Yale University Press, 1998). Cannadine discusses the nuances of class and the notion of respectability.

1. Catherine Hall, *Cultures of Empire: A Reader: Colonisers in Britain and the Empire in Nineteenth and Twentieth Centuries* (Manchester: Manchester University Press, 2000); Frederick Cooper and Ann Laura Stoler, *Tensions of Empire: Colonial Cultures in a Bourgeois World* (Berkeley: University of California Press, 1997), 1-45, notes the transactional relationship in terms of identiy between metropole and perifery; Mary Louise Pratt, *Imperial Eyes: Travel Writing and Transculturation* (London: Routledge, 1992), 6-7. 'Contact zone' and 'transculturation' describe meaning drawn from encounters across space and culture. I use the term overseas to refer to this diversity of locations.
2. Alison Twells, *The Civilising Mission and the English Middle Class, 1792-1850: The 'Heathen' at Home and Overseas* (Basingstoke: Palgrave Macmillan, 2009), 5. uses the terms 'missionary philanthropy' and 'civilising mission'; Jenny Daggers, 'The Victorian Female Civilising Mission and Women's Aspirations Towards Priesthood in the Church of England', *Women's History Review* 10, no. 4 (2001): 625.
3. In *Friendship's Highway; Being the History of the Girls' Friendly Society* (London: Girls' Friendly Society, 1926), 82, Mary Heath-Stubbs quotes Mary

'civilising mission' encapsulates the assumption of superior values and standards of behaviour and an assumed authority to impose them on groups categorised as deficient.[1] This book considers Mary Sumner's interplay with mission through these three interconnected strands, domestic, philanthropic and engagement with distant spaces.

The inception and growth of the Mothers' Union occurred at a time when educational provision expanded and reformed in ways that were contested. It was also a period in which the understanding of childhood was subject to change. Mary Sumner's views on the nature of childhood and pedagogy have received little attention. Her activism, via the MU, relates to key themes in education, the contest for power in the educational field between the Established Anglican Church, other denominations and the state in mass elementary education.[2] Her advocacy for the home as a site of religious education and for the mother as a religious educator also occurred in the context of expansion in the provision of schooling for middle and upper-class girls and the articulation of aspirations for higher education amongst women. This involved the negotiation of gendered identities and roles and the development of contingent curricula deemed to be appropriate. The expansion of professional and voluntary roles for women within the sphere of education, whether as mistresses in middle-class schools, elementary teachers or as philanthropic 'workers' and members of school boards, was related to women's increasing pedagogic

---

Townsend, the GFS founder, discussing the 'missionary element which is the secret of our society'. Angela Georgina Burdett-Coutts, *Woman's Mission: A Series of Congress Papers on the Philanthropic Work of Women by Eminent Writers*, facsimile reprint, Portrayer Publishers 2002 ed. (London: Sampson Low, Marston and Company, 1893). Mary Sumner's 'Responsibilities of Mothers' was one of the papers; Mary Sumner, *To Mothers of the Higher Classes* (Winchester: Warren and Sons, 1888), 5. She asserts the 'exalted mission' of child rearing 'the sphere which God has appointed for her in the home'.

1. Gill, *Women and the Church of England*, 131-145; Martha Vicinus, *Independent Women: Work and Community for Single Women: 1850-1920* (London: Virago, 1985), 36. 'Underpinning all women's work was a sense of religious commitment.'
2. James Murphy, *Church, State and Schools in Britain 1800-1970* (London: Routledge and Kegan Paul, 1971); W.B. Stephens, *Education in Britain, 1750-1914* (Basingstoke: Macmillan, 1998), 6; Terence Copley, *Spiritual Development in the State School: A Perspective on Worship and Spirituality in the Education System of England and Wales* (Exeter: University of Exeter Press, 2000), 17; John Hurt, *Education in Evolution Church, State, Society and Popular Education 1800-1870* (London: Rupert Hart-Davis, 1971), 20; Murphy, *Church, State and Schools.*

authority and thus bound up in the negotiation of the purpose and practice of women's education. Religion mediated women's educational experience in several ways. It informed assumptions about women's spiritual, emotional and sexual nature, as well as their intellectual capacity, and it legitimised domesticated roles and the notions of self-restraint and service. In so doing it framed responses to the purpose and practice of education for women.[1] These issues can be located against a context of increasing literacy and mass print communication, in which media were used to assert contested religious and secular orthodoxies.[2] Mary Sumner qualifies as a popular educator according to a definition that encompasses informal means such as philanthropy and the dissemination of materials intended to change behaviour amongst the populace.[3] In this book I explore and locate her educational ideas in context and analyses the strategies she deployed in the dissemination of her educational message.

Mary Sumner's identity was informed and her activism was negotiated in relation to other agents and to social structures invested with power that included the family, the Church and philanthropic organisations. She can be linked with a number of significant individuals through kinship, social milieu or affiliation to interest groups. Her life trajectory intersects with a number of 'churchwomen' of distinction,

1. Dale Spender, *The Education Papers: Women's Quest for Equality in Britain 1850-1912* (London: Routledge and Kegan Paul, 1987), 10-31; Sara Delamont, 'The Domestic Ideology and Women's Education', in *The Nineteenth-Century Woman: Her Cultural and Physical World*, ed. Sara Delamont and Lorna Duffin (London: Croom Helm, 1978); Joan Burstyn, *Victorian Education and the Ideal of Womanhood* (London: Croom Helm, 1980), 99-118; Carol Dyhouse, *Girls Growing up in Late Victorian and Edwardian London* (London: Routledge, 1981); Deborah Gorham, *The Victorian Girl and the Feminine Ideal* (London: Croom Helm, 1982), 18-19, 78-79; Gill, *Women and the Church of England*, 112-130.
2. Richard D. Altick, *The English Common Reader: A Social History of the Mass Reading Public, 1800-1900* (Columbus: Ohio State University Press, 1998); Sarah C. Williams, '"Is There a Bible in the House?": Gender Religion and Family Culture', in *Women, Gender and Religious Cultures in Britain, 1800-1940*, ed. Sue Morgan and Jacqueline de Vries (London: Routledge, 2011).
3. Sjaak Braster, 'The People, the Poor, and the Oppressed: The Concept of Popular Education through Time', *Paedagogica Historica* 47, no. Nos. 1-2 (2011); Alejandro Tiana Ferrer, 'The Concept of Popular Education Revisited – or What Do We Talk About When We Speak of Popular Education', ibid., no. 1-2; Harold Silver, 'Knowing and Not Knowing in the History of Education', *History of Education* 21, no. 1 (1992).

including novelist Charlotte Yonge, educationalist Charlotte Mason and imperialist Ellen Joyce, who exemplify the religiously inspired philanthropic or educational activism that was a characteristic feature of women's negotiation of agency at the time. A situation that affirms the relevance of Barbara Caine's advocacy for looking at individuals in the context of their familial and social networks in order to illuminate the intersecting boundaries of private lives and public action. The incidence of connected lives also suggests the utility of an approach that draws on prosopography to identify shared attitudes or attributes common to a given group.[1]

Mary Sumner's Mothers' Union and The Girls Friendly Society, as networks of women with common goals seeking to influence public policy via lobbying and the distribution of information, exhibit characteristics that can be located within Margaret Keck and Kathryn Sikkink's category of 'advocacy network'. Their claim that network actors contribute ideas and offer discourses which may serve to change perceptions of the category they represent, thereby mediating behaviour towards them in state and society, is of interest to an analysis of Mary Sumner that seeks to position her activism in relation to agency and change in relation to women's horizons of possibility.[2] Eckhardt Fuchs identifies 'exchange theory', which assumes that organisations establish voluntary relations for the transfer of desired resources, as in the case of Keck and Sikkink's category of advocacy network. He also notes the contrasting 'power dependency theory' which asserts that relations are based on competition for advantage and thus involve conflict and power.[3] Both categories may be applied to advocacy which seeks to win adherence to one view in opposition to alternative perspectives, as is the case with Mary Sumner's Mothers' Union. For Fuchs, a key purpose of the study of networks is to illuminate the interaction between individuals and structures, both social and organisational, and the unofficial social interactions which consist of less well documented or quantifiable data,

1. Barbara Caine, 'Feminist Biography and Feminist History', *Women's History Review* 3, no. 2 (1992); Peter Cunningham, 'Innovators, Networks and Structures: Towards a Prosopography of Progressivism', *History of Education* 30, no. 5 (2001). Short biographical notes on women mentioned in the text, are included in Appendix 2.
2. Margaret Keck and Kathryn A. Sikkink, *Advocacy Networks in International Politics Activists Beyond Borders* (Ithaca and London: Cornell University Press, 1998), 2.
3. Eckhardt Fuchs, 'Networks and the History of Education', *Paedagogica Historica* 42, no. 2 (2007); Keck and Sikkink, *Advocacy Networks*, 8-10.

notions in accord with Caine's advocacy for seeing a life in context and pertinent to the examination of Mary Sumner's negotiation of agency, and claims to authority in relation to the Anglican Church and in a gendered and socially stratified social context.

Interpreting Mary Sumner's life requires a conceptual framework that accommodates the perspectival nature of the sources; positions her activism in the context of social structures, institutions and significant others; interrogates assumptions of value and belief; and engages with the negotiation of agency and considers on whose behalf it was enacted. I draw on the conceptual tools and theoretical stance of Pierre Bourdieu to address the challenges of understanding Mary Sumner's negotiation of constraint and agency, and her position in upholding and transacting power across domestic, local and global spaces in relation to the fields of religion, mission, and education with motherhood as a connecting theme. In the following chapter I outline my interpretation of Bourdieu's key concepts and relate his 'thinking tools' to the analysis of a temporally situated subject.

I then begin to 'think with Bourdieu' in order to examine Mary Sumner's life trajectory not as a linear narrative but in relation to the strands of religion, mission and education which form an organising framework for analysing aspects of her activism. These strands are seen as related, for doctrinal preference provides and informs a mandate for activism in support of religious goals via mission, and mission itself, in seeking converts to religious knowledge or religiously authorised conduct, is educational in intent and practice. Furthermore, religious preference defines what constitutes legitimate knowledge and mediates who has access to it. In Chapter 2, I focus on exploring Mary Sumner's experience of religion in family life and locating the Anglican faith that underpinned her MU activism against a context of evangelical revival and competition for allegiance amongst rival denominations. Chapter 3 also focuses on doctrinal preference but moves the focus outward to consider notions of good womanhood, the role of women in the Church, and Mary Sumner's strategies for establishing the Mothers' Union in the Anglican religious field. Chapter 4 explores Mary Sumner's formative experience of understandings of mission in relation to gendered roles and philanthropic traditions in family life. The chapter engages with Mary Sumner as a traveller and gives further context to her activism through the MU by documenting the views and practices of the GFS in relation to 'civilising mission' through philanthropy and engagement overseas. Chapter 5 takes the theme of 'Missionary Mothers' and explores how notions of mission and constructions of identity drawn from transactions between the British imperial metropole and periphery informed MU practice and claims to authority. Mary Sumner is positioned as an advocate for empire, and the MU as an imperial organisation is related to Church power. Chapter 6 introduces the theme of education with a focus on Mary Sumner's personal experience of education and attitude to the education of women encountered in family life. The chapter also explores her understanding of childhood and views on child rearing. The following chapter considers Mary's strategies through the MU to promote education of the populace and positions her and her organisation in relation to state-sponsored mass elementary education, denominational education and higher education for girls. The book concludes by thinking with Bourdieu to reflect on Mary Sumner's life and activism in relation to power agency and change.

Chapter 1
Thinking Mary Sumner with Bourdieu: Habitus, Field, Capital, Pedagogic Authority, Symbolic Violence and Reproduction

Bourdieu's ideas were initially framed within the disciplines of anthropology and sociology, drawing upon the work of Weber, Durkheim and Marx on the objective structures of society. The ideas of Marx were a particular influence on Bourdieu's conception of an economy of symbolic 'goods'.[1] As an anthropologist Bourdieu was also responsive to, but also critical of, Levi-Strauss's ideas concerning the generating rules of the structures in society. He also reacted against the existentialism of Sartre as inadequate in accounting for the objective structural realities and the pragmatism inherent in the negotiation of the social world. Bourdieu was influenced by Merleau-Ponty's ideas on understanding the social world as inscribed and embodied in persons, and drew on the ideas of Gaston Bachelard concerning the contextual relation of epistemology in time and space, and in the location of the thinker. Ervin Goffman's notions of dramaturgy, which concern self-presentation by the individual as mediated by the situations in which they are located, also influenced Bourdieu's understanding of the transaction between the person and social structures.[2] In this chapter I seek to synthesise Bourdieu's ideas and demonstrate that his thinking tools and conceptualisation of the way life choices are informed and power transacted, provide a useful 'tool kit' for the historian and are an appropriate framework for interpreting the life of Mary Sumner.

---

1. Pierre Bourdieu and Jean-Claude Passeron, *Reproduction in Education, Society and Culture*, Rev. ed. / preface to the 1990 edition by Pierre Bourdieu. (London: Sage, 1990), 183; Pierre Bourdieu, *The Field of Cultural Production: Essays on Art and Literature* (Cambridge: Polity Press, 1993), 74-76. The symbolic economy in which assets are accumulated and exchanged for advantage will receive further elaboration in later paragraphs.
2. Michael Grenfell and Cheryl Hardy, *Art Rules: Pierre Bourdieu and the Visual Arts* (Oxford: Berg, 2007), 25, 27; Richard Jenkins, *Pierre Bourdieu* (London: Routledge, 1992), 19.

Bourdieu insists that theorising follows the observation and analysis of practice and describes his approach as 'a philosophy of action', which is 'condensed in a small number of fundamental concepts, habitus, field, [and] capital and at its cornerstone is the two way relationship between objective structures (those of social fields) and incorporated structures (those of habitus)'.[1] These categories seek to overcome simplistic oppositions of freedom or constraint and dominance or submission. They provide tools for conceptualising how identity is informed and agency negotiated that I apply to analysing how Mary Sumner occupied and negotiated these different positions. The category of capital pertains to valued attributes, their deployment, and negotiation towards securing advantage. Bourdieu makes frequent use of the analogy of game-playing when explaining his ideas and theoretical interpretation of how society works.[2] This encapsulates his interest in agents as 'players' who seek advantage (capital) on the (structural) field of play within the constraints of the 'rules of the game'. I draw on this analogy in exploring the assets and strategies that Mary Sumner drew upon in establishing and promoting the Mothers' Union.

Habitus concerns the subjective understanding of social reality vested in the 'player' or collectively in 'players'. Habitus can be understood as those unthinkingly assumed habits of mind that the individual acquires through socialisation within their contextual back ground. Habitus concerns the practical, situational negotiation of life. For Bourdieu, the concept of habitus was intended to:

> account for practice in its humblest forms – rituals, matrimonial choices, the mundane economic conduct of everyday life, etc. – by escaping both the objectivism of action understood as mechanical reaction 'without an agent' and the subjectivism which portrays action as the deliberate pursuit of a conscious intention, the free project of a conscience positing its own ends and maximising its utility through rational computation.[3]

The significance of habitus is its mediating function between the individual and the structures in social reality, which exists in time and place, as well as inside and outside agents. Habitus is ontologically specific, being realised through individuals, yet epistemologically generalisable

1. Pierre Bourdieu, *Practical Reason: On the Theory of Action* (Cambridge: Polity Press, 1998), vii.
2. Pierre Bourdieu and Loic J.D. Wacquant, *An Invitation to Reflexive Sociology* (Cambridge: Polity Press, 1992), 23-24, 98-100.
3. Ibid., 121.

to social and cultural structures. It is relational as well as mediating. It concerns where one is in time, space and circumstances, who one knows and what one thinks proper or possible. This acknowledges a 'knowing subject' within what Morwenna Griffiths, in her assertion of the significance of the multiple influences, contexts and relationships in the establishment of identity, has conceived of as a cultural 'web'.[1] Habitus implies an accumulation of collective understandings and assumptions, which are durable dispositions that are embodied in individuals or collectively.[2] Bourdieu uses the terms 'doxa' and 'doxic relations' to explain the embodiment of social and cultural messages and practices within habitus. Doxa concerns the apparent self-evidence of social reality which in its habitual familiarity goes unquestioned.[3] Habitus is generative of dispositions in that it structures and normalises unconscious assumptions of how the world is, and thus orientates the agent towards interpretation of the social world. Habitus informs logical preferences for action against culturally historically determined possibilities, and is a 'practical sense of the game'.[4]

Habitus does not rule out a measure of calculation of opportunity but this is defined in relation to the structuring perception of the habitus itself, which predisposes the agent towards the recognition of horizons of possibility and likely outcomes of certain choices.[5] However, Bourdieu refutes claims that this is a deterministic view.[6] He insists that habitus is not merely passively received social inheritance, for the dispositions thus acquired by the individual (despite their durability and the tendency of experience to affirm them) allows for 'regulated improvisation'.[7]

> Habitus is not the fate that some people read into it. Being the product of history, it is an open system of dispositions that is constantly subject to experiences, and therefore constantly affected by them in a way that reinforces or modifies its structures.[8]

1. Morwenna Griffiths, *Feminisms and the Self: The Web of Identity* (London: Routledge, 1995).
2. Pierre Bourdieu, *The Logic of Practice* (Cambridge: Polity, 1990), 53, 54.
3. Ibid., 20.
4. Bourdieu and Passeron, *Reproduction*, 95; Bourdieu and Wacquant, *An Invitation*, 120, 124; Bourdieu, *Logic of Practice*, 66.
5. Bourdieu, *Logic of Practice*, 53.
6. Bourdieu and Wacquant, *An Invitation*, 131.
7. Bourdieu, *Logic of Practice*, 57.
8. Bourdieu and Wacquant, *An Invitation*, 133.

One aim of this book is to position Mary Sumners' activism in relation to change or conservation of the religious and social doxa characteristic of her habitus. To this end I locate Mary Sumner's in relation to her religious upbringing, education, experience of family relationships and married life. Her social status and relationships, and clerical and philanthropic networks will also be considered in relation to identifying attributes of the wider group habitus in which she was positioned.

Mary Sumner's activism was realised within the spheres of religion, philanthropy and education. Thinking with Bourdieu, these may be conceptualised as fields; that is, structured systems of social relations that exist in relation to one another. A field consists of a set of objective, historical relations anchored in certain forms of power (or capital).[1] Fields are related to habitus because fields structure the location in which identity is established and agency is enacted. Fields mediate between the practices of the participants and their social and economic context, and are consequently sites of cultural engagement and differentiation. Many fields are interrelated, and fields may have sub-fields within them. A defining characteristic of fields, if the game analogy is pursued, is that the players have a common tacit belief in the game, 'a recognition that escapes questioning'.[2] This recognition is constitutive of the boundaries of the field, which is the sum of what is valued within it. Fields are locations for the production of value, knowledge or symbolic goods.[3] Fields assert value for the purpose of legitimising and upholding their ascendancy, and in so doing, they construct an epistemology of social reality, and determine who and what is within them. They are sites for the acquisition of advantages and of competition for them.[4]

Mary Sumner's activism on behalf of the Anglican Church, whether through parochial work in support of her husband, or through organisations such as the Church of England Temperance Society (CETS), the Girls' Friendly Society or the MU, locates her in the field of religion. She is associated through her kin and social contacts to those with high status within the Anglican Church, a dominant presence in the field of religion. Mary Sumner is also located in the field of education through her engagement in disseminating religious knowledge via her publications for the MU, her engagement in parish educational initiatives, and her

1. Ibid., 16.
2. Ibid., 98; Bourdieu, *Logic of Practice*, 67-68.
3. *The Field of Cultural Production*, 78, 121.
4. *Logic of Practice*, 68; Moishe Postone, Edward LiPuma, and Craig J. Calhoun, 'Introduction', in *Bourdieu: Critical Perspectives*, ed. Craig J. Calhoun, Edward LiPuma, and Moishe Postone (Cambridge: Polity Press, 1993), 10.

involvement in the CETS and GFS, all of which aimed to inculcate religious values. Her male relatives connect her by association to the fields of political power (her father-in-law, a bishop, sat in the House of Lords) and economic power (her father was a retired banker and landowner).

In seeking to explain how power is upheld and transacted within fields, Bourdieu uses the term capital in relation to transactions of value and the pursuit of advantage in the field. The notion of symbolic capital expands on a market analogy from Marxist theory to suggest that capital allows the possession or acquisition of that which is perceived to have a value.[1] Despite acknowledging his appropriation of economic terminology, Bourdieu refutes a classical economic Marxist model of capital because he considers that it fails to acknowledge attributes other than material goods that may accrue from, and be transacted for, advantage. Capital and field are mutually constituting and relational. Capital consists of attributes individuals (and groups) seek to acquire. It refers to those qualities and credentials that are valued in the field and are recognised as accruing advantages (power) to the players of the game.[2] It is the field itself that defines and legitimises those assets that will be valued within it. Conversely, the assets acknowledged within it are constitutive of the field itself. These assets can be exchanged for advantage. Moreover, position in the field will possibly define the capital of an individual or group and affects dispositions (habitus) and opportunities for its further acquisition.[3]

Bourdieu presents capital as being of three basic forms.[4] These are economic, cultural and social but he states 'we must add symbolic capital which is the form one or another of these species takes when it is grasped through categories of perception that recognize its specific logic or, if you prefer, *misrecognise* the arbitrariness of its possession and accumulation'.[5] Symbolic capital is associated with the acquisition of prestige and social honour. Economic capital is the most material and least symbolic, for it

1. Michael Grenfell and David James, *Bourdieu and Education: Acts of Practical Theory* (London: Falmer Press, 1998), 20.
2. Bourdieu and Wacquant, *An Invitation*, 119, 199.
3. Grenfell and Hardy, *Art Rules*, 31. Capital is symptomatic of field positioning according to a hierarchy logically defined by the field.
4. Bourdieu and Passeron, *Reproduction*. This work, published in French in 1970 and in English in 1977, was Bourdieu's first use of linguistic capital and cultural capital understood as relating to legitimate knowledge. Bourdieu has since identified further kinds of capital; Pierre Bourdieu, *Language and Symbolic Power* (Cambridge: Polity Press, 1991). First published in France 1982, this work identifies symbolic, social, economic, personal, political, linguistic and cultural capital.
5. Bourdieu and Wacquant, *An Invitation*, 119.

appertains to financial wealth. Economic capital may be advantageous towards securing other kinds of capital but it does not necessarily equate to the possession of cultural capital. Bourdieu defines cultural capital as varieties of legitimate knowledge. It would be possible to be affluent but to be perceived, according to the logic of other fields, as lacking the cultural capital recognised as prestigious in education, taste or forms of behaviour.[1]

Bourdieu subdivides cultural capital into embodied, objectified or institutionalised capital.[2] Embodied capital is vested in agents. It could appertain to attributes such as piety, taste or being 'of good family', for which the agent may receive recognition and secure advantage. Embodied attributes such as gender or 'race' may serve to mediate capital. Objectified capital is associated with prestigious things invested with meaning and value. Institutionalised capital is vested in structures or in organisations such as museums or religious bodies which have the authority to bestow advantage or prestige. Social capital refers to the sum of the resources and networks of personal relations, acquaintance and recognition which an individual connects. Social capital concerns lasting relations in a sphere of contact. High social capital is characterised by relations with significant others who are bearers of status. Examples of social capital could be popularity, 'good breeding', and respectability.

Capital is symbolic not just because it can designate non-material attributes such as reputation but because it works through a process of acknowledgement and recognition of what Bourdieu terms the imposed cultural arbitrary, which is perceived as legitimate and which will be discussed below. Attributes may be intangible, such as in the case of piety, as designated with the religious field, but have exchange value because they are recognised in the field as having worth or securing advantage.[3] Capital is transferable from one field to another. The notion of capital is also helpful in interpreting the archival sources relating to Mary Sumner, much of which are perspectival. Thinking with Bourdieu, these sources can be interpreted as assertions of capital and hence signposting the possession of attributes deemed desirable by their authors, or claiming capital by association with bodies of individuals perceived as invested with, or embodying, desirable or prestigious attributes. A key intention of the book is to identify Mary Sumner's embodied and accumulated capital and to explore how it was accrued and transacted in relation to her activism.

1. Bourdieu, *The Field of Cultural Production*, 3, 39, 68; *Practical Reason*, 19.
2. Bourdieu and Wacquant, *An Invitation*, 119.
3. Beverly Skeggs, 'Exchange, Value and Affect: Bourdieu and "the Self"' in *Feminism after Bourdieu*, ed. Linda Adkins and Beverly Skeggs (Blackwell, 2004).

Bourdieu's interest in the transmission of culture and the durability of social structures and advantage vested in certain groups, stimulated by his own location as an academic, led him to engage with epistemology and to investigate the construction and status of knowledge. His interest extends to education via both formal systems and informal means for the construction and transmission of legitimate knowledge, and to the relationship these have to social reproduction. Bourdieu drew from empirical research into the relationship of scholastic attainment and social factors within the French education system, to inform his theory of symbolic violence and the concept of the cultural arbitrary, explained in *Reproduction in Education and Society*.[1] Bourdieu also identified the concepts of pedagogic work, pedagogic action and pedagogic authority. He sees these concepts, although initially framed in the context of, and applied to, a formal education system, as being relevant to 'any social formation, understood as a system of power relations and sense relations between groups or classes'.[2] This book considers Mary Sumner in relation to these concepts and positions her as subject to pedagogic work by institutions and pedagogic action and simultaneously an agent of pedagogic action invested with pedagogic authority.

For Bourdieu, all culture (systems of symbolism and meaning) is arbitrary. In one sense culture is arbitrary because there are no underlying objective principles to be found in culture; it is the accumulated sum of the practices of a group over time and owes its existence to the social conditions that produced it.[3] Culture is also arbitrary in that it is an imposition, which rests ultimately on force (albeit symbolic), of the values and meanings of the dominating group. It serves to sustain and reproduce their position of domination. Bourdieu claims 'every established order tends to the naturalisation of its own arbitrariness' through the assertion of its self-defined attribution of value and in a stable society this is misrecognised as self-evident.[4] Bourdieu refers to this as symbolic violence, which disguises the arbitrary nature of domination by presenting it as legitimate:[5]

> The conservation of the social order is decisively . . . reinforced by . . . the orchestration of categories of perception in the social world which being adjusted to the divisions of the established

1. Bourdieu and Passeron, *Reproduction*. Other major works on education include *La Misere Du Monde* (Paris: Seuil, 1993); *Homo Academicus* (Paris: Editions de Minuit, 1984).
2. Bourdieu and Passeron, *Reproduction*, 4.
3. Bourdieu and Passeron, *Reproduction*, 8.
4. Pierre Bourdieu, *Outline of a Theory of Practice* (Cambridge University Press, 1979), 164.
5. Bourdieu and Passeron, *Reproduction*, 5.

> order, (and therefore to the interests of those who dominate it) and common to all minds structured in accordance with those structures, impose themselves with all appearances of objective necessity.[1]

Symbolic violence only acts on social agents with their complicity. Through the effect of pedagogic work, they are habituated towards unthinking recognition or misrecognition of the authority of the dominating structure.[2] Thus the dominated may uphold those structures which dominate them because they acknowledge the dominating authority as legitimate. They misrecognise the arbitrary nature of the legitimising values of the dominating structure. The complicity of the dominated is reinforced by offering rewards such as material, cultural or social advantage. These are capital assets asserted through pedagogic action which the dominating majority has the power to award. Yet domination is not merely power over a given group. 'The violence is symbolic because, it is a relationship of *meaning* between individuals in which (mis)recognition of legitimacy ensures the persistence of power.'[3] It is also the case that those exercising domination do so because they also misrecognise its arbitrary nature. This is achieved through what Bourdieu terms pedagogic action. Bourdieu sees every pedagogic action as an act of symbolic violence, in that it seeks to impose the cultural arbitrary. For Bourdieu, pedagogic action functions in three modes: family education, and diffuse education (which are acquired by interaction with socially competent members within a social context), and institutionalised education (which is acquired by the pedagogic action of structures and organisations). The rites of the Church, such as confirmation or marriage, which Mary Sumner advocated, may be conceived of as institutional education. The success of pedagogic action lies in its ability to reproduce and endorse the dominant culture.[4]

Pedagogic work is the longer-term inculcation of the cultural arbitrary; its product is a durable transposable habitus, achieved 'without resorting to external repression or, in particular, physical coercion'.[5] Pedagogic work cannot be accomplished without pedagogic authority.

1. Pierre Bourdieu, *Distinction: A Social Critique of the Judgement of Taste* (London: Routledge & Kegan Paul, 1984), 471.
2. Bourdieu and Wacquant, *An Invitation*, 162.
3. Frank Poupeau, 'Reasons for Domination: Bourdieu Versus Habermas' in *Reading Bourdieu on Society and Culture*, ed. Bridget Fowler (Oxford Blackwell, 2000), 71, 72.
4. Bourdieu and Passeron, *Reproduction*, 5-10.
5. Ibid., 31-54.

Pedagogic authority, which is contested in field manoeuvres that deploy capital to assert legitimacy, is invested in those who are recognised or misrecognised as agents authorised to speak on behalf of, and invested with the authority accruing to, the group or institution whose cultural arbitrary they wish to enforce through pedagogic action.[1] In this book I apply these categories to Mary Sumner and argue that she was, as is the case with all social agents, a recipient of pedagogic action through her family and social context. As an upholder of a socially stratified society and the values of the Church of England she was habituated by pedagogic work to aspects of the cultural arbitrary. She was also a pedagogic worker in her strategies for the promotion of religious values and behaviour, which drew together family education and institutional education. Analysing the assets and attributes that allowed her pedagogic authority is a central concern of this book.

In *Reproduction in Education and Society* and in *Language and Symbolic Power*, Bourdieu refers to linguistic capital and explains his understanding of language as both a product of and a medium for social interaction that must be considered in relation to its context and the circumstances of its production. Agents may be bearers of linguistic capital and located within a linguistic habitus which may or may not accord with the 'code' prioritised by perpetrators of the cultural arbitrary.[2] Fields may prioritise particular varieties of linguistic capital that can be used for differentiation and for the reproduction of a cultural arbitrary.[3] As such, language is a medium for symbolic violence and the dispositions of habitus allow this to be misrecognised. Bourdieu associates language with pedagogic authority: '[T]he power of words is nothing other than the delegated power of the spokesperson, and his speech – that is the substance of his discourse . . . is testimony to the guarantee of delegation which is vested in him.'[4] The notion that by using legitimised language the speaker claims (and thereby gains) legitimisation as having the right to speak, and for the authority of the message, has relevance to Mary Sumner's use of the rhetoric of motherhood and religion in securing recognition for the Mothers' Union and to the gendered discourses delineating the women's domestic containment as 'mission'.

1. Ibid., 11-31.
2. Bourdieu and Wacquant, *An Invitation*, 184-149.
3. Bourdieu and Passeron, *Reproduction*. See Chapter 1, 'Cultural Capital and Pedagogic Communication', 71-106 and Chapter 2, 'The Literate Tradition and Social Conservation', 107-139.
4. Bourdieu, *Language and Symbolic Power*. 'The Production and Reproduction of Legitimate Language', 43-65. Ibid,. 107.

Bourdieu's attention to religion is contained within a selection of articles and chapters.[1] In 'Genesis and Structure of the Religious Field', Bourdieu includes religion within the definition of a field and extends his definition of capital to include religious capital. For Bourdieu religious capital, which he terms the 'goods of salvation', includes the sacraments and a sense of legitimisation and non-material well being acquired through membership of a recognised congregation which promises salvation.[2] This understanding is also developed in 'The Laughter of Bishops' and 'On the Economy of the Church' in *Practical Reason*.[3] The chapter 'Authorised Language: The Social Conditions for the Effectiveness of Ritual Discourse' in *Language and Symbolic Power* draws on religious terminology to assert the notion of consecrated language in a discussion of the authorisation of discourse.[4] Bourdieu asserts that:

> Religious institutions work permanently, both practically and symbolically to euphemise social relations, including relations of exploitation (as in the family), by transfiguring them into relations of spiritual kinship or of religious exchange. . . . Exploitation is masked.[5]

In the religious field, Bourdieu believes competition is over the ownership of the 'goods of salvation' in that it seeks to inculcate in the practice and world view of lay people a particular religious habitus.[6] Terry Rey's interpretation is that religion 'provides a way for the under-classes to make sense of their lot. Religion thus contributes to the misrecognition of the social order as legitimate, although religion can and at times does trigger major social change'.[7] Beate Krais similarly observes that 'religious specialists inculcate in the laity a religious habitus that permits

1. 'Legitimation and Structured Interest in Weber's Sociology of Religion' in *Max Weber, Rationality, and Modernity*, ed. Scott Lash and Sam Whimster (London: Allen and Unwin, 1987), 119-136; 'Genesis and Structure of the Religious Field', *Comparative Social Research* 13, no. 1 (1991); 'Authorised Language: The Social Conditions for the Effectiveness of Ritual Discourse', in *Language and Symbolic Power* (Cambridge: Polity Press, 1991).
2. Terry Rey, 'Marketing the Goods of Salvation: Bourdieu on Religion', *Religion* 34, no. 4 (2004): 337.
3. Bourdieu, *Practical Reason*, 112-126. Appendix: Remarks on the Economy of the Church, 124-126.
4. *Language and Symbolic Power*, 107-116.
5. *Practical Reason*, 117.
6. Bourdieu and Passeron, *Reproduction*; Bourdieu, *Language and Symbolic Power*, 126.
7. Rey, 'Marketing the Goods of Salvation: Bourdieu on Religion', 333.

orthodoxy's and the economic and political elite's "misrecognized domination".[1] Religious specialists create the illusion that elites are religious and therefore moral and thus deserving of their power.[2] Rey asserts the relationship of religion to gender, 'race' and colonial conquest in his advocacy for the application of Bourdieu's thinking tools to institutional religion, which he sees as closely bound up with class and the legitimisation of domination.[3] I apply these concepts to positioning Mary Sumner as a self-aligned Churchwoman in relation to constraint and agency as both subject to, and agent of, domination.

Mary Sumner's activism cannot be conceived of in the context of a single sex, nor is it divorced from class. Her agency was realised within male dominated power structures and upheld notions of womanhood authorised by patriarchal religious authority, yet her educational mission to reform national life articulated expectations of manliness, advocated improvement in the conduct of men as well as women, and engaged with public issues. Gender is a relevant lens to apply to the making of meaning around sexual difference that is evident in Mary Sumner's negotiation of agency and authority. Bourdieu is clear that gender is a site for the perpetuation of domination.[4] The asymmetry of status he ascribes to gender reveals his anthropological perspective. Bourdieu maintains that women as a category are treated as objects of symbolic exchange and invested with a symbolic function. As goods themselves women are forced to preserve their symbolic value by conforming to male ideas. 'The liberation of women must involve questioning the foundations of the production of symbolic capital.'[5] Bourdieu, in accord with Sue Morgan and John Tosh, sees gender as a construct embedded within the social field applicable to the categories of 'men' and 'women'.[6] For Bourdieu 'the logic of gender domination . . . seems to be the paradigmatic form of

1. Beate Krais, 'Gender and Symbolic Violence: Female Oppression in the Light of Pierre Bourdieu's Theory of Social Practice' in *Bourdieu: Critical Perspectives*, ed. Craig Calhoun, Edward LiPuma, and Moishe Postone (Cambridge: Cambridge Polity Press, 1993), 177. Punctuation as source.
2. Rey, 'Marketing the Goods of Salvation: Bourdieu on Religion', 334.
3. Ibid.; *Bourdieu on Religion: Imposing Faith and Legitimacy* (London: Equinox Pub., 2007).
4. Pierre Bourdieu, *Masculine Domination* (Cambridge: Polity Press, 2001).
5. Bourdieu and Wacquant, *An Invitation*, 174.
6. Sue Morgan, 'Theorising Feminist History: A Thirty Year Retrospective', *Women's History Review* 18, no. 3 (2009); John Tosh, *A Man's Place: Masculinity and the Middle-Class Home in Victorian England* (New Haven, Connecticut; London: Yale University Press, 2007).

symbolic violence'.[1] He sees 'men the dominant . . . equally constrained by the roles and identities according to the dominant taxonomy, they were supposed to incarnate'.[2] Bourdieu considers masculine domination so structurally embedded as to be misrecognised as the natural order:

> the concordance between the objective structures and the cognitive structures, between the shape of being and the forms of knowledge . . . apprehends the social world and its arbitrary divisions, starting with the socially constructed division between the sexes as natural, self-evident and as such contains a full recognition of legitimacy.[3]

Gender permits acknowledgement of 'race', class, affluence, education and religion as mediating factors in access to opportunity or exclusion from power.[4] Bourdieu's ideas have been drawn on by scholars who acknowledge gender as a mediator of opportunity and a constituent aspect of domination.[5] Terry Lovell claims that Bourdieu over-emphasises the durability of the bodily inscription of the habitus, yet acknowledges that the durability of structural domination may be usefully conceptualised with Bourdieu's conceptual tools.[6] Krais and Toril Moi consider Bourdieu's conceptual tools a means of interrogating gender in relation to power and domination. According to Moi, gender, like class, is a location for the exercise of symbolic violence. It can be theorised in the same way as social class, as not a field in itself but as part of the general social field. It is always a relevant factor but not always the most relevant. Moi sees

1. Bourdieu and Wacquant, *An Invitation*, 170.
2. Jeremy F. Lane, *Pierre Bourdieu: A Critical Introduction* (London: Pluto, 2000), 133.
3. Bourdieu, *Masculine Domination*, 9.
4. Joan Scott, *Feminism and History* (Oxford: Oxford University Press, 1996), 3.
5. Joan W. Scott, 'Gender: A Useful Category of Historical Analysis', *American Historical Review* 91, no. 5 (1986); Toril Moi, *'What is a Woman?' And Other Essays* (Oxford: Oxford University Press, 1999); Andrea Jacobs, 'Examinations as Cultural Capital for the Victorian School Girl; Thinking with Bourdieu', *Women's History Review* 16, no. 2 (2001); Joyce Goodman and Jane Martin, 'Networks after Bourdieu: Women, Education and Politics from the 1980s to the 1920s', *History of Education Researcher* 80, no. November (2007); Lisa Adkins and Beverley Skeggs, *Feminism after Bourdieu* (Oxford: Blackwell, 2004); Beverly Skeggs, 'Context and Background: Pierre Bourdieu's Analysis of Class, Gender and Sexuality', *The Sociological Review* 52 (2004); Krais, 'Gender and Symbolic Violence.'
6. Terry Lovell, 'Thinking Feminism with and against Bourdieu' in *Reading Bourdieu on Society and Culture*, ed. Bridget Fowler (Oxford: Blackwell, 2000).

Bourdieu's perspective as assuming gender as relational and carrying varying amounts of social capital in different contexts.[1] The concept of the symbolic economy is helpful for understanding the negotiation or transformation of power and relationships that may be accomplished through the transactions of capital.[2] For Moi, although a woman may lose some legitimacy through her gender, she may still have enough capital to make an impact in the field.[3] This is the case for example, when women of high social capital engage in patronage and philanthropy, a category that applies to Mary Sumner.

Bourdieu interprets biographical events as a life trajectory which he sees as a 'series of successive locations, moves and field positions'.[4] He describes this process as social ageing which accompanies biological ageing. Biographical events, locations and individual moves are not detached from structures or other agents.[5] He maintains agents can only be understood as social beings and refers to the 'fallacy' of biography that treats the individual as singular and detached from context.[6] In Bourdieu's view, this approach fails to engage with the structural properties of the field, and its logic and claim to legitimacy which intersects with the habitus of the agent in question to inform their horizon of possibilities. This understanding that an agent is linked to the collection of other agents engaged in the same field and facing same realm of possibilities accords with Barbara Caine's advocacy for a collective approach in order to avoid the potential distortion of a focus on an individual exceptional subject detached from context.[7] Bourdieu's insistence that the life of an individual agent should be placed in context also acknowledges the significance of networks and supports the prosopographical analysis of an agent that seeks, through assembling and comparing evidence on agents sharing common characteristics, to understand them relationally and in context and to illuminate values, attitudes and meanings.[8] Evidence relating

---

1. Krais, 'Gender and Symbolic Violence', 156; Moi, *What is a Woman?*, 269, 291.
2. Joan Wallach Scott, *Gender and the Politics of History* (New York: Columbia University Press, 1999).
3. Moi, *What is a Woman?*, 293.
4. Bourdieu, *The Field of Cultural Production*, 189.
5. Bourdieu and Wacquant, *An Invitation*, 297-298.
6. Pierre Bourdieu, 'The Biographical Illusion' in *Identity: A Reader* ed. Paul Du Gay, Jessica Evans, and Peter Redman (London: Sage, 2000), 304.
7. Barbara Caine, 'Feminist Biography and Feminist History', *Women's History Review* 3, no. 2 (1992).
8. Peter Cunningham, 'Innovators, Networks and Structures: Towards a Prosopography of Progressivism', *History of Education* 30, no. 5 (2001); Bourdieu, *The Field of Cultural Production*, 8, 180-181, 193.

to others of similar habitus is relevant to locating the agent in focus within and against the dominant doxa with Bourdieu's understanding of social reality and his notion of field is also compatible with Fuchs's identification of networks as concerned with the interplay of agents and structures and the production of knowledge, as Joyce Goodman and Jane Martin illustrate in their application of Bourdieu's conceptual tools to intellectual exchange, and the role and authority of key women in relation to organisational networks in a wider political context.[1]

Bourdieu favours engagement with agents and structures that are historically situated. He draws attention to the embedded historical aspect within habitus and fields,[2] and considers that 'the separation of sociology and history is a disastrous division, and one totally devoid of all epistemological justification: all sociology should be historical and all history sociological'.[3] His advocacy for a history 'which finds in each successive state of the structure under examination both the product of previous struggles to maintain or to transform this structure and the principles, via the contradiction, the tensions, and the relations of force which constitute it, of subsequent transformations' is in other words a call to engage with what historians conceptualise as, cause and consequence and change and continuity.[4] Bourdieu's thinking tools provide a means for unpicking structures, struggles and transformations and I apply them to an analysis of Mary Sumner's life and activism that seeks to engage with issues of constraint, agency and empowerment.

The historiography of the categories of 'women's', 'feminist' and 'gender' history,[5] and of education demonstrates that historians are, like the subjects they chose for enquiry, time and value bound. Bourdieu uses the concept of reflexivity which calls for 'conscious self referencing' in an attempt to reduce biases from social origin and references, academic location (power and status) and intellectual

1. Eckhardt Fuchs, 'Networks and the History of Education', *Paedagogica Historica* 42, no. 2 (2007); Goodman and Martin, 'Networks after Bourdieu: Women, Education and Politics from the 1980s to the 1920s'.
2. Bourdieu and Wacquant, *An Invitation*, 124.
3. Ibid., 90.
4. Ibid., 91.
5. Sue Morgan, ed. *The Feminist History Reader* (London: Routledge, 2006); Ruth Watts, 'Gendering the Story: Change in the History of Education', *History of Education* 34, no. 3 (2005); Joyce Goodman, 'The Gendered Politics of Historical Writing in History of Education', ibid., 41, no. 1 (2012).

assumptions.[1] This applies to agents and to the disciplinary structures in which they operate and challenges practitioners to address presuppositions systematically in the 'unthought categories of thought which delimit the thinkable and predetermine the thought'.[2] This idea relates to history, as practiced by agents temporally located, subject to assumptions of value [habitus] and seeking recognition [symbolic capital]. Bourdieu's concept of reflexivity resonates with Sue Morgan's call for the 'perpetual interrogation of dominant historical concepts and categories'.[3]

Bourdieu recognises that the act of theorising is not a detached activity but an act of practical involvement with the subject and I acknowledge my location in respect of Mary Sumner.[4] Mary Sumner's views on religion, gender roles, sexual morality and social stratification are at some distance to my values as a secular feminist formed in the twentieth century. Yet her activism may be interpreted as contributing towards the opening of the horizons of possibility available to me. Her views on parenting and educational entitlement resonate to some degree with my own beliefs and experience as a teacher. Her writings reveal glimpses of warmth and humour, yet the religious agenda and rhetoric of much of her archive means that her inner life remains intriguingly elusive. Bourdieu's attitude to engagement with the study of a life trajectory encapsulates my intention:

> To try to really situate one's mind in the place the interviewee occupies in the social space from necessity by starting to question them from that point, in order to take their part in it in some way . . . is not to project oneself into others in the way that phenomenologists claim. It is to give oneself a generic and genetic understanding of who they are, based on the theoretical and practical command of the social conditions which produced them.[5]

To this end, I follow Bourdieu in being conscious of the fallacy inherent in an unthinking assumption of objectivity, and acknowledge his observation that there is no point outside the system from which to

1. Bourdieu and Wacquant, *An Invitation*, 38.
2. Ibid., 40.
3. Morgan, 'Theorising Feminist History: A Thirty Year Retrospective', 339.
4. Craig J. Calhoun, Edward LiPuma, and Moishe Postone, eds., *Bourdieu: Critical Perspectives* (Cambridge: Polity Press, 1993), 6.
5. Grenfell and James, *Bourdieu and Education*, 174. Translation from Bourdieu's *La Misere du Monde*.

gain a neutral disinterested perspective.[1] Yet in presenting arguments rooted in evidence I strive to achieve a methodological approach and a theoretical perspective towards understanding Mary Sumner as a woman of her times that is respectful to her and to the disciplinary traditions of historical scholarship and so contributes to and participates in an ongoing construction of her archive. Bourdieu's theoretical understanding that agents or structures seek to maintain domination, which he expresses in the term 'reproduction', frames analysis of Mary Sumner as an advocate for the religious values of the Established Church. As she conformed to, and advocated, religiously authorised notions of behaviour mediated by class and gender, the concepts of symbolic violence and misrecognition are also relevant. Bourdieu suggests that the analysis of a field which seeks to conceptualise the process of participation in, and the reproduction and transformation of, social systems and power could be approached through a three-level analysis. This involves analysing the position of the field vis-à-vis the field of power and secondly mapping the structure of relations between the positions occupied by agents competing for authority in the field. The third level focuses on the habitus of agents, the systems of dispositions they have acquired by internalising a determinate type of social and economic condition and which find in a definite trajectory within the field under consideration a more or less favourable opportunity to become actualised.[2] I apply these analytical steps in reverse order, moving broadly from informative habitus, horizons of possibility, and activism realised through 'field manoeuvres' to an examination of agency and achievement in relation to upholding or transforming the doxa and the interest of dominant groups. These steps are deployed in chapters relating Mary Sumner to the themes of religion, mission and education.

Analysis of Mary Sumner's MU in relation to power is informed by the following assumptions. The field of power is understood to relate to the state apparatus of government personified by the monarch as the symbol of the nation. Power implies political power in a broad sense but not exclusively so. The notion of the field of power as power to dominate and reproduce advantage overlaps with power in the economic field, the power of ownership and the political, cultural, and educational advantages that economic power may be transacted towards. The Anglican Church has power in the religious field but also in the political field because as the Established Church it has

1. Calhoun, LiPuma, and Postone, *Bourdieu: Critical Perspectives*, 6.
2. Bourdieu and Wacquant, *An Invitation*, 104-105.

representatives in the legislature. Anglicanism is regarded as a major sub-field in relation to the religious field as a whole. In this book, the MU as an organised official body representative of a specific interest group is regarded as a sub-field within Anglicanism.

Part 1

Religion

Mary Sumner, Margaret Lady Heywood, Heywood Sumner, 'Loulie' Louisa Gore Browne, and George Sumner Golden Wedding, 1898

Old Alresford Rectory c. 1900

Chapter 2
A Family Affair: Mary Sumner, Religious Habitus, Evangelical Enthusiasm and Anglican Advocacy

2.1 Family life, living religion, capital assets and symbolic gifts

Mary Sumner's religious preferences were framed against a context of attention to matters of religion within the home and to the public performance of perceived religious obligations. Her initial encounters with religion in home life were under the guidance of her parents, Thomas and Mary Heywood, former Unitarian converts to Anglicanism. From the age of twenty (1848) Mary's experience of religion in home life, and in matters of doctrinal interpretation, was also informed by the Sumner family. Her marriage placed her in proximity to her husband's views on religion and to the authoritative views of his uncle, the Archbishop of Canterbury, and his father, the Bishop of Winchester. Both families exemplify the contemporary evangelical enthusiasm in their approach to religion, characteristic across a range of denominations at a time of 'religious revival' and contested authority in the field of religion. This chapter explores religion in the daily conduct of home life and public affairs that Mary Sumner experienced in childhood and married life. The evangelical enthusiasm and Anglican affiliation of Mary Sumner's kin is related to notions of religious capital particularly in relation to women. The chapter then moves outwards to locate the doctrinal preferences prioritised in Mary Sumner's kinship network against a context of contested religious capital. Attention is given to the field of religion within which members of her kinship and social network manoeuvred. The contextual circumstances which framed these manoeuvres are noted as they inform Mary Sumner's notions of capital and horizons of possibility and are thus pertinent to her activism via the MU.

Mary Elizabeth Heywood was born on December 31st 1828 in Swinton, near Manchester. Mary's mother Mary Elizabeth Barton (d. 1870) was the daughter of John Barton of Swinton, a Unitarian land owner. Her father Thomas (1797-1861) was the third son of the banker

Nathaniel Heywood and had attended Manchester Grammar School before becoming, in 1818, a partner in the family bank.[1] Prior to their conversion circa 1832, her parents had been prominent members of the influential Manchester Unitarian Cross Street Chapel. Unitarians did not believe in the virgin birth or the doctrine of the Trinity, nor did they use the Book of Common Prayer. They were also distinctive in denying the doctrine of original sin. For Unitarians, Jesus was not divine but represented the most perfect human; humanity was envisioned as perfectible and living religion was perceived as an application of reason to improve the individual and society.[2] However, as in the evangelical tradition within Anglicanism, social ills were seen as attributable to bad habits and the remedies were to be sought in personal efforts towards improvement. The Cross Street Chapel congregation, led by William Gaskell between 1828 and 1884, represented powerful families from the commercial and industrial elite of the town who were committed to social reform, civic improvement and the removal of the cultural and political disadvantages attendant on their denominational preference.[3] What Helen Plant encapsulates as 'the quest by Unitarian men to achieve "gentleman" status, and occupy the positions of leadership within the new urban middle class to which their growing affluence seemed to entitle them', an aspiration supported by joining the Established Church, appears to be exemplified in the careers of Thomas Heywood and his elder brother Sir Benjamin Heywood (1793-1865), also a convert to Anglicanism.[4] Benjamin had been created a baronet in acknowledgement of his parliamentary support of the 1832 Reform Bill. Thomas Heywood likewise achieved public office as Borough Reeve of Salford in 1826 and as High Sheriff of Herefordshire in 1840. Whilst David Bebbington attributes Sir Benjamin's conversion

1. C.W. Sutton and Alan G. Crosby, 'Thomas Heywood (1797-1866)', *Oxford Dictionary of National Biography* (Oxford University Press, 2010), [http://www.oxforddnb.com/view/article/13191, accessed November 27th 2012].
2. Kathryn Gleadle, *The Early Feminists: Radical Unitarians and the Emergence of the Women's Rights Movements, 1831-51* (Basingstoke: Macmillan, 1995), 7, 26.
3. Ruth Watts, *Gender, Power and the Unitarians in England, 1760-1860* (London: Longman, 1998). Isabel Mary Heywood and Sir Thomas Percival Heywood, *Reminiscences, Letters and Journals of Thomas Percival Heywood, Baronet. Arranged by His Eldest Daughter (Isabel Mary). With a Preface by the Rev. George Body* (printed for private circulation: Manchester, 1899), 4-5.
4. Helen Plant, '"Ye Are All One in Christ Jesus": Aspects of Unitarianism and Feminism in Birmingham, c. 1869-90', *Women's History Review* 9, no. 4 (2000): 723.

to the Established church to the attraction of liturgy rather than status, the conversions of Benjamin and Thomas Heywood did coincide with advances in their social and political status.[1]

Piety and scrutiny of conscience feature prominently in *Mary Sumner: Her Life and Work* and *A Short History of the Mothers' Union,* but there is no reference to Mary Sumners' Unitarian heritage. This is an understandable omission, given that both sources are written with the intention of asserting the superiority of Anglican approaches to liturgy and belief. Although Joyce Coombs acknowledges the Nonconformist tradition of the family, her assertion that the Heywoods all 'returned to the Church of England' is incorrect. The younger brother of Thomas and Benjamin, James Heywood, a liberal MP noted for his efforts to revoke the Test Acts (which permitted only Anglican communicants to obtain English university degrees), remained active as a Unitarian.[2] James does not feature in Mary Sumner's recorded recollections of family interaction. However, the emphasis on culture, self-improvement and philanthropy characteristic of Unitarian belief are evident in the Heywoods' conduct of private life and public affairs, and Katherine Gleadle's view that Unitarian beliefs were significant in influencing attitudes to the spiritual status, role and education of women resonates with Mary Sumner's experience.

In 1833 Thomas Heywood retired from the bank and assumed the life of a country landowner at Hope End near Ledbury in Herefordshire. The previous owner of the 500-acre estate, Edward Moulton-Barrett (who later assumed the surname Browning), had built the house in 1815 in an oriental, Moorish style that incorporated minarets at the eastern end. However, Moulton-Barrett, whose fortune derived from the ownership of sugar plantations in Jamaica, was forced to sell when financial difficulties brought about by slave emancipation led to his mortgage being foreclosed. His daughter, the poet Elizabeth Barrett Browning, commemorated her childhood home at Hope End in *The Lost Bower,* a detail that Mary Sumner recorded in her biographical notes. This celebrity connection was reproduced in *Mary Sumner: Her Life and*

1. Watts, *Gender, Power and the Unitarians in England, 1760-1860*; David W. Bebbington, 'Unitarian Members of Parliament in the Nineteenth Century' (2009), [http://hdl.handle.net/1893/1647, accessed May 17th 2017].
2. Joyce Coombs, *George and Mary Sumner: Their Life and Times* (Westminster: Sumner Press, 1965), 37; M.C. Curthoys, 'Heywood, James (1810-1897)', *Oxford Dictionary of National Biography* (Oxford: Oxford University Press, 2009), [http://www.oxforddnb.com/view/article/56315]. James Heywood kept his Unitarian faith and sources relating to Mary Sumner suggest there was no contact between them.

Work. It was at Hope End that Mary remembered galloping her pony Strawberry and boating on the lake in what is recorded as 'a girlhood that was not only happy, but was also characterised by an amount of freedom', with her elder sister Maggie and brother Tom.[1]

The Heywoods were personally attentive to their children's religious and cultural education. The children were included in trips to the continent. Mary an accomplished musician, spoke several languages and was encouraged to enjoy history by her antiquarian father, an early member of the Chetham's Society and the collector of a library of tracts and pamphlets.[2] Bible study was directed by Mrs Heywood and the children's upbringing also reflected Thomas Heywood's commitment to philanthropy as a means of social improvement. The establishment of a school and the funding of the Anglican Church on his estate at Wellington Heath were projects that the Heywood children were encouraged to support.[3] The emphasis on philanthropy, education and culture characteristic of Unitarians is also demonstrated by Sir Benjamin Heywood, a noted promoter of Mechanics' Institutes.[4] The themes of philanthropy and education in relation to Mary Sumner's activism are the subject of following chapters.

In the winter of 1846 the Heywoods were in Rome with their daughters Margaret and Mary, where they were introduced to George Sumner (1824-1909) at a party given by his cousin Mrs Wilson, a daughter of John Bird Sumner (1780-1862), who became Archbishop of Canterbury in 1848. George, then aged 22, was enjoying a period of travel after graduating from Balliol College, Oxford, prior to taking Holy Orders. George was the son of Charles Sumner (1790-1874), Bishop of Winchester from 1827 until 1867, and formerly chaplain to George IV.[5] George and Mary were married on July 26th 1848 at the Church of St James's the Great, Colwall, in a ceremony presided over by the bridegroom's father. Mary Sumner reproduced in full what she referred to the 'glowing and amusing terms' with which the *Herefordshire Journal* reported the festivities to

1. Mary Porter, Mary Woodward, and Horatia Erskine, *Mary Sumner: Her Life and Work and a Short History of the Mothers' Union* (Winchester: Warren and Sons, 1921), 4-6.
2. Sutton and Crosby, 'Thomas Heywood (1797-1866)'.
3. Mary Sumner, 'Account of Her Early Life at Hope End 1828-46' in *Mothers' Union* (Lambeth Palace Library).
4. Watts, *Gender, Power and the Unitarians in England, 1760-1860*, 91. Mary Sumner's parents were Thomas Heywood (1797-1866), formerly of Heywood's Bank in Manchester, and Mary Elizabeth Barton (d. 1870).
5. Porter, Woodward, and Erskine, *Mary Sumner*, 9-10.

its readers in her memoir of her husband. That this was written more than sixty years after the wedding suggests, somewhat poignantly, that Mary had retained the clipping from the newspaper. In addition to a faithful report of the attire of the bride and bridesmaids, the *Journal* recorded a 'sumptuous déjeunér' served to sixty friends and family. The *Journal* article gives an indication of the extent of the Heywood's estate in recording that:

> More than 600 people partook of the lavish hospitality provide by Mr and Mrs Heywood for their tenants and labourers with their wives and children from Wellington Heath, Munsley, Coddington, Bosbury and Colwall. Games and amusements of varied kinds were provided after the repast in a large field near the upper lodge and were cheered by the strains of an excellent band.[1]

George and Mary Sumner lived for two years at Crawley near Winchester, where George served as curate to Canon Jacob. Following the death of Mrs Charles Sumner, George, Mary and their baby daughter Margaret Effie (born 1849) moved to Farnham Castle where, with George's unmarried sister Emily, they became part of the bishop's household. The birth of their second daughter, Louisa 'Loulie' Mary Alice, in 1850 enlarged the family. George's official position in the Castle was as his father's domestic chaplain and at this time he was also appointed as a chaplain to his uncle the Archbishop.[2] So Mary was positioned at the heart of a kinship circle representing the highest authority in Anglicanism, in a prestigious location, where family life and the family business of administrating and upholding the ascendancy of the Established Church coexisted.

After two years at Farnham, Bishop Sumner appointed his son to the living of Old Alresford, a large rural parish a few miles from the cathedral city of Winchester. George and Mary set up home in the twelve-bedroom rectory where they were to live for the next thirty five years. It was here in 1853 that their son Heywood, who in later life became an artist associated with the Arts and Crafts movement and a noted archaeologist, was born. They socialised amongst the local gentry and were regular guests in local country houses but maintained connections

1. *Hereford Journal* August 2nd 1848, 3; Mary Sumner, *Memoir of George Henry Sumner, D.D., Bishop of Guildford: Published for His Friends by Special Request* (Winchester: Warren and Son, 1910), 8-10.
2. Mary Sumner, *Memoir of George Henry Sumner, D.D., Bishop of Guildford: Published for His Friends by Special Request* (Winchester: Warren and Son, 1910), 8-14.

with the network of social and clerical contacts established by association with their ecclesiastical kinsmen. Although removed from the Bishop's residence, the family business of religion continued to be centred on and conducted from home. As mistress of her own household, twenty-three year old Mary embraced the duties of 'helpmeet' and practical assistant to her husband in efforts to promote adherence to the Church and instil religious principles in the conduct of parish life.

Bishop Charles Sumner and Archbishop John Bird Sumner (1780-1862), are considered highly influential evangelicals; representative of what Owen Chadwick considers 'the strongest force in British life', significant because in inspiring religious enthusiasm across a range of denominations it affected the conduct of public affairs.[1] Within Anglicanism there were different emphases on the interpretation of doctrine: Lower Church understanding was closer to the Protestantism of Methodists and other Nonconformist denominations, whereas High Church (Anglo-Catholic) positions were closer to Roman Catholic practice. Evangelicals believed that in order to achieve salvation the depravity of man and the sacrifice of Christ as atonement for sin must be accepted. Evangelical believers sought a purposeful and worthy life in order to be able to give a satisfactory account of their lives at judgement day. This was realised through an emphasis on demonstrably 'living' religion in the home sphere and public life. This imperative for accountability also encouraged a sense of 'mission' and an appetite to spread the 'joys of living religion' which was frequently pursued through philanthropic activity or educational initiatives.[2]

The evangelical impulse had its roots in the emotionally experienced religion of John Wesley but the evangelical tradition upheld by the Sumner family remained firmly within the Anglican Church and drew inspiration from the influential Clapham sect, so called in reference to the location of the church that formed the locus for members' worship. Reforming rather than radical, 'Claphamites' were dedicated to the improvement of society through the practical application of religion to current affairs. The exercise of power should be mediated by conscience

1. Owen Chadwick, *The Victorian Church Part I, 1827-1859* (A&C Black, 1966), 5. See also Kenneth Hylson-Smith, *Evangelicals in the Church of England, 1734-1984* (T&T Clark, 1988); D.W. Bebbington, *Evangelicalism in Modern Britain: A History from the 1730s to the 1980s* (London: Routledge, 1988).
2. Ian Bradley, *The Call to Seriousness: The Evangelical Impact on the Victorians* (London: Jonathan Cape, 1976), 21. Bradley notes William Wilberforce pressing his son Samuel, the future Anglican bishop, for evidence of his religious awakening.

and moral conduct. Foremost amongst prominent members of the sect was William Wilberforce (1759-1833) the distinguished campaigner against the slave trade.[1] The Sumners were related to the Wilberforce family by marriage. Wilberforce's wife Judith was the aunt of Hannah Bird Sumner, the mother of Charles and John Bird Sumner. The family connection was sustained over the following generations through ecclesiastical patronage and friendship. William's son Samuel, later Bishop of Oxford and successor to Charles Sumner at Winchester, was given the livings at Brightstone and Alverstoke, and appointed to the post of archdeacon of Surrey in 1839 by his second cousin. In later years Samuel was to be a regular visitor at Old Alresford rectory and his son Ernest and his second wife Emily were to feature as key players in the recount of genesis of the diocesan Mothers' Union.

The practice of recording biographies of notable male family members was common to both the Heywoods and the Sumners. These functioned as mementos for the numerous members of their extended families. Mary's eulogistic *Memoir of George Sumner, D.D., Bishop of Guildford,* 'written for his friends by special request' and 'published for private circulation' in 1910, is certainly in this category and may also be interpreted as a means for articulating her grief.[2] George Sumner, the author the 1874 *Life of C.R. Sumner, D.D., Bishop of Winchester During a Forty Years' Episcopate,* was not only his father's biographer but also completed a memoir of Sir Benjamin Heywood on behalf of his father-in-law.[3] Thomas Heywood's own *Reminiscences* were edited by his daughter Isabel, Mary Sumner's niece. Her claim that: 'It will help many a one to know how a layman, living in the world . . . and sharing the ordinary pleasures of a country gentleman, can yet fulfil the command; "What so ever ye do, do all to the Glory of God"';[4] illustrates the assertion of symbolic religious capital, a characteristic common to all the Heywood and Sumner memoirs. Both families presented religion as a public practice and as integral to the conduct of harmonious domestic

1. David Spring, 'The Clapham Sect: Some Social and Political Aspects', *Victorian Studies* 5, no. 1 (1961); Anne Stott, *Wilberforce: Family and Friends* (Oxford: Oxford University Press, 2012).
2. Sumner, *Memoir of George Sumner.*
3. Thomas Heywood, Sir Benjamin Heywood, and George Sumner, *A Memoir of Sir Benjamin Heywood . . . By His Brother, T.H. With Two Chapters of Domestic Life, and Letters, 1840-1865* (Manchester: printed for private circulation, 1888); George Henry Sumner, *Life of C.R. Sumner, D.D., Bishop of Winchester, During a Forty Years' Episcopate* (London, 1876).
4. Heywood and Heywood, *Reminiscences*, x.

life. The memoirs publicise private devotion as a public virtue. The *Memoir of Sir Benjamin* Heywood includes '*Two Chapters of Domestic Life*'. Mary Sumner's references to religion in daily life, as a child and in her married life recalled in her manuscripts *Early Life at Hope End and Account of the Founding of the Mothers' Union and Parochial Work at Old Alresford*, accord with the emphasis on earnest religion recorded by other members of her family, and by George Sumner as a feature of his evangelical upbringing.

All the memoirs follow a pattern. In addition to recording the observance of religious practice in home life, attention to religious education and scrutiny of conscience, they communicate the valuing of warm family relationships. A happy childhood guided by affectionate pious parents, is followed by domestic harmony in marriage, and a career featuring religious and educational good works. Finally, family members (and servants) gather for a peaceful deathbed parting and testimonials to the character of the deceased from worthy sources are quoted. Mary affirmed the affectionate relations in the Sumner family by commenting on her own reception as a daughter in law:

> There never could have been a more united family than the Sumners, and it was remarkable that the sons and daughters who entered into the home life at Farnham Castle, were each one treated as part of the family quite as much as the real sons and daughters.[1]

Mary and George maintained strong links with their Heywood and Sumner relatives through regular visits. From 1850 they took annual holidays with Bishop Sumner, which included visits to Geneva, Rome and Seville, whilst their children stayed with their Heywood grandparents 'who made them supremely happy' at Hope End.[2] Mrs Heywood, Mary's mother, when widowed in 1866, moved to Old Alresford Rectory. Kinship ties were reinforced through the rituals of christenings, weddings and funerals. Intermarriage between relatives was not unusual. Just how close connections could be is exemplified by the marriages of Mary's elder sister Margaret (d. January 30th 1894) and daughter Margaret Effie. Margaret married Sir Benjamin's son, her cousin (Sir) Thomas Percival Heywood (MP for Salford), on May 19th 1846 and Margaret Effie (1849-1916) married Arthur Percival Heywood, the eldest son of her aunt Margaret, in 1872. The remarriage of widowers within close kinship, social and professional networks was also common. In 1837 George

1. Sumner, *Memoir of George Sumner*, 11.
2. Ibid., 25-27.

Sumner's sister Louisanna married the Reverend William Gibson, who had previously been married to her cousin Eliza. George and Mary's daughter Louisa became the second wife of Barrington Gore Browne, the son of Bishop and Mrs Harold Browne of Winchester in 1882.[1]

The Heywoods and Sumners were on cordial terms. The former Unitarianism of Mary's parents and uncle was not perceived as a difficulty by the Sumner family, despite their prominence in the Anglican hierarchy. Thomas Heywood and his brother Sir Benjamin, who was considered by Charles Sumner to be 'most devotionally minded and kind hearted',[2] were accepted as committed Anglicans. George acted as chaplain to his brother-in-law, Thomas Percival Heywood, in his role of High Sherriff of Lancashire (1851), and gave his funeral sermon in 1897.[3] Although Mary Sumner did not refer to the conversion of her parents, her cousin Thomas Percival Heywood's *Reminiscences* acknowledged the Unitarian background of his parents with respect: 'To this day I hear with pain and impatience any abuse of Unitarians. . . . My father and mother were faithful and devoted servants of God before they became members of the Church.'[4]

The value placed on religious sensibility characteristic of evangelicals is illustrated by Mary Sumner choosing to recall her mother's girlhood religious awakening after a dream of judgement (when still a Unitarian) in her 'Memoir of Early Life at Hope End'. Mary's references to the solemnity of confirmation and communion also accord with the personal experience of 'vital religion' professed by evangelicals, and also affirm the advocacy for communion expressed by her husband and father-in-law. She recalled the birth of her daughter, Margaret Effie, in 1849 as a religious experience: 'My first thought when my first child was born was of an awful sense of responsibility – God had given an immortal soul in to our keeping it was a blessed solemn moment the joy was quite unspeakable.'[5] The evangelical belief in active efforts

1. Heywood and Heywood, *Reminiscences*, 27-30, 40, 261. Louisanna and William Gibson's daughter Ella Sophia married Henry, a son of Sir Benjamin Heywood; Sumner, *Memoir of George Sumner*, 10, 135-6; Heywood Sumner, 'Memorials of the Family of Sumner from the Sixteenth Century to 1904' (Southampton 1904). Porter, Woodward and Erskine give 1871 as the date for Margaret Effie's marriage, in contradiction to other sources.
2. Sumner, *Life of C.R. Sumner*, 425.
3. Heywood and Heywood, *Reminiscences*, 43, 264-75.
4. Ibid., 4-5.
5. Mary Sumner, 'Account of the Founding of the Mothers' Union and Parochial Work at Old Alresford' in *Mothers' Union* (Lambeth Palace Library).

towards securing salvation is illustrated in her other writing. In a talk directed to mothers on 'Obedience' she drew on biblical authority to assert that: 'Our Father in Heaven shows by his training of us, his grown up children that life was meant to be a place of discipline and self-conquest.'[1] As a young wife Mary kept a card on her dressing table as prompt towards religious endeavour and although she recalled this in her public recollections on the genesis of the MU, it was at the time, a private exercise.[2] Similar scrutiny of conscience is noted in Jennie (Mrs Charles) Sumner's response to the Bishop's translation to Winchester in 1827: 'humility fills my mind my prayer is most earnest that we may be kept humble . . . more talents added to our charge calls for redoubled vigilance and activity', a sentiment repeated by George Sumner when, as Bishop of Guildford, he urged clergy not to overlook their own private prayer and improvement.[3]

Religion was presented as a comfort and a good death signified a good life. Mrs Heywood was sustained in her final illness by her son-in-law's sermons and ministration. Preparation for, and anticipation of, the afterlife were mentioned frequently. George Sumner was described as 'sailing placidly to eternity in absolute submission to the will of God'.[4] Jennie Sumner approached death with expressions of 'joyful hope and expectation' in a 'happy state of semi-entrancement'. The death of her husband was similarly an occasion for family participation, with George Sumner taking Holy Communion at his father's bedside amidst children and servants waiting to be wished farewell by the dying bishop.[5] The joyful anticipation of the afterlife was similarly recorded in the later account of Mary Sumner's own death, which notes 'the vision must have been wonderful'.[6] The sorrows of parting were alleviated by the comfort of the family circle and the conviction that a life well lived would assure salvation and reunion in the hereafter. The attention to preparation for what Mary Sumner referred to as 'the Home above' involved the

1. 'Obedience' in *Home Life* (Winchester: Warren and Sons, 1895), 33. Romans 16, 'We are the children of God'; Hebrews 16, 'Whom the Lord loveth he chasteneth'.
2. Porter, Woodward, and Erskine, *Mary Sumner*, 13.
3. Sumner, *Life of C.R. Sumner*, 126; Sumner, *Memoir of George Sumner*, 108-9. Charge by the Bishop of Guildford.
4. *Memoir of George Sumner*, 13, 28, 153-4.
5. Sumner, *Life of C.R. Sumner*, 324, 479. Jennie Sumner died in 1849; Charles in 1874.
6. Louisa Gore Browne, 'Letter to Mrs Hubert Barclay in Response to Condolence Letter on the Death of Mary Sumner, August 1921' in *Mothers' Union* (Lambeth Palace Library).

observance of religious ritual in the earthly home.[1] Sunday was observed as a quiet day for spiritual refreshment; two services were attended even whilst on holiday. The habit of family prayer, in which servants were included, shared by both the Heywoods and Sumners, was sustained by George and Mary Sumner in their own household. In 1886 their new home was consecrated by a religious service and the reading of a prayer specially composed by George to mark the occasion.[2]

The evangelical emphasis on individual efforts towards salvation prompted reflection on the religious natures of men and women. William Wilberforce's 1797 publication A *Practical View of the Prevailing Religious System of Professed Christians in The Higher and Middle Classes of this Country Contrasted with Real Christianity* was influential in asserting a heightened religious sensibility in women, which was thought to suit them to the domestic sphere, as providers not only of physical respite but a moral refuge from the competitive masculine world of work and public affairs. The trope of the 'Angel in the House', a phrase originating from Coventry Patmore's poem extolling loving domesticity, encapsulated this conception of womanhood which became a dominant discourse during the nineteenth century.[3] The evangelical focus on the home as a site of religious observance, far from suggesting a division of separate spheres, involved greater emphasis on domestic relations, including the negotiation of marriage and the role of fathers in home life; issues that Mary Sumner addressed in much of her writing.[4]

---

1. Mary Sumner, 'Marriage Address 2' in *Home Life* (Winchester: Warren and Sons, 1895), 24.
2. *Memoir of George Sumner*, 21, 16, 84.
3. Eileen Janes Yeo, 'Some Paradoxes of Empowerment' in *Radical Femininity; Women's Self Representation in the Public Sphere*, ed. Eileen Janes Yeo (Manchester: Manchester University Press, 1998), 4; Sean Gill, *Women and the Church of England: From the Eighteenth Century to the Present* (London: Society for Promoting Christian Knowledge, 1994), 29-31; Deborah Gorham, *The Victorian Girl and the Feminine Ideal* (London: Croom Helm, 1982), 3, 7-9.
4. 'Evangelical Christianity was a domestic religion [which] articulated a new masculine norm against which men's conduct has been measured ever since.' John Tosh, *A Man's Place: Masculinity and the Middle-Class Home in Victorian England* (New Haven, [Conn.]; London: Yale University Press, 2007), 6, 11; see also Frances Knight, *The Nineteenth Century Church and English Society* (Cambridge: Cambridge University Press, 1995), 41. Knight notes the large volume of religious publication as evidence for the home as a site of religious observance; Stephanie Olsen, 'The Authority of Motherhood in Question: Fatherhood and the Moral Education of Children in England, c. 1870-1900', *Women's History Review* 18, no. 5 (2009).

The focus on religion in the home that positioned parents as religious educators and acknowledged the influence of women was evident in the Sumner and Heywood families. Charles Sumner, as Rector of Highclere in 1817, circulated an address to parents emphasising the importance of religious home example on children.[1] The Heywoods also modelled religious conduct to their children. Mary Sumner wrote: 'I never remember disobeying my parents. Such a course seemed to be made impossible . . . by their example of high principle as regards obedience, truth and honour.' She noted the 'debt of gratitude' owed to Mrs Heywood for the thorough religious training that she and her siblings Tom and Maggie had received, which included daily Bible reading. Mary created a picture of childhood as a time of innocence and playfulness, and parental care as affectionate. She also noted the affection shown by her father-in-law to her baby daughter, Margaret Effie, [2] which accorded with George Sumner's recollection of his parents' enjoyment of holidays with their children. He included an extract from a letter written by his mother, Jennie Sumner, in the memoir of his father:

> We are greatly enjoying ourselves walking – rambling over the rocks still more by being with our children and permitted to enjoy their society as we can never do at home to be so much with my dear husband and to see him thus surrounded with our children and delighting to hear them converse freely are sources of happiness.[3]

Mary Sumner's experience of family relationships demonstrated that the role of mother and helpmeet was esteemed. Jennie Sumner regarded married love as blessed and sanctified by God, and George Sumner's grandmother, Hannah Bird Sumner, is quoted as stating: 'no life can be happier than that of a private clergyman's wife – when the parties are tenderly united by a bond of rational affection, not expecting unchequered felicity (which in no station here below is attainable).'[4] Accounts of family life, couched in conventional religious rhetoric, refer to the contribution of wives and mothers and extol their virtues as religious exemplars to their families. At Farnham Castle, George Sumner's home from 1827-1848:

1. Sumner, *Life of C.R. Sumner*, 34.
2. Sumner, 'Early Life'; *Memoir of George Sumner*, 14; Porter, Woodward, and Erskine, *Mary Sumner*, 8.
3. Sumner, *Life of C.R. Sumner*, 220. Extract from a letter from Mrs Charles Sumner included in the memoir without addressee or date.
4. Ibid., 220, 23.

> There never was a house where domestic happiness was more beautifully seen . . . who can forget the joyous radiance of Mrs [Charles] Sumner of whom it may be truly said, that she was the centre of a system of gladness, which influenced the whole circle as it moved harmoniously around her.[1]

Mary Sumner drew on a well-worn cliché in referring to her mother as the 'Angel in the house to us all'. She further eulogised her mother by describing her as 'winning people of all sorts and kinds, rich and poor by her tender sympathy, her charm of manner, her cleverness and humour, and her quick appreciation of all that was good and interesting in those who approached her'. Mrs Heywood was also celebrated for her 'very decided religious convictions' which 'moulded her whole tone of thought and manner of life and were an influence to those with whom she came in contact'.[2] Her endeavours as a spiritual helpmeet were acknowledged by her husband on his deathbed: 'It is all through you that I die in faith and peace – God bless you we shall soon meet again.' Jennie, Mrs Charles Sumner was similarly commended; her moral influence on students tutored by her husband was considered worthy of comment in the memoir of his life.[3] According to George Sumner: 'She was a true mother in Israel and throughout her married life a helpmeet to the husband that she dearly loved both in domestic and public life.'[4] A eulogy signed by 684 clergy publicly acknowledged her contribution to family life and her husband's career:

> She 'consecrated all to the service of her heavenly master' and well did she work with him [the Bishop] by her loving holy influence. The Golden thread of principle, the fear and love of God was woven into the Farnham daily life, and made it very attractive to all who shared in it.[5]

George Sumner's conduct as a parish clergyman, which involved the 'heart to heart' work of taking religion into the homes of parishioners by visiting, leading family prayer, and winning over men, upheld the evangelical stance of his father, for whom ministry was more than the public act of preaching 'for hearers only' once a week. It involved 'attention to the

1. Ibid., 199. Reminiscence of Reverend Charles Hume.
2. Sumner, 'Early Life'.
3. Sumner, *Life of C.R. Sumner*, 37.
4. Sumner, *Memoir of George Sumner*, 28, 12.
5. Sumner, *Life of C.R. Sumner*, 324; Mary Sumner repeats the anecdote, see Sumner, *Memoir of George Sumner*, 12.

young and all that general parochial superintendence which is implied in what is termed the cure of souls'.[1] Mary was brisk in her dismissal of the previous absentee incumbent of Old Alresford, who personified the spiritual laxity and financial abuses that Charles and John Bird Sumner sought to eradicate in a revitalised Church. Francis North, the sixth Earl of Guildford, had held the livings of Old Alresford, New Alresford and Medstead for over fifty years. The beneficiary of the patronage of his father Brownlow North, a former Bishop of Winchester, he also received income as the incumbent of St Mary's Southampton, as a Prebendary of the Cathedral and, more lucrative still, as Master of St Cross, the alms houses which were the subject of the 1851 financial scandal satirised by Anthony Trollope in his novel *The Warden*. The rectory was to be 'no longer the land of lotus living ease' but 'a centre of parochial usefulness'.[2] This was realised through a number of projects in the years between 1851 and 1886 that aimed to foster religious knowledge and behaviour, such as the village reading room (1878). Even the 'Cottage Garden Society' can be interpreted with the promotion of the religiously approved virtues of thrift and temperance in mind. The Sumners' approach to parochial work assumed that, following the pattern of her mother-in-law, Mary would be an active helpmeet in the parish. According to her memoir of life at Old Alresford, George 'greatly approved' of the mothers' meeting, 'which went through catechism, baptismal and Holy Communion services, the marriage service and special passages from the Bible and Prayer Book'.[3] An accomplished musician, she served as church organist and directed the choir. A married men's meeting and a branch of the GFS (1875) were also under her direction.

2.2 Anglican advocacy and contested authority in the field of religion

George and Mary Sumner's presence in the Bishop's household and years of parish ministry occurred against a context of religious controversy. At the time of the inauguration of the Girls' Friendly Society (1875) and the parochial genesis of the MU (1876), the Established Church had been facing sustained challenges to its dominance in the religious field. These were posed by the increase of non-Anglican denominations (as

1. *Memoir of George Sumner*, 111; Sumner, *Life of C.R. Sumner*, 171.
2. Sumner, *Memoir of George Sumner*, 15.
3. 'Founding.' The membership cards introduced in 1876 were an innovation to an existing meeting for which the date is unspecified. A later chapter will discuss philanthropy in relation to Mary Sumner's understanding of mission.

revealed in the 1851 census) and their increasingly favourable treatment in law.[1] Bishop Charles Sumner and his brother, the Archbishop of Canterbury, were, as agents with high field position, at the forefront of manoeuvres to support the status and authority of the Anglican Church. They were also engaged in negotiating struggles over authority within Anglicanism which concerned doctrinal interpretation and preferred forms of worship. The views advanced by adherents of the Tractarian movement, so-called after the 1833 '*Tracts for the Times*', published by Oxford scholars John Keble, Richard Hurrell Froude, William Palmer and John Henry Newman formed a key focus for controversy. The repercussions of these struggles directly affected Mary Sumner and her kinship network. They informed her personal experience of religion and the aims and practices of the Anglican organisations in which she was active.

Tractarians were motivated by a desire to defend the priestly authority of the clergy against the incursions of government intervention. They also sought to revitalise and beautify the Anglican Church of England, an aspiration embodied in the ornate adornment of churches exemplified in the gothic revival style of Augustus Pugin. As in the case of evangelical Low Church views, Tractarianism was a stimulus to religious revival in its reaction against lack of rigour in religion and morals. The Anglo-Catholic Anglicanism asserted by Tractarians challenged the Protestant ascendancy of the reformation and stimulated scrutiny of the core Anglican beliefs of apostolic succession, the sacraments of baptism, communion, marriage and the use of the Book of Common Prayer. This attention to identity involved the taking of frequently hostile 'party' positions amongst Anglicans.

The Anglican 'evangelical party' (notably Archbishop John Bird Sumner and Bishop Charles Sumner) perceived Tractarianism as a threat to the authority and unity of the Church of England.[2] Tractarian belief in transubstantiation (the objective presence of the body and blood of Christ in the mass), the sacrificial role of the priest, priestly authority, and baptism as automatically regenerative was close to

1. Key legislation included the Repeal of the Test Acts 1828, Catholic Emancipation Act 1829 and Irish Disestablishment 1871. See also Nigel Scotland, *John Bird Sumner: Evangelical Archbishop* (Leominster: Gracewing, 1995), 67-80. Scotland details other legislation that affected the financial status of the Church and Sumner's response to social legislation.
2. Ibid., 81-94. Scotland explains Sumner's strong oposition to Tractarian ideas; see also Michael Chandler, *An Introduction to the Oxford Movement* (New York: Church Publishing, 2003), 99-106.

Roman Catholic doctrine. The High Church Anglo-Catholicism of Tractarianism associated with a scrutiny of conscience did culminate, in several cases, in conversion to Roman Catholicism. Notable converts close to the Sumner's circle were future Roman Catholic Cardinal Henry Manning, Bishop Samuel Wilberforce's brother-in-law, and his brothers Henry, William, and Robert.[1] Despite the relaxation of legal restrictions on denominational participation in public institutional life, there remained intense anti-Roman Catholic suspicion. Whilst the prevalence of Roman Catholicism in the urban lower orders might be attributed to deficiencies of education, class or 'race', when practiced by the ruling classes and members of the Anglican hierarchy it was a cause of political as well as spiritual unease because it asserted the authority of the Pope as transcending national boundaries.[2] Clerical celibacy was also a focus for concern as it was perceived as a challenge to the patriarchal governance of the family; an institution regarded by Anglicans and evangelicals, including Mary Sumner, who wrote 'the home is God's own institution ordained and founded by him at the beginning', as divinely ordained and a bulwark of social order.[3]

'Correct' form in baptism, communion and ritual in worship was disputed by Low Church evangelicals (such as Bishop Charles Sumner and Archbishop John Bird Sumner), who emphasised individual effort towards salvation, and High Church Tractarians, who favoured ritual and priestly authority. The effect of Charles Sumner's antipathy to those suspected of Tractarian views, which included the exclusion of ladies from philanthropic projects, is recalled by Charlotte Moberly, a friend of novelist Charlotte Yonge, who wrote:

> Bishop Charles Sumner had not long been Bishop of Winchester. He and almost all the clergy wives were of the Evangelical School. He had entirely made up his mind that Mr

1. D. Newsome, *The Parting of Friends: A Study of the Wilberforces and Henry Manning* (London: Murray, 1966); see also Arthur Rawson Ashwell and Reginald Garton Wilberforce, *Life of the Right Reverend Samuel Wilberforce, D.D: Lord Bishop of Oxford and Afterwards of Winchester, with Selections from His Diaries and Correspondence* (London: John Murray, 1880).
2. See Eileen Janes Yeo, 'Protestant Feminists and Catholic Saints' in *Radical Femininity: Women's Self Representation in the Public Sphere*, ed. Eileen Janes Yeo (Manchester: Manchester University Press, 1998), 127, for the hysterical reaction of a lady passenger seeing the architect Pugin crossing himself whilst on a train; 'Guard, guard, let me out!', and for the attitude of the Unitarian Reverend Samuel Gaskell to the threat of his daughter converting.
3. Sumner, 'Marriage 2', 20.

> Keble would go over to Rome and was dreadfully afraid of him. The Tractarian Oxford movement was just beginning [1833] and the new Headmaster [of Winchester College, Charlotte's father George Moberly] had the reputation of being connected with it and being full of Romish tendencies so for many years he had a hard time of it in Winchester.[1]

The strength of feeling associated with establishing the exact doctrinal interpretation of the Anglican Church and, by implication, defending its spiritual authority is demonstrated by the Gorham case. In 1850, after three years of dispute, Archbishop John Bird Sumner supported Reverend Gorham's view that baptismal regeneration was upheld by living the baptismal promise, rather than by virtue of the rite itself, which had been legally contested by Tractarian Bishop Henry Phillpotts as against Anglican doctrine.[2] George Sumner devoted nine pages of biography to justifying Charles Sumner's support for his brother's judgement which, by implication, emphasised the role of parents and godparents in preserving baptismal grace and protecting the child from sin,[3] a view that Mary Sumner was to make central to the 'Objects' of the Mothers' Union.

The conversion of senior Anglican clerics to the Roman Catholic Church affirmed Charles Sumner's fear that Tractarianism led to Rome. The sense of threat to the Established Anglican Church was heightened by the establishment of the Roman Catholic hierarchy in England, the so called 'papal aggression' of 1850. Charles Sumner considered it to be an invasion of the Queen's supremacy as head of the Church of England. His aversion to the 'corruption of Rome' was reflected in his objection to the use of Marian iconography, and he perceived Roman Catholic priests as an assault on the paternal authority of the family:

---

1. C.A.E. Moberly, *Dulce Domum: George Moberly, His Family and Friends* (London: John Murray, 1911), 58-59, 83. See Appendix 2. Charlotte Yonge was spiritually mentored by John Keeble when he was vicar of Hursley, a parish near Winchester. By the time Charlotte Yonge took over the editorial of *Mothers in Council* in 1890, feelings were not running so high.
2. Bradley, *The Call to Seriousness*, 13, 26. The case went to the Ecclesiastical Court of Arches and the Privy Council. Philpotts threatened to excommunicate Sumner after his ruling. It was this controversy over baptismal regeneration that was the catalyst for the conversion of Henry Manning, the Wilberforce brothers and several others.
3. Sumner, *Life of C.R. Sumner*, 331-40.

> The system of the confessional is foreign to the spirit of the gospel. . . . Englishmen will never endure to see the weaker members of their families subjected to an authority which, if it does not taint and confuse the moral sense, will subdue the mind to the extinction of all independent volition and chains it captive with passive submission to the will of a spiritual director.[1]

In 1876 Mary Sumner's sister Margaret converted to Roman Catholicism. According to the account written by Margaret's daughter Isabel Heywood: 'Of this act and of the mental agony which it caused to herself and to my father, both having been always of one heart and of one mind working together for God and His Church, I cannot write.'[2] There is no surviving record of Mary Sumner's view on this, but her writings for the MU reveal her to be in accord with her father-in-law's views on Roman Catholicism. She averred that 'the father should be the priest in the house.'[3] Similarly, when discussing the use of images in relation to MU materials, she insisted that the Madonna should only be represented with the infant Jesus:

> She was most blessed as Mother of our Saviour but RC's worship her. Our Lord clearly showed that he did not wish this during his life . . . he always showed respect to her – but as an honoured human being – let us guard against worshiping the Virgin Mary as the RC's do.[4]

Mary also felt that Roman Catholic attempts to 'win our people' were a threat to be resisted, and whilst she could respect Nonconformist Protestants, she was strongly opposed to Mormonism and the 'deadly heresy' of Christian Science.[5]

The death of Tractarian John Keble in 1866 within the Anglican Church may have alleviated local tension in Winchester but the struggle for authority over doctrine and related field manoeuvres, remained current

1. Ibid., 345-6, 286-7, 380.
2. Heywood and Heywood, *Reminiscences*, 125-6. This was the same year Mary Sumner initiated the membership card at her mothers' meeting.
3. Mary Sumner, 'To Husbands and Fathers' in *Mothers' Union* (Lambeth Palace Library, n.d.).
4. 'Letter to Mrs Maude Central Secretary of the Mothers' Union 1917' in *Mothers' Union* (Lambeth Palace Library).
5. 'Letters to Mrs Maude' in *Mothers' Union* (Lambeth Palace Library, 1908-1920); 'Secular Education', *Mothers in Council* (October 1894); 'Letter to Mrs Maude Re Christian Science May 25th 1909' in *Mothers' Union* (Lambeth Palace Library).

within Mary Sumner's family. In 1868 George Sumner edited *Principles at Stake*, a collection of essays by anti-Tractarian scholars. George's essay, 'The Doctrine of the Eucharist Considered, with Statements Recently Put Forward Concerning the Sacrament', reflected the evangelical view in its argument against transubstantiation:

> If the wicked only eat the sign or sacrament of the body of the Lord without being in any wise partakers of Christ then it seems to follow that consecration cannot so change the elements of bread and wine as that they shall be themselves the body and blood of Christ. . . . Eucharist is not a sacrifice but a sacrament, a symbolic receiving, to the heart of the believer the sacrifice is of praise and thanksgiving not body and blood [as Tractarians and Roman Catholics believed].[1]

Despite a refutation of the doctrine of transubstantiation, evangelicals within the Anglican Church promoted communion, according to Charles Sumner: 'more frequent administration of the Holy Sacrament is much to be desired, so that the well-disposed . . . may have many opportunities of drawing near to the table of the Lord'. An increase of communicants was regarded as a measure of Episcopal success, and Mary Sumner thought it relevant to comment on the uplifting effect of her husband's confirmation addresses.[2] Taking communion was advocated on the MU membership card.

The refurbishment of churches was a typical practice amongst George and Mary Sumner's kin and social network. Charles Sumner (1844 Hale), Thomas Heywood (1840 Wellington Heath), and the Yonges (1872 Otterbourne), all endowed or improved churches. However, the appropriate adornment of churches was a matter for dispute between opposing doctrinal factions.[3] Thomas Percival Heywood, who

1. George Henry Sumner, ed. *Principles at Stake: Essays on Church Questions of the Day* (London, 1868), 161. The word 'stake' evoked Protestant martyrs Latimer and Ridley 'whose blood had been shed for the pure truth of God'. Ibid., 170.
2. Sumner, *Life of C.R. Sumner*, 173. The confirmation drive extended to repentant prisoners at Parkhurst Reformatory. Ibid., 319; Sumner, *Memoir of George Sumner*, 83-84.
3. Sumner, *Life of C.R. Sumner*, 135. Charles Sumner 'preached the restoration and adornment of churches so shortly to be monopolised by the opposite school of thought', 170; Sumner, *Memoir of George Sumner*, 16-18; Georgina Battiscombe, *Charlotte Mary Yonge: The Story of an Uneventful Life* (London: Constable & Co., 1943), 48-49.

sponsored the (1874) church refurbishment that was the catalyst for a legal challenge to the legitimacy of the form of (allegedly Tractarian ritualistic) worship conducted by the incumbent, was directly caught up in the bitter controversy of the 'Miles Platting Affair'; which finally concluded in 1882. His daughter, Isabel, recorded the grievance felt at perceived interference on the part of an extreme anti-Tractarian Low Church faction.

> My Father's efforts, both public and private, in defence of the clergy and people of St. John's during the cruel and unjust persecution which they had to undergo were generous and untiring; they were also entirely unselfish. He was not contending for a ritual which he personally preferred, for he was no ritualist. . . . But he could not, and would not, endure to see a united congregation, with its devoted parish priests, insulted and molested by persons who had nothing to do with the church or parish, and relentlessly persecuted for obeying, in perfect good faith, the rubrics of The Book of Common Prayer.[1]

The 1871 church restoration funded by George and Mary Sumner at Old Alresford avoided controversy: 'there was neither excessive ornamentation nor severe plainness'. The avoidance of 'severe plainness' illustrates the Sumners' rejection of views tending towards more extreme Protestantism; although evangelical in earnestness they rejected a Nonconformist emphasis on preaching. The church was a '*House of Prayer*' (Mary Sumner's italics) not a 'House of preaching'.[2] The appointments of Samuel Wilberforce (1869), and Edward Harold Browne (1873) in succession to Charles Sumner (1827-69) brought a perspective to the interpretation of doctrine more accommodating to Higher Church views which George, who had attempted a conciliatory tone in *Principles at Stake*, adapted to. As archdeacon (1885) he was described as a 'moderate High Churchman', and on his appointment as Bishop of Guildford (1888), 'a champion of no party or sect'.[3] Despite taking the Bible as inspiration, the Sumners were also to accept the theological interpretation that accommodated the scientific understanding of evolution which emerged towards the latter years of

1. Heywood and Heywood, *Reminiscences*, 138-9.
2. Sumner, 'Prayer', 127.
3. Sumner, *Principles*, 153. 'What I have said [on transubstantiation] has been, I hope urged in a spirit of brotherly candour and charity. Hard names convince no one.' Sumner, *Memoir of George Sumner*, 51, 71.

the century. As with their interpretation of the sacraments of baptism and communion, belief in 'the sense not the letter' allowed them to recognise the non-literal 'Higher Criticism' approach to biblical interpretation as advocated (amongst others) by their acquaintances, Archbishop William Temple and Charles Kingsley.[1]

2.3 Synopsis: religious habitus and capital

Mary Sumner's habitus was located in a milieu in which agents upheld the doxa of Anglicanism. Her network included clergymen who, as holders of official positions in the field of the Church, were invested with symbolic social capital accruing to high office and pedagogic authority by virtue of their institutional attachment. The enthusiastic advocacy for living religion, evident in Mary Sumner's kinship network, indicates that lay members of her family were also habituated to mis/recognise the religious cultural arbitrary as legitimate. Their attention to the public assertion of scrutiny of conscience, piety, service and charity as symbolic religious capital indicates that these attributes were esteemed within kinship and wider networks. In Mary Sumner's experience of marriage and family, symbolic capital assets accrued to women as helpmeets and maternal exemplars of religious values. Possession of this symbolic capital was rewarded by esteem within the family, and the hope of a happy reunion in the 'hereafter'. The symbolic violence of patriarchal domination was masked by the conformity of men to gendered expectations of protectiveness, chivalrous behaviour and concessionary delegation of some authority to women that could be realised in the pedagogic action of philanthropy or parish work. Capital thus earned gave reputation (and thereby a degree of pedagogic authority) for the individual women. It also added to the collective capital of the family because it was recognised within the social milieu and field of the Church, which were structurally informative of the habitus of Mary Sumner and her kin.

Mary Sumner's dispositions of habitus were informed at a time when the ownership of the 'goods of salvation' was bitterly contested. The temporal durability of this contest indicates the high capital value accorded to the possession of 'correct' doctrinal interpretation within the evolving field of religion as a whole, and within the sub-field of the Anglican Church. The struggles for authority in matters of doctrine could (and did in Mary Sumner's kinship and close social network) have

1. Sumner, *Principles*, 158; Owen Chadwick, *The Victorian Church Part 2, 1860-1901*, 2nd ed. (London: A&C Black, 1972), 87-110.

professional, legal, and personal repercussions. Her relatives participated in field manoeuvres to uphold the established status of the Anglican Church and in advocacy for an interpretation of doctrine which rejected both ornate ritual and austerity in forms of worship. For Mary Sumner and her kin (with the notable exception of her sister), orthodoxy, and thus the religious capital of most worth, lay in Anglican belief. Thus Mary Sumner's activism was informed by an evangelical emphasis on living religion in the home and an evangelical appetite to promote living religion in the public sphere, contextualised by an imperative to uphold the doctrine of Anglicanism as interpreted by her authoritative relatives against encroaching rival denominations and interpretations.

Chapter 3
Anglican Motherhood for Church and Country: Mary Sumner, Religious Networks and the Mothers' Union

3.1 Introduction

Mary Sumner's kin were not the only mediators of her denominational preference and contingent expectations of the appropriate roles and conduct of women. Social life was bound up with religious observance and Anglicanism was the denomination of 'the establishment'. The Sumners identified themselves with the upper classes; a position substantiated by the affluence of Mary's father, her titled uncle, George's Episcopal relatives and his education at Eton and Oxford. Old Alresford, a living worth £560 a year, was sufficient to sustain the lifestyle of a gentleman. Although Mary pointed out in the memoir of her husband that 'this good income' was by no means excessive given the 'claims made upon it', she made sure to signal her own and her husband's social capital by enumerating the titled persons and gentry amongst their circle. At Old Alresford, 'the clergy and their wives were ever welcomed and many pleasant gatherings were held for church work'.[1] Supporting church and philanthropic projects was consequently a source of capital. It demonstrated the discharge of charitable obligations to social inferiors but also signalled participation in upholding the structure of society to peers and social superiors.

The chapter places Mary Sumner in the context of a group habitus that prioritised Anglicanism as the preferred religious doctrine, and shared understanding of social stratification and obligations. It identifies Anglican notions of 'good' womanhood and the position of women in the Church. It notes how Mary Sumner's notions of religious capital accruing to women as wives and mothers upheld the Anglican religious doxa and were articulated through the MU. The chapter explores her

1. Mary Sumner, *Memoir of George Henry Sumner, D.D., Bishop of Guildford: Published for His Friends by Special Request* (Winchester: Warren and Son, 1910), 2-7, 15, 23-25.

views on the negotiation of marriage and the role of fathers. How capital was transacted towards pedagogic authority in Mary Sumner's strategies to promote recognition of the MU within the Anglican Church are examined. Networking with other agents and organisations in relation to the field of religion are considered. The MU as an Anglican organisation is located in relation to the Anglican Church in the field of religion. The relationship of Anglicanism to power invested in the state is examined.

3.2 Mary Sumner's wider habitus, networks and establishing the Mothers' Union

Mary Sumner's first involvement with a women's religious organisation was through the Girls' Friendly Society. The GFS had originated in 1874, following discussions at Lambeth Palace between a committee that included its 'foundress', Mary Townsend, Catherine Tait (wife of the Archbishop of Canterbury), Elizabeth Harold Browne (wife of Edward Harold Browne, the Bishop of Winchester), and philanthropist Mrs Jeanie Elizabeth Nassau Senior. The society was officially instigated the following year with the Diocese of Winchester taking a leading role. Avowedly Anglican but not denominationally exclusive for its rank and file membership, the GFS aimed to prevent unmarried working class women and girls from 'falling' and so protect them from the forfeiture of symbolic (and possibly economic) capital occasioned by loss of chastity.[1] This preventive agenda was to be achieved through religious guidance, employment training, and opportunities for social contact under the supervising patronage of a woman of higher social status. The GFS spread through Mary Townsend's efforts to mobilise women of similar class and religious interests to initiate and run branches in the role of 'Associate'.[2] Mary Sumner, socially advantaged and with high status clerical contacts, was typical of the constituency of women who were approached, and her Old Alresford Branch was one of the first in the diocese.

Mary Sumner visualised the Mothers' Union extending the preventive work undertaken by the GFS into the homes of married women, who she felt, would influence their children and indeed husbands and neighbours

1. Agnes L. Money, *History of the Girls' Friendly Society*, New and rev. ed. (London: Wells Gardner, Darton, 1905), 4, 6. GFS rule three insisted on chastity.
2. Money, *History of the Girls' Friendly Society*, 11. 'Every Branch was organised in direct communication with her. For several years she never took so much as a week's holiday from GFS correspondence.' See Appendix 2, Mary Townsend.

towards religious observance, morality and temperance. She drew on her social contacts as a means of publicising the idea of the MU and 'seized every opportunity that offered itself of seeking to interest personal friends far and near.'[1] GFS events and personnel were an obvious channel for promoting the MU and Mary continued to be involved with the GFS after the MU was adopted as a diocesan organisation. It was not uncommon for women to be active in both organisations. Winchester GFS 'Founding Associates' Mrs Harold Browne, the novelist Charlotte Yonge, and Ellen Joyce, the promoter of emigration, were members of the Winchester Diocesan Mothers' Union Committee. **Table 1** illustrates women, many of them Bishops' wives, who were simultaneously active in the GFS and MU.

The networking amongst women to promote mutual aims, which was instrumental in expansion of both societies, was reflected in their 'Objects'. GFS 'Object' 1 was: 'To band together in one Society, women and girls as Associates and Members, for mutual help, (religious and secular), for sympathy and prayer.' The Mothers' Union's third 'Object' was similar: 'To organize in every place a band of mothers who will unite in prayer, and seek by their own example to lead their families in purity and holiness of life.' At the first MU Diocesan Conference in 1887 at Winchester's George Hotel, Mary Sumner said: '[T]hose who join are asked to try and interest others in the union, and persuade them to become members.'[2] Personal connections with bishops, who embodied both social capital and pedagogic authority as figures of distinction in the Anglican Church, contributed to the genesis and development of the MU and the GFS. In 1873, the Sumners' kinsman, Bishop Samuel Wilberforce, had been instrumental in stimulating Mary Townsend to conceive of the GFS.[3] Mary Sumner's speech at the 1885 Portsmouth Church Conference was delivered at the instigation of her friend, Bishop Ernest Wilberforce. The suggestion that the MU should be adopted as a diocesan body occurred at a social gathering and, with the sanction of Bishop Harold Browne, was enacted the following day.[4] Positioned

1. Mary Heath-Stubbs, *Friendship's Highway: Being the History of the Girls' Friendly Society* (London: Girls' Friendly Society, 1926), 6; Mary Porter, Mary Woodward, and Horatia Erskine, *Mary Sumner: Her Life and Work and a Short History of the Mothers' Union* (Winchester: Warren and Sons, 1921), 27, 28; Mary Sumner, 'Vice Presidential Speech to the G.F.S. Diocesan Conference at the George Hotel', *G.F.S. Associates Journal* 8.
2. Porter, Woodward, and Erskine, *Mary Sumner*, 30-31.
3. Money, *History of the Girls' Friendly Society*, 4.
4. Testimony of Mrs Wilberforce in Porter, Woodward, and Erskine, *Mary Sumner*, 21.

through marriage in a clerical milieu that included Church leaders, Mary felt authorised to write 'personally to most of the Diocesan Bishops, explaining the aims of the new venture, and asking for their approval and support' following the initial adoption of the MU in Winchester. Mary Sumner's expanding links with bishops through kinship, friendship, or through her husband's career in the Church are illustrated in **Table 2**.

The Mothers' Union, unlike the GFS, was not immediately a fully structured, centralised body. For several years it was an informal network instigated on the initiative of interested women who were recruited through social events such as the 'drawing room meeting' or through correspondence between friends and acquaintances for whom Mary Sumner was the central contact. Her 1888 publication *To Mothers of the Higher Classes* explained branch and diocesan organisation, and the role of organising Associates 'who may be married or unmarried ladies' but 'must be members of the Church of England'. According to her biographers Mary Sumner's vision for the Mothers' Union drew widespread support: 'Very rapidly other dioceses followed the lead given by Winchester and they generally accepted the Winchester organisation.' However, Louise Creighton, a generation younger than Mary Sumner and who, as a Bishop's wife, felt obliged to start a 'MU campaign' in Peterborough in 1891, did not like the idea of conforming to a central authority and in particular disapproved of the idea of Associates as she wished 'all to join on an equal footing'.[1]

The keystone of the 'work' was at parish level and reflected traditions of rural philanthropic patronage which Louise Creighton found objectionable and outdated.[2] The *Hampshire Chronicle* reported a meeting hosted by Charlotte Yonge which combined a social event with launching a Mothers' Union branch:

> OTTERBOURNE Mothers' Meeting – On Tuesday last Miss Yonge entertained about 60 'mothers of young children' at tea in the school room. After the tables had been cleared a meeting was held, at which an earnest and impressive address was delivered by Mrs Sumner, wife of the Archdeacon of Winchester.[3]

1. Mary Sumner, *To Mothers of the Higher Classes* (Winchester: Warren and Sons, 1888), 65-69; Porter, Woodward, and Erskine, *Mary Sumner*, 107; Louise Creighton, *Memoir of a Victorian Woman: Reflections of Louise Creighton 1850-1936* (Bloomington and Indianapolis: Indiana University Press, 1994), 112-113.
2. Jessica Gerard, 'Lady Bountiful Women of the Landed Classes and Rural Philanthropy', *Victorian Studies* 30, no. 2 (1987); F.K. Prochaska, *Women and Philanthropy in Nineteenth Century England* (Oxford: Clarendon Press, 1980).
3. Hampshire Chronicle, 'Otterbourne Mothers Meeting', *Hampshire Chronicle*, Saturday February 13th 1886.

Once Mothers' Union branches had been established, typical practices local level included:

> holding periodical meetings which are addressed by various ladies on the objects of the union generally, lectures are given under its auspices on questions of health and sanitation: classes are held on Sunday afternoons for the religious instruction of members so that they may be able to impart religious teaching to their children.[1]

The Mothers' Union message was also publicised at larger scale meetings. Dioceses with MU organisation held annual conferences and women associated with the MU were regular speakers at Church Congress meetings for women after 1885. Following her Portsmouth debut, Mary Sumner spoke at Hull in 1890, Liverpool in 1904, Weymouth in 1905 and Southampton in 1913. Another key strategy for promoting the MU was through the dissemination of printed materials. Numerous pamphlets by Mary Sumner were distributed through MU branches and she made a habit of enclosing them with her correspondence.[2] *The Mothers' Union Journal* was conceived as a newsletter from Mary Sumner to all members. Published initially in leaflet form in 1888, by the following year it had a circulation of 46,000.[3] MU identity was also promoted through the use of a logo. The first, designed by Heywood Sumner (c. 1888), consisted of a mother and child encircled by the words 'train up a child in the way he should go'. A decade later, the tradition of the Mothers' Union brooch was initiated with a design produced under Mary Sumner's close supervision.[4]

In 1892, the Winchester Diocesan Committee, invested with authority as the first Mothers' Union organisation and home diocese of the 'Foundress', resolved that a central organisation and constitution were

1. *Hearth and Home*, 'Leading Societies and Their Work: The Mothers' Union', *Hearth and Home: An Illustrated Weekly Journal for Gentlewomen*, Thursday January 28th 1892.
2. Mary Sumner, 'Letter to Mrs Crawford June 19th 1917' in *Winchester Diocesan Mothers' Union* (Hampshire Record Office); 'Letter to "My Dear Marion" (A.K.A. Basdell) December 23rd (Surmised) 1916' in *Winchester Diocesan Mothers' Union* (Hampshire Record Office).
3. Mothers' Union, *Fifty Years* (Westminster: The Mothers' Union, 1926), 10-12. 'Practically all the dioceses adopted . . . a Diocesan Cover for local news.' Published quarterly, it sold 8,000 in 1888 and 46,000 the following year.
4. Mary Sumner, 'Letter to Mrs Maude Concerning Lady Hillingdon's Drawing Room Meeting' in *Mothers' Union* (Lambeth Palace Library, 1909). Written from Bournemouth, February 23rd 1909.

desirable in order to promote cohesion between dioceses and to ease the administrative burden on Mary Sumner. Negotiations towards this commenced with the establishment in 1893 of a Committee of Presidents, who gathered for meetings at the Church House, Westminster.[1] In 1896, after three years of negotiation, a formal constitution was agreed that enabled the MU to present a corporate stand on issues relating to morality and family life. Mary Sumner continued to personify the MU after centralisation and its campaigns on divorce, secular education and temperance reflected her views.[2] She served as its Central President until 1909 when she resigned in order to nurse George through his final illness. However, she found it hard to relinquish control of the organisation which her husband had referred to as her 'youngest child', and after his death continued to intervene on the policies and practices of the organisation by expressing her views in letters to her presidential successors Lady Chichester and Emily Wilberforce, and to the Mothers' Union Central Secretary Mrs Maude.[3]

Mary Sumner was, despite her stature in the Mothers' Union, obliged to compromise over the issue of revising the wording of membership cards. The revision sought to reword and combine the original two versions, worded for different social classes, in to one version suitable for all members. Mary was resistant to change and wrote to her friend Minnie, Lady Addington in 1910, 'Naturally I would prefer the cards we have always had.' Another letter from 1912 reveals her distress: 'I am so grieved at all the discussion and varying opinions about the card, it is really a great trial to me and I long for peace concerning it.'[4] It was unusual for Mary to reveal feelings that were less than positive, or to show weakness. Her disappointment that 'the Mothers' Union has not

1. Mothers' Union, 'Minute Book', ibid. (Lambeth Palace, 1892-1901); Lady Horatia Erskine, 'A History of the Mothers' Union', ibid. (Lambeth Palace Library, 1919).
2. Mary Sumner, 'Marriage Address I' in *Home Life* (Winchester: Warren and Sons, 1895); Mary Sumner, 'Secular Education', *Mothers in Council* (October 1894); Sumner, 'Temperance'.
3. *Memoir of George Sumner*, 142; 'Letters to Lady Chichester Central President of the Mothers' Union' in *Mothers' Union* (Lambeth Palace Library, 1913-15). Sent between 1909-1911: 'Letters to Mrs Wilberforce' in *Mothers' Union* (Lambeth Palace Library). Sent between 1916-20: 'Letters to Mrs Maude' in *Mothers' Union* (Lambeth Palace Library, 1908-1920). 1909-1921.
4. 'Letter to "Dearest Minnie" Concerning Revision of Mothers' Union Constitution April 14th 1910' in *Mothers' Union* (Lambeth Palace Library); 'Letter to "Dearest Minnie" Concerning Revision of the Mothers' Union Cards 1912' in *Mothers' Union* (Lambeth Palace Library).

gripped London' which she expressed to Mrs Maude in 1912 was to be kept 'strictly private'.[1] However, Mary's programme of travelling and speaking for the MU at large scale meetings affirmed the esteem in which she was held by members. She was greeted with a standing ovation at the 1908 Mass Meeting in the Albert Hall and at the York MU Conference in 1913, and after an extensive tour of northern towns her visit was likened to a royal progress.[2]

Mary Sumner's key field manoeuvre for promoting her organisation was mobilising agents whose class affiliation and allegiance to Anglicanism framed a group habitus in which notions of social and religious capital were recognised collectively. She drew on individual agents invested with social capital and pedagogic authority (possessed by virtue of social status, philanthropic activism, marital association, or as holders of office within the Church), working outwards from her own immediate circle in an expanding network, to give authority to the MU. The notion of capital by association (forwarded through Mary Sumner's field manoeuvres; speeches, publication and notably correspondence) not only endorsed the message and status of the organisation but served to make it attractive to an extended network of activists and a wider membership. As the revered 'foundress' of the MU, Mary Sumner was a beneficiary of this spiral of increasing capital. A timeline showing Mary Sumner's activism and the durability of her involvement in the MU in relation to its corporate development is included in the introductory pages.

3.3 The Mothers' Union as an Anglican organisation: women in the Church, capital and field manoeuvres

The adoption of the Mothers' Union as a diocesan organisation was facilitated by Mary Sumner's social position amongst a network of clerical contacts. This was given impetus by George's promotion to Archdeacon and the subsequent move to the Cathedral Close in Winchester, a physical location invested with diocesan authority. The MU's diocesan adoption also reflects an acknowledgement by senior churchmen, which the instigation of the GFS and the introduction of a dedicated women's section at the 1881 Newcastle-Upon-Tyne Church Congress illustrate, that women had a pastoral role in the ministry of the

---

1. 'Letter to Mrs Maude on the Mothers' Union in London Failing to Reach Educated Mothers September 28th 1917' in *Mothers' Union* (Lambeth Palace Library).
2. Porter, Woodward, and Erskine, *Mary Sumner*, 52, 71-72.

church.[1] The Church Congresses had been instigated in 1861 by John Bird Sumner as a forum in which clergy and laymen could meet and air topical issues. The Congress format involved a week-long programme of religious services and public talks held annually in towns around the country under the presidency of the bishop of the host diocese. Conference proceedings were covered in the press and published in full in an 'official report' so the text of speeches could be disseminated beyond the conference audience and retained for reference. Recurrent themes in the programmes included the poor, leisure, education and temperance. The role of women in the Church was a matter for ongoing discussion. Deaconesses, district visitors and sisterhoods were on the agenda of the 1883 Reading Church Congress. Whilst the clergy participating in the debate were comfortable with women as 'district visitors' engaged in parish philanthropy, there was some ambivalence about an organised system of deaconesses that accrued around boundaries of authority and reflected a reluctance to acknowledge that ladies might require payment. Organised sisterhoods, especially those that involved taking vows, were regarded with suspicion as too close to Roman Catholic practice. The lifelong separation of the sexes was similarly regarded with distaste.[2] For the majority of Anglican clergy and laymen, the role and duty of women lay in supporting the family.

The Church Congresses were a popular from of respectable entertainment and attracted substantial audiences. The public talks were targeted to different class and gendered categories including mothers and working women.[3] The conferences also had a social dimension and offered an opportunity for clerics and their spouses and female relations to meet old acquaintances and, as Louise Creighton, an enthusiastic participant in the Congresses, noted, 'get to know more about church people generally and to understand more about church affairs'.[4] Women

---

1. Sean Gill, *Women and the Church of England: From the Eighteenth Century to the Present* (London: Society for Promoting Christian Knowledge, 1994), 131-145.
2. Charles Dunkley, *The Official Report of the Church Congress, Held at Reading: On October 2nd, 3rd, 4th, and 5th, 1883* (London: Bemrose & Sons, 1883), 319-320.
3. *The Official Report of the Church Congress Held at Birmingham on October 3rd, 4th, 5th, and 6th, 1893* (London: Bemrose & Sons, 1893). Introduction table of Church Congress attendance figures; 'Church Congress', *The Morning Post*, October 2nd 1885. Readers were reminded that passengers with congress tickets were entitled to discounted railway tickets and that ladies could secure platform tickets for sixpence.
4. Creighton, *Memoir of a Victorian Woman: Reflections of Louise Creighton 1850-1936*, 112.

had a role as organisers and hostesses at the social gatherings for conference guests, local civic dignitaries and distinguished speakers that were a feature of the conferences. Mary Sumner's friend Lady Laura Ridding, the wife of the Bishop of Southwell, recorded the headaches she faced finding accommodation for guests at the Nottingham Church Congress.[1] It was also customary for women to be seen (if not heard) on the Congress platforms beside their husbands. This public performance of family life added a civilising dignity and respectability to the assembly of the Church and endorsed its patriarchal authority, seemingly affirming its 'inclusiveness' and 'Christian Chivalry'. The limited participation conceded to women as hearers and helpers reflected the Anglican emphasis on wives and daughters prized as helpmeets, subject to but complicit with patriarchal authority.[2]

The recollection of Mary Sumner's debut speech at the 1885 Portsmouth Conference, as presented by her biographers, enhances and elaborates on the text recorded in the Church Congress Official report, which makes no reference to the Mothers' Union. The biography account does, however, illustrate the negotiation of authority (or observance of social conventions of propriety) by women speakers. Biographers Porter, Woodward and Erskine include Mrs Emily Wilberforce's report of her husband's (Bishop Ernest Wilberforce) 'inspiration' in asking a woman to address women. Emily Wilberforce emphasises Mary Sumner's modest reluctance to speak until urged to do so by the bishop.[3] Mary's own account also made sure to signal male authorisation; 'my dear husband was not in the hall but I knew he would approve' [of her speaking].[4] She was not the only woman to speak at the conference. Although Mr Townsend spoke about the GFS on behalf of his wife, Ellen Joyce, a widow no longer subject to the authority of her husband, delivered her own paper on emigration.[5]

The notion that religious authority was unwomanly was rooted in Scripture and the interpretation of St Paul. The Pauline position derived from Genesis and woman's secondary creation from Adam's rib as his

1. Lady Laura Ridding, 'Diaries' in *Selborne Papers* (Hampshire Record Office). Saturday September 25th 1897.
2. Simon Morgan, *A Victorian Woman's Place: Public Culture in the Nineteenth Century* (London: Tauris Academic Studies, 2007), 160, 168.
3. Porter, Woodward, and Erskine, *Mary Sumner*, 21.
4. Mary Sumner, 'Account of the Founding of the Mothers' Union and Parochial Work at Old Alresford' in *Mothers' Union* (Lambeth Palace Library).
5. Ibid.; Joyce Coombs, *George and Mary Sumner: Their Life and Times* (Westminster: Sumner Press, 1965), 82; Church of England, 'Official Report of the Church Congress Held at Portsmouth' (London: Church of England, 1885), 449.

companion. Further, because of her susceptibility to temptation, woman was responsible for loss of innocence and sin according to the Bible (Timothy 2.14) 'Adam was not deceived but the woman being deceived was in transgression'. Charlotte Yonge wrote in 1877: 'I have no hesitation in declaring my full belief in the inferiority of woman, nor that she brought it upon herself.'[1] Mary Sumner, likewise, misrecognised the legitimacy of gendered Anglican doctrine and affirmed her agreement that women should 'be sober, to love their husbands, to love their children. To be discreet, chaste, keepers at home, good, obedient to their own husbands, that the word of God be not blasphemed' by using this Biblical quotation as a subheading to a written address.[2] She upheld paternal authority as divinely ordained:

> Home life is a monarchy the husband and father is the sovereign of the small realm – he and his wife together wield a sceptre of divine power – the exercise of this power in the human father is intended to express and typify in each home the greater rule of the Almighty.[3]

Although according to Scripture, it was 'a shame for women to speak in the church' (1 Corinthians 14:35), it was considered appropriate, like Dorcas, 'to be full of good works' (Acts 9:36). This position was demonstrated by the favourable attitude of the Sumners and Heywoods to female participation in parochial work and philanthropy while excluding women from institutional power. This stance exploited women's contributions to religious life as, in the words of George Sumner, 'handmaids of the church'.[4] Bishop Harold Browne, although progressive in initiating a stipendiary deaconess in his Ely diocese in 1869, noted that she should set aside 'all unwomanly usurpation of authority in the church'.[5] In 1890, there was still a guarded reaction to women's activism.

1. Charlotte M. Yonge, *Womankind*, 2nd ed. (London: Walter Smith and Innes, 1898), 1; Gill, *Women and the Church of England*, 15.
2. Mary Sumner, 'Mothers' Work Outside the Home' in *Home Life* (Winchester: Warren and Son, 1895). The biblical reference heading the chapter is Titus 2:3-5.
3. 'To Husbands and Fathers' in *Mothers' Union* (Lambeth Palace Library n.d.).
4. George Sumner, 'Speech to the Annual G.F.S. Diocesan Conference at the George Hotel Winchester', *Girls' Friendly Society Associates Journal*, January 1885.
5. Frances Knight, *The Nineteenth Century Church and English Society* (Cambridge: Cambridge University Press, 1995), 197. Harold Browne appointed stipendiary deaconess Fanny Elizabeth Eagles 'to seek out poor and impotent folk and intimate their names to the curate, instruct the young in school or otherwise, minister to those in hospitals and setting aside all unwomanly usurpation of authority in the church, should seek to edify the souls of Christ's people in the faith'. E.H. Browne, Charge to the Clergy of the Diocese of Ely, 1869.

The English Woman's Review reported to its readers on the proceedings of the Hull Church Conference, at which Archdeacon Emery

> wanted to speak in favour not of special societies, or guilds, or sisterhoods, or deaconesses, but in favour of the old district visiting system. . . . What they wanted was the clergyman's wife to feel she was one with her husband.[1]

Mary Sumner drew on this understanding of capital to claim pedagogic authority in her manoeuvres to secure the position of the MU as a recognised body within the (Anglican) religious field. Speaking on the same platform, Mary Sumner asserted her respect for the paternal authority vested in both family and Church:

> It must be self-evident that the Mothers' Union is a work of women to women, of mothers to mothers and that we could hardly summon fathers of all ranks and classes, as well as mothers to our meetings we should be considered presumptuous and impertinent if we were to do so. It would be outside our province as women.[2]

She was, however, 'deeply grateful to clergymen and laymen who are helping us' and drew on the pedagogic authority of churchmen. Ways to encourage the clergy to endorse Mothers' Union parish branches were discussed at Diocesan Committee meetings and in MU publications disseminated amongst clergy wives and rural deaneries.[3]

Mary Sumner's advocacy for the doctrinal beliefs of the Anglican Church was articulated in her writing. In 1888 she urged *Mothers of the Higher Classes* to uphold the sacraments of the Church, and in 1895 she wrote, referring to baptism and communion: 'If Mothers would hope to fulfil their duty to their children they must not neglect any one of the means of Grace.'[4] The 1876 MU membership card began with the exhortation, 'Remember that your children are given up body and soul, to Jesus Christ in Holy Baptism', and concluded:

---

1. English Woman's Review, 'Record of Events Report of the Church Congress at Hull', *English Woman's Review*, October 15th 1890.
2. Mary Sumner, 'Paper Read at the Church Congress in Hull 1890' in *Mothers' Union* (Lambeth Palace Library).
3. Ibid.; Winchester Diocesan Mothers' Union Committee, 'Minute Book 1886-1910' in *Diocese of Winchester Mothers' Union* (Hampshire Record Office).
4. Sumner, *To Mothers of the Higher Classes*, 67; *Home Life* (Winchester: Warren and Son, 1895), 8.

> If you repent truly of your sins, and desire with all your heart to love and follow the Lord Jesus, come to the Holy Communion and feed on him by faith, then will your soul be strengthened and refreshed. Jesus said 'Do this in remembrance of me;' It was His dying command.[1]

Anglican identity was promoted by the insistence that the Subscribing Members who formed the leadership of the MU at local, diocesan and central level should be communicants of the Church of England. Protestant Nonconformists could join as ordinary members as long as they accepted the sacrament of infant baptism. Bishops were secured as diocesan patrons, and clergy officiated at MU services. Mary Sumner sought the presence of 'powerful' clerics and laymen to endorse the MU message at conferences and mass meetings.[2] MU practice also drew on the forms and language of the Church to substantiate its claims to pedagogic authority, although it did not, in keeping with its misrecognition of the superiority of paternal clerical authority, engage with intellectual theological debate.[3] Enrolment into the MU involved a ritual prayer and used a question and answer format reminiscent of the catechism and was conducted either by a clergyman in church or an Enrolling Member. Annual services were held from 1888 in Winchester and Annunciation Day (March 25th), an anniversary marked in the Church calendar, was adopted by the Central Council in 1897 as a 'Day of Prayer and Thanksgiving'. Territory was also claimed through the display of banners in parish churches. In a letter dated 1915, Mary Sumner expressed her view that 'the Mothers' Union ought to have its centre in the Church House – it is one of the most important of the Church organisations'.[4] The instigation of an annual service at St Paul's Cathedral and the 1917 opening of the central headquarters by the Bishop of London indicate the success of field manoeuvres to

---

1. *Home Life*, 6. Membership card original wording.
2. 'Letters to Lady Chichester.' 'Some powerful men speakers. . . . Would the Bishop of London help or the Bishop of Southwell who is a warm friend of mine? . . . A good powerful layman should be chosen.'
3. *Home Life*, 7-8; Cordelia Moyse, *A History of the Mothers' Union: Women Anglicanism and Globalisation, 1876-2008* (Woodbridge: Boydell Press, 2009), 59. Moyse discusses Higher Criticism and Theology in reference to the MU Annual Conference of 1896, 44-6, regarding Mary Sumner's views as being in accord with mainstream Anglican liberal thought.
4. Sumner, *To Mothers of the Higher Classes*, 66; Porter, Woodward, and Erskine, *Mary Sumner*, 109; Sumner, 'Letters to Lady Chichester', October 20th 1915.

secure the MU's recognition as a Church body. In 1926 seven bishops under the leadership of the Archbishop of Canterbury officiated at the MU jubilee celebrations.[1]

The Mothers' Union treated landmarks in family life as occasions for religious thanksgiving and in the case of prominent figures, adopted them as shared corporate events that were reported in MU publications.[2] Mary Sumner's golden wedding anniversary was celebrated with the Eucharist and afterwards 'a large gathering was assembled by the Diocesan Council of the Mothers' Union, at the palace of Wolvesey, whereat the Bishop and Mrs Sumner were the honoured guests'. The following day a special service in the Cathedral and 'tea under an enormous tent' was attended by 1,200 Diocesan MU members.[3] George and Mary's diamond wedding anniversary was celebrated with the presentation of a screen endorsed with royal signatures. Death and bereavement amongst prominent officials in the organisation and in the royal family were also treated as occasions for public recognition.[4]

In working to secure the recognition of the Mothers' Union as a Church organisation Mary Sumner avoided assertions contrary to notions of gendered patriarchal authority legitimised by the Church and embedded in social practice. She built on the recognition by individual clergymen that women could contribute to the pedagogic action of the Church through field manoeuvres which identified the MU with its spaces, ritual and language and she sought further endorsement from its highest officials, invested with pedagogic authority, as speakers, celebrants and advisers. Her organisation also asserted domestic celebrations (notably her own wedding anniversaries) to signal religious capital because they commemorated successful upholding of the religious sacrament of marriage. Thus, not only did the MU speak for the Church but the Church spoke for and sanctified the MU and thereby endowed the women speaking on its behalf with pedagogic authority.

1. Porter, Woodward, and Erskine, *Mary Sumner*, 110, 178; Mothers' Union, *Fifty Years*, 50-52.
2. Mary Sumner, 'Letter to Mrs Maude Thanking Her for Birthday Wishes' in *Mothers' Union* (Lambeth Palace Library, 1919). Mary Sumner wishes her birthday greetings and her response to be published in the *Mothers' Union Journal*.
3. *Memoir of George Sumner*, 138-143; Porter, Woodward, and Erskine, *Mary Sumner*, 42-43. Second MU London President Horatia Erskine also had her golden wedding marked by the Society, 126.
4. Sumner, *Memoir of George Sumner*, 151-153; Porter, Woodward, and Erskine, *Mary Sumner*, 53, 70, 110, 158.

3.4 The province of women: morality, motherhood, marriage and the symbolic capital of purity

Women's authority was vested in their upholding the Christian construction of what were deemed desirable womanly qualities; raising children, nurturing family life and demonstrating piety and self-restraint.[1] The inception of the Diocesan Mothers' Union occurred after Mary Sumner had demonstrably discharged her duties as mother and helpmeet to the Rector. She assumed marriage and motherhood as a desirable destiny for women and the role of woman was hardly differentiated from that of mother. A good mother 'shines like a light in this dark world. She receives the flame straight from Christ Himself – she reflects His Image. Husband, children and neighbours rise up and call her blessed'.[2] However, unmarried women could act in a motherly role by contributing to the management and ethos of 'The Home' or by performing duties associated with the home sphere, such as education or philanthropic activity. 'Mothers' work often devolves on unmarried women'; 'we have many married women without children in our Mothers' Union and good unmarried who are <u>mothering</u> children as Godmothers or Guardians.[3] In conflating womanhood with motherhood, Mary Sumner was in accord with clerical authority. For Bishop Thorold, quoted in an undated MU leaflet, 'maiden aunts are the human angels of childhood . . . if she is not a mother she had yet the motherly heart which is womanhood's priceless possession'.[4]

Mary Sumner's promotion of motherhood as a spiritual, educative vocation reflected her experience of maternal influence and the home as a site for living religion. She considered that children should be reverenced as the handiwork of the Creator: 'The child has a soul, that soul will live

1. Mary Sumner, 'In Memoriam Mrs Wordsworth', *Mothers in Council*, 1894. Mary Sumner enumerates these virtues as exemplified by Mrs Wordsworth; George Henry Sumner, *Life of C.R. Sumner, D.D., Bishop of Winchester, During a Forty Years' Episcopate* (London, 1876), 324; Sumner, *Memoir of George Sumner*, 12; Isabel Mary Heywood and Sir Thomas Percival Heywood, *Reminiscences, Letters and Journals of Thomas Percival Heywood, Baronet. Arranged by His Eldest Daughter (Isabel Mary). With a Preface by the Rev. George Body* (printed for private circulation: Manchester, 1899), 45; Mary Sumner, 'Account of Her Early Life at Hope End 1828-46' in *Mothers' Union* (Lambeth Palace Library).
2. *To Mothers of the Higher Classes*, 57.
3. 'Letter to Mrs Sharme' in *Mothers' Union* (Lambeth Palace Library, 1911).
4. C.M. Hallett, 'The Mothers' Union, How It May Be Furthered in a Parish by Associates', ibid. (n.d.).

forever. God gives to each little child a conscience – a religious instinct, and the wish to love and serve him. Our duty is to cultivate this divine instinct and train our children for the battle of life.'[1] The 1876 card issued to mothers urged church attendance, Bible study and family prayer and instructed mothers to teach their children to be 'truthful, obedient and pure'.[2] For Mary Sumner, this involved protecting them from the loss of innocence caused by bad companions and temptations such as drink. The card noted: 'You are strongly advised never to give your children beer, wine or spirits without the Doctor's orders or to send them to the public house.'[3] Her 1895 address on 'Temperance' warned that: 'Bad people often give beer or spirits to young girls in order to ruin them.'[4] The MU card also advised that 'Blasphemy, coarse jests and slander' were to be avoided, as were 'bad books' and material dealing with what were considered to be scandalous topics.[5] In Mary Sumner's view, these were not only an incentive to vice but would corrupt the national as well as individual character.[6]

Purity as a desirable attribute, particularly (but not exclusively) for women, was understood to mean, above all else, chastity. Rule IV on the MU card made explicit the need to protect the chastity of girls before marriage and to 'keep them from the streets and lanes at night, unprotected'. Mary Sumner's lengthy elaboration on virginity demonstrates her prioritisation of this capital attribute:

> Tell her [the daughter] what a *priceless* jewel it is; which once lost or spoiled can never be regained other things when lost or spoiled may be made good, but a girl's character never; once lost it is lost forever; the girl may repent and by the mercy of our Saviour she may be forgiven, she may do her utmost to retrieve her character, but she can never be the same; her innocence is gone, gone forever: she may marry; she may be a good wife and mother; but she can never be in God's sight or in man's sight, or in her own sight, what

1. Mary Sumner, 'A Mother's Greatest Duty' (London: Mothers' Union, n.d.).
2. *Home Life*, 6, 7.
3. Ibid., 6. The wording for 'poorer mothers' was 'in accordance with their different state of life . . . no lady would be tempted to send her child to the public-house'.
4. 'Temperance', 70.
5. *Home Life*, 6.
6. 'Letter to the Editor, *The Times*, "Improper Books", December 9th 1909'; Mary E. Sumner, Horatia E. Erskine, and Emily Wilberforce, 'Letter to the Editor, *The Times*, "Undesirable Literature".'

> she was in the happy days of her *innocence*. Therefore dear friends warn your girls and warn them in time.[1] (Mary Sumner's punctuation and italics.)

The GFS was equally concerned with securing the symbolic capital of an elevated standard of womanhood for its members. Central Rule Three (1875) stated: 'No girl who has not borne a virtuous character to be admitted; such a character being lost, the Member to forfeit her Card.' This was not entirely uncontested, Agnes Money, the first historian of the GFS, commented on the challenge to GFS recruitment posed by this high standard:

> There had been in some minds strong objections to Central Rule Three as unchristian, as likely to foster a pharisaicial spirit in its members. These objections seemed to be dying out, and it seemed to be very generally acknowledged that a national society on any other basis would not be the least the same power for good, and could not create that public opinion which is such a safeguard to those classes in which it exists, and the absence of which, in too many communities of the working classes has left their girls so much exposed to temptation.[2]

Mary Sumner had no doubts about the value of chastity. In her capacity as Vice President of the Diocesan GFS she 'spoke strongly on the injuries done to the Society by the admission of those who would bring it into disrepute. It should be looked upon as an honour to belong, rather than as an institution for the training of rough girls'.[3] The importance of individual members upholding the collective reputation of the Society was also emphasised in the MU. Mary Sumner noted:

---

1. Sumner, 'Discipline', 80; Eileen Janes Yeo, 'Some Paradoxes of Empowerment' in *Radical Femininity; Women's Self Representation in the Public Sphere*, ed. Eileen Janes Yeo (Manchester: Manchester University Press, 1998), 8. Yeo notes the paradox of spiritual womanhood contrasted with Eve the sinner. Women seeking religious authority needed to prove their incorruptibility, hence the distance created between the virtuous and fallen woman. See also Gill, *Women and the Church of England*, 25, 125.
2. Money, *History of the Girls' Friendly Society*, 18-19. 'But now the difficulty arose in a fresh form as the work of the GFS took root in some of the large towns where the standard of morality was at an exceptionally low ebb and where constant changes of residence made the difficulty of knowing the past character of girls. I will not refer to this . . . for it leads to the sundering of friends and the hindering of work.'
3. Sumner, 'Vice Presidential Speech to the G.F.S. Diocesan Conference at the George Hotel'.

> In many branches an excellent rule has been made that no mother can be admitted who has only been married to her husband before a registrar . . . and it is needless to say that no unmarried mother could ever be a Member of the Society.[1]

Moreover 'no person should be admitted, who is known to be living in open sin, or causing gossip'. The following rule from the Organisation Leaflet, which Mary Sumner quoted in the preface to her 1895 *Home Life,* noted that: '[I]f any Member or Associate persists in breaking the rules, or causes a scandal, it may be necessary to ask them to return their card, and remove their name from the lists.'[2] Individual reputation contributed to, as well as drew from, the collective. The emphasis placed on 'purity' in the Mothers' Union (and the GFS) reflected their stance as preventive societies. Seeking religious authority as associations of spiritual women, it was important to demonstrate the incorruptibility of members and to distinguish them from sexually transgressive 'fallen' girls and women, a category subject to the rescue work undertaken by Josephine Butler, who lived in the Winchester Cathedral Close between 1882 and 1890. Josephine Butler concentrated on opposing the Contagious Diseases Acts, sex trafficking and organised prostitution topics regarded as too unsavoury for respectable women. Despite Mary Sumner's vociferous advocacy for chastity, Butler considered Mary Sumner her 'good friend and neighbour' and both women were advocates of equal standards of morality for men and women.[3]

Mary Sumner's view that Christian marriage legitimised sexual relations was reflected in MU literature. In 1895, she envisaged marriage as a 'mystical union instituted of God in the time of man's innocency, signifying unto us the bond that is between Christ and His church'. Her view references Ephesians 5, which sanctified marriage as a transition from innocence that safeguarded the reputation of women. According

1. Winchester Diocesan Mothers' Union Committee, 'Minute Book 1886-1910'. November 21st 1890 'In the case of immorality it would be best if the member resign her card.'
2. Sumner, *Home Life*, 4-7, 5.
3. Jane Jordan, *Josephine Butler* (London: John Murray, 2001), 207. The Contagious Diseases Acts legalised the forcible medical examination of women suspected to be prostitutes in garrison towns. Butler's resistance to this and organised prostitution caused her to be reviled and on occassion physically assaulted; Coombs, *George and Mary Sumner: Their Life and Times*, 91-94. Coombs asserts that the Sumners supported Josephine Butler and notes that Mary visited Hope Cottage, a 'Home of Rest' established in Winchester by Butler for the rehabilitation of prostitutes.

to Mary: 'The first wedding was that of Adam and Eve, and God himself married them in the Garden of Eden and started Home Life.' Thus marriage was a bond of 'the deepest solemnity'; marriage as 'the result of a marketable transaction also called a satisfactory match' could not be considered a true bond. It was not 'a mere contract to end at will, when either party grows tired of the other, or when there is unkindness and quarrelling and incompatibility of temper'. The vow of marriage was 'absolute, irrevocable, [and] indissoluble'.[1] An undated leaflet produced by the London Diocesan MU noted: 'the whole position of women stands or falls with the sanctity of marriage and the respect due to family life'.[2] Mary Sumner believed that the divine institution of marriage upheld social order and she was concerned that: 'the sanctity of marriage is being undermined and trifled with by the increasing number of divorce cases and attacks made on marriage by certain writers of the day'. 'We all know how seriously the Divorce Act of 1857 has sapped the foundations of family life. . . . It is causing the degradation of parents, widespread misery and cruel injury to the character training of children'. She saw this as 'flooding the country with immorality' which would lead to 'fatal results' in national as well as home life. [3]

For Mary Sumner, notions of desirable womanly capital were predicated on the misrecognition of the legitimacy of the prevailing religious doxa which assumed, in accord with prevailing social practice, that marriage and motherhood was the appropriate role for women. Women as 'spiritual mothers' could demonstrate their possession of symbolic religious capital by demonstrating piety through prayer, church attendance and encouraging children in Bible study. Capital was also to be acquired by protecting children from the sins of intemperance and blasphemy and, in so doing, raising them to uphold religiously authorised standards of morality. Foremost amongst the capital of the Christian woman was chastity, which Mary Sumner considered (in common with her co-workers in the GFS and MU) an absolute marker of the capital of women collectively as well as individually. The possession of this religiously framed symbolic capital was an essential pillar of the MU claim for pedagogic authority.

Mary Sumner's view of appropriate relations between men and women in marriage reflected the Anglican assumption of the divinely ordained authority of men over women: 'The husband and Father is

1. Sumner, 'Marriage I', 2-4,11, 12; 'To Husbands and Fathers.'
2. Mrs Maude, 'Leaflet Number 4 for Subscribing Members', ed. Diocese of London Mothers' Union (n.d.).
3. Sumner, 'Marriage 1', 13; 'The Home' (Winchester: Warren and Son, n.d.).

the head of the house his example and influence should be to his family the type and pattern of divine rule.' Yet, her vision of marriage included the Pauline exhortation 'husbands, love your wives' (Ephesians 5:25).[1] Mary saw marriage as a benign institution for the love, honour, comfort and exclusive status of the wife, who was 'the weaker member and needs sympathy and protection'.[2] She envisaged marriage as a religious partnership: '[H]ow beautiful is a home where peace and love prevail, where a married pair are the entire world to each other, and live faithfully under God's laws.'[3] In her second 1895 address on marriage she asserted the rewards of loving domesticity:

> It would be well if husbands and wives could treat each other as they did in their courting days and try to remain *lovers* all their life long so that love grows sweeter and stronger, as like Darby and Joan, they walk hand in hand down the hill of life together, and prepare for the Home above.

She advocated prayer as a way for couples to keep their marriage vows in mind: 'There are some happy couples who begin the habit of praying together on their wedding day and have never left off.'[4]

Although Mary Sumner was enthusiastic in her advocacy for marriage, but she acknowledged that it was 'not the whole object of life. . . . It is better to remain single than to marry unhappily or unwisely. No woman is justified in joining her herself to a man who is victim of a fatal passion and bringing down misery on her family.' She accepted that domestic life, caring for children and keeping one's husband from temptation could be hard, but once married the couple should make the best of their situation, 'for no two people can be joined together for life without meeting trials and difficulties . . . there is always the need of mutual forbearance'.[5] The onus was on the woman to lead by example. Wives were recommended to avoid nagging and to counter the ill temper of the husband with 'sweetness and evenness of temper'. The remedy to marital discord lay in forbearance, civilising through example and prayer. Self-restraint should also be exercised in keeping difficulties private. 'Beware of ever talking about your husband's faults to anyone – even your own mother . . . you can speak to God about them.'[6]

1. 'To Husbands and Fathers.'
2. 'To Husbands', 141.
3. 'Marriage I', 14.
4. 'Marriage 2', 23. Mary Sumner's italics.
5. 'Marriage I', 16, 17.
6. 'Marriage 2', 20, 21.

Despite Mary Sumner's assertion to a Church Congress audience in 1890 that it was 'presumptuous' to summon fathers ('of all classes') to meetings, her actions suggest that she was referring to men other than those from the working class, which indicates class as a mediating factor in gendered hierarchy.[1] According to her reminiscence of parochial life between the years 1851-86, she had spoken (with her husband's 'cordial approval'), to a parish Bible class of labourers. She recalled this in a 1917 letter to MU central Secretary Mrs Maude.[2] Working men were also addressed in the articles 'To Husbands' and 'To Fathers' (1895) and the undated pamphlet *To Husbands and Fathers*. She had high expectations for Christian manhood: 'Boys should be modest and pure quite as much as girls.'[3] In 'To Fathers' she asserted that men had a duty of respect, love and fidelity to their wives and they also had a role as exemplars of religious living to their children. In 'To Husbands' she wrote that:

> True religion is needed here, which will inspire men with Christian chivalry, and make them good and tender and sympathetic husbands and fathers, temperate in their habits, providing for the home needs themselves, and placing the wife in her true position in home life – honoured, shielded, and protected.

This included (especially for the poor man, whose wife lacked the help of servants) being:

> Ready and willing to put his shoulder to the domestic wheel, to cheer with kind words the suffering weary hearted mother, and even through the night to relieve her sometimes of the fretful baby or the sick child, and set things to rights in the morning before he starts off to work again.[4]

For Mary Sumner, the good husband and father was domesticated and religious. The attributes she recognised as the capital assets of the Christian man, sexual continence, temperance, and involvement in family prayer, reflected the evangelical prioritisation of religion

1. 'Paper Read at the Church Congress in Hull 1890'; Mrs Sumner, the Close, Winchester, in Charles Dunkley, *The Official Report of the Church Congress, Held at Hull on September 30th, and October 1st, 2nd, and 3rd, 1890* (London: Bemrose & Sons, 1890), 256-261.
2. Sumner, 'Founding'; 'Letter to Mrs Maude Central Secretary of the Mothers' Union 1917' in *Mothers' Union* (Lambeth Palace Library).
3. 'Purity', 44.
4. 'To Husbands', 149, 150.

in the home and the emerging emphasis on paternal involvement in family life.[1] The good father exemplified these behaviours as a model to his children. Other sources for the acquisition of symbolic capital lay in providing for the material needs of the household and treating the wife with courtesy and consideration. The rewards for conforming to standards of Christian manliness were the symbolic gifts of companionship and comfort within the domestic circle, respect there and in the community, and the hope of salvation.

3.5 The patriotic Mothers' Union: Church, state and the field of power

Mary Sumner's intention that the MU should 'awaken in Mothers a sense of their great responsibility . . . in the [religious] training of their boys and girls (the future fathers and mothers of England)', and in so doing 'reform the morals and raise the tone of this country through the homes', revealed her belief in the contribution of women to national life.[2] This understanding of women's citizenship was predicated on a concern for and participation in community improvement that reflected the evangelical focus on good living and social improvement through good works. Whilst focussing on duties rather than the achievement of civil rights, the emphasis on contribution to social well-being, which Mary Sumner saw as dependent on Christian values and conduct, was a claim for the recognition of women's 'work' as wives and mothers.[3] It was also an assertion that public matters overlapped with issues of concern in the home which permeated the rationale and practice of the MU.

The Established Church of England, which Mary Sumner sought to uphold through the MU, had a privileged relationship to the state. State and Church power were embodied in the monarch. Authorised by temporal power, Anglicanism, in turn, legitimised monarch and

1. See John Tosh, *A Man's Place: Masculinity and the Middle-Class Home in Victorian England* (New Haven, Connecticut; London: Yale University Press, 2007); Stephanie Olsen, 'The Authority of Motherhood in Question: Fatherhood and the Moral Education of Children in England, c. 1870-1900', *Women's History Review* 18, no. 5 (2009).
2. Sumner, *Home Life*, 10, 14. Objects of the Mothers' Union. In 1902 'England' was replaced by 'Empire'. This will be discussed in the following chapter on mission; *To Mothers of the Higher Classes*, 69.
3. See Catriona Beaumont, *Housewives and Citizens: Domesticity and the Women's Movement in England, 1928-64*, Gender in History (Manchester: Manchester University Press, 2013), 4-43, 47-52. Beaumont discusses citizenship and the MU after 1928.

state by association with divine authority and Christian values.[1] Mary considered the Christian family as the bulwark of well-ordered society. In 1895 she claimed: 'Every man in the land who is ruling himself and his home in accordance with the faith and obedience of Christ is a tower of strength to his country.'[2] George Sumner's remarks at the 1890 Hull Church Conference communicate a perception that there was a need to promote social cohesion: he claimed that the MU 'tends to unite the classes and in these days of social inequality and difficulty, anything that tends to unite the classes together should certainly be welcomed by us who have the interests of society at stake.'[3] For Mary, this reflected the notion of respectability in which classes were united by adherence to the moral and social values endorsed by the Church. She illustrated her vision of a cohesive (but stratified) society with reference to Aesop's fable of 'the Body and its Members', a view that echoed the commitment to 'faithfulness to employers' advocated by the GFS in their 'Objects':

> The connection of every class of society is required to the support and well-being of the whole. . . . In fact, the union of all classes is necessary to that maintenance of authority, respect for the public law, and stability of government on which the safety of property to individuals and the continuance of the national prosperity alike depend.[4]

Misrecognising the legitimacy of social stratification, she asserted the social and spiritual inclusiveness of the MU, where 'Even the poorest mother will remember her life is of infinite value', for 'the mysterious gift of influence is granted to all wives and mothers in extraordinary measure, rich and poor, educated and uneducated.'[5] Mary Townsend likewise stated in 1885 that the GFS was 'intended to embrace . . . not one class only but any of those maidens of our land who are bravely going forth to earn their livelihood in different posts of honourable work.'[6]

---

1. Sumner, *Memoir of George Sumner*, 5, 62, 85; Sumner, *Life of C.R. Sumner*, 109, 124.
2. Sumner, 'Prayer', 161.
3. George Henry Sumner, 'Address at the Church Congress in Hull 1890' in *Mothers' Union* (Lambeth Palace Library); ibid., 286-287.
4. Sumner, 'Prayer'; For a discussion of respectability as demarking social status see David Cannadine, *Class in Britain* (New Haven; London: Yale University Press, 1998), 92-94.
5. Sumner, *Home Life*, 1, 139, 'Every Member Should be a Worker'.
6. Mary Elizabeth Townsend, 'Department for Members in Professions', *Girls Friendly Society Associates Journal*, February 1885. The GFS faced more difficulties negotiating status amongst different categories of working

Although, as Charlotte Yonge noted in her 1887 article on the MU, it was desirable to enrol 'ladies, farmers' wives, and village tradespeople, as well as the poor', this did not mean that social divisions were dismantled. When travelling, Mary Sumner requested a first class railway ticket for herself, whilst her maid travelled third class.[1] However, competence and loyalty in servants was regarded as laudable and used to illustrate the virtues and (symbolic) rewards of accepting and fulfilling the obligations of one's (divinely ordained) place in society, whether high or low. Being a good master was also recognised as a source of capital.[2] Relationships across social strata could be warm, as Mary Sumner's correspondence with her former maid Marion Basdell, illustrates: 'Dearest B, I am longing to hear about you, how you are and how dear baby is. . . . Ever I am, with love and best wishes, your affectionate as of old, M.E. Sumner'.[3]

Mary Sumner assumed that leadership would follow class divisions. Her view was that 'reforms come from the head of the body politic and circulate through the masses'. The responsibility of the upper classes to set a good example to social inferiors was a recurring theme in her writing. In *To Mothers of the Higher Classes,* she wrote:

> Let me entreat the more educated, more influential women to give a helping hand in spreading the principles of the Mothers' Union, each in her own circle among her equals, and among her poorer neighbours. . . . They must take the ignorant and weaker Mothers by the hand, and by prayer and example teach them how to do their duty by their children.[4]

This message was repeated in *Home Life*: 'Mothers of the Upper Classes are asked to take their place in the van . . . if they join and act as leaders, it will be easier to win all sorts and conditions of Mothers to see their responsibility'.[5] The parish meetings of the MU exemplified the patronage assumed by 'ladies' for those within their sphere of influence.

---

women who were sensitive to nuances of class status – both Societies were rather tentative in relations with the middle classes.

1. Charlotte Yonge, 'Conversation on the Mothers' Union', *The Monthly Packet of Evening Readings for Younger Members of the Church of England* Thursday September 1st 1887; Sumner, 'Letter to Mrs Maude Central Secretary of the Mothers' Union 1917'.
2. *Memoir of George Sumner*, 26, 51-52.
3. 'Letters to Marion Basdell "Bassie" Hutchings Ereaux' in *Diocese of Winchester Mothers' Union* (Hampshire Record Office, n.d.). Mary Sumner was godmother to 'dear baby'.
4. *To Mothers of the Higher Classes*, 11, 57.
5. *Home Life*, 3.

Mary interpreted the response of her married men's group as acceptance of her class-based assumption of authority, which she recalled in a 1917 letter: 'I hold that a lady has such power over the married men – I shall never forget their inborn chivalry to me – they treated me like a queen. Many were tough looking men.'[6] Her friend and fellow worker, Lady Laura Ridding, held similar views. In an address delivered to the 1887 Wolverhampton Church Congress she claimed: 'The mother owes it to her children and her households to teach them. . . . Character training is her work.' At the Exeter Church Congress in 1894 she noted that this responsibility extended to the workplace where, ideally, 'the girls look up with a happy smile of friendship as the owner's wife goes through the rooms where she watches with motherly Christian care'.[7]

Mary Sumner's assumptions concerning class were also embedded in the early Mothers' Union cards, which addressed a membership categorised as ordinary members who were referred to as 'poorer' or 'cottage mothers' and 'subscribing members' referred to as 'educated mothers' or 'mothers of the higher classes'. As can be seen in **Table 3**, their cards had slightly different wording, for 'no lady would be tempted to send her child to the public house'.[8] The later publication of magazines (from 1888 and 1891) replicated the differentiation between these social categories. Class stratification was also reflected in the distinction made (as noted in 1888 in *To Mothers of the Higher Classes*) between Subscribing Associate members and the 'poorer' members who were not obliged to pay.[9] In 1895, this was qualified with the amendment, 'unless they like to'.[10] The two-tier system followed the approach taken by the GFS.[11] It was not until 1912 that, after some resistance from Mary Sumner, the MU cards were revised into a single version for all members.[12] The organisation was slow to adopt democratic processes. Mary Sumner's undisputed leadership was acknowledged with her installation as Central President in 1896, and the appointment of her successor, Lady Alice Chichester,

6. 'Letter to Mrs Maude Central Secretary of the Mothers' Union 1917.'
7. Lady Laura Ridding, 'Home Duties and Relations of the Educated Woman; an Address to the Wolverhampton Church Congress on Women Workers 1887' in *Selborne Papers* (Hampshire Record Office); 'The Guardianship of Working Girls Paper Read to the Church Congress Exeter 1894' in *Selborne Papers* (Hampshire Record Office).
8. Sumner, *Home Life*.
9. *To Mothers of the Higher Classes*, 66.
10. *Home Life*, 4.
11. Money, *History of the Girls' Friendly Society* 4-5.
12. Sumner, 'Letter to "Dearest Minnie" Concerning Revision of the Mothers' Union Cards 1912'; Porter, Woodward, and Erskine, *Mary Sumner*, 129.

in 1910 did not involve an election. Social status, network contacts and record of service contributed to the pedagogic authority necessary for leadership, and responsibility was presented as an obligation to be upheld rather than sought for personal aggrandisement.[1]

The Mothers' Union, like the Girls' Friendly Society, secured royal patronage from Queen Victoria in 1897, Queen Alexandra in 1901, and Queen Mary in 1910. Mary Sumner used Queen Victoria and Prince Albert as an example of desirable religious as well as social capital to endorse the MU message: '[T]heir true love and their noble high minded standard of righteous living [were] a pattern of what married life should be.'[2] She repeated Queen Victoria's views on the corrupting effect of reports from the divorce courts in her own anti-divorce pamphlet 'Good Homes and Faithful Marriages':

> These cases which must necessarily increase, when the law becomes more known, fill now almost daily a large portion of the newspapers and are of so scandalous a character that it makes it almost impossible for the newspaper to be trusted in the hands of a young lady or boy. None of the worst French novels, from which careful parents would try to protect their children, can be as bad as what is daily brought before and lands upon the breakfast table of every educated family in England and it is evident must be pernicious to the public morals of the country.[3]

Princess Christian of Schleswig-Holstein (Queen Victoria's third daughter Helena) was Patron of the Mothers' Union in the Diocese of London from 1908, gave the MU support as a speaker, and corresponded with Mary Sumner. In the context of opposition to divorce in 1911, she wrote: 'Yes I will come and come gladly to a special meeting.' She also shared Mary Sumner's view that the leaders of society should set a moral standard and that sensational publicity was damaging: '[T]he good of our class is not brought before the masses but all our sins, vices, silliness [and] bad manners are put upon them in very crude colours.'[4] Royal patronage, as enumerated in **Table 4**, endorsed the MU's definition of itself as an

1. *Mary Sumner*, 117, 137, 138, 158.
2. Sumner, *To Mothers of the Higher Classes*, 12.
3. 'Good Homes and Faithful Marriages' in *Mothers' Union* (Lambeth Palace Library).
4. Princess Christian of Schleswig Holstein, 'Letter to Mrs Sumner', ibid., n.d., surmised 1911 in context of other correspondence on topics discussed in the letter.

organisation with interests in upholding national life. In a letter to the Mayoress of Birmingham, written in 1910, Mary Sumner drew on King George V's rhetoric to support her claim to the contribution of the work of mothers to national life: 'The strength of a nation lies in the homes of its people.'[1]

The association of temporal and spiritual power was reflected in the Anglican Church's endorsement of the army, which was symbolised in the ceremonial blessing of regimental colours by distinguished clergymen. When officiating at such a ceremony in 1886, George Sumner said: '[I]t would be an evil day when Christianity was supposed to be separated from the military profession . . . the true soldier of the Queen might be a true servant of the King and Lord of Lords.'[2] The Mothers' Union established Army Branches (1894) and, in 1918, Navy Branches, which were instrumental in spreading the organisation overseas. The MU demonstrated its overt patriotism by publishing leaflets to support recruitment to the armed services in 1914.[3] Mary Sumner was in no doubt of the religious justification for the 1914-18 hostilities and claimed 'the army fighting to save England from being conquered by the cruel Germans' had divine sanction. She was not alone in holding this view. MU Vice President Horatia Erskine referred to 'the Kaiser's unholy ends', and Laura Ridding's *War Chronicle*, a wartime diary, documented instances of alleged German atrocities.[4] Mary Sumner saw the war as a stimulus towards religious belief, writing to Edith Randall in 1915: 'This terrible war gives an opportunity of getting hold of and influencing the mothers in their time of sorrow and anxiety.' However, she feared the effect of wartime conditions on the morals of girls: 'Soldiers are more moral than

1. Mary Sumner, 'Letter to the Mayoress of Birmingham December 13th 1910', ibid.
2. *Memoir of George Sumner*, 62, 125. See also Sumner, *Life of C.R. Sumner*, 293-294.
3. Mothers' Union, 'To British Mothers: How They Can Help Enlistment' (London: Mothers' Union, 1914); 'Brave Women' (London: Mothers' Union, 1914); The GFS was also patriotic and mobilised its members to support the war effort in practical ways. See Chapter XII, 'The Motherland's call to the pilgrims', in Heath-Stubbs, *Friendship's Highway*, 91-105.
4. Sumner, 'Letter to "My Dear Marion" (A.K.A Basdell) December 23rd (Surmised) 1916'; 'Letter to Mrs Crawford June 19th 1917'; Lady Horatia Erskine, 'Letter to Mrs Sumner' in *Mothers' Union* (Lambeth Palace Library); Lady Laura Ridding, 'The War Chronicles Part I 1914' in *Selborne Papers* (Hampshire Record Office, 1914). Laura Ridding, *The War Chronicles*, 1919. Selborne Papers, Hampshire Record Office 9M68/95. 'Corpse Factories with bodies rendered for fat.' January 12th.

girls of a certain class now. I am sick at heart over the type of young women now disgracing the nation.' Presumably her assertion in the same letter that 'Every girl can show her patriotism by becoming a mother' applied only to those who were married.[1] Retaining divine blessing for a successful outcome to the war required demonstration of moral fitness. Mary Sumner's view in 1915 was that 'Until the Nation humbles itself and turns to God we cannot expect Victory and Peace'. She was in favour of a national day of prayer and humiliation. Her assertion that victory should be earned by moral rectitude, and advocacy for a day of national humiliation, reflected her evangelical emphasis on atonement and her belief that Protestant, preferably Anglican, Christianity was integral to national identity and that it legitimised and contributed to the authority of the state.[2]

Traditionally, the Anglican Church was associated with conservative political values. George Sumner described himself as a conservative 'of a somewhat liberal type' but insisted 'it was not the wish of the Church simply to vote Tory, [clergy were] Churchmen first politicians second'. There were nevertheless occasions when Church (and Mothers' Union) interests overlapped with divisions of opinion on party political lines. Moves to disestablish the Church in Wales from 1895, which were opposed locally by George Sumner in Winchester and nationally by the MU, were associated with Liberal party policy.[3] The secularisation of education, so feared by Mary Sumner and which was the subject of discussion in her address 'Secular Education', was similarly associated with the Liberal party. However, despite this (and the presence women of Tory opinions including Laura Ridding and notably Ellen Joyce, a stalwart supporter of the Conservative Primrose League in the membership) the MU was not an overtly party political organisation. Consistent with the emphasis on women's citizenship as service to society rather than seeking rights, the MU avoided the issue of suffrage. Mary Sumner was not an enthusiast for it. She considered that caring for children gave women a more exalted status than the achievement of

1. Sumner, 'Letter to Mrs Sharme': 'the beautiful thing is how religious most of the men are – they have daily prayers in some of the trenches!'; 'Letter to Dearest Edith (Randall)' in *Mothers' Union* (Lambeth Palace Library).
2. 'Letters to Lady Chichester', July 2nd 1915: 'Until the Nation humbles itself and turns to God we cannot expect Victory and Peace. Do you think a universal day of humiliation can be arranged?'
3. *Memoir of George Sumner*, 128-130. George Sumner was speaking at a meeting held in Winchester to protest against the proposed disestablishment of the Church in Wales.

political rights. Her friend, Lady Horatia Erskine, agreed. Even Laura Ridding, a committed suffragist, expressed reservations about lowering the age for women voters in 1919.[1] The MU position was encapsulated in a speech by the Countess of Airlie that was reproduced in the 1891 debut issue of *Mothers in Council*:

> Consider what power has been given to women by God and how far greater it is than the powers that man can accede to them. The moulding of the future generation lies mostly in their hands if they care to exercise their influence.[2]

The Mothers' Union sought to influence government policy on topics such as the (1902) legalisation of marriage to the 'Deceased Wife's Sister', which they opposed, and relaxation of divorce law in 1903, 1908-12, 1917, and 1921, which was also resisted. Support was voiced in favour of raising the age of consent in 1910 and the 'threat of Mormonism' was highlighted the following year.[3] Mary Sumner's correspondence reflects the scope of concern, with moral issues ranging from the secularisation of education (1902 and 1906) and anti-Christian 'Socialist' Sunday Schools (1912) to the 'Disestablishment of our Dear Anglican Church in Wales' (1911), the 'White Slave Trade' (1912), and 'bad books'.[4] Temperance was also an issue prioritised by Mary Sumner. The Mothers' Union responded to the increase in drinking amongst women in wartime with the appointment, in 1917, of Mrs Russell (the daughter of Emily and Ernest Wilberforce) as a Temperance correspondent. It was in favour of legislation intended to increase the age of consent (1910).[5] The scope of MU interests and its professionalisation in matters of procedure was represented by the establishment of diverse committees. The brief of the 'Watch Committee', instigated by Lady Laura Ridding in 1912, was 'to watch and give information and advise the Council as to desirable action

1. *Mothers in Council*, January 1891; Erskine, 'Letter to Mrs Sumner'; Ridding, 'Diaries', July 6th 1919. At this time only women over 30 could vote in British parliamentary elections.
2. Countess of Airlie, 'Report of Speech by the Countess of Airlie', *Mothers in Council*, January 1891.
3. Porter, Woodward, and Erskine, *Mary Sumner*, 11, 12, 119-128, 142, 154.
4. Sumner, 'Letters to Lady Chichester', April 24th 1915; 'Letter to "Dearest Minnie" Concerning Revision of the Mothers' Union Cards 1912'; 'Letters to Lady Chichester', January 7th 1913, 'Every member of the Mothers' Union is against the White Slave traffic – if she were not she would not be a member; 'Letter to the Editor, *The Times*, "Improper Books", December 9th 1909.'
5. Porter, Woodward, and Erskine, *Mary Sumner*, 141. Mrs Wilberforce was Central President of the MU at the time.

with regard to legislative proposals in Parliament concerning matters affecting the welfare of the mothers of the nation'.[1] The MU sought to influence policy through gathering evidence to present to government commissions (notably the 1909 Gorell commission on divorce), securing the support of influential individuals and sending delegates and speakers to conferences.[2] It also cooperated with other organisations, such as the GFS. This cooperation and the overseas dimension of the MU's networking will be explored in following chapters.

Mary Sumner considered that divorce was not only sinful but 'tends to fatal results in domestic and national life'.[3] Opposition to divorce reform from 1903 was foremost amongst MU campaigns. As in the years prior to the centralisation of the MU between 1886 and 1896, the strategy of writing directly to influential clergy or laymen in authority was deployed. In 1909 Mary Sumner drew on her acquaintance with Archbishop Cosmo Lang of York and the Bishop of London, Randal Davidson (the husband of the London Diocesan MU President), to seek advice on raising an anti-divorce petition. The same year, Mary Sumner and members of the MU Central Council expressed their view to Lord Gorell, the chairman of the Royal Commission on Divorce and Matrimonial Causes, and presented evidence gathered by enquiry at diocesan and branch level. Mary Sumner's views on divorce were still being heard in 1920, when her daughter, Mrs Gore Browne, passed on her views on indissolubility of marriage to the Mothers' Union central council under their new president Mrs Hubert Barclay.[4] In rationale and campaigning strategy, opposition to divorce reform encapsulates the agenda and practices of the MU, which reflected the views of the 'foundress' and the durability of her influence.[5] It also illustrates the field position that she and the MU achieved in relation to the Church and to temporal authority. In 1926, the author of *Fifty Years* considered that the MU had been influential in mediating legislative reform:

1. Ibid., 127.
2. Mothers' Union, *Fifty Years*, 26, 30, 43. Lady Laura Ridding spoke on issues of interest to the Mothers' Union from 1887 when she addressed the Wolverhampton Chuch Congress on 'Home Duties of the Educated Woman'.
3. Sumner, 'The Home'.
4. Porter, Woodward, and Erskine, *Mary Sumner*, 119-123, 154. Evidence was presented to the commission by Mrs Church an MU worker in the east end of London, MU Central Vice-President Evelyn Hubbard and Mrs Emeline Francis Steinthal, PNEU activist and friend of Charlotte Mason, who in this instance was acting in her capacity as Honorary Secretary of Rippon Diocesan MU.
5. Beaumont illustrates the durability of Mary Sumner's views in MU policy, *Housewives and Citizens*, 77-79.

> Those who govern our nation have realised that, in dealing with the marriage laws of our country, they have to reckon with a very large section of women who banded together in the Mothers' Union have pledged themselves to defend their country from legislation which is in direct contradiction to the law of God more than once since 1910 the prompt action of the Mothers' Union has prevented the increase of divorce facilities and its influence has been felt with regard to other Bills before parliament which have concerned the moral welfare of our country.[1]

The author of *Fifty Years* might also have concluded that the Mothers' Union, now numbering 490,000 worldwide, represented a force to be reckoned with within the Church. Yet those amongst the clerical hierarchy might also have been relieved that the MU accepted a limited delegation of authority within traditional gendered church and social doxa and did not at this point represent pressure for radical change.

3.6 Synopsis: wider habitus, transactions of capital, entering the field

The Anglican religious doxa legitimised the cultural arbitrary of patriarchal dominance by asserting the authority of men over women as divinely ordained. It drew on biblical interpretation to identify chastity as an absolute marker of female symbolic capital. Mary Sumner's writings on marriage (which were produced with advocacy for the Mothers' Union in mind) illustrate her misrecognition of patriarchal domination as both divinely ordained and 'the natural order'. Her writings on marriage emphasise the symbolic (but also practical) rewards of conforming to religiously authorised gendered conduct. Her complicity with the cultural arbitrary of religion (and with the associated arbitraries of class and gender differentiation) is demonstrated in the agenda of the MU and by her support for the GFS. This complicity may be attributed to the effectiveness of pedagogic action in securing the misrecognition of gendered arbitraries as legitimate and masking the symbolic violence to which she was subject. However the sanctions for transgression against the arbitrary of chastity could be severe. There was a high degree of correspondence between the pedagogic action of family, social milieu and as institutionalised in the Church, in the misrecognition of legitimate authority and capital assets and in the imposition of sanctions for transgression.

1. Mothers' Union, *Fifty Years*, 26-27.

The authorisation of the Mothers' Union by clerics representing institutional pedagogic authority, and its promotion through the mobilisation of Christian ladies, demonstrates that Mary Sumner's capital was recognised by agents within her habitus, who collectively misrecognised the dominant cultural arbitraries of Church, gender and class hierarchy and sought to reproduce them through symbolically violent pedagogic work. The instigation of 'her' MU and the GFS is reflects a perception that the religious doxa and the indices of religious womanly capital were contested and in need of defending. This mutual recognition of desirable capital was fundamental to the success of Mary Sumner's field manoeuvres. Her possession of social and religious capital allowed her the authority to recruit support amongst an extending network of personal contacts with a shared interest in upholding Anglicanism, to endorse the MU. The endorsement she secured from agents possessed of high social capital or invested with religious pedagogic authority as churchmen, served to present association with the MU as a means for the acquisition of social and religious capital. This accumulation of capital accrued not only to the MU as a body but was embodied in Mary Sumner as its iconic 'Foundress'. The wide circulation of the publications through which she asserted the significance of women as moral exemplars, without challenging the gendered doxic values of Anglicanism, was also a successful field manoeuvre. In speaking for an official Church organisation and drawing on the language of the Church, Mary Sumner may be considered not just a pedagogic worker, a helpmeet on behalf of the Church, but as an agent of distinction, invested with pedagogic authority.

The Anglican Church of England, in which Mary Sumner was raised and into which she married, was associated with the state and upheld the cultural arbitrary of royal power. The monarch was affirmed in temporal power by the rite of coronation. This was presided over by clergy of the highest rank who were political appointees and members of the higher legislative chamber. The Church also legitimised the armed forces, the ultimate bastion of state power, through religious ceremonials. Religious authority was drawn on to sanction the moral right of the nation in time of warfare against its enemies.

The Church represented the interests of the dominant social group. It perpetuated the cultural arbitrary of class privilege by promoting a doxa that asserted social stratification as divinely ordained. In return for 'knowing ones place' it offered paternalistic philanthropy and salvation. Mary Sumner identified with 'the upper classes' and saw behaviour in accordance with religious principle as related to social well-being. Social ills were interpreted as indicative of moral failings rather than systemic disadvantage. Conformity to, and complicity with, the symbolic violence of religiously approved standards of behaviour, such as sexual continence and temperance, would avoid the misery of prostitution, violence and poverty and thus served the interests of the state. For Mary Sumner, the dominant position of those with temporal power was legitimised by their demonstrable possession of religious capital. Much of her pedagogic action was directed at the upper and middle-classes with the aim of securing their conformity to the religious cultural arbitrary. This may be interpreted as action to legitimise social domination by associating it with religious capital. Mary Sumner's pedagogic action can be seen as defending the cultural arbitrary of religion against secular values. The MU and to a lesser extent the GFS, which placed less emphasis on Anglican sacraments, may be perceived as pedagogic work towards perpetuating the Anglican cultural arbitrary. As avowedly patriotic organisations they also engaged in pedagogic work towards upholding the privileged status of the Anglican Church in relation to the state.

Mary Sumner represents a category of conservative, religious woman of upper or middle-class status, who identified with, and claimed alliance to, 'upper-class' interests and perceived privileges and responsibilities. The MU offered these women, within gendered parameters, opportunities for the acquisition of symbolic capital through religious activism. In exchange for mis/recognising the legitimacy of arbitrarily ascribed gender roles and characteristics (that accrued around the notion of spiritual motherhood) that they sought to perpetrate, it offered the rewards of usefulness, capability and expertise and reputation in a territory of their own, dedicated to lobbying on issues they considered relevant. The foremost beneficiary of these rewards as the revered 'foundress' was Mary Sumner herself. She was innovative in securing her own recognition as a pedagogic authority not just within the MU but in the Anglican Church and the field of religion.

In establishing the MU as a recognised body within the Anglican religious field, Mary Sumner may be seen as mediating doxic assumptions on the role of women. Whilst the capital asserted as desirable in women was conceived of within the existing gendered religious and social doxa, the worth of this capital was asserted as significant to national life. Through drawing on the authority conferred by institutional attachment to the Church and royal endorsement, the MU made the presence of women at mass gatherings, and as speakers on public platforms, not only familiar but respectable. It identified women as collectively organised within the Church. It also normalised the collective action of women in relation to public issues. It could also claim to represent a body of opinion and lobbied to influence policy at a time when women had no direct political voice.

The voices of rank and file members of the organisation are underrepresented in the record, yet evidence of support for the pedagogic work of the MU and recognition of the pedagogic authority of Mary Sumner can be drawn from the rapid expansion of membership nationally and overseas. In exchange for the misrecognition of the legitimacy of a religious doxa which upheld patriarchal and class domination, and enforced absolutes in gendered standards of behaviour, the MU offered tangible advantages and symbolic gifts. Members of the MU were offered a discourse of empowering motherhood and could accrue the social honour of belonging to an organisation which (like the GFS) upheld a standard of high moral conduct. They were also given a space for respectable socialisation and offered entertainment and instruction through its magazines. Celebrity endorsement was given to the organisation by titled ladies and members of the royal family. In Mary Sumner members could identify with a leader who combined a distinguished public profile with the ability (via her writing, speaking and correspondence) to give members a sense of sympathetic personal connection. She appeared to embody the capital assets and symbolic gifts that she asserted as a reward for upholding religiously authorised notions of womanhood and religious piety.

Mary Sumner's activism was dedicated to, and authorised by, upholding the gendered and socially stratified doxic values of the established Anglican Church. Despite this dual position as recipient and perpetrator of symbolic violence, the MU was a conduit for the articulation of a collective woman's point of view and a means, albeit framed within gendered notions of maternal womanliness, for women to develop expertise, exercise authority and assert their value. Mary Sumner's stature as a female celebrity speaker to mass audiences, and the leader of a religious worldwide mass organisation, makes her a figure of distinction in the context of her times and remarkable in any period.

Original members of the MU being entertained at Upton House c. 1898

Part 2

Mission

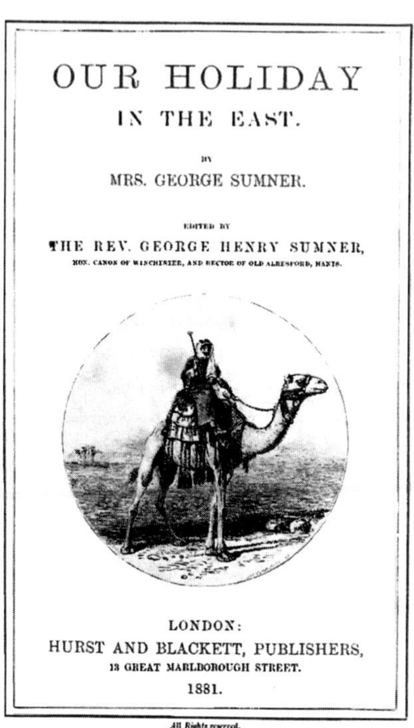

OUR HOLIDAY

IN THE EAST.

BY

MRS. GEORGE SUMNER.

EDITED BY

THE REV. GEORGE HENRY SUMNER,

HON. CANON OF WINCHESTER, AND RECTOR OF OLD ALRESFORD, HANTS.

LONDON:

HURST AND BLACKETT, PUBLISHERS,

13 GREAT MARLBOROUGH STREET.

1881.

All Rights reserved.

The title page of Our Holiday in the East *by Mary Sumner*

Chapter 4
Home and Abroad: Mary Sumner and Traditions of Philanthropy, Evangelical Religion and Civilising Mission

4.1 Introduction

Mary Sumner's activism through the MU was framed against a context of a proliferation of philanthropic activity stimulated by evangelical religious revival, in which women were participants. It also occurred at a time of expansion in British imperial rule and transnational engagement in which religious preference figured as both a stimulus and legitimising rationale. The term mission evokes religious enterprise, and it was used to label the domestic role assigned to women delineated by assumptions of their intellectual and spiritual nature that were informed and legitimised by religious authority. Mission also relates to varieties of philanthropic activism 'out of the house'.[1] It relates to the provision of religious ministry for expatriate communities and concerns the activity of missionaries and missionary societies seeking converts overseas. Mission in this sense invites consideration of identities (racial and gendered), relations and transactions of meaning and power between metropole and periphery, 'home' and overseas.[2] This chapter seeks to contextualise the notions of mission as they related to women's roles and moral improvement through

1. Frank Prochaska, *The Angel out of the House: Philanthropy and Gender in Nineteenth-Century England* (Charlottesville and London: University of Virginia Press, 2002).
2. Catherine Hall, *Cultures of Empire: A Reader: Colonisers in Britain and the Empire in Nineteenth and Twentieth Centuries* (Manchester: Manchester University Press, 2000); Frederick Cooper and Ann Laura Stoler, *Tensions of Empire: Colonial Cultures in a Bourgeois World* (Berkeley: University of California Press, 1997), 1-45, note the transactional relationship in terms of identity between metropole and periphery; Mary Louise Pratt, *Imperial Eyes: Travel Writing and Transculturation* (London: Routledge, 1992), 6-7. 'Contact zone' and 'transculturation' describe meaning drawn from encounters across space and culture. I use the term overseas to refer to this diversity of locations.

philanthropic pedagogic action in the domestic and more distant spaces that Mary Sumner was to operationalise through the Mothers' Union. Focussing on habitus and capital, this chapter explores these aspects of mission as Mary Sumner experienced them in the years prior to the adoption of the Mothers' Union as a diocesan organisation in 1885.

The term 'Victorian female civilising' mission encapsulates the expansive range of activity undertaken by women into the world beyond the home. Religion was bound up with philanthropy, for in framing notions of good womanhood as maternal and spiritually nurturing, it authorised charitable outreach. Religion, given stimulus by the evangelical revival, which crossed denominational boundaries, was 'the moral engine' for reform. Jane Jordan and Sue Morgan respectively have explained the religiously-motivated reforming ambitions of notable 'spiritual women', Josephine Butler, the campaigner against prostitution, and purity advocate Jane Ellice Hopkins of the White Cross Crusade, in seeking equal moral standards between men and women, a theme that can be identified in Mary Sumner's aims for the MU.[1] As Mary Ryan notes, 'It is to the domain of the public that women turn to achieve and protect their private as well as public objectives', an analysis highlighted by the MU's engagement in legislation on moral issues.[2]

Philanthropic activity offered an outlet for ladies seeking to be useful, and an opportunity for the evangelically minded to pursue the imperative of seeking converts to 'vital religion'.[3] Much philanthropy was organised along denominational lines and reflected the desire

---

1. Jane Jordan, *Josephine Butler* (London: John Murray, 2001), 207. Butler concentrated on opposing the Contagious Diseases Acts; Sue Morgan, *A Passion for Purity: Ellice Hopkins and the Politics of Gender in the Late-Victorian Church* (Bristol: Centre for Comparative Studies in Religion and Gender, University of Bristol, 1999). Hopkins wrote on behalf of the MU. See Appendix 2.
2. Mary P. Ryan, 'The Public and the Private Good across the Great Divide in Women's History', *Journal of Women's History* 15, no. 1 (2003); Cordelia Moyse, *A History of the Mothers' Union: Women Anglicanism and Globalisation, 1876-2008* (Woodbridge: Boydell Press, 2009), 69-77, 116-126, 170-181, 188-192, 230-133 are the main sections dealing with divorce.
3. Jenny Daggers, 'The Victorian Female Civilising Mission and Women's Aspirations Towards Priesthood in the Church of England', *Women's History Review* 10, no. 4 (2001); Sean Gill, *Women and the Church of England: From the Eighteenth Century to the Present* (London: Society for Promoting Christian Knowledge, 1994), 84. See also Ian Bradley, *The Call to Seriousness: The Evangelical Impact on the Victorians* (London: Jonathan Cape, 1976), 119.

to rectify social disorder by imparting religious preferences and contingent standards of conduct upon others.[1] Philanthropic activity was also mediated by class. Lucy Bland has drawn attention to the application of a moral agenda to material aspects of social improvement in attempts to modify working-class culture, notably with regard to temperance, an analysis that will be traced in Mary Sumner's habitus.[2] Jessica Gerard interprets the exercise of philanthropy by the 'landed classes', a definition equating to the upper and upper-middle classes, as legitimising the permanent inequality of a stratified society. Likewise, Diana Kendall sees a tradition of benevolence upholding social stratification.[3] Themes relevant to social reproduction are explored in this and the following chapter.

Susan Thorne considers missionary intelligence to be a distinguishing feature of Victorian culture and makes the association with religion, mission and empire by noting that 'Victorians learned much of what they knew about empire in church'.[4] Elizabeth Prevost, who gives substantial attention to the MU in her treatment of colonial Africa, sees mission as 'a crucial vector by which Britons experienced the non-western world'. She also considers that religion was the framework by which women 'conceptualised, articulated and challenged other social categories'.[5]

---

1. Gill, *Women and the Church of England*, 131-145; Brian Heeney, *The Women's Movement in the Church of England, 1850-1930* (Clarendon, 1988), 19; Susan Mumm, 'Women and Philanthropic Cultures' in *Women, Gender and Religious Cultures in Britain, 1800-1940*, ed. Sue Morgan and Jacqueline de Vries (London: Routledge, 2010); see also Eileen Janes Yeo, 'Some Contradictions of Social Motherhood' in *Mary Wollstonecraft: 200 Years of Feminisms*, ed. Eileen Janes Yeo (London and New York: Rivers Oram Press, 1997).
2. Lucy Bland, 'Purifying the Public World: Feminist Vigilantes in Late Victorian England', *Women's History Review* 1, no. 3 (1992); see also Nigel Scotland, *Squires in the Slums: Settlements and Missions in Late Victorian Britain* (London: I.B. Tauris, 2007), 253-254.
3. Jessica Gerard, 'Lady Bountiful Women of the Landed Classes and Rural Philanthropy', *Victorian Studies* 30, no. 2 (1987); Diana Kendall, *The Power of Good Deeds: Privileged Women and the Social Reproduction of the Upper Class* (Boston: Rawman Littlefield, 2002).
4. Susan Thorne, 'Religion and Empire at Home' in *At Home with the Empire: Metropolitan Culture and the Imperial World*, ed. Catherine Hall and Sonia O. Rose (Cambridge: Cambridge University Press, 2006), 145.
5. Elizabeth E. Prevost, *The Communion of Women: Missions and Gender in Colonial Africa and the British Metropole* (Oxford: Oxford University Press, 2010), 159.

The exercise of philanthropy at home is seen by Alison Twells not only to draw on the metaphor of foreign mission but to be part of the same project and informative of middle-class identity and culture.[1]

According to Andrew Porter, British imperial pre-eminence was bound up with assumptions of cultural and racial superiority which informed the view that the 'improvement' of less civilised and unchristian societies was an obligation.[2] The influence of the periphery in the construction of identities in the British metropole, demonstrated by Hall and Rose as a relational transaction bound up with religion, is explored in this chapter with a focus on the Girls Friendly Society, which Julia Bush identifies as having an imperial identity, and explored further in the following chapter through the Mothers' Union.[3]

The decade 1880-1890 marked a high point in the production of women's travel narratives. Perceptions of 'otherness' by European travellers and the constructions of identity drawn from them by travellers and their audiences have been analysed by Mary Louise Pratt and Billie Melman. Melman sees the trope of travel writing as autobiographical in constructing, locating and affirming the identities of their protagonists as they responded to the 'other' in the 'imaginary geography' of a culturally constructed gendered and hierarchical 'orient', an oppositional binary to the 'occident'.[4] Jane Rendall, too, sees gender identities related to imperial identities. She argues that British women used the zenana as a powerful symbol of women's oppression in heathen society, which was seen as evidence of the cultural superiority of Christian values and, by implication, to vindicate imperial rule. Paradoxically, the constraint of zenana women provided white women with the opportunity to occupy

---

1. Alison Twells, *The Civilising Mission and the English Middle Class, 1792-1850: The 'Heathen' at Home and Overseas* (Basingstoke: Palgrave Macmillan, 2009), 5.
2. A.N. Porter, *The Imperial Horizons of British Protestant Missions, 1880-1914* (Grand Rapids, Michigan: Wm. B. Eerdmans, 2003), 2.
3. Catherine Hall and Sonia O. Rose, eds., *At Home with the Empire: Metropolitan Culture and the Imperial World* (Cambridge: Cambridge University Press, 2006), 2, 5, 6; Julia Bush, *Edwardian Ladies and Imperial Power* (London: Leicester University Press, 2000), 142-143; Catherine Hall, *Civilising Subjects: Metropole and Colony in the English Imagination, 1830-1867* (Cambridge: Polity, 2002); Thorne, 'Religion and Empire at Home'.
4. Pratt, *Imperial Eyes*; Billie Melman, *Women's Orients: English Women and the Middle East, 1718-1918: Sexuality, Religion and Work*, 2nd ed. (Basingstoke: Macmillan, 1995).

a role exclusive to women in missionary societies.[1] Mary Sumner's published report of her *Holiday in the East* which included first-hand observations of zenana life will be contextualised against these interpretations.

The chapter is organised into three sections. The first section begins with a consideration of circumstances that informed Mary Sumner's habitus and examines the three aspects of mission (outlined above) as understood in, and experienced by, Mary Sumner in her kinship network. It then moves outward into wider networks both informal and formal, to locate Mary Sumner amongst other agents and organisations during her years of parochial life. The second section of the chapter then moves outwards and gives attention to Mary Sumner's understanding of non-Christian religion and attitudes to 'race' and the work of missionaries as discussed in accounts of her travels, in particular her visit to the Holy Land in 1880 (prior to the diocesan launch of the MU), which provided the material for the published account *Our Holiday in the East*. In the third section of the chapter, Mary Sumner's views on 'woman's mission', philanthropy, overseas engagement and imperial identities are contextualised through attention to the GFS (Girls' Friendly Society), the organisation in which she was active for nine years prior to the inception of the MU as a diocesan organisation. Following the transnational and spatial expansion of the MU, the societies collaborated on overseas projects.

4.2 Philanthropy and mission in family life; parochial philanthropy via organisations 1851 to 1886

The Unitarian traditions upheld by the Heywoods prior to their Anglican conversion were characterised by the application of religious principles to all aspects of life, belief in human perfectibility and contingently, aspirations for self and societal improvement. These were frequently realised through philanthropy. The Manchester Cross Street Chapel to which the Heywoods had been affiliated, was a noted centre for projects that sought to promote individual welfare and

1. Jane Rendall, 'The Condition of Women, Women's Writing and the Empire in Nineteenth Century Britain' in *At Home with the Empire: Metropolitan Culture and the Imperial World*, ed. Catherine Hall and Sonia O. Rose (Cambridge: Cambridge University Press, 2006), 104; see also Bush, *Edwardian Ladies and Imperial Power*, 122. Bush comments on the association of assumptions of cultural superiority with gendered racial attitudes; Gill, *Women and the Church of England*, 181-197.

accomplish civic improvement.[1] These were compatible with Anglican practice, particularly amongst believers of an evangelical mind, who demonstrated their inner faith through public acts. Thomas Heywood and his elder brother, Sir Benjamin, following conversion to Anglicanism (c. 1834) realised their philanthropic impulses in the building of parish churches, in addition to providing schools and facilities for the poor.[2] The Heywoods (and the Sumners), motivated by their religious beliefs, considered that their advantaged position within society both qualified and obliged them to exercise responsibility for the material and spiritual welfare of the population in the locality. A feature of the memoirs in both the Heywood and Sumner families is the enumeration of philanthropic achievements to signal religious capital. Mary Sumner noted: 'Uncle Benjamin [Sir Benjamin Heywood] and [cousin] Oliver [Heywood] spent their lives in working for God and their fellow creatures.' She also recorded that her cousin and brother-in-law Thomas Percival Heywood was 'a lifelong philanthropist'. Mary's father, Thomas Heywood, similarly demonstrated his philanthropy through building a church and schoolroom for his tenants in the village of Wellington Heath, a hitherto 'neglected district' on his Hope End estate.[3]

Mary Sumner and her niece Isobel emphasised philanthropic activity as ministry undertaken by their parents as married couples. Mary recorded that her parents 'took a never failing interest in all the poor around them' and 'kept actively at work for the good of the poor people'.[4] Isobel Heywood similarly recorded that her parents, used 'to visit diligently and make friends with the poor'.[5] Children in the family were

1. Alan J. Kidd and K.W. Roberts, *City, Class and Culture: Studies of Social Policy and Cultural Production in Victorian Manchester* (Manchester: Manchester University Press, 1985); Ruth Watts, *Gender, Power and the Unitarians in England, 1760-1860* (London: Longman, 1998); Kathryn Gleadle, *The Early Feminists: Radical Unitarians and the Emergence of the Women's Rights Movements, 1831-51* (Basingstoke: Macmillan, 1995). The educational dimension will be discussed in the following chapter.
2. Mary Sumner, 'Account of Her Early Life at Hope End 1828-46' in *Mothers' Union* (Lambeth Palace Library); Anita McConnell, 'Heywood, Sir Benjamin, First Baronet (1793-1865)', *Oxford Dictionary of National Biography* (Oxford University Press, 2004), [http://www.oxforddnb.com/view/article/1317911, accessed November 20th 2012].
3. Sumner, 'Early Life.'
4. Ibid., 32, 33.
5. Isabel Mary Heywood and Sir Thomas Percival Heywood, *Reminiscences, Letters and Journals of Thomas Percival Heywood, Baronet. Arranged by His Eldest Daughter (Isabel Mary). With a Preface by the Rev. George Body* (printed for private circulation: Manchester, 1899), 31.

also encouraged to participate in philanthropic activity. Mary and her sister were expected to help in the Sunday school run by their mother. They also helped in practical fund raising. Mary recorded that when 'a large bazaar was held at Hope End to help in getting the church at Wellington Heath finished . . . I had a stall of canary birds and flowers and made £12'.[1]

The conceptualisation of philanthropy as mission is evoked by the language in which philanthropic activity is described, which is evocative of endeavour, and venture to regions deemed to be in need of moral improvement. Mary Sumner considered that her parents' interventions 'were the means of transforming a wild district into a respectable community'.[2] The district reformed by her sister Maggie and her husband was described by their daughter Isobel Heywood as: 'A sort of "no man's land" out of the way of good influences; drinking, fighting, and all sort of wickedness went on there unnoticed and unrebuked'.[3]

Missionary valour is evoked in anecdotes recalling the personal witness of religion. Mrs Heywood's 'wonderful act of piety and love' in nursing and bringing spiritual comfort (but not, unfortunately, physical recovery) to a typhoid victim, signalled her willingness to engage in an unpleasant and possibly perilous activity in the discharge of Christian duty that was consistent with notions of 'woman's mission'.[4] The Sumners shared a similar outlook towards the participation of women in philanthropic activity. George Sumner's mother was publicly commended for her competence in administrating the annual charitable distribution of clothing to the poor from the Bishop's Palace: 'the clergy were obliged to allow that the lady had been the best general'.[5]

As evangelical Anglicans, the Sumners also saw their religious preference as a mandate for working towards the improvement of others. Charles Sumner applied himself to modifying public conduct by eliminating 'abuses', such as the 'profanation of the Sabbath' by cricket matches and Sunday trading. He opposed the 'Hop Sunday' festival in Farnham on the grounds that it provoked excessive drinking,

---

1. Sumner, 'Early Life'. See also Charlotte Mary Yonge, 'A Real Childhood', *Mothers in Council*, January 1892. MU and GFS co-workers Charlotte Yonge and Ellen Joyce were similarly expected to contribute to philanthropic 'work' as children. Yonge taught Sunday school and Joyce sewed for an emigrant.
2. Sumner, 'Early Life'.
3. Heywood and Heywood, *Reminiscences*, 64.
4. Sumner, 'Early Life'.
5. George Henry Sumner, *Life of C.R. Sumner, D.D., Bishop of Winchester, During a Forty Years' Episcopate* (London, 1876), 155.

immorality and rowdiness.[1] For Charles Sumner, whose success in filling an empty church by the earnestness of his evangelical preaching is recorded by his son George, 'clergy were not placed just to live an ordinarily respectable life but to save souls'. Dissent, understood as the favouring of denominations other than Anglicanism, should be actively countered, for 'others in the field are ready to pick up gleanings'. The Anglican priest 'must preach more earnestly, more simply, more affectionately'.[2]

Charles Sumner approached his Episcopal duties with missionary enthusiasm. In 1829 he made the first visit by the incumbent Bishop to the Channel Islands which formed part of the extensive diocese of Winchester. The purpose of the visit was to resist adherence to rival denominations. It was also intended to promote confirmation and the taking of communion in a region where this aspect of sacramental observance had been neglected.[3] The conception of the nature of these visits as missionary is evoked not only by the agenda of improving religious participation but by the emphasis on the travail and hazard involved in gaining the destination. The sense of distant venture is heightened by the fact that French 'or a sort of patois' was the first language of the working class population, some of whom were 'somewhat primitive in their manners and customs, but singularly free from vicious habits'. Mrs Jennie Sumner and two of their children 'were of course included' in the Bishop's travels. Her contribution to his ministry by correcting his French in order to aid his communication with catechumens is noted, and her stalwart behaviour at moments of danger is also recorded as a laudable attribute.[4] George and Mary Sumner accompanied Bishop Charles Sumner on one of these visitations, which included the islands of Guernsey, Jersey, Alderney and Sark, in 1850. As his father's chaplain, George 'preached and spoke for the SPG [Society for the Propagation of the Gospel] and CMS [Church Mission Society]'.[5] Once again in 1859

1. Ibid., 175.
2. Ibid., 33, 176.
3. Ibid., 184, 187. Visits were subsequently undertaken every four years.
4. Ibid., 181-184. Geneva born, Jennie Fannie Barnardine Sumner had French as her first language. In 1829 Charles and Jennie had six children: John born 1816, Louisanna 1817, Charles 1819, Robert 1821, Sophia 1823 and George 1824. Emily was born three years later in 1832. The account does not specify which children were included in the visit.
5. Mary Sumner, *Memoir of George Henry Sumner, D.D., Bishop of Guildford: Published for His Friends by Special Request* (Winchester: Warren and Sons, 1910), 14.

George and Mary joined Charles Sumner in a tour of what were referred to as 'missionary districts' in Ireland. The tour was undertaken in 1859 to support the (Anglican) 'Society for Irish Church Missions to Roman Catholics'. The Bishop was pleased to note that as a result of the 'patient forbearance and endurance of the missionaries . . . the influence of the priests is much diminished'.[1]

Charles Sumner was an enthusiast for foreign as well as domestic missions. He had preached on behalf of the evangelically aligned CMS in 1827, and was active in support of both the CMS and the SPG, increasing the diocesan funding for the latter from £70 at the start of his episcopate to £4061 in 1866.[2] Diocesan contributions to the CMS by that time totalled £8,964. At the start of the twentieth century, Sumners were contributing man power as well as funds to missionary enterprises overseas. George Sumner's nephew, Alan George Sumner Gibson, was Coadjutor Bishop of Capetown in 1904 and his great-nephew, Edward Harold Etheridge, was in 1900, a missionary in Mashonaland (Zimbabwe).[3]

George and Mary Sumner, like their relatives, realised their religiously motivated philanthropy by providing facilities for education and worship. They maintained an emphasis on personal intervention in relations with parishioners. George 'gained their hearts in many cases by sympathy in their family joys and sorrows. . . . He was a personal friend and advisor as well as their clergyman.'[4] Parish work at Old Alresford reflected the trend towards participation in organisations that sought to promote religiously-approved conduct in order to remediate perceived social ills. In 1855, George Sumner, the Honorary Secretary for the

1. Sumner, *Life of C.R. Sumner*; see David W. Bebbington, 'Atonement, Sin and Empire 1880-1914' in *The Imperial Horizons of British Protestant Missions, 1880-1914*, ed. Andrew Porter (Michigan: Wm B. Eerdmans, 2003), 22, 27, for evangelical aversion to Roman Catholicism as a stimulus for missionary activity
2. Sumner, *Life of C.R. Sumner*, 139-141; Brian Stanley, *The Bible and the Flag: Protestant Missions and British Imperialism in the Nineteenth and Twentieth Centuries* (Leicester: Apollos, 1990), 55-84. See 'The Gospel for the Globe' for the origins of the evangelical Anglican CMS (1799) and the Society for the Propagation of the Gospel in Foreign Parts (1701), which originated to provide Anglican clergy for British subjects in the colonies. It was associated with the 1699 Society for Promoting Christian Knowledge. Stanley associates evangelical revival with missionary expansion.
3. Heywood Sumner, 'Memorials of the Family of Sumner from the Sixteenth Century to 1904' (Southampton, 1904).
4. Sumner, *Memoir of George Sumner*, 16-17, 19. See previous chapter.

initiative in Hampshire, published an account of 'Book Hawking', a scheme which, according to Mary Sumner, 'did useful work in sending men round the villages with Bibles, prayer books and good literature.' George Sumner also served on mission-related committees. He was a member of the Diocesan Mission Council for promoting parochial missions in the Diocese and was Vice President of the Winchester Diocesan Branch of the SPG.[1]

The Church of England was conscious that working-class men were under-represented in congregations and attention was given to their recruitment.[2] Old Alresford had a Young Men's Association, and Mary Sumner drew attention to the participation of men in parish life as a marker of the success of her husband's (and her own) parochial work: 'It was often observed how great was the number of men who attended Old Alresford Church.' She notes that it was at the request of the husbands of members of her Mothers' Meeting that her Bible study group for married men was started.[3]

During and following the years of Mary and George's parochial work, the perceived social evils of drink provided a focus for campaigns by those who perceived the inculcation of moral and religious conduct as a remedy for social ills. For Mary Sumner, poverty, violence and immorality could be attributed to drink because it caused loss of

1. George Henry Sumner, *Book Hawking; as Conducted in Hampshire* (London: Wertheim and Macintosh, 1855). Book hawking was a Church of England initiative dating from c. 1855. See also Sumner, *Memoir of George Sumner*, 20, 149; Henry George De Bunsen, 'The Bookhawker: His Work and His Day: Being a Paper Read at the Conference of the Church of England Bookhawking Union, Held at Derby, Sept. 21, 1859', (published for the Church of England Bookhawking Union, Aylott and Sons, 1859); James Randall, *Book-Hawking: A Means of Counteracting the Evils of the Day* (1862); D.R. Mackarill, 'Book-Hawking – A Moral Enterprise', *Antiquarian Book Monthly* 27, no. 7; ISSU 309 (2000).
2. Sumner, *Memoir of George Sumner*, 117-120. Charge by the Bishop of Guildford Church of England Men's Society c. 1901; see also Owen Chadwick, *The Victorian Church Part 2, 1860-1901* (London: S.C.M., 1987), 222, 223, 226; Gill, *Women and the Church of England*, 84-87, discusses attempts by 'muscular Christians' such as Charles Kingsley to reconcile a gentle Jesus and a feminised church with masculinity. The issue of the lack of appeal of the Established Church also accrued around perceptions that it was not socially inclusive.
3. Sumner, *Memoir of George Sumner*, 16, 18; 'Account of the Founding of the Mothers' Union and Parochial Work at Old Alresford' in *Mothers' Union* (Lambeth Palace Library).

self-control. Advocacy for temperance (and mothers as promoters of temperance) was embedded from 1876 in the cards produced for members of the Mothers' Meeting and later asserted in Mary Sumner's writing.[1] At Old Alresford, the 'cause' was supported indirectly by the promotion of respectable entertainments, such as the Cottage Garden Society, the Reading Room and village concerts. It was overtly promoted through a branch of the Church of England Temperance Society (established in Winchester 1877) which did 'not seek to enforce teetotalism on all . . . simply moderation in the use of intoxicants as a condition of membership'.[2] However, Mary Sumner regarded total abstinence with approval. Her advocacy for temperance was shared by her daughter Louisa (also an activist in the MU) and her husband Canon Gore Browne, who 'stopped the whole village going to the pub'.[3] By 1886, Mary Sumner was taking a leading role in the Winchester Juvenile Union of The Church of England Temperance Society. The *Hampshire Chronicle* reported:

> A gathering in Canon Street rooms of the children of the Juvenile Union established three years ago for the benefit of children who do not attend the National Schools in Winchester, over which Mrs Sumner who is president of the Union for 1886 most kindly presided. Mrs Sumner addressed the children and gave most excellent reasons why they should remain steadfast to their principles and expressed the hope that each of the children would try and get some more children to join.[4]

---

1. 'Temperance' in *Home Life* (Winchester: Warren and Son, 1895); see Brian Harrison, *Drink and the Victorians: The Temperance Question in England, 1815-1872* (London: Faber and Faber Ltd, 1971); see also Gill, *Women and the Church of England*, 133-134, for discussion of temperance and Church of England women.
2. Anon, 'Church of England Temperance Society', *Hampshire Chronicle*, Saturday April 7th 1877.
3. Mary Elizabeth Sumner, *Our Holiday in the East* (London: Hurst & Blackett, 1881), 74. 'As the majority of the party were total abstainers . . . a kettle was soon boiled and excellent tea with milk, provided.' M.G. Evans and Austin Whitaker, 'Winchester Life Histories No. 31 Mrs M.G. Evans' in *Winchester Memories* (Hampshire Record Office, 1971). The parish in question was Michelmersh in Hampshire.
4. Anon, 'Winchester Juvenile Union of the Church of England Temperance Society', *Hampshire Chronicle*, Saturday January 16th 1886. National Schools were sponsored by the Church of England.

The imperative towards the improvement of others through religion, evident in both the Heywood and Sumner families, was mediated by their social status but informed, above all, by evangelical enthusiasm typified by a belief in the application of religious practice for the improvement of public as well as private life. Their philanthropic projects may be considered as a mission in that they sought to promote adherence to standards of moral conduct informed by religion. The misrecognition of the superiority of Anglican doctrine informed the categorisation of 'others' as deficient in religious capital and legitimised this perpetration of symbolic violence through pedagogic action. Those categorised as unenlightened, that is in need of winning for (Anglican) Christianity, could be local or further afield. For the Heywoods and Sumners, involvement in philanthropy could accrue and indicate possession of symbolic capital, both religious and social. For Mary Sumner, parochial work affirmed dispositions of habitus towards religious outreach. Acting as the helpmeet to her husband in his parochial ministry provided an opening into the field of philanthropy through which she accumulated religious and social capital. This authorised her to exercise pedagogic authority on her own account, notably through her involvement in the GFS (1875) and Mothers' Meeting which, with the issue of membership cards in 1876, marked the genesis of the Mothers' Union. Mary Sumner's transaction of this pedagogic authority into pedagogic work through the diocesan MU is the subject the following chapter.

4.3 Travels in the 'East': Mary Sumner in the 'contact zone', the habituated gaze, religious and cultural capital

In 1880 Mary Sumner had an experience that confirmed her religious preferences and advocacy for mission work in foreign lands. It also contributed to her pedagogic authority as an expert in religious matters. She published an account of what she described as 'our pilgrimage to the Holy Land' in *Our Holiday in the East*. Mary was accompanied by her husband, George, their daughter, Louisa, two Heywood cousins and the Reverend (later Archdeacon) Stanhope and his daughter. This 'charming party of intimate friends and relations', styling themselves 'The Happy Seven', set out on a three month adventure to Egypt, Palestine, Syria and Lebanon.[1] By visiting the 'Orient', Mary Sumner was engaging in a pastime of increasing popularity amongst the upper

1. Sumner, *Our Holiday*, 4, 70; Sumner, *Memoir of George Sumner*, gives an edited account and documents a trip to Algiers in 1892-3.

and upper-middle classes. The practice of providing a written account of travels through which the audience 'at home' could imagine and construct notions of identity and difference was also familiar.[1]

The Sumners were in the category of Christian travellers (particularly those of an evangelical mind) who 'saw' the Holy Land in terms of an illustration to revealed Scriptural truth. Throughout her narrative, Mary Sumner emphasises the possession and accumulation of religious capital. In camp George led Sunday services and twice-daily prayer. Her assertion of the sense of religious solemnity experienced at sites associated with Scripture is encapsulated in this entry:

> Good Friday in Jerusalem was a day never to be forgotten. The English services were well attended and the [Anglican] Bishop of Jerusalem preached an earnest sermon on the great subject of the crucifixion. It seemed wonderful and solemn to be commemorating the great central fact of our holy faith in the very place where Our Blessed Lord laid down his Life.[2]

There were occasions when there was a deficit between Mary Sumner's aspiration for spiritual affirmation and the actuality of experience: 'When face to face with a holy site on which the mind has dwelt during a lifetime, it is somewhat disappointing not to have a stronger sense of enthusiasm at such moments.'[3] However, her comment that, 'the difficulty of realising the exquisite scriptural stories in modern degraded Palestine was a constant source of disappointment' hints that poor government and cultural and religious deficiencies, rather than the lack of religious sensibility on the part of the travellers, was the reason for this disillusionment.[4]

The Sumner party's cultural capital was signalled in reports of enthusiastic and even intrepid sightseeing at historic sites. Mary Sumner described George and daughter Louisa making the hazardous and undignified ascent of a pyramid and reported George's swim in the Red

---

1. Mary Sumner's friend Lady Laura Ridding also visited Egypt and the Holy Land in 1886. Lady Laura Ridding, 'Account of Travels to Egypt and the Holy Land' in *Selborne Papers* (Hampshire Record Office, 1886); Melman, *Women's Orients*, 25-56. 165-190. See 'A Prosopography of Travel, 1763-1914'; 'Evangelical Travel and the Evangelical Construction of Gender'.
2. Sumner, *Our Holiday*, 143. See also 22, 37, 42, 72, 87, 90, 103, 110, 123, 151, 183, 193 for similar evocations of religious experience and sensibility.
3. Ibid., 162.
4. Ibid., 80.

Sea as an amusing anecdote.[1] The narrative communicates her relishing the freedom and adventure of travel on horseback and 'bohemian' living under canvas. However, this did not mean abandoning comfort: the ladies had bought their own saddles and 'india-rubber baths, soap tins, beds, sponges and looking glasses' were amongst the equipment dealt with by the numerous servants employed to organise the Sumners' transport, accommodation and catering.[2] She also took pleasure in the perceived quaintness and exoticism of the 'East' and its inhabitants. In Alexandria, she 'felt very much as if we had waked [sic] up in another planet . . . full of interest and delight'.[3] Cairo donkey boys 'were as full of fun as an Irish car driver', Arabs had 'noble countenances' and their artistic drapery was a pleasure to look at. Mary considered that they exhibited 'a strange sort of majesty and loftiness' and noted with approval that 'a Bedoueen [sic] is always true to his word'.[4] She singled out their 'handsome and loyal' Syrian guide for praise. Of Hani, 'it was impossible to speak too highly'. Hani's estimable qualities were associated with his profession of Christianity: 'Hani always tried to join in these [religious] Tent Services, and when they parted he said to Canon Sumner. "I never had such a successful journey before. . . ." He then said pointing to Canon Sumner's breast pocket, "That's what kept us safe. It was the Bible you always read and your prayers"'. [5]

Convinced of the superiority of her own religious, national, cultural and even aesthetic notions of value, Mary Sumner felt able to record generalised judgements of categories (religious, racial/national) of person based on limited examples of behaviour. English characteristics (conceived as work ethic, as well as moral and physical hygiene) were seen to have the advantage even in comparison with other Europeans. She portrayed Italians at Brindisi as exhibiting an 'inconceivable want of energy' and her condemnation of Port Said as 'very new, very French and very wicked' reveals her association of France with laxity

1. Ibid., 26-30.
2. Ibid., 24, 296.
3. Ibid., 16.
4. Ibid., 14, 121, 224; Emma Raymond Pitman, *Missionary Heroines in Eastern Lands: Woman's Work in Mission Fields* (London: S.W. Partridge & Co., 1895), 131-137. Miss Whatley's view of Egypt corresponds almost exactly with Mary Sumner's responses in interpretation of the exotic scene, both refer to dreaming and describe camels, drapery and 'native countenances'.
5. Sumner, *Memoir of George Sumner*, 7, 51. Mary Sumner records a visit to Hani's family in 'Beyrout' and notes correspondence with Hani in years after the holiday. Hani's children were Selim, Maron, Ayoob, Foudoulla, Regina, Bechara and 'little Josef'.

in morals.[1] Cleanliness was a measure of 'civilised' behaviour. Even Christian pilgrims going to Jerusalem were noted as exhibiting manners and customs that 'were not altogether appetising'.[2] Mary was shocked at villages in Alexandria: 'The Arab villages are deplorable children of all ages and degrees of nudeness roll about in the dust heaps . . . how they can live in such degrading dirt, and with habits so uncivilized, is almost inconceivable to Europeans.'[3]

Lack of refinement was noted by Mary Sumner in culture, too. She considered that 'Orientals seem to have no musical gifts'. Seeing a performance by dancers at Jericho, who 'with their tattooed faces, glaring eyes, dark complexions and dishevelled hair . . . looked like savages', the Sumner party (who had not enjoyed the concert) thought they 'had found ourselves in central Africa'. The Sumners countered by singing 'a selection of glees and songs'. Mary reported that these efforts were applauded but the thoughts of the indigenous audience on the Sumners' artistic efforts and conduct are a matter for speculation.[4] Lack of self-control was also interpreted as a sign of racial inferiority; Mary noted that 'Easterns are subject to paroxysms of wrath'. 'Orientals' were also categorised as childlike and the narrative included:

> An incident worth noting as illustrative of native character . . . Al Raschid having been kicked by a horse burst into tears . . . it was only a scratch which an English lad would have laughed at but the great childlike Syrian be-pitied himself greatly, and his pathetic and dramatic gesticulations were quite touching.[5]

Mary Sumner indicated the social standing of her party by distinguishing it from organised groups of 'Cook's Tourists'. She also signalled confidence in their status as English travellers by noting that 'the Union Jack floated over the central tent, and gave éclat to our encampment'.[6] The Sumners claimed access to indigenous people

---

1. Sumner, *Our Holiday*, 4, 64; 'French' was synonymous with lax morals and 'French novels' exemplified unsuitable literature. For examples of this view, see Mrs Knight, 'On High Schools and Home Education', *Mothers in Council*, April 1891; Mary Sumner, 'Good Homes and Faithful Marriages' in *Mothers' Union* (Lambeth Palace Library, n.d.); *To Mothers of the Higher Classes* (Winchester: Warren and Sons, 1888), 18; Lesley Hall, *Sex, Gender and Social Change in Britain since 1880* (Basingstoke: Macmillan, 2000), 44-45.
2. Sumner, *Our Holiday*, 66.
3. Ibid., 12, 14.
4. Ibid., 101, 124-125.
5. Ibid., 223. For references to 'orientals' as childlike, see 108, 215 and 278.
6. Ibid., 71, 122.

of high social standing and authority. *Our Holiday* records visits to the Governor of Nablus and the Mufti of Damascus, amongst other notables.[1] In Egypt they were entertained by the Khedive who had 'the good sense to apply to one of our great public schools in England, [for a tutor for his sons] . . . an ex-master of Winchester College'. The narrative implies that superior class equates with civilised behaviour and thus the appreciation of (English, Christian) values as represented by the Sumner party.[2]

Mary Sumner's observations reflect her preference for Protestant Anglican observance.[3] Roman Catholic iconography was not to her taste: 'At Gethsemane the only things that jarred upon us were the pictures of our Lord's sufferings at the Latin stations. These poor representations seemed puerile and impertinent.' She also disapproved of Greek Orthodox Church ritual and the lack of restraint shown by its worshipers.[4] Positioned as non-believers, Muslims and Jews were also subject to critical scrutiny. Mary Sumner condemned 'the utter lack of reverence and decorum' at a Jewish funeral. At the 'Wailing' [Western] Wall in Jerusalem she noted: 'Jews from all parts of the world . . . many with almost Saxon features . . . but all having the subtle Jewish look which is unmistakable'. She also commented on what was, to her, their mistaken profession of faith. 'Their forefathers had crucified the Lord of Glory, and they knew it not: the true Light is Shining, and they see it not: the Messiah for whom they sigh has come, but they believe it not.'[5]

Muslims also exhibited what for Mary Sumner was a regrettable lack of decorum in worship. She condemned the religious fervour of an Egyptian festival as a 'barbarous and disgusting rite' and, at a Muslim funeral, 'four veiled women astride on donkeys [were] uttering wails. Great indeed was the contrast between this scene and our reverent English funerals. The wailing too had an artificial ring about it, which did not denote true sorrow.' Muslim stories and legends 'did not to say the least, consort well with the facts of scripture'. Moreover, she averred that 'religious liberty is abhorrent to Moslems'. [6] However, 'It was impossible not to be struck by their fearless profession [of faith] or to

1. Ibid., 185, 264, 169, 249, 263, 267, 306.
2. Ibid., 47-49, 50-51; Sumner, *Memoir of George Sumner*, 41-42.
3. Mary Sumner's remarks illustrate Cooper and Stoler's 'grammar of difference', see Cooper and Stoler, *Colonial Cultures*, 2-4.
4. Sumner, *Our Holiday*, 172. Ibid., 98
5. Ibid., 113, 145, 147.
6. Ibid., 47, 52, 104, 186.

help wishing that members of our pure Church would be equally bold in their Christian ritual.' She was also impressed by the devotion exhibited by a group of 'dervishes' but qualified her approbation by noting that:

> In our minds was a deep longing that such evident religious fervour might be gathered up with our own holy faith and that the yearnings of these fanatics should be satisfied by a real and intelligent knowledge of the unknown God whom they ignorantly worship.[1]

Despite George Sumner's claim in his preface to *Our Holiday*, that no attempt 'to solve the knotty questions connected with the holy sites in Palestine' was intended, Mary associated what she perceived as the failings of the Ottoman government with religious deficit: 'Bad government may account for much, a false religion may account for more'. Missionary work offered a solution. She considered that:

> We as Christians must try more zealously to raise up the banner of the Cross in the midst of a land so dear to Our Lord. . . . Only thus will light break forth out of the present darkness, and Palestine take its rightful place amongst Christian kingdoms. If the holy land were governed by Christian rulers a great religious revival would in all probability soon begin.[2]

A recurrent theme in Mary Sumner's assertion of the superiority of (Protestant) Christianity concerned the treatment of women. For her, 'eastern' social practice demonstrated a 'barbaric want of chivalry'.[3] It was also her view that 'eastern' religious forms of observance denied women participation in worship and spiritual inclusion. She described a Jewish service as 'very much lacking in devotion . . . the mother sat apart and hardly seemed to join in the service at all'. At the 'Wailing' [Western] Wall there were only 'a few women who kept in the background'.[4] Despite declaring that 'No

1. Ibid., 54, 276.
2. Ibid., 90.
3. Sumner, *Memoir of George Sumner*, 98-99.
4. Sumner, *Our Holiday*, 151,145; Melman, *Women's Orients*, 194-209. Melman's chapter '"Domestic Life in Palestine": Evangelical Ethnography – Faith and Prejudice' refers to women's writing on Moslem and Jewish women that puts Mary Sumner's views in a context of evangelical disapproval of the treatment of 'orientals'. Melman identifies (amongst numerous examples) Mrs Mott's 1865 *Stones of Palestine: Notes on a Ramble through the Holy Land;* Suzette Lloyd and Harriet Smith's 1872 *Daughters of Syria: A Narrative of the Efforts of the late Mrs Bowen Thompson for the Evangelisation of Syrian Females*

religion treats women fairly but the Christian religion', her reservations on the practices of the 'eastern' Orthodox Churches extended to the treatment of women. In a Greek Orthodox Church, 'there was a gallery at the back very high up where women can worship unseen. Even the Christian women here follow the Moslem custom and entirely veil their faces.'[1]

Muslim practice drew Mary Sumner's strongest disapproval. She considered that the zenana system, which she had observed at first-hand in Egypt, Palestine and Syria, symbolised the low social and spiritual status of women. For Mary Sumner, the zenana condemned women to a life that was 'vacant and debilitating . . . dreary, useless, childish [and] inane.'[2] Women were 'kept in ignorance and practical imprisonment . . . employing their time in little else than idle gossip, and the jealousies and inanities of their miserable life. We never saw a book or a bit of needle work in any harem we visited.' She condemned what she called 'forced marriage' and commented 'daughters are puppets in their parents' hands.' This state of affairs demonstrated the need for missionary intervention, 'the inestimable value of zenana work.'[3] These views were reiterated in her 1910 memoir of George: 'It is frequently asked by men and women of the world; "What is the good of Missions? Why not leave the Easterns to live up to their own religions?" These people . . . do not know the fate and sorrow of the eastern woman.'[4] Mary Sumner's experience in Algeria (also recalled in the memoir), which included a covert visit to observe worship in a mosque, affirmed the view she asserted in the account of *Our Holiday* and was also drawn upon as evidence towards her authority on the subject:

> During our time in Algeria, as in the East we were deeply moved by the condition of wives and mothers. It is terribly sad, for where the Christian religion does not prevail, their lot is indeed hard, and fills one's heart with sympathy. A woman is never seen inside a mosque. I believe she is supposed to have no soul,

---

and Countess Ellesmere's *Journal of Tour in the Holy Land in May and June 1840* as works which reflect this view. These works are dated prior to Mary Sumner's 1880 journey.

1. Sumner, *Memoir of George Sumner*, 50; Sumner, *Our Holiday*, 81.
2. *Our Holiday*, 310, 128. Miss Stanhope's 'exhibition of first rate riding' to an Arab audience is used by Mary Sumner to indicate the freedom accorded to Christian women.
3. Ibid., 266, 303. See Guli Francis-Dehquani, 'Women Missionaries in Persia: Perceptions of Muslim Women and Islam, 1884-1934' in *The Church Mission Society and World Christianity, 1799-1999*, ed. Kevin Ward and Brian Stanley (Grand Rapids, Michigan; Cambridge: Wm. B. Eerdmans, 2000).
4. Sumner, *Memoir of George Sumner*, 50.

> for in speaking to a dervish (the native village schoolmaster at Sidi-ben-Madin) he said, when asked why there were only boys in school, 'OH girls do not need it; they have no souls; they die like dogs.' I do not suppose this is the universal opinion of Easterns; but it would account in some measure for the treatment of women in Mohamedan countries. All honour to Missions which are working for the salvation of women.[1]

Accounts of visits to missions and missionaries feature in both *Our Holiday* and in the record of Mary Sumner's time in Algeria.[2] Women taking leading roles in missionary schools feature prominently, and she noted that the missionary, Mr Macintosh, was 'greatly helped in his work by his wife'.[3] In Egypt, Mary visited a school run by the 'brave, indomitable' Miss Whatley, who had been 'abused insulted and cursed in the streets by fanatical Moslems'. She was impressed by Miss Whatley's achievement in the face of 'difficulties which would have completely disheartened a less heroic spirit'.[4] She also commended Mrs Bowen Thompson, the founder of the British Syrian Schools, for her mission school in Damascus where 'the sphere is one of great difficulty and danger, and requires much tact as well as Christian Courage'. In 'Beyrout', mothers at Mrs Mott's school for girls 'sent a kind message to the members of my Mothers' Meeting at home about which I had told them'.[5] For Mary Sumner, the valorous example of missionaries was a standard to be lived up to and she warned of the discredit that failure to uphold Christian standards engendered in the eyes of non-believers. In 1910, when the Mothers' Meeting mentioned in 1880 had grown into a worldwide organisation, she wrote:

1. Mary Sumner observed the Grand Mufti leading 'the last important ceremony of ramadan' and noted, 'very properly the Bishop [George Sumner] was not invited.' Ibid., 93. Capitalisation as source. See also 94-95 and 99: according to the testimony of English missionaries, 'the homelife of women . . . was sad indeed'.
2. Sumner, *Our Holiday*, 110, 112, 119, 146, 204-206, 210-211. These are in addition to other references mentioned in the body of the text.
3. Ibid., 273.
4. Ibid., 44-45; 'Mary Louisa Whatley: The Story of Her Mission Life and Work in Egypt', Pitman, *Missionary Heroines*, 129-160. Miss Whatley was the daughter of the Archbishop of Dublin. She worked in Egypt from 1856 to 1889, having begun her mission work in Ireland during the famine of 1846 to 1851 on behalf of the Irish Anglican Church Mission among Roman Catholics.
5. Sumner, *Our Holiday*, 273, 302. Mrs Mott, Mrs Bowen Thompson, Mrs Henry Smith and Miss Lloyd of the British Syrian Schools were sisters; Pitman, *Missionary Heroines*, 40-72. Mrs Bowen Thompson's *Missionary Work Among the Daughters of Syria*.

> If *all* English women showed the Easterns what the home life of a true wife and mother is, and if in every country possessed by the English, the Christian religion has always been openly lived and honoured by the English Government, and taught in the schools which were started by our Government in the conquered lands, by this time Christianity would have won so many hearts and homes that the present troubles assailing the British rule would, in all probability, be unknown.[1]

Mary Sumner also considered Christianity to contribute to good government, as exemplified by the rule of England, for her the highest exemplar of a Christian nation. Moreover, English men and women needed to embody the standards of morality that made English rule superior. Mary Sumner also prioritised the cultural and social capital of 'Englishness' above those of different nationality, religion and ethnicity. In her accounts of *Our Holiday* and the visit to Algiers, she asserted herself and her associates as bearers of desirable cultural, social and religious capital by positive assertions of engagement with cultural symbols, association with persons of status, and anecdotes of religious sensibility. Defining herself as a traveller, and presenting her account in print, was, in itself, an assertion of capital (implicitly economic and cultural and also signifying intrepidity). In addition, possession of (assumed) superior symbolic capital was affirmed and asserted in contrast to examples of difference perceived as indicative of deficiency. So, for Mary Sumner, the 'east' signified dirt, ignorance, heathenism, passion, childishness and the oppression of women, whereas 'English' signified cleanliness, education, self-control, maturity and 'freedom' for women. With the Bible as her guidebook, she approached her journeys misrecognising Protestant Christianity and 'Englishness' as superior and legitimating of domination, and like others of similar habitus, saw what she came looking for.

4.4 Mary Sumner: habitus, wider network, and mission via the Girls' Friendly Society

In 1874, Mary Sumner had become one of the original 'Associates' of the GFS.[2] She sustained a parochial GFS branch at Old Alresford until 1886 and served as Winchester Diocesan Vice President in 1885 and then as President in 1887 and 1888.[3] Her daughter, Louisa Gore

1. Sumner, *Memoir of George Sumner*, 50-51. Mary Sumner's italics.
2. Mary Heath-Stubbs, *Friendship's Highway: Being the History of the Girls' Friendly Society* (London: Girls' Friendly Society, 1926), 218.
3. Ibid., 214.

Browne, (daughter-in law of Mrs Harold Browne, wife of the Bishop of Winchester and member of the inaugural GFS committee), was also active in the GFS.[1] In 1911, Margaret Gore Browne, Mary Sumner's granddaughter (b. 1886, later Mrs Evans) became Diocesan GFS President.[2] The GFS and key figures in its leadership were a continuing presence in Mary Sumner's life. The GFS informed and affirmed Mary Sumner's dispositions of habitus pertinent to notions of 'women's mission' and engagement overseas that were realised through the MU. It also exercised pedagogic action on the members of the GFS who were likely after marriage to become MU members. Scrutiny of the GFS also locates Mary Sumner within a context of views on Empire and 'race', which, while diverse in emphasis, are united in prioritising religious capital as legitimising of gendered roles, philanthropy, mission and empire. Although the GFS preceded the diocesan MU by a decade, overseas expansion of the societies was largely contemporaneous (c. 1890-1914) and collaboration occurred between them in field manoeuvres to promote a mutual religious agenda 'at home' and overseas. The GFS was notable for its promotion of women's emigration to imperial destinations. As noted in the previous chapter, there was an overlap of GFS and MU personnel, notably in the context of engagement overseas exemplified by Charlotte Yonge, an enthusiast for missionary work, and imperialists Laura Ridding and Ellen Joyce.

In the account of the GFS published in *Friendship's Highway* (1926), its 'foundress', Mary Townsend, is reported as saying, 'I have always conceived of the GFS work as the nature of a Mission, the Mission of Women to Women'.[3] To prevent 'tales of shame and misery, of wasted lives spent in the service of sin or vanity instead of in the service of Christ', GFS 'lady' Associates would promote religious knowledge and observance amongst working-class 'girls' by acting as moral guardians and through providing 'respectable' leisure opportunities and education.[4] GFS Associates' shared habitus gave them, in addition to class identity and religious affiliation as Anglican communicants, an expectation of, and an appetite for, service. Mary Townsend's assertion

1. Winchester Diocesan Girls' Friendly Society, 'Winchester Diocesan GFS Council Minutes' in *Winchester Diocesan Girls' Friendly Society* (Hampshire Record Office).
2. Heath-Stubbs, *Friendship's Highway*, 214.
3. Ibid., 82.
4. Agnes L. Money, *History of the Girls' Friendly Society*, New and rev. ed. (London: Wells Gardner, Darton, 1905), 4, 6. See previous chapter; GFS rule three insisted on chastity.

that 'hundreds and hundreds of devoted women are labouring for their young sisters' welfare' is given credence by the personal column of *The Monthly Packet* of August 1875 (the inaugural year of the GFS), the magazine edited until 1890 by GFS Associate and 'Literature Correspondent', Charlotte Yonge. Whilst 'Emilie would be grateful for linen or books to distribute amongst her poor people', 'PC' offers thanks for donations for her 'Winter Home for Consumptives'.[1] For Edith Moberly, GFS Diocesan President for Salisbury between 1880 and 1887, philanthropic involvement was central to her sense of worth. The thought of being obliged to give up such 'work' left her feeling bereft.[2] The admission by Miss Lucy Olivia Wright, who made a career as Central Secretary of the GFS from 1880 until her death in 1896, that '*I love the GFS*' [italics as source] also suggests that philanthropic work was experienced as affirming identity and sense of purpose, and points to a role and position in the field of philanthropy through which unmarried women could contribute their 'maternal' talents to social improvement.[3]

Despite the extensive range of practical welfare work undertaken by the GFS its identity as a Church of England society remained to the fore; it looked upon itself as 'one portion of that great army of Christ, humbly

1. Agnes Louisa Money, *History of the Girls' Friendly Society* (London: Wells Gardner, Darton, 1902), 5; Anon Monthly Packet, 'Correspondence August 1875', *The Monthly Packet of Evening Readings for Younger Members of the Church of England*; Charlotte Yonge, *Womankind*, 2nd ed. (London and New York: Macmillan, 1890; first published 1876), 85-90. The chapter 'Charity' asserts almsgiving as a religious duty and provides examples of how young ladies may achieve this through the support of missions 'at home' or overseas even if parents forbade direct contact with the poor. F. K. Prochaska, *Women and Philanthropy in Nineteenth Century England* (Oxford: Clarendon Press, 1980), 1-17; see also Midori Yamaguchi, *Daughters of the Anglican Clergy: Religion, Gender and Identity in Victorian England.*
2. C.A.E. Moberly, *Dulce Domum: George Moberly, His Family and Friends* (London: John Murray, 1911), 213. The Moberleys were friends of Charlotte Yonge. In 1869, Edith responded to the thought of giving up her boys' class with 'I am done for'; Money, *History of the Girls' Friendly Society* 45; Yeo, 'Some Contradictions of Social Motherhood,' 122-123; see also Prochaska, *Women and Philanthropy*, 6-8, 41, 124, for the 'maternal' role of unmarried women and philanthropy as a rewarding and expected outlet for their energies.
3. Yeo, 'Some Contradictions of Social Motherhood', 122-123; see also Prochaska, *Women and Philanthropy*, 6-8, 41, 124, for the 'maternal' role of unmarried women and philanthropy as a rewarding and expected outlet for their energies.

seeking the spread of his kingdom'.[1] It engaged in manoeuvres to promote its moral standards into the wider public sphere, both nationally and overseas. 'We are,' said Mrs Townsend, 'a fighting fellowship'.[2] Members were exhorted to active witness of the religiously sanctioned capital of chastity, temperance, thrift and prayer, which the GFS espoused, and Mary Sumner advocated for Mothers' Union members. GFS Associates believed that their girls should, and did, provide an example of desirable public conduct. According to Charlotte Yonge, reporting a conversation with a local farmer, 'the reason that the boys in this village are so much better than they were, is because the GFS has a great deal to do with it, for if the boys are not steady they say the girls will not speak to them'.[3] The GFS gave conspicuous public demonstrations of its values by running wartime temperance canteens, through the 1920 pageant at the Albert Hall, and via participation in the White Crusade, a campaign for moral regeneration, in which the Mothers' Union also participated. The 'White Horse' project, which converted a public house in the socially disadvantaged east end of London to a social centre, also suggests a 'mission' intent.[4]

The GFS belief in 'Purity as the true standard for the womanhood of the world' [5] [capitalisation as source] reflected the spread of members (and potential members) whose work took them abroad and the presence of expatriate potential Associates, frequently wives of clerics or government officials, who sustained the GFS network of overseas branches and lodges.[6] The GFS organised 'departments' to address different aspects of members' needs such as employment training and accommodation. The department for girls emigrating was initiated in 1886 (the year of the diocesan adoption of the MU), under the supervision of Ellen Joyce.[7]

1. Money, *History*, 47. '. . .because the sin we are specially banded to combat is ravaging the fold of Christ . . . lives should be devoted to this work'; For examples of GFS cooperation with government on employment and training see ibid., 12, 44, and Chapter V, 'The Pilgrims and Work', in Mary Heath-Stubbs, *Friendship's Highway*, 33-41.
2. *Friendship's Highway*, 4.
3. Winchester Diocesan Girls' Friendly Society, in *Winchester Diocesan Girls' Friendly Council Minutes* (Hampshire Record Office, 1892-1896).
4. Heath-Stubbs, *Friendship's Highway*, 91-105, 111-112. See Chapter XII, 'The Motherland's Call to the Pilgrims', for patriotic fundraising, the provision of hostels and service canteens and cooperation with uniformed services.
5. Ibid., 8.
6. Ibid., 226. GFS branches started in Scotland 1875, Ireland and the USA 1877, Canada and Australia 1883, New Zealand 1884, South Africa 1889, Argentina and the West Indies 1910.
7. Money, *History*, 44.

The GFS took inspiration from the work of missionary organisations and those working on their behalf, who were seen to exemplify piety, devotion to others and fortitude in hardship, in their engagement with overseas endeavour. This reflected an interest in missionary work overseas. It was Mary Townsend's view that 'Helping to sustain the work of church and the GFS in distant lands [was] – a wide and most legitimate field.' According to Mary Heath Stubbs, 'from the early days individual branches undertook the support of Missions.[1] GFS support for promoting Christianity overseas varied according to location. A key difference was between the colonies (notably India), or transnational spaces where a non-white indigenous population was prolific, and the white settler colonies (later Dominions) of Australia, Canada, New Zealand and South Africa within the Empire.[2]

The GFS supported overseas missions in collaboration with the SPG and the CMS. The first was in India at Lahore in 1885 and contributions were made to a Church of England Zenana Mission Society (CEZMS) initiative dating from 1895. In 1897, the GFS undertook fundraising for mission work in Japan following the appointment of Bishop Awdry, husband of GFS Central Council member Mrs Awdry, to the diocese of Osaka. In China, the GFS supported one (1911), then two (1919) CMS workers; by 1924 this had increased to eight. The GFS claimed their own missionary martyr, Dr Alice Marval, who, in 1903 at Cawnpore, 'lost her life, owing to her indefatigable labours among the plague stricken natives.'[3] GFS manoeuvres in support of missions, in collaboration with the MU as initiated under the leadership of Mary Sumner, are noted the following chapter.

1. Heath-Stubbs, *Friendship's Highway*, 82; Judith Rowbotham, 'Ministering Angels, Not Ministers: Women's Involvement in the Foreign Missionary Movement, c. 1860-1910' in *Women, Religion and Feminism in Britain, 1750-1900*, ed. Sue Morgan (Basingstoke: Palgrave Macmillan, 2002). Rowbotham notes not all women workers on behalf of missions were official missionaries. Women tended to work in an auxiliary capacity as 'civilising agents' rather than evangelising.
2. Caroline Elkins and Susan Pedersen, 'Introduction Settler Colonialism: A Concept and Its Uses' in *Settler Colonialism in the Twentieth Century; Projects, Practices, Legacies* (New York; London: Routledge, 2005). Settler colonialism (as in South Africa and Australia) is defined as differing from expansion by military domination or trade, and an attempt to establish communities identified by ties of ethnicity and faith in lands (despite the presence of an indigenous population) perceived of as 'empty'. Attitudes to indigenous populations are thus characterised by attempts to eliminate or exclude, rather than economic exploitation, which are codified in law. Settler colonies may, although dependent on the site of metropolitan power, seek autonomy from it.
3. Money, *History*, 67-69; Heath-Stubbs, *Friendship's Highway*, 83-85.

Overseas links were drawn upon to consolidate the field position of the GFS 'at home'. Through the magazine *Friendly Leaves*, GFS members were encouraged to identify with missionary activity as exemplifying desirable capital, envisage links between 'home' and overseas, and to note their own capital advantages defined in contrast to indigenous women. In 1907 the column, 'Our Own Affairs', included correspondence from a GFS member working as an SPG missionary in Simla and news of '*Our Own Worker* [italics as source] in Japan' who 'has a daily class of sixty-eight policemen . . . who learn English and have a Bible lesson. Support for missionary activities and the adoption of overseas GFS branches by home branches were also featured. There were also articles by missionary workers.[1] 'Foreign Missions' and 'Missions – India' were set as comprehension questions for members following the GFS Elementary Reading Union course. In answer to the question 'Name some contrasts between the lives of English and Indian girls', the candidates wrote:

> to express thankfulness for the privileges which come to them as born in our island kingdom, with the religious and social opportunities which are theirs; whilst one emphatically declares that it should make them wish to do all they could for their Indian sisters. It is to be hoped that those who answered so well the questions on missionary work will keep up their interest in it all their lives.[2]

The reference to the work of missionaries and missions in the official histories of the GFS also emphasised the links between home and overseas. In 1905 Agnes Money, reporting on GFS work in India, noted that 'few as yet of the native Christian girls have joined', but she made a particular and somewhat poignant reference to Eurasians to assert the inclusiveness of the GFS:

> Our Government classes them as Europeans; they are Christians; they dress like ourselves, and their daughters go to the High Schools with our English girls. They have the greatest love for England and for all that belongs to it, and will speak of England as 'home' though they have never seen

1. Girls' Friendly Society, 'Our Own Affairs, India, Ceylon, Ireland', *Friendly Leaves*, April 1907, 147. Anon, 'Our Own Affairs News from Japan', ibid., March 1907, 115; Edith Scott, 'Work at Lahore', ibid., May 1907; Anon, 'Our Worker in Japan', ibid.
2. 'Elementary Reading Union Foreign Missions and Course II Missions in India,' *Friendly Leaves*, July 1907.

> it, and know that they can never expect to do so. . . . We are rejoiced to welcome these girls to our Society which is for girls of the English Empire everywhere.[1]

GFS worker Miss Kathleen Townend gave a report of her 1904 visit to India to a meeting of Branch Secretaries. She combined an evocation of an exotic setting with an assertion of the role of the society in the imperial project and associated the growth of empire with the spread of Christianity. Like Money's, hers was a vision of Christian inclusiveness, and she also claimed a space for women in the imperial field:

> In that great work which England today is doing for her Indian Empire, I have proud hopes that our GFS may play its part, helping to break down racial distinctions, binding together Anglo-Indian, Eurasian, and Christian native with its chord of love and sympathy and prayer . . . shall there not be room in this work for women by women? For after all is not our GFS a section of that greater and fairer Temple, the Church of Christ, 'whose Builder and Maker is GOD'?[2]

The GFS as a patriotic organisation identified with empire and used emigration as a manoeuvre to extend its position in the imperial field. GFS associates included keen imperialists. In addition to Mary Sumner, Laura Ridding, and Ellen Joyce was Lady Knightly of Fawsley, a member of the pro-Imperial Primrose League and editor of the British Women's Emigration Association's magazine *Imperial Colonist*.[3] The 'settler' destinations of South Africa, Australia, and Canada were of particular interest to the GFS which promoted emigration through its own department. *Friendly Leaves'* column for members emigrating advocated travelling with Mrs Joyce's escorted parties which fixed contacts in the country of destination. In June 1907 the column concluded with a warning in bold type: 'Caution – Agencies are not always to be depended on: trust your own society.' The GFS emigration department linked with Ellen Joyce's Winchester Emigration Society (to which Mary Sumner subscribed), which later became part of the BWEA.

---

1. Money, *History*, 66-67. Money's comment overlooks the reality of racial prejudice against Anglo-Indians; see Elizabeth Buettner, '"Not Quite Pukka": Schooling in India and the Acquisition of Racial Status' in *Empire Families: Britons and Late Imperial India* (Oxford: Oxford University Press, 2004). Buettner's analysis suggests that the prejudice against Anglo-Indians was intense because their presumption of 'whiteness' was perceived as an encroachment on the status of British expatriates.
2. Money, *History*, 70-71.
3. Bush, *Edwardian Ladies and Imperial Power*, 142-143. See Appendix 2.

Emigration was seen as an opportunity for members to better themselves and contribute to the imperial project by populating the Empire with 'the right sort of woman', Christian, chaste, domesticated and (implicitly) white.[1]

For Ellen Joyce, who misrecognised the superiority of British cultural and (Anglican) religious capital and conflated this with supposed racial attributes, emigration was a civilising religious mission. It was, 'missionary work done by hundreds rather than units'.[2] This missionary work was to be achieved not just by professing the faith and upholding the implicitly 'civilised' culture of 'home'; to ensure its success, it required the physical reproduction of the 'race' in sufficient numbers. In 1920 she wrote:

> If England believes herself and the English speaking people to be the power entrusted with the evangelization of that vast part of the globe that is entrusted to their jurisdiction, then the duty of fully populating the fringes of the huge Oversea [sic] Empire becomes paramount. If again, it is the exponent of Purity, it must focus its efforts to distribute its daughters under protection, where they can find their mates and help make homes pure, happy, and Christian.[3]

The project of White Australia instigated in the decade following Australia's commonwealth status in 1901 introduced legislation excluding non-whites from migrating to Australia. It codified for the first time British imperial citizenship according to colour. It was intended to protect the white man's preferential status. It was perceived as a defence of 'higher civilisation' by white settlers fearful of being 'swamped' by 'black and yellow races'.[4] The implication for white women was to exalt

1. Anon, 'Winchester Emigration Society Appeal for Funds', *Hampshire Chronicle*, April 10th 1886. The Sumners subscribed £5 to the Society. Mary gave a further pound to the Ladies' Committee clothing scheme; Heath-Stubbs, *Friendship's Highway*, 219; Julia Bush, '"The Right Sort of Woman": Female Emigrators and Emigration to the British Empire, 1890-1910', *Women's History Review* 3, no. 3 (1994).
2. Money, *History*, 57; Heath-Stubbs, *Friendship's Highway*, 70.
3. *Friendship's Highway*, 76. See also Katie Pickles, *Female Imperialism and National Identity: Imperial Order Daughters of the Empire* (Manchester: Manchester University Press, 2002). Pickles notes the activities of the pro-imperial IODE, which included the promotion of white emigration and motherhood.
4. S.R. Mehrotra, 'On the Use of the Term "Commonwealth"', *Journal of Commonwealth Political Studies* 2, no. 1 (1963); Marilyn Lake and Henry Reynolds, 'White Australia Points the Way' in *Drawing the Global Colour Line: White Men's Countries and the International Challenge of Racial Equality* (Cambridge: Cambridge University Press, 2008), 137-165.

them as mothers: 'Whereas white mothers were feted and remunerated in the Commonwealth of Australia, Aboriginal women's race was invoked to deny their capacity for motherhood.'[1] Ellen Joyce not only asserted the moral contribution of women to the Empire but made the racial dimension of the role of women explicit. In 1921 she asserted:

> the absolute necessity in the cause of religion and morality, of stimulating the Protected Migration of members, to parts of the Empire where good women are really needed to preserve in those far parts of our possessions a high standard of morals, [and] in equalising the sexes, to multiply a race practicing religious habits, and in one part of our vast Dominions to keep for King and Empire a 'White Australia'.[2]

The notion of 'women's mission' upheld by the GFS was informed by the gendered doxa of Anglicanism, supported by the socially dominant class. GFS organising Associates, in their misrecognition of this religiously circumscribed notion of pure maternal womanliness, were themselves subject to the symbolic violence that they perpetrated. Yet, the capital accrued by being 'good church women' gave them pedagogic authority and the opportunity for self-realisation and power in a sphere of their own. GFS members were encouraged to support missionary philanthropy 'at home' and the work of missionaries overseas. In so doing, they could contribute to the pedagogic work of Christianity by demonstrating their elevated standards of morality and conduct in public 'at home' and overseas.

Despite assertions of spiritual inclusivity for Christian indigenous populations in colonies and other contact zones, the GFS was in accord with the misrecognition of whiteness as superior racial capital. GFS emigrants to white settler colonies and dominions were presented as pioneers participating in the valorous project of exporting 'English'

---

1. 'White Australia Points the Way', 156. See also 157-159 *Citizen Mothers* for discussion of eugenics, the promotion of white motherhood and the maternity bounty of £5 which was paid only to white mothers from 1912 onwards.
2. Ellen Hon Joyce, 'Letter to President of Winchester Diocesan G.F.S. Council November 5th 1921' in *Winchester Diocesan Girls' Friendly Society* (Hampshire Record Office); Julia Bush, 'Edwardian Ladies and the 'Race' Dimensions of British Imperialism', *Women's Studies International Forum* 21, no. 3, May-June (1998). Joyce's view, so out of step with contemporary global Anglicanism, may explain why her Winchester Cathedral memorial has been moved to the obscurity of the cathedral crypt.

culture and Christianity to empty lands. It was also implicit that these women would reproduce a white population. The spread of Christianity was understood as an obligation, which served as a legitimising rationale for imperial rule. The GFS used notions of gendered religious capital to claim space for women in the imperial field: it asserted the significance of Christian women as exemplars of superior capital and the notion of maternalism could be employed to euphemise the symbolic (and actual) violence inherent in the prioritisation of a white Christian English cultural arbitrary. GFS Associates also drew upon their social status and location close to individuals in positions of authority; they also secured pedagogic authority as experts in the field of emigration. Their misrecognition of British/English racial and cultural superiority mirrored their acceptance of social stratification. At grassroots level, in return for their misrecognition of a religious doxa of class and gender stratification, GFS members could perceive themselves as belonging to a religious, and contingently cultural and racial elite.

4.5 Synopsis: capital assets and 'missionary' habitus

The previous chapter identified religion as a significant in contributing to Mary Sumner's dispositions of habitus and thereby informing notions of desirable capital. Members of her kinship network upheld the prevailing (religious) doxa of the dominant social group in their allegiance to Anglicanism. Mary Sumner's wider social network was also Anglican and predominately clerical. The evangelical enthusiasm of the Sumners (which is also evident in the Heywood family) attached high symbolic capital value to the public witness of faith, and action towards securing religious awakening or conversion of others. This religiously motivated intervention, which in Mary Sumner's kinship network was predominantly realised through philanthropic initiatives, designated here as missionary philanthropy, can be interpreted in Bourdieu's terms as pedagogic action.

Missionary philanthropy, as practiced in Mary Sumner's kinship and wider social network, sought to impose the doxa of Anglicanism, the preferred doctrine within the cultural arbitrary imposed by the dominant group. It was pedagogic action, an instrument of symbolic violence, as it aimed to encourage conformity to approved doxic standards and remediate the views and conduct of those perceived as deficient. Initially exercised in local space, towards employees and tenants at parish level, this pedagogic action (located in a wider context of pedagogic work institutionally via the Church) extended spatially and organisationally to the support of, or participation in, missionary philanthropy. Deficiency concerned failure to conform to the cultural arbitrary of the dominant group, the group to which Mary Sumner and her kin claimed allegiance. Some deficiencies of capital, such as intemperance, were perceived as being particularly threatening to the cultural arbitrary upheld by Mary Sumner and her kin and were a stimulus for remediating pedagogic action. The missionary philanthropy of Mary Sumner's kinship and wider network aimed to remediate these infractions and thus defend of the doxa of the dominant cultural arbitrary, which they misrecognised as legitimate. Symbolic religious and social capital could be accrued from missionary philanthropy by men and women. Gendered notions of desirable womanly capital, informed by religious and social doxa allowed women with sufficient capital to extend their 'women's mission' beyond the home to exercise pedagogic authority via missionary philanthropy.

Mary Sumner's responses to other Christian denominations and non-Christian religions encountered in 'the contact zone' demonstrate her complicity (in common with agents of similar habitus) with the doxic values of Anglicanism. She misrecognised the social, political and cultural attributes of 'Englishness', which the Anglican religious doxa endorsed as superior. Possession of capital thus defined was assumed to give agents the pedagogic authority to assert the superiority of this capital over others perceived as deficient. This legitimised the symbolic violence perpetrated by the pedagogic work of missionaries. It also legitimised colonial rule, as long as the Anglican doxa was upheld. For Mary Sumner and those of similar habitus, complicit with the Anglican religious doxa, missionaries, perceived as pious, self-sacrificing and brave, were invested with high religious capital.

The symbolic capital Mary Sumner possessed by virtue of her social class and successful performance of her 'woman's mission' as wife, mother and helpmeet to the Rector, allowed her to exercise pedagogic authority in parochial work. As a traveller in, and published author on, places associated with Scripture, she was invested (amongst those of similar habitus) with symbolic religious and cultural capital. This enhanced her pedagogic authority by entitling her to speak from experience on the 'East'. She had sufficient capital to authorise her participation in organised missionary philanthropy in the CETS, although in the gendered area of the juvenile section. It is indicative of her capital assets that Mary Sumner was approached to be a 'Founding Associate' of the GFS. Her achievement of presidential office at diocesan level in the GFS (in the inaugural diocese of Winchester at a time when her husband was Archdeacon) was a measure of, and a source of, increasing capital. It contributed to a level of pedagogic authority upon which Mary Sumner drew to establish the MU.

The Honourable Ellen Joyce

Chapter 5
Mary Sumner, Missionary Mothers and Imperial Aspirations

5.1 Introduction

Prior to the adoption of the MU as a diocesan organisation, Mary Sumner had accumulated symbolic capital through her involvement in the GFS and the CETS in which she achieved positions of distinction. Travel to the Holy Land had further enhanced her pedagogic authority. Mary Sumner invested her experience in the Girls' Friendly Society to inform the organisation of the Mothers' Union. She also made use of the opportunities that the GFS provided for promoting the MU and recruiting Associates. As with the GFS the MU took inspiration from and appropriated the language of mission, and aligned its philanthropic activity as a mission by and to women. The MU also shared the GFS's imperial aspirations and their identification with the work of the Church overseas. This chapter builds on the previous exploration of Mary Sumner's dispositions of habitus concerning mission, contextualised against her domestic and parochial life prior to the inception of the diocesan Mothers' Union. It focusses on how Mary Sumner's notions of women's mission were realised through the Mothers' Union and positions the MU in relation to mission 'at home' and overseas, Church and empire.

The Mothers' Union grew from an existing tradition of philanthropic social patronage exercised by 'ladies' and fits the category of missionary philanthropy as defined by Alison Twells in that its aims and practices were evangelical.[1] Elizabeth Prevost considers that despite not being an official missionary organisation, the MU promoted missionary enterprise though reinforcing Christian values, upholding purity, and

1. F.K. Prochaska, *Women and Philanthropy in Nineteenth Century England* (Oxford: Clarendon Press, 1980); Frank Prochaska, *The Angel out of the House: Philanthropy and Gender in Nineteenth-Century England* (Charlottesville and London: University of Virginia Press, 2002).

offering protective education.[1] It also supported overseas missionary workers and, in common with the GFS, reported on missionary enterprise in its publications. The transnational expansion of the MU has been comprehensively documented by Cordelia Moyse, who comments on the way the MU associated imperial rule with Christian service in order to validate and inspire responsible mothering. The conduct of the good mother was associated with the physical as well as moral fitness of the future citizen and Moyse also notes the association of the MU with a 'positive eugenics' that linked imperial greatness with the quantity and quality of the population.[2] Julia Bush emphasises the symbolic significance of maternal discourse as central to imperialism. For Bush, Queen Victoria embodies the notion of the mother country and the association of the domestic family with the family of empire. Bush identifies Ellen Joyce, who saw the emigration of Christian women as a civilising influence on male colonists and the indigenous population, as an exponent of imperial motherhood.[3] Both Anne O'Brien and Brian Heeney point to the remarkable expansion of the MU in the imperial context: 'With its roots in a tradition of English philanthropy revived by late nineteenth century fears of social disorder, the MU's growth worldwide in the thirty years before the first world war was phenomenal.' For Sean Gill, Mary Sumner is 'representative of a Late Victorian Anglicanism that benefited from the upsurge of imperialist sentiment.'[4]

1. Elizabeth E. Prevost, *The Communion of Women Missions and Gender in Colonial Africa and the British Metropole* (Oxford: Oxford University Press, 2010).
2. Cordelia Moyse, *A History of the Mothers' Union: Women, Anglicanism and Globalisation, 1876-2008* (Woodbridge: Boydell Press, 2009), 83-86; see Anna Davin, 'Imperialism and Motherhood', *History Workshop* 5 (1978) for the eugenic motivation behind the education of working-class mothers in St Pancras; see also Lesley Hall, *Sex, Gender and Social Change in Britain since 1880* (Basingstoke: Macmillan, 2000) for further discussion of morality and eugenics.
3. Julia Bush, '"The Right Sort of Woman": Female Emigrators and Emigration to the British Empire, 1890-1910', *Women's History Review* 3, no. 3 (1994); 'Edwardian Ladies and the "Race" Dimensions of British Imperialism', *Women's Studies International Forum* 21, no. 3 May-June (1998); *Edwardian Ladies and Imperial Power* (London: Leicester University Press, 2000); Lisa Chilton, *Agents of Empire: British Female Migration to Canada and Australia, 1860s-1930* (Toronto; Buffalo: University of Toronto Press, 2007). Chilton emphasises the networking of women involved in emigration through the BWEA and GFS.
4. Anne O'Brien, 'Militant Mothers: Faith Power and Identity in the Mothers' Union in Sydney 1896-1950', *Women's History Review* 9, no. 1 (2000): 37; Brian Heeney, *The Women's Movement in the Church of England, 1850-1930*

The chapter begins by noting Mary Sumner's articulation of the role of women and motherhood validated as a religious mission. It locates the Mothers' Union in the field of philanthropic organisations 'at home' and notes Mary Sumner's assertion of the distinctive contribution of the MU in the field of domestic mission/philanthropy. The growth of the MU overseas and the appropriation of missionary endeavour in contact zones to validate the MU message and sanctify mothers' work by associating it with missionary identity are examined. The chapter then notes the MU involvement in promoting mission work and examines relations with other organisations, including the GFS and the Anglican Church, and evidence of networking practices in relation to mission. These are regarded as field manoeuvres related to secure recognition of the MU as a Church organisation. The position of the Church overseas and its relation to the imperial project is considered and the MU is located in the wider fields of power represented by the Anglican Church and the Empire. Mary Sumner's attitudes to Empire, race, non-Christian religion and non-Protestant Christian denominations as reflected in, and promoted through, the MU will be located in relation to the reproduction or negotiation of a dominant cultural arbitrary with attention being given to gender, class, religion and race.

5.2 Mary Sumner: women's mission, the Mothers' Union, and the field of philanthropy

The account of Mary Sumner's first Church Congress speech, in the officially authorised *Mary Sumner: Her Life and Work*, signals a significant point of expansion in the Mothers' Union story, and its heightened language and dramatic structure evokes missionary enterprise. The location of the October 1885 Church Congress at Portsmouth, 'a great densely populated sea port', illustrates Church outreach into an urban district in which the parochial structure and the personal sway of squire and cleric was less robust than in its rural strongholds.[1] The account, 'Mrs Wilberforce's Narrative', conjures need and deprivation in its description of the audience, 'many of them with

---

(Clarendon, 1988), 44, 45; Sean Gill, *Women and the Church of England: From the Eighteenth Century to the Present* (London: Society for Promoting Christian Knowledge, 1994), 104.

1. Portsmouth was the kind of urban territory associated with poverty and moral peril subject to attention from university and public school missioners via the settlement movement. See Nigel Scotland, *Squires in the Slums: Settlements and Missions in Late Victorian Britain* (London: I.B. Tauris, 2007).

sad anxious faces, or bearing some unmistakable sign of poverty's cold grip'. It also suggests missionary valour in its reference to Mary Sumner's conquest of fear, and by allusion to religious inspiration: 'we who listened to her felt that the Holy Spirit was manifestly guiding and strengthening her, in an undertaking which at that time called for no little courage'.[1] The text of Mary Sumner's address recorded in the *Official Record of the Church Congress* demonstrates that she (after a lifetime's familiarity with examples and exponents of the form) was able to structure a sermon and deploy religious rhetoric. Experience in the Church of England Temperance Society Juvenile Section and the GFS would have given her direct experience of public speaking. Her Vice Presidential address from the platform of the Winchester Diocesan GFS earlier in the year illustrate her rationale for the MU, which saw homes as a territory where endeavour to promote allegiance to religiously sanctioned standards of behaviour was needed in order to conquer immorality.[2]

Mary Sumner's Portsmouth speech also reflects her perception that there were social ills, notably drunkenness and immorality that needed remediation, themes that were articulated in the Objects and rules of the Mothers' Union. She begins by lamenting the 'terrible want of purity and high tone amongst the women of this country', then she attributes blame to neglectful mothers, advocates temperance and suggests good maternal example as the remedy to immorality and drunkenness. The speech then changes tone by articulating sympathy for the trials of mothering and concluding with the hopeful message that comfort is to be found in Christ. Her claims that 'the reformation of the country' was in the hands of mothers and that the 'country can only be leavened by the mothers' aligns them with a missionary role.[3] The Portsmouth speech also articulates her perception of 'women's mission', terminology that was used to legitimise assertions concerning the domestic and maternal roles of women as divinely ordained, and to signal that women performing these roles as exemplars of Christian values had a pedagogic function:

1. Mary Porter, Mary Woodward, and Horatia Erskine, *Mary Sumner: Her Life and Work and a Short History of the Mothers' Union* (Winchester: Warren and Sons, 1921), 22. Mrs Wilberforce's Narrative.
2. Mary Sumner, 'Vice Presidential Speech to the G.F.S. Diocesan Conference at the George Hotel', *G.F.S. Associates Journal* 18.
3. Charles Dunkley, *The Official Report of the Church Congress, Held at Portsmouth: On October 6th, 7th, 8th, and 9th, 1885* (London: Bemrose & Sons, 1885), 448-449. See Appendix 1 for full text.

> You should look solemnly at your child and say to yourself, 'This is God's child; I have to nurse it for Him and for heaven.... God will ask you at the last great day, "What have you done with that child – those children – I gave you to train for Me?"'[1]

It was not only children who needed winning for God: the Mothers' Union third object required mothers to lead not just their children but their families 'in purity and holiness of life'. Writing on marriage, Mary Sumner emphasised the role of the wife as a religious influence on her husband by referring to St Monica's conversion of her husband to Christianity, and by asserting that 'the Bible tells us "the unbelieving husband is sanctified by the wife"'.[2] She returned to this theme in other addresses and extolled the importance of public prayer 'as especially blessed' for 'very often a churchgoing wife makes a churchgoing husband'.[3] Setting an example here was one way the Mothers' Union member could exert a moral influence beyond the home and contribute to a national reformation of life and morals. Mothers were (for example) exhorted to restrain the public behaviour of their children and to exercise civic responsibility by alerting school teachers to rude behaviour. They were also urged to encourage temperance and to avoid gossip.[4] Mary Sumner used her eulogy of Mrs Wordsworth (a GFS Activist and wife of the Bishop of Salisbury) as an occasion for asserting the contribution of homemakers to the wider common good: 'She held firmly to the belief that to touch the life of the community at large, it was absolutely necessary to begin with the home, and to influence the wife and mother.'[5]

The Mothers' Union drew on the tradition of philanthropic patronage exercised by 'ladies' to social subordinates in the same way (and frequently via the same personnel) as the GFS. In her 1888 book, *To Mothers of the Higher Classes*, Mary Sumner attempted to mobilise socially advantaged women towards the religious reform of 'ignorant and weaker mothers'.[6] She also used her personal influence to keep MU workers active. In a letter to Mrs Sharme, a local Branch President she wrote:

---

1. Ibid., 449.
2. Mary Sumner, 'Marriage Address 2' in *Home Life* (Winchester: Warren and Sons, 1895), 21, 22.
3. 'Churchgoing' in *Home Life* (Winchester: Warren and Sons, 1895), 126; 'Prayer' in *Home Life* (Winchester: Warren and Son, 1885), 106.
4. 'Purity', 45, 46; 'Words' in *Home Life* (Winchester: Warren and Sons, 1895), 59.
5. 'In Memoriam Mrs Wordsworth', *Mothers in Council*, No. 16 October 1894, 202.
6. *To Mothers of the Higher Classes* (Winchester: Warren and Sons, 1888), 57.

> I should be so glad if you could tell me personally what has been done in your branch . . . meetings held . . . any fresh members . . . it is vital that there should be weekly or fortnightly religious meetings held for Bible and Prayer book teaching for members and any other mothers they can bring with them.[1]

Mary Sumner evoked a sense of missionary identity for the society and its members by identifying mothers as workers for a religious cause, through comments in her writing, in committee minutes, and in material published in the *Mothers' Union Journal.* The minutes of a diocesan MU Council Meeting in 1898 recorded that: 'Members of every class should feel that they are workers for the Mothers' Union both inside and outside their homes by their influence and example.' In a letter to an overseas president, Mary Sumner was even more explicit: 'We must get the members of our Mothers' Union to act as missionaries amongst their relations and friends, helping to bring the Christian life into the darkened homes where as yet our dear Lord is not loved and honoured.'[2] She considered the Mothers' Union as essentially a spiritual society, distinguished by the three 'Objects', but upholding these were seen to achieve practical improvements. Writing in the *Mothers' Union Journal,* Mary quoted an Associate correspondent reporting that: 'The whole of my neighbourhood has been raised since we started a Mothers' Union.' In her undated leaflet, *What is the Mothers' Union?*, she justified the MU in the populous field of other philanthropic initiatives:

> How does the Mothers' Union affect the success of other societies and organizations – it is at the root of every one of them – if home life is good and the mother is a Christian woman – cruelty to children will be checked, morality will be taught (girls self-respect, boys chivalry and self-control) – kindness to animals inculcated.[3]

---

1. 'Letter Mrs Sharme August 22nd 1915' in *Mothers' Union* (Lambeth Palace Library). Ellipsis as source.
2. Winchester Diocesan Mothers' Union Committee, 'Minute Book 1886-1910' in *Diocese of Winchester Mothers' Union* (Hampshire Record Office). Council Meeting at The Close, November 15th 1898; Porter, Woodward, and Erskine, *Mary Sumner*, 41.
3. Mary Sumner, 'Hints to Associates', *Mothers in Council*, April 1891, 116; *What is the Mothers' Union?* (London: Gardner Darton and Co, n.d. surmised after 1896). HRO 38M499/E7/106, surmised date after 1895.

Mary Sumner defended the Mothers' Union's identity and position as the sole Anglican organisation for mothers. In 1893 the Winchester Diocesan Committee resolved that 'it was not advisable to affiliate a Mothers' League which has been started in one part of Bournemouth'.[1] Twelve years later, the suggestion from a Mr Corbett in the *Church Family Newspaper* that there should be an additional Church organisation for women prompted a flurry of protest from Mary Sumner. In a letter to Lady Chichester, the then president of the MU, she wrote: 'I do trust you will stop another society . . . the pamphlets [enclosed] are likely to convince Mr Corbett against the fresh society proposed.' She repeated these sentiments in letters to Princess Christian and Mrs Maude, the central secretary of the MU: 'I do trust the Mothers' Union is not going to unite with other leagues and clubs.'[2] However, the Southwell Women's League, started by Mary Sumner's friend Laura Ridding, who as a married woman without children could not comfortably lead mothers as a specific category, was given a dispensation to use the MU prayer.[3]

The Mothers' Union was sympathetic towards the aims of organisations such as the CETS and the British Committee of the International Federation for the Abolition of State Regulation of Vice, which opposed

1. Winchester Diocesan Mothers' Union Committee, 'Minute Book 1886-1910'. November 8th 1893. HRO 145M85/C2/1.
2. Princess Christian of Schleswig-Holstein, 'Letter to Mrs Sumner' in *Mothers' Union* (Lambeth Palace Library). Princess Christian asks for clarification as to why Mr Corbett's views are 'so objectionable'; Mary Sumner, 'Letters to Lady Chichester Central President of the Mothers' Union', ibid. (1913-15), July 26th 1915; 'Letters to Mrs Maude' in *Mothers' Union* (Lambeth Palace Library, 1908-1920), April 8th 1915. Despite Mary Sumner's desire to keep the MU as the exclusive organisation for Anglican women, the MU Central Committee responded to concerns that the MU was failing to attract younger women by agreeing to the initiation of a Young Women's fellowship in 1917 and a Young Wives Committee in 1921. See Moyse, 134-36. See Louise Creighton, *Memoir,* 122, for an account of the short-lived Women's Diocesan Association and the more successful Girls' Diocesan Association, an organisation she initiated with the purpose of interesting young educated women in social issues. Its first president was her daughter Beatrice. For collaboration between the GDA and the GFS, see Mary Heath-Stubbs, *Friendship's Highway; Being the History of the Girls' Friendly Society* (London: Girls' Friendly Society, 1926), 21.
3. Winchester Diocesan Mothers' Union Committee, 'Minute Book 1886-1910', MU Council Meeting November 26th 1890. As a married woman without children, Laura Ridding could not comfortably lead a branch of the MU. Her solution was the Southwell Women's League, which had similar religious aims to the MU.

the continental system of legalised prostitution.[1] Although distinct from the GFS, the MU did have a close relationship with it in matters relating to women's welfare: MU members were to be warned of the dangers posed by unscrupulous employment registries to their daughters and the GFS Registry Office list was suggested as a safe alternative. The organisations collaborated in seeking state regulation of employment registries.[2] As noted in chapter three, the MU and GFS were united in protesting against easier facilities for divorce, supporting an increase in the age of consent and in issuing a joint 'Protest' in opposition to proposed legislation to allow marriage to the sister of a deceased wife. In 1914 their joint appointment of a moral 'Vigilance Worker' for the 'home nation' of Ireland reflected an established practice of supporting mission workers overseas.[3]

The mission of the Mothers' Union and its achievements were publicised in Church and philanthropic forums and via the press.[4] MU workers and sympathisers, including Mary Sumner herself, Laura Ridding, and Ellen Joyce, were a presence at Church Congresses and the words of platform speakers were disseminated in the official published conference record, and conference proceedings were reported back to diocesan MU committees.[5] Mary Sumner's paper, 'The Responsibilities of Mothers', was included in philanthropist Baroness Angela Burdett-Coutts' 1893 compendium of writing on diverse aspects

---

1. C.B. Mayne, 'Letters from the British Committee of International Federation for the Abolition of State Regulation of Vice' in *Mothers' Union* (Lambeth Palace Library). Josephine Butler was a supporter.
2. Winchester Diocesan Mothers' Union Committee, 'Minute Book 1886-1910', November 1898.
3. Mary Heath-Stubbs, *Friendship's Highway; Being the History of the Girls' Friendly Society* (London: Girls' Friendly Society, 1926), 170.
4. Mary Sumner, 'Letters to Mrs Maude' in *Mothers' Union* (Lambeth Palace Library), April 8th 1915; Beatrice Temple, E., Mary Sumner, E., and Eleanor Chute, J., 'Letters to the Editor – Women Workers for India', *The Times*, September 27th 1907; Anon, 'Record of Events Report of the Church Congress at Hull', *English Woman's Review*, October 15th 1890; 'Leading Societies and Their Work: The Mothers' Union', *Hearth and Home: An Illustrated Weekly Journal for Gentlewomen*, Thursday January 28th 1892; Charlotte Yonge, 'Conversation on the Mothers' Union', *The Monthly Packet of Evening Readings for Younger Members of the Church of England*, Thursday September 1st 1887.
5. Winchester Diocesan Mothers' Union Committee, 'Minute Book 1886-1910'. Report from Mrs Joyce on the Rhyl Church Conference women's work for women section. November 29th 1891.

of women's philanthropic work, 'Woman's Mission Congress Papers'. The overlapping set of activists between the MU and the GFS has already been noted but MU (and GFS) women also connected via other advocacy networks, such as the Worlds Purity Federation Congress in Kentucky to which Miss Lucy Soulsby was sent as the MU delegate in November 1917.[6] MU representatives participated in the conferences of the National Union of Women Workers (NUWW) from its inception in 1895 under the Presidency of Louise Creighton, a MU diocesan President. As the forum for women's philanthropic groups (including the GFS), the NUWW asserted the contribution of this 'work' to the nation. With a constituency of delegates that included keen imperialists MU and GFS activists Laura Ridding and Ellen Joyce, the notion of nation was understood to include empire.[7]

5.3 Mary Sumner and the Mothers' Union: missionary identities at home and overseas, missionary organisations, colonies and contact zones, and attitudes to indigenous members

Mary Sumner, through the Mothers' Union, engaged with the extension and reconfiguration of fields in colonies and empire and to the perception of that expansion in the British metropole. The MU not only drew from the endeavour of missions and missionaries overseas to dignify, legitimatise and valorise its stance on women's roles and its domestic agenda but saw the possession of religious capital as a mandate for outreach to the imperial periphery. The MU sought recognition as a transnational organisation. Its expansion overseas was associated with the dispersal of women of the social and religious category from

6. Angela Georgina Burdett-Coutts, *Woman's Mission: A Series of Congress Papers on the Philanthropic Work of Women by Eminent Writers*, facsimile reprint, Portrayer Publishers, 2002 ed. (London: Sampson Low, Marston and Company, 1893); Porter, Woodward, and Erskine, *Mary Sumner*, 141.
7. Winchester Diocesan Mothers' Union Committee, 'Minute Book 1886-1910', October 4th 1895. The NUWW was instigated by Emily Janes; its first president was Louise Creighton, an activist in the GFS and MU, and Laura Ridding was its president between 1909 and 1911; Lady Laura Ridding, 'The Early Days of the National Union of Women Workers' in *Selborne Papers* (Hampshire Record Office, n.d.). Bush, *Edwardian Ladies and Imperial Power*, 176-177. Bush draws attention to the number of ladies active in the pro-Imperial Victoria League, Primrose League, and BWEA who took leadership positions in the NUWW. She notes, amongst others, Maude Selborne (Laura Ridding's sister-in-law), Frances Balfour, Edith Lyttleton, Millicent Fawcett, and Lady Frederick Cavendish.

which MU Associates were drawn. This was linked to the presence of the armed forces, and the outreach of the Church in colonies, imperial dominions, or in areas of missionary endeavour and emigrant destinations. In 1914, MU literature was being provided for emigrant passengers on the ships of the White Star and Cunard lines. The initial focus of MU mission was to promote the upholding of Christian values amongst expatriate mothers, such as soldiers' wives. The initiative of individual activists in starting branches overseas was, as at home, significant. The first individual overseas branches were established in the white settler colonies of Canada (Ontario) and New Zealand (Christchurch) in 1888.[1] In 1891, Mary Sumner celebrated branches for expatriates in India, Africa, Tasmania and Australia. By 1895, the MU was organised in Ceylon. Following the central organisation of the MU in 1896, an Overseas Committee was established and it was at this time that the first branches for indigenous (rather than expatriate) members were initiated in Hong Kong and India. The first conference of overseas members was in 1897. By 1899, the West Indies, Japan, Cairo, Malta and South America had MU branches.[2] The end of the South African 'Boer' War in 1902 was the catalyst for attempts at reconstruction in South Africa that raised questions about the conduct of colonial rule and the negotiation of civil rights and social hierarchies mediated by constructions of 'race'. It also stimulated popular enthusiasm for, and awareness of, the imperial project. It was in this year that the MU was first organised in South Africa, but, as Laura Ridding observed during her 1908 tour, branches were racially segregated.[3]

As in the GFS, the field manoeuvres to extend the Mothers' Union overseas also served to support the society 'at home'. The theme of connecting 'home' and overseas runs through MU literature, corporate practice, and the personal networking of Mary Sumner (and other members). MU members were to see themselves as part of a network connected by their allegiance as Christian women. The Winchester Diocesan Council passed a resolution to request 'friends going to South Africa to become members before they go and to start branches on their arrival'. The resolution was proposed by Mrs Eleanor Chaloner Chute and seconded by Mrs Joyce, who were both prominent in the GFS, and,

1. Porter, Woodward, and Erskine, *Mary Sumner*, 133, 111.
2. Mary Sumner, 'Introduction', *Mothers in Council*, January 1891; Porter, Woodward, and Erskine, *Mary Sumner*, 41, 36; Moyse, *History of the Mothers' Union*, 84.
3. Lady Laura Ridding, 'South African Note Book' in *Selborne Papers* (Hampshire Record Office, 1908-9).

in the case of Ellen Joyce (as previously noted), a promoter of emigration.[1] The network offered channels of communication whereby intelligence from overseas ventures could be relayed 'home', and 'home' news and values exported. The practice of twinning a 'home' and overseas branch began to develop. In 1915, Mary Sumner wrote to the MU secretary, Mrs Maude, concerning a letter she had received:

> from a branch called Sumner in New Zealand asking me if they could be linked with a Home Branch connected with me personally. I wrote to Mrs Preston [Old Alresford] asking if it were possible . . . are there any special forms or papers when a Home Branch is just linked with a foreign one? [2]

The MU magazines were an important networking medium for providing members, especially those separated by distance, with a sense of contact and unity of purpose. The *Mothers' Union Journal* (for ordinary members) included references to missionary activity in reports from branches such as the 'interesting address by Miss O'Connor, a medical missionary' given at Rochester and the 'lantern entertainment' on 'The Mothers' Union in Many Lands' with which the Reverend Miller had entertained the Manchester branch.[3] Reports also came from branches overseas. The January 1908 edition featured reports from South Africa, India and the West Indies, illustrating that MU lantern slides were used as an aid to recruitment. In India back copies of the *MUJ* were 'so much appreciated by soldiers' wives'. In 1917, *Mothers in Australia* was started but, according to biographers Porter, Woodward and Erskine, writing in 1921, 'many members, however, especially those not long from their home country, still take the *MUJ*'.[4]

Under the editorial guidance of Charlotte Yonge, who had invested the proceeds of her 1854 bestseller the *Heir of Redclyffe* in the missionary ship *Southern Cross* and was the biographer of the martyred missionary Bishop Patteson of Melanesia, *Mothers in Council* (for 'educated' members) also featured reports from overseas.[5] A report from the MU

---

1. Winchester Diocesan Mothers' Union Committee, 'Minute Book 1886-1910', June 25th 1901. Eleanor Chaloner Chute was Central President of the GFS 1901-1916.
2. Sumner, 'Letters to Mrs Maude', February 13th 1915.
3. Anon, *Mothers' Union Journal*, January 1901, 23, 22; ibid., January 1908, 7-8.
4. Porter, Woodward, and Erskine, *Mary Sumner*, 144.
5. Talia Schaffer, 'Taming the Tropics: Charlotte Yonge Takes on Melanesia', *Victorian Studies* 47 (2005); Teresa Huffman Traver, 'The Ship That Bears through the Waves', *Women's Writing* 17, no. 2 (2010).

in New Zealand hoped that 'the Union may be especially useful in the colony in helping to keep up family ties'.[1] *MIC* readers were also given news relating to mission themes, such as the report of celebrated traveller Mrs Isabella Bird Bishop's address, 'Home Life in Foreign Countries'. It asserted that, although women in Asia (Japan, China and India) had little status, European influence, without high Christian standards, was corrupting to indigenous people, a view in accord with Mary Sumner's position.[2] Later, the formal involvement of the MU in work with missionary organisations was also reported. Letters to Mary Sumner from Miss Gertrude King, the SPG missionary and MU worker, featured in the 1906, 1909, 1910 and 1912 editions. As in the GFS, accounts of missionary success emphasised the joyfulness and simplicity of the faith of converts. One of Gertrude King's 'dear old ladies preparing for Holy Baptism . . . was disappointed after her first class because she had not been confirmed', but commented 'my heart will ascend to God'. Gertrude King noted: 'It is wonderful to see their faces change as they grow nearer the realities of the faith.'[3]

Missionary activity overseas was also drawn upon to inspire activism and create a sense of missionary identity 'at home'. Mrs Malden's article, 'Wanted: Some Educated Mothers', catalogued the good work of 'bands of mothers over the Empress Queen's Dominions', before asserting the need for more Associates 'at home'. In the October 1898 edition, Mary Sumner advocated support for missions by prayer and subscription and suggested that MU members might be mission workers themselves.[4] Missionary exploits were also featured in the stories that appeared in the *MUJ* to signal what the MU considered to be desirable attributes. The October 1902 edition recounted 'a true story of missionary work in prison', and the heroism of missionaries in upholding religious values in adversity was referred to in the story 'Mother's' Teaching'.[5] 'The Missionary Mother' recounted the story of a 'poor tired Mother' who takes her son, as a treat, to hear a missionary speaker. The boy is inspired and overcomes many difficulties to achieve his dream of becoming a

1. Anon, *Mothers in Council*, January 1893, 57; October 1893, 254; October 1892, 190.
2. Isabella Bird Bishop, 'Report of Mrs Bishop's Address Home Life in Foreign Countries', *Mothers in Council*. October, 1893, 249. See Appendix 2.
3. Gertrude King, 'Reports from Miss King in Madagascar', *Mothers in Council*, October 1906, 253; January 1909, 49; January 1910, 57-59; October 1912, 248.
4. Mrs Malden, 'Wanted: Some Educated Mothers', *Mothers in Council*, October 1893, 263; Mary Sumner, ibid., October 1898, 211-213.
5. *Mothers' Union Journal*, October 1902, 84; April 1901, 27.

missionary in China. After winning many converts and plaudits from his Bishop, he succumbs to martyrdom during the Boxer uprising, leaving his mother to be comforted by the thought of the great work he did for God, and the anticipation of reunion in heaven.[1]

Support for missions was a way to demonstrate Christian virtues through philanthropy and the promotion of the faith. Support for missions was also a way to indicate concern for, and difference from, those considered to fall within a 'deficit' category. Mary Sumner's enthusiasm for the work of overseas missions as expressed in her travel diary, *Our Holiday in the East,* and affirmed by her experiences in Algeria in 1892/3, was reflected in an 1898 Winchester Diocesan MU Committee resolution: [2]

> That it would be well to bring before members the duty of the Mothers' Union to help in sending women medical missionaries to try to raise home life in Zenanas and Harems – It is strongly agreed that Mothers' Union members support Mission Zenana work through the SPG or Church of England Zenana Society.[3]

Mary Sumner, like Charlotte Yonge, gave personal financial support to missionary enterprise. The 'Buttress Fund', dedicated as a memorial to George Sumner, collected funds from MU members and supporters, including those overseas to support restoration work on Winchester cathedral. Mary Sumner donated the £250 surplus from the fund to 'overseas work' in 1915.[4]

The MU and GFS jointly provided funding for workers and as 'at home' individual women gave their support to both societies. Mary Sumner fostered network contacts with 'GFS ladies who are speaking for the Mothers' Union in India so that they might join the Mothers' Union as Associates'.[5] In 1907, Mary Sumner wrote jointly to *The Times,* with Eleanor Chute of the GFS and Beatrice E. Temple of the SPG, detailing

1. Anon, October 1901, 78-85.
2. Mary Elizabeth Sumner, *Our Holiday in the East* (London: Hurst & Blackett, 1881); Mary Sumner, *Memoir of George Henry Sumner, D.D., Bishop of Guildford: Published for His Friends by Special Request* (Winchester: Warren and Sons, 1910), Chapter X, 'Buxton and Algiers'.
3. Winchester Diocesan Mothers' Union Committee, 'Minute Book 1886-1910', February 24th 1898.
4. Mothers' Union, *Fifty Years* (Westminster: The Mothers' Union, 1926), 31; Porter, Woodward, and Erskine, *Mary Sumner*, 134; Sumner, 'Letters to Lady Chichester'.
5. 'Letter to Lady Horatia Erskine' in *Mothers' Union* (Lambeth Palace Library).

the existing collaboration between the societies. The article canvassed lady volunteers of means, 'as full stipends cannot be paid', to contribute to nurturing the faith of expatriate and converted women. Whilst Mary Sumner and her co-authors noted that it 'was not direct missionary work', it was 'work for the Master', and the letter claimed that: 'The uplifting of the tone of those who are representative of the Christian religion in a heathen country must tend to the spread of the Gospel of Christ.'[1]

The Mothers' Union, working in collaboration with the Anglican SPG, CMS and CEZMS, provided further financial support for an increasing number of what were referred to as mission workers, thereby contributing to the recognition of the contribution of women in the field of mission. The MU's Overseas Department dealt with 'the vast amount of correspondence' from overseas and was a conduit for passing on missionary news to the MU membership.[2] The earliest MU African Branch for indigenous women was instigated by Miss Gertrude King circa 1901 in the French colony of Madagascar.[3] From 1909, Miss Rix, at the request of the SPG, was supported by the MU in work in Southern India, and Miss Davis, a worker under the direction of the CMS, 'beloved by many hundreds of friends and supporters both at home and in southern India', was appointed in 1913. Miss Loader, a worker in China amongst Christian converts, was also supported. In 1918, a third worker for India was funded. Miss Gibson of the CEZMS was appointed to work specially for the MU and 'endeared herself and her work to many MU members during her furlough in England – a time that was much prolonged owing to her illness'. In 1920, Miss Norah Short was appointed to work with railway workers and their families in Southern Africa and by 1925, 'six Mothers' Union Workers were wholly maintained by our overseas fund'.[4]

Just as the Queen Empress embodied the Empire, Mary Sumner personified the Mothers' Union. Her biographers Mary Porter, Mary Woodward and Horatia Erskine eulogised 'Mrs Sumner's part in the world wide extension of the Mothers' Union [through] her personal share by her pen, by her prayers, and by that true mother's love that went out to all the daughter branches of her beloved union in far off lands'.[5]

1. Temple, Sumner, and Chute, 'Letters to the Editor – Women Workers for India', *The Times*, September 27th 1907.
2. Mothers' Union, *Fifty Years*, 30.
3. Gertrude King, 'Letters to Mary Sumner' in *Mothers' Union* (Lambeth Palace Library), March 25th 1902.
4. Porter, Woodward, and Erskine, *Mary Sumner*, 130, 146; Mothers' Union, *Fifty Years*, 50.
5. Porter, Woodward, and Erskine, *Mary Sumner*, 36.

The networking that Mary Sumner deployed to promote the organisation included giving influential workers and rank and file members a sense that they were remembered and valued by 'the Foundress'. This 1917 letter to Mrs Crawford from Adelaide is typical of Mary Sumner's approach in style and content (including the inclusion of leaflets):

> Your letter has given me very great pleasure and I heartily thank you for your love and belief in our 'Mothers' Union' – How thankful I am that you tell me that the union is strong in S. Australia! And will you give my heartfelt and affectionate Good Wishes when you write. I was so glad to be introduced to you at the dedication of our 'Mary Sumner House' and I trust it will be the means of spreading our Christian faith in Hearts and Homes throughout our Nation and Empire . . . will you give my very special sympathy and love to the dear mothers in Adelaide Diocese who are sending their husbands and sons to fight with our home troops . . . I remember them daily in prayers and I feel God is blessing us in this Righteous war. . . . Remember me to the Bishop of Stafford; will you accept a copy of my leaflet on religious education and one besides to give away?[1]

Three years later in 1920 (aged 91), she was still seeking to pursue overseas contacts and was 'anxious to get in touch with Bishops' wives who are coming from overseas' for the Lambeth conference of Anglican bishops. The MU timed its own conference of overseas workers to coincide with the Lambeth gathering, as many Diocesan Presidents were also wives of bishops.[2]

Overseas members could identify with Mary Sumner as a celebrity. Mementoes and anecdotes of Mary Sumner kept her 'linked with the loneliest member and the remotest branch'. New Zealand members appreciated 'photographs of Winchester Cathedral and particularly the one showing your own [Mary Sumner's] home'.[3] An Australian Diocesan President, quoted by Porter, Woodward and Erskine, gives further testimony to Mary Sumner as embodying the organisation and a link with the 'mother country':

1. Mary Sumner, 'Letter to Mrs Crawford' in *Winchester Diocesan Mothers' Union* (Hampshire Record Office); see also 'Letters to Mrs Maude', August 5th 1917. Mary Sumner would like to see the President of the Ottawa MU and asks for her address.
2. 'Letters to Mrs Wilberforce' in *Mothers' Union* (Lambeth Palace Library), June 7th 1920.
3. Porter, Woodward, and Erskine, *Mary Sumner*, 40.

> So many of our mothers lived in England once, and some have been here quite a short time: and it is so touching the way they come up to me at meetings, and tell me of the English Branch to which they belonged and how – in many cases they 'once' heard you speak or 'once' saw you.[1]

Links with members in colonial or other contact zones (such as China and Madagascar) emphasised the spatial construct of 'home' and distant places. As with the settler colonies, Mary Sumner's maternal personification of the organisation and personal touch was applied to indigenous members of the MU, as well as to expatriates nostalgic for the 'mother country'. Miss Rix from India noted that Mary Sumner's letter to mothers had been translated into Tamil. Correspondence between Mary Sumner and indigenous members reflects her 'maternalistic' attitude to non-white women and suggests her misrecognition of the legitimacy of a hierarchical stratification of 'race' and culture.[2] The adoption of Christianity by indigenous people, in what were perceived from the British/English metropole as exotic, less civilised locations, was for Mary Sumner an achievement to be celebrated. News of MU success overseas was a useful conversational gambit in clerical company: 'Do you know I have 500 dear black daughters in Madagascar?'[3] The presentation of this material in her 1921 memoir and the account of the development of the MU indicate that this was considered worthy of celebration and 'bringing home to' members. The MU branch established in Madagascar (then under French colonial rule) was notable as the earliest in Africa. It was started by Miss Gertrude King, the sister of the Bishop of Madagascar, working under the aegis of the SPG. The Malagasy mothers

---

1. Ibid., 41.
2. Ibid., 40; Moyse, *History of the Mothers' Union*, 140-141, 149. Moyse comments on the 'colonial mentality' of the Mothers' Union leadership in the period 1910-1940, which she sees as being reinforced by the insistence on monogamy, chastity and Western notions of the nuclear family. She also notes 'the different treatment of indigenous members on the basis that they were new to Christianity and, by implication, to civilized standards of female behaviour'.
3. Porter, Woodward, and Erskine, *Mary Sumner*, 37; See Brian Stanley, 'Church State and the Hierarchy of "Civilization": The Making of the World Missionary Conference, Edinburgh 1910' in *The Imperial Horizons of British Protestant Missions, 1880-1914*, ed. A.N. Porter (Grand Rapids, Michigan: Wm. B. Eerdmans, 2002). Stanley notes the acceptance without challenge of imperial power as a given and the embedded assumption of racial superiority and the categorisation of races and cultures according to perceived degrees of 'civilisation'.

were encouraged to evangelise their faith and act as role models for other mothers with recruitment in mind, in a way that accorded with what was expected of English MU (and GFS) members.[1] Miss King corresponded with Mary Sumner via the Overseas Committee.[2] Miss King's testimony is drawn on by Porter, Woodward and Erskine:

> From the moment our foundress heard of the need of a Mothers' Union work in Madagascar, she took the Malagasy mother to her heart. Needless to say they idealised her, and she became to them the embodiment of all that is highest and best in motherhood. Wonderful letters passed between them, Mrs Sumner always began, 'My dear daughters' and ended as 'your loving white mother'. [3]

The Malagasy mothers did not challenge Mary Sumner's assumption of parental authority; they replied to Mary Sumner's letter of welcome to the MU: 'We, your children, were very pleased to receive your letter of welcome into the Mothers' Union.' Porter, Woodward and Erskine include further references to appreciation of Mary Sumner as a figure of maternal authority. Chinese members wrote:

> We feel it was God's grace that you were allowed to begin such a Union, thus showing your great love to the little, little children of China, and by this means also to teach us women of China good methods of carefully bringing up, and educating our children – a work beyond our human strength (divine help needed).[4]

The conceptualisation of a parent-child relationship and difference in colour was not only signalled by Mary Sumner. Following the themes of gratitude, Porter, Woodward and Erskine recorded that following the 1914-18 war:

> Touching presents of money came also from native and coloured members in South Africa for fellow members at home, to convey, in the gift-language of the child-races, their sympathy for white mothers in the bereavements of war.[5]

---

1. Prevost, *Communion of Women*, 123-155. Prevost considers that the MU engagement in Madagascar under Miss King enlarged the status, opportunity and authority of women in missionary work.
2. King, 'Letters to Mary Sumner'.
3. Porter, Woodward, and Erskine, *Mary Sumner*, 37. See previous chapter for other references to 'childlike natives'.
4. Ibid., 38, 39.
5. Ibid., 144.

How this 'gift language of the child races' differed from the donation of a writing table and other gifts from Mothers' Union members 'at home' to Mary Sumner on the occasion of her Golden Wedding anniversary is not specified.[1]

5.4 Mary Sumner, the Mothers' Union, empire and the Church overseas

The Mothers' Union's overseas development was bound together with the growth of Empire. Its spread was frequently initiated by women with spouses associated with the enforcement of imperial rule via the army. It was also associated with women close to authority in imperial government, such as Lady Victoria Buxton, wife of the Governor of South Australia, an instigator of the Adelaide MU, and the Countess of Glasgow, the wife of the Governor-General of New Zealand.[2] The MU, like the GFS, was a patriotic organisation. Its establishment of a central constitution in 1896 gave the society a national identity. It had royal patronage from 1897. Until 1901, this was in the maternal figure of the Queen Empress, who singularly personified both head of state and head of Church. For Mary Sumner and others in her network, Christianity and nation were synonymous, as were whiteness (with Englishness prioritised) and cultural superiority.[3] Imperial rule was justified as Christian mission, and the articulation of this as the obligation of the enlightened towards those in 'darkness' illustrated the appropriation of legitimising religious language.[4] The Queen as maternal icon and the

1. Ibid., 42-43.
2. Moyse, *History of the Mothers' Union*, 80. Mothers' Union Handbook and Central Report 1897, 50, 56.
3. Bush notes Cecil Rhodes, Charles Dilke, J.R. Seeley, Alfred Milner and Joseph Chamberlain as key imperial propagandists. Bush, *Edwardian Ladies and Imperial Power*, 1, 107-110. 'Intrinsic to the imperial outlook was a self definition of the British (often, interchangeably "Englishmen") as a peculiarly gifted race with an insatiable need to exercise their colonizing genius for the benefit of less fortunate others.' Bush also notes the 'gradual elision of racial and national identities. Anglo-Saxons were assumed to be British and indeed usually English'. She also draws attention to notions of racial hierarchy related to social Darwinism and eugenics.
4. Sumner, *Memoir of George Sumner*, 50-51, 93; Agnes L. Money, *History of the Girls' Friendly Society*, New and rev. ed. (London: Wells Gardner, Darton, 1905), 57; Heath-Stubbs, *Friendship's Highway*, 70, 71, 76; Lady Laura Ridding, 'The Call of Empire' in *Selborne Papers* (Hampshire Record Office, 1909); Pierre Bourdieu, 'Authorised Language: The Social Conditions for the Effectiveness of Ritual Discourse' in *Language and Symbolic Power* (Cambridge: Polity Press, 1991).

rhetoric of the 'mother country' were drawn on to identify and assert the contribution of mothers to the imperial project. If, as Mary Sumner asserted, 'Eastern races' were 'paralysed by ignorance' and the 'advance of the nation greatly depended on the domestic life and personal influence of the mother', Christian mothers had much to contribute to the Empire as exemplars of desirable standards.[1]

Mary Sumner was convinced of the superiority of the 'sterling purity of British Character, a character on which our national prosperity has been built'. She wrote: 'As a nation we pride ourselves on our truthfulness, and not without reason. An Englishman's word is held to be sacred, and men trust us.' She believed that 'the English home was said to be model for the world'.[2] For Mary Sumner, laudable 'English' characteristics were attributable to the religious identity of the nation and were the rationale for imperial rule. This ideal needed to be upheld. Mary Sumner exhorted '*all* [italics as source] English women' to set an example of the highest standards of Christian behaviour. She saw this as important because the English reputation and therefore the moral legitimacy of imperial rule were at stake.[3]

The South African War of 1899-1902 was significant for the Mothers' Union, GFS, and other women's organisations in serving to focus enquiry into South Africa, raise questions concerning racial coexistence and to engender enthusiasm for Empire.[4] In 1902, the year of British victory and the coronation of Edward VII, the MU signalled its imperial identity with an amendment to its second object. The words 'the Empire' were substituted for 'England' so that it read: 'To awaken in mothers a sense of their great responsibility as mothers in the training of their boys and girls (the future fathers and mothers of Empire).' In 1904, Mary Sumner claimed at the MU Central Council that the organisation was a presence in nearly every British colony. In the MU Handbook and Central Report of the same year, Mrs. Philip's account of her mission to South Africa averred that the MU had an imperial mission.[5] MU (and GFS) activist

1. Moyse, *History of the Mothers' Union*, 80-86; Bush, *Edwardian Ladies and Imperial Power*, 69; Mary Sumner, 'Secular Education', *Mothers in Council* (October 1894).
2. Mary E. Sumner, Horatia E. Erskine, and Emily Wilberforce, 'Letter to the Editor, *The Times*, "Undesirable Literature"'; Sumner, 'Truth', 41; See Bush, *Edwardian Ladies and Imperial Power*, 105-110; Mary Sumner, 'The Home' (Winchester: Warren and Sons, n.d.).
3. *Memoir of George Sumner*, 51-52.
4. See Bush, *Edwardian Ladies and Imperial Power*, for details of The Victoria League and South African Colonisation Society.
5. Violet Lancaster, *A Short History of the Mothers' Union* (London: Mothers' Union, 1958), 115; Moyse, *History of the Mothers' Union*, 83.

Laura Ridding, a supporter of the 1903 South African Colonisation Society (SACS), undertook an extended tour of South Africa in 1908. While there, she kept a notebook which included reflections on social and educational issues and 'the native problem'.[1] In her 1909 paper, 'The Call of the Empire', she asserted an aspirational vision of empire and explained the virtues of empire and women's role in it, an ideal not matched by the realities of colonial rule in the recent South African conflict, nor in other parts of the Empire.[2] For Laura Ridding, the Empire should be 'a federation of free peoples under one flag or crown governed by their willing consent', and she considered that 'the British government was the only one which stands for freedom for native races'.[3] While subscribing to Christian notions of spiritual inclusiveness she was less certain about temporal equality. She noted the failure of the MU to engage with coloured and native girls, which she attributed to the low standard of morals amongst the indigenous people and to the reluctance of whites to mix with them.[4] Her notion of what constituted 'freedom for the native races' did not mean a rejection of notions of racial cultural and social hierarchy. Her vision was of humane improving trusteeship and did not challenge the higher status conferred by whiteness. Laura Ridding also thought that the 'Call of the Empire' was 'to fulfil our special duty as women, to be guardians of the moral standard of the Empire'.[5]

---

1. Ridding, 'South African Note Book,' 33. December 1908. See Appendix 2 for further details of Laura Ridding activism and South African connections.
2. A.N. Porter, *The Oxford History of the British Empire, Volume III: The Nineteenth Century* (Oxford: Oxford University Press, 1999). For select examples, see Imperial India, 422-446; Southern Africa, 597-623; and Australia and the Western Pacific, 546-572. The chapter on New Zealand and Polynesia details conflict, resistance and dispossession despite colonisation and colonialism 'being less brutal that some', 573.
3. Ridding, 'The Call of Empire'.
4. 'South African Note Book', 33; Bush, *Edwardian Ladies and Imperial Power*, 113-114. Bush locates Ridding's view and anecdotes relating to fear of black men recorded in the notebook in relation to a context of 'Black Peril scares' between 1893 and 1913.
5. Ridding, 'The Call of Empire'; Ridding's view of trusteeship on behalf of 'natives' replicates her attitude to those of lower social class. See 'Home Duties and Relations of the Educated Woman; an Address to the Wolverhampton Church Congress on Women Workers 1887' in *Selborne Papers* (Hampshire Record Office); see also Andrew Ross, 'Christian Missions and the Mid-Nineteenth Century Change in Attitudes to Race: The African Experience' in *The Imperial Horizons of British Protestant Missions*, ed. Andrew Porter (Grand Rapids Michigan and Cambridge: Wm. B. Eerdmans, 2003), 92. Ross

The development of an imperial identity for the Mothers' Union was associated with the overseas and imperial aspirations of the Anglican Church. MU and Anglican manoeuvres in the field of Empire sought to expand their organisations and shared common religious aims. Mary Sumner canvassed the support of overseas bishops just as she had with bishops 'at home'. The 1897 Lambeth Conference, which gathered colonial and overseas Bishops and their wives (several were MU Diocesan Presidents), was used by the MU as an occasion to advertise its presence overseas to an audience of clerics, as well as to the MU membership.[1] The Pan-Anglican Conference of 1908 provided the MU with the opportunity for a conspicuous demonstration of their allegiance to, and presence alongside, the Church overseas. The Conference had been instigated by the pro-imperial secretary of the SPG, Henry Montgomery, whose vision was of a worldwide imperial Anglican Church, inclusive of other 'races' but led by 'racially superior' Anglo-Saxons. He saw missionary work as a source of inspiration for this and a potentially unifying initiative in Anglicanism.[2] He had formerly been the Bishop of Tasmania (1889 and 1910), where his wife Maud had served as MU Diocesan President. Mary Sumner and Lady Chichester joined Maud Montgomery on the Women's General Committee of the conference. Louise Creighton, also a MU official, was in the chair.[3] In the autumn following the conference, the MU organised a mass meeting at the Albert Hall to which many wives of overseas delegates had been invited. Mary Sumner gave an address:

---

notes trusteeship as the acceptance of responsibility for perceived 'lower races' who should be treated humanely, as expressed in Kipling's poem 'The White Man's Burden'.

1. Malden, 'Wanted: Some Educated Mothers', July 1897, 194-209.
2. Steven Maughan, 'Imperial Christianity? Bishop Montgomery and the Foreign Missions of the Church of England, 1895-1915,' in *The Imperial Horizons of British Protestant Missions 1880-1914*, ed. A.N. Porter (Grand Rapids, Michigan: Wm. B. Eerdmans, 2003).
3. MU members were strongly represented on the Women's General Committee of the congress. Louise Creighton was the chair; other members included Mary Sumner, Lady Chichester and two other MU Associates. Moyse, *History of the Mothers' Union*, 85. See Appendix 2. Maud Montgomery was the mother of General Bernard Montgomery of Alamein. Ironically, Bernard regarded his upbringing as abusive and denied his mother any contact with his own children. See John Bierman; and Colin Smith, *Alamein: War without Hate*. (London: Penguin, 2002), 223-230.

> They had now nearly covered the Empire with their number of over a quarter-of-a-million members and associates, and 6000 branches . . . besides that she was glad to say their objects and their rules had been translated into twelve different languages, and they were winning a way in other countries.[1]

The inclusion of Mrs Oluwole, the 'wife of the African Bishop of Lagos', who was not, as readers of the Mothers' Union Journal might suppose, 'a poor ignorant heathen', as a platform speaker was recorded as significant.[2] Her speech noted:

> the deep appreciation felt by her fellow country women in Western Equatorial Africa for the Mothers' Union and of the help it brought to Christian mothers of every race and colour uniting them in an unbreakable bond of fellowship and prayer.[3]

It may also have been gratifying to the audience to hear the Bishop of the West Indies, speaking at a MU reception at Church House, say that: 'Nothing could be of greater use to his country and the colonies than the Mothers' Union.'[4]

The activity of missionaries was used to inspire, affirm identity, and enhance authority in the metropole. Cooperation with Anglican Missionary Societies and the financial support of the pedagogic work of women missionary workers strengthened the identification of the Mothers' Union (and its members) with the Church. Both the Church and the MU drew on imperial popularity and interest engendered in mission work to raise enthusiasm for their aims 'at home' and overseas. In locating itself as an imperial organisation, the MU was acting in accord with its patriotic identification with royalty and nation, an association with state power. Mary Sumner's attitudes to indigenous members of the MU, which resonate with the views expressed in MU publications and by other MU activists, were maternalistic. Indigenous members were welcomed into the MU on the understanding that they misrecognised the imposition of the MU's gendered religious doxa as legitimate. In this, and in the repeated use of colour and immaturity as a signifiers of difference, Mary Sumner and others associated with the MU appear complicit with the assumption of whiteness as superior

1. Porter, Woodward, and Erskine, *Mary Sumner*, 113.
2. *Mothers' Union Journal*, January 1909, 23.
3. Porter, Woodward, and Erskine, *Mary Sumner*, 114-115.
4. *Mothers in Council*, October 1908, 93.

and associated with the possession of preferred cultural capital, in a hierarchical ordering of cultural attributes. The demonstration of, and propagation of, perceived higher religious and cultural standards were asserted by Mary Sumner and in her lifetime by the MU as a standard for 'Englishmen' and women to live up to and as legitimising imperial rule.

5.5 Synopsis: pedagogic authority, field manoeuvres and symbolic violence

Mary Sumner's achievement of presidential office at diocesan level in the GFS (in the inaugural diocese of Winchester at a time when her husband was Archdeacon) was a measure of, and a source of, increasing capital. It represented a level of pedagogic authority upon which Mary Sumner drew to establish the Mothers' Union and so claim the promotion of motherhood as a distinct category in the fields of philanthropy and the Anglican Church. Whilst cooperating with agents or groups that she felt might advance the position of the MU, she asserted its superiority over other organisations that might compromise its pre-eminent position.

Mary Sumner evoked religious missionary endeavour to dignify the role of mothers fulfilling their domestic 'women's mission', by associating it with the sacred, thus consecrating the symbolic capital of motherhood. This served to assert the value of maternal capital in public and to MU members (and their spouses). By associating mothers with the work of missionaries, the MU offered the white mother the symbolic capital of identification with a cultural and 'civilising' moral elite which evoked connotations of valorous endeavour and participation in work for God. For the non-white mother, the symbolic violence of conformity to the values of the dominant imperial/colonial power which prioritised Christian religion, 'western culture', and, implicitly, 'whiteness', categories associated with 'civilisation', education, socio-political maturity and equitable gender relations, was euphemised by fellowship and the inclusion in a moral elite that promised eternal salvation.

The sponsorship of women missionary workers by the Mothers' Union and the GFS (sometimes in collaboration), in conjunction with Anglican missionary organisations, was a direct intervention in the missionary field which served to affirm (and publicise) the contribution of women workers in in the CMS and SPG and other overseas 'church work'. It proclaimed the symbolic capital of women engaged in missionary philanthropy and, by association, those working for Christian life in the home. The MU, like the GFS, sought to consolidate its position in the religious field both 'at home' and further afield by linking identities and transacting notions of esteemed capital between metropole and periphery. As in the MU and GFS, missionary activity served the dual purpose of seeking to impose religious doxa in Empire and contact zones but also of promoting allegiance to it 'at home'.

In a previous chapter, the notion of the field of power was associated with the state and the ruler as symbolic of the nation. In this chapter, the notion of the field of power is extended to reflect the overseas expansion of British domination encapsulated in the term empire. Empire was predicated on the perpetuation of the cultural arbitrary of British rule, which connects with assumptions of value, capital and legitimacy. It existed as an idea as well as an entity. The economic, political and military circumstances conducive to British colonial expansion could be both rationalised and legitimised by asserting domination as a 'civilising' mission by claiming the superiority of the symbolic gifts, the 'civilisation' and salvation it had to bestow on those complicit with its domination. Thus empire became associated, for those habituated to misrecognise the cultural arbitrary imposed by British rule as legitimate, with positive notions of improvement and redemption. Mary Sumner and others in the MU and GFS, in common with authoritative agents within the Anglican Church, saw the upholding of, and propagation of, religious standards as the legitimising rationale for imperial rule.[1] Mary Sumner saw in settler colonies an opportunity to extend the field position of the MU by securing wider membership and asserting its presence within, and contribution to, the patriotic imperial project. For the Anglican Church, as with the MU and GFS, missionary activity served the dual purpose of seeking to impose religious doxa in Empire and contact zones but also, by association with its esteemed capital, of promoting allegiance to it 'at home'. Moves within the Established Anglican Church to position itself as an imperial church were likewise an assertion of position within the wider field of religion and an extension of the identification with state at power 'at home'.

Women's organisations, including the MU and the GFS, led by women with high social capital, played a significant part in the reproduction of the values of the dominant imperial power.[2] The legitimising of the imperial project was highly gendered. The chastity, moral sensibility and motherliness attributed to the Christian woman were asserted as exemplifying the superiority and benignity of English imperial rule.

1. David W. Bebbington, 'Atonement, Sin and Empire 1880-1914' in *The Imperial Horizons of British Protestant Missions, 1880-1914*, ed. Andrew Porter (Grand Rapids, Michigan: Wm B. Eerdmans, 2003).
2. See Bush, *Edwardian Ladies and Imperial Power*, for other women's imperial organisations.

Christian English women were offered as examples of desirable capital to their 'sisters' in colonies and contact zones although the enthusiasm of converts was offered as an object lesson in the rewards of faith. The emphasis on motherliness and nurture served to euphemise the symbolic and actual violence perpetrated by imperial rule.

Mary Sumner was confident that the doxa of the cultural arbitrary to which she claimed allegiance was valid transnationally and its capital superior, a superiority that was thought not only to justify attempts to impose it in extending spaces, countries and overseas, but made it a duty to do so. Assumptions of superiority based on 'race' were masked by attribution to perceived deficit in cultural and religious capital. Mary Sumner was complicit with the perpetration of symbolic violence towards indigenous people and non-Christian believers. The imperial doxa assumed a hierarchy of 'race' and culture, just as the women of Mary Sumner's habitus misrecognised class stratification as legitimate. Mary Sumner drew on the association with Empire to enlarge the symbolic capital offered by the MU to its members. By associating themselves with the category of Christian womanhood, in which 'white' and 'English' were preferred qualities, MU members in the metropole were encouraged to feel a sense of participation in the Empire as exemplars of benign rule. Work associated with empire could be, for women of Mary Sumner's network and similar habitus, a means of enhancing symbolic capital and exercising pedagogic authority. Association with the agencies of imperialism served as an opportunity for women leaders to accrue capital as experts in a field. This was notably the case in the GFS, which was consulted by imperial government on matters relating to emigration and employment. However, despite asserting the universality of motherhood and the worth of maternal capital, the MU included women of 'lesser' non-white 'race' if they were apparently complicit with the values of the white English Christian 'civilised' dominant cultural arbitrary. The MU was an instrument of domination as its pedagogic work and the pedagogic action of its agents, notably Mary Sumner, perpetrated symbolic violence by seeking to reproduce the dominant arbitrary by securing the misrecognition of its legitimacy.

The MU's enhancement of women's capital through association with empire is less tangible but it did secure a position in the imperial field by securing a presence all over and beyond the Empire, thus making women visible. This served to identify mothers as citizens and contributors to the imperial project. The MU and the GFS gave specific opportunities for mission workers and contributed towards the normalisation of women as missionaries in their own right, rather than as missionary wives or associate workers. Through her association with the work of missionaries, the Church overseas, colonial settlement and the Empire as an ideal, Mary Sumner secured her authority and the prominent position of her organisation, within the fields of philanthropy and the Anglican Church. She could also claim to have placed her organisation in the field of religion worldwide, where by virtue of mass membership it could claim a high field position. In achieving recognition as the personification of the organisation that she founded by hundreds of thousands of women worldwide, Mary Sumner could claim considerable capital.

Part 3

Education

Mary Sumner with her daughter Louisa Gore Browne, Diocesan GFS president, and granddaughter Margaret Evans (with son Harold), GFS Diocesan President, 1911

Chapter 6
'Education Begins at Home': Educational Habitus, Childhood and Childrearing

6.1 Introduction

Mary Sumner's life and activism occurred against a context of change and contested authority in the field of education: religion, gender and class were significant mediators of educational opportunity. Previous chapters have identified the importance of religion in Mary Sumner's habitus and her proximity to figures of distinction in the Anglican hierarchy. Anglican doctrine drew on biblical authority to legitimise assumptions on the emotional, spiritual and intellectual capacities of women and their contingent domestic role. It informed curricula and protected the patriarchal hegemony of theological authority. Until the latter years of the century, education for most women of the middle and upper classes was not only for home but largely undertaken at home, yet despite this, some girls were able to achieve a high standard of learning in 'papa's study'.[1] The domestic ideology continued to pervade notions of appropriate curricula for girls, even after the expansion of more intellectually aspirational schooling for girls that developed from the 1860s.[2] The rationale for, and rhetoric of, girls' education continued to legitimise education as preparation for women's mission as good wives and mothers.[3] Scrutiny of educational practice was not confined to a consideration of the purpose of education for girls. The work of key thinkers Heinrich Pestalozzi (1746-1827) and Friedrich Froebel (1782-1852) was influential in stimulating reflection on the nature of the child and review of appropriate methods for learning.

1. Deborah Gorham, *The Victorian Girl and the Feminine Ideal* (London: Croom Helm, 1982), 21, 22-24. Mary Sumner is in this category; Mary Sumner, 'Account of Her Early Life at Hope End 1828-46' in *Mothers' Union* (Lambeth Palace Library).
2. Sara Delamont, 'The Domestic Ideology and Women's Education' in *The Nineteenth-Century Woman: Her Cultural and Physical World*, ed. Sara Delamont and Lorna Duffin (London Croom Helm, 1978).
3. Gorham, *The Victorian Girl*, 105-109.

Education seen as a means through which to accomplish religious and social objectives relates to power. Control of education allows arbitration of who has access to institutions; it means having the power to set curricula, define what counts as knowledge, and prioritise what kind of knowledge is esteemed. Educational provision is contested by interest groups of differing perspectives seeking to authorise their preferred notions of esteemed capital and achieve or reproduce dominance in the field. During Mary Sumner's lifetime, competition for dominance in the field of education reflected a struggle for religious authority: contested between Anglicans and non-conformists and, with the systematic intervention by the state in mass elementary education following the 1870 Forster Act, between advocates of denominational education, notably the Anglican Established Church, and those favouring secular schooling. This chapter focuses on locating Mary Sumner's educational habitus, notions of educational capital and horizon of gendered educational possibilities against a context of change and negotiation of authority in which religion was a significant mediating factor. The following chapter explores how Mary Sumner as a popular educator operationalised her aims through the Mothers' Union. This chapter begins by locating Mary Sumner in relation to her experiences of education in childhood and earlier married life. It identifies attitudes to childhood, women's education, women as educators and notions of educational capital amongst her kinship network. The chapter then moves outward to consider parochial educational initiatives and the broader context of educational affairs, notably the instigation of 'Board schools' that were at odds with Mary Sumner's understanding of educational capital. The next section of the chapter focuses on Mary Sumner's notions of childhood, the responsibilities of mothers as home educators, appropriate parenting and methods for teaching, and what to teach girls and boys.

6.2 Mary Sumner's experience of childhood, educational capital, attitudes to women and education, educational activism in her kinship network

Mary Sumner's 'Account of Early Life at Hope End' reveals her notions of desirable educational and cultural capital by enumerating the assets possessed by her family as exemplary parents, possessors of elite cultural knowledge and educational philanthropists.[1] The 'Account of Early Life' also provides evidence that Mary Sumner experienced what, in the context of the time (pre-1850), may be seen as a conventional but

1. Sumner, 'Early Life'.

privileged and relatively extensive home education. Both her parents took an interest in her education. As former Unitarians they would have experienced a tradition which acknowledged women's intellect and valued their education, despite envisaging women's roles within family life. It was also a tradition that acknowledged women as educators.[1] Mary's retrospective account of her early life, written in the context of a proposed memoir of her life when the Mothers' Union had been long established, emphasised the attention given to the religious education of her son and daughters by Mrs Heywood. It underscored the key aim of the MU to encourage mothers in the religious education of their children and can be seen as a field manoeuvre intended to validate Mary Sumner's pedagogic authority.

Mary Sumner advertised the educational and cultural credentials of her father, who was recognised as an art collector, antiquarian, a German linguist and, as she noted, 'a remarkable historian'. Thomas Heywood shared his enthusiasm for history with his daughter. Daily lessons, including readings from Gibbon's *Decline and Fall of the Roman Empire,* were held in his library when Mary's brother, Tom, was home from Eton. Thomas Heywood also encouraged the education of his family through travel abroad, which included the fashionable winter destination of Rome, given cultural distinction by its classical associations. In visits to Germany and France, Mary noted that 'French and German were spoken all the time' by the family,[2] circumstances likely to have contributed to her proficiency in languages. Mary considered it relevant to note that she was taught literature by her governess, Miss Parker, and recorded being tutored in more conventional ladylike accomplishments by 'Masters' of various kinds in London, including Herr Kroff who taught singing. Mary showed promise as a soloist and enjoyed further training in operatic singing whilst in Italy. In later life, she was recognised for her proficiency as a musician. She drew on Herr Kroff's lessons when teaching others and noted that: 'I taught his system to Loulie [daughter Louisa] who has a

1. Ruth Watts, *Gender, Power and the Unitarians in England, 1760-1860* (London: Longman, 1998), 115-118, 165.
2. Sumner, 'Early Life'. Tom's schooling at Eton was a departure from family tradition and reflected their upward social mobility. Mr Heywood had been educated at Manchester Grammar School. His brother James, who remained a Unitarian, attended Cambridge but, as a Nonconformist, was barred from taking his degree in England. Benjamin Heywood secured university education in Glasgow where the religious test did not apply and his sons went to Eton.

lovely voice.' The cultural aspect of life at Old Alresford rectory was also signalled by references to social encounters with Thackeray, Carlyle, Ruskin, Charles Kingsley, Landseer and Sir Frederick Leighton.[1]

Mary Sumner's recount of early life records participation in educational philanthropy to signal merit. In addition to daily Bible study for her own children, Mrs Heywood also taught village children at Sunday school, a project to which her own son and daughters were expected to contribute. Mary also recorded the educational initiatives of other members of her family, much of which was for the improvement of the working class, such as the village school built by Mary's father, or the larger-scale support of Mechanics' Institutes, which aimed to promote science, undertaken by her uncle, Benjamin Heywood.[2] These initiatives may be interpreted as reflecting the Unitarian belief in education as a means towards individual 'betterment', and progress through education to public welfare, but the aspiration for improvement did not mean detachment from class perspectives. The educational philanthropy of the members of the Heywood family that Mary identifies was exercised after, as well as before, conversion to Anglicanism. Thomas Percival Heywood's funding of Denstone School, as part of Canon Woodard's initiative to build Anglican schools for the middle classes, illustrates the prioritisation of denominational religious truth as a form of knowledge and class stratification as a mediator of schooling and curricula.[3]

---

1. Mary Porter, Mary Woodward, and Horatia Erskine, *Mary Sumner: Her Life and Work and a Short History of the Mothers' Union* (Winchester: Warren and Sons, 1921), 16-17; Mary Sumner, *Memoir of George Henry Sumner, D.D., Bishop of Guildford: Published for His Friends by Special Request* (Winchester: Warren and Sons, 1910), 24.
2. 'Early Life'; see Alan J. Kidd and K.W. Roberts, *City, Class and Culture: Studies of Social Policy and Cultural Production in Victorian Manchester* (Manchester: Manchester University Press, 1985); Anita McConnell, 'Heywood, Sir Benjamin, First Baronet (1793-1865)', *Oxford Dictionary of National Biography* (Oxford University Press, 2004), [http://www.oxforddnb.com/view/article/1317911, accessed November 20th 2012].
3. Isabel Mary Heywood and Sir Thomas Percival Heywood, *Reminiscences, Letters and Journals of Thomas Percival Heywood, Baronet. Arranged by His Eldest Daughter (Isabel Mary). With a Preface by the Rev. George Body* (printed for private circulation: Manchester, 1899), 32-33; Brian Heeney, *Mission to the Middle Classes: The Woodard Schools 1848-1891* (London: S.P.C.K, 1969). These secondary boarding schools, largely for boys, were intended to promote allegiance to the Anglican Church. Woodard was a Tractarian sympathiser. The 1868 Schools Inquiry (Taunton) Commission into middle-class schooling for boys envisaged a three-tier system for lower,

The Sumners, whose family tree included headmasters of Eton and Harrow,[1] like the Heywoods, celebrated and advertised their educational and cultural capital. They also saw education, mediated according to class and with religion as an essential component, as a means for the betterment of individuals and society. The value of education for women within the 'womanly sphere' was acknowledged and women's contribution as religious educators by example recognised.[2] The men of the family were educated in elite institutions. As an Etonian, George Sumner followed his father and uncle but differed from them in having his university education at Balliol, Oxford, rather than at Cambridge. Heywood Sumner followed his father to Eton and Balliol but his sisters, Margaret Effie and Louisa, were educated at home where a French governess was employed.[3] George Sumner's biography of his father, Charles, identifies him as a man of culture, 'well read in English and foreign literature' and an enthusiast for botany and horticulture. Charles Sumner's promotion of public education was also noted. In his Hampshire parish (1816-20) he established a village school, researched educational practice, and in countering opposition to education for the poor, may be seen to have favoured the evangelical emphasis on both education in religion for individual salvation and for training in respectable social conduct.[4]

Charles Sumner wished for an educated helpmeet who could offer intellectual companionship. In a letter to his bride-to-be, he requested not to be troubled with the details of domestic management and added:

---

middle and upper-middle class pupils. This followed the 1864 Public Schools (Clarendon) Commission. Delamont, 'The Domestic Ideology and Women's Education,' 172; James Murphy, *Church, State and Schools in Britain 1800-1970* (London: Routledge and Kegan Paul, 1971), 46.

1. Heywood Sumner, 'Memorials of the Family of Sumner from the Sixteenth Century to 1904,' (Southampton 1904).
2. George Henry Sumner, *Life of C.R. Sumner, D.D., Bishop of Winchester, During a Forty Years' Episcopate* (London, 1876), 34, 25-26, 37.
3. Anon, 'Old Alresford Parish Census 1861' in *Old Alresford* (Hampshire County Record Office, 1861). Amongst their seven resident servants, Mary and George Sumner employed a nursemaid, Eliza Simpson, and a French governess, Valle Laiore.
4. Sumner, *Life of C.R. Sumner*, 30, 33, 34. There was resistance to the education of the poor on the grounds that it might promote questioning of the established social order. Hannah More's teaching of reading was criticised from this perspective although she was no radical. John Lawson and Harold Silver, *A Social History of Education in England*, reprinted. ed. (London: Methuen, 1978), 231, 235; Ian Bradley, *The Call to Seriousness: The Evangelical Impact on the Victorians* (London: Jonathan Cape, 1976).

'Nor can I conceive of anything greater than the disappointment of a man who admires a woman for her mental resources of cultivation of mind, but finds on marriage she degenerates into a mere intendente de maison.'[1] Evidence of Charles Sumner's favourable attitude to educated women is given by his daughter Louisanna, who in later life published on religious themes. Louisanna's ability to give her younger brother George (prior to his entry to Eton in 1836) lessons in Latin and Greek, subjects not usually a standard part of the female curriculum, indicates that her education was more intellectually challenging than that experienced by most home or school educated middle- and upper-class women at the time.[2]

In Mary Sumner's kinship and social network, the appreciation of literature, art, music, history, languages, and the classics were celebrated as cultural capital. For women of higher social status, individual educational capital (and a degree of intellectual capital) was recognised if acquired and invested in ways legitimised by religiously and socially mediated notions of appropriate gendered behaviour. The provision of educational opportunities, or facilities for others less socially advantaged was asserted as a source of symbolic capital for the benefactors.

6.3 Educational context, parochial work, and initiatives relating to educational habitus and Mary Sumner's horizons of possibility

Mary Sumner's activism began in the 'Board School era' (1870-1902) when Anglican pre-eminence in the field of elementary education was subject to challenge by the emergence of state sponsored, non-denominational schools, administered by locally elected Boards.[3] Yet agents with authority in the Church in Mary Sumner's kinship network had been participants in pedagogic action and field manoeuvres to support Anglican ascendancy, in a contest for control of educational provision which had been ongoing from early in the nineteenth century. This contest in the field of education provides the contextual background to Mary Sumner's habitus and her later trajectory of activism through the diocesan MU.

---

1. Sumner, *Life of C.R. Sumner*, 25-26.
2. Sumner, *Memoir of George Sumner*, 144. Louisanna Gibson (1817-1899), married in 1837 and widowed in 1862, was the author of 'Simple Sketches of England and her Churchmen in the Middle Ages' and 'First Teachings about the English Church'; Gorham, *The Victorian Girl*, 23, 24; June Purvis, *A History of Women's Education in England* (Milton Keynes: Open University Press, 1991), 65-68.
3. David Wardle, *English Popular Education, 1780-1970* (London: Cambridge University Press, 1970).

The Anglican position on education may be seen within the wider context of attempts to maintain its spiritual authority and position in the wider field of power in the face of challenge from other Christian denominations. The instigation of the British and Foreign Schools Society in 1808 by the Quaker Joseph Lancaster, which sought to promote a non-denominational curriculum, challenged the assumption that the Anglican Church should have a monopoly of educational provision.[1] As Anglicanism was traditionally aligned with the Tory landowning class representative of the 'establishment' there was a political dimension to the Society. It drew support from Whigs, radicals and socialists seeking to change the social order. Religious hostility and political opposition were frequently aligned. The Anglican Church had sought to educate the poor in its doxa through Sunday schools, which served as an outlet for the philanthropic pedagogic action of socially advantaged women such as Mary Sumner and Charlotte Yonge. The explicitly titled National Society for Promoting the Education of the Poor in the Principles of the Church of England was the Anglican response to the threat presented by the Nonconformist British and Foreign Schools Society to its domination of popular education. Its goal was to build on existing provision to establish an elementary school in every parish staffed by communicant Anglican teachers.[2] The committee of what was known as the 'National Society' was composed of bishops and archbishops of England and Wales. It was 'in effect the education committee of the Anglican Church'.[3] Through this manoeuvre the Anglican Church was relatively successful in maintaining its position as a key provider of working class elementary education outside cities, until the further challenge represented by the 1870 legislation. However, state intervention in educational provision continued to be negotiated between interested parties, both religious and political.[4]

1. Murphy, *Church, State and Schools*, 4-6. Susan Mumm, 'Women and Philanthropic Cultures' in *Women, Gender and Religious Cultures in Britain, 1800-1940*, ed. Sue Morgan and Jacqueline de Vries (London: Routledge, 2010). Sumner, 'Early Life'; Charlotte Mary Yonge, ' A Real Childhood', *Mothers in Council*, January 1892, 15-19.
2. John Hurt, *Education in Evolution Church, State, Society and Popular Education 1800-1870* (London: Rupert Hart-Davis, 1971), 11-38. Chapter 1 'Schism and Cohesion' for the National Society's negotiation with the state and competition with the British and Foreign Schools; Not all Anglican Schools were National Society schools. Murphy, *Church, State and Schools*. Chapter 1.
3. Hurt, *Education in Evolution*, 17. See also 39-45
4. Murphy, *Church, State and Schools*. Chapters 2 and 3 explain the complexities of these negotiations and legislation.

Anglicanism was also influential in the education of upper-class boys through its association with elite public schools, which had undergone a religious revival in the mid-nineteenth century.[1] Anglican clergy formed the majority of headmasters, and headmasters often became bishops, a trend illustrated by Mary Sumner's 'warm friend', George Ridding, of Winchester College, subsequently Bishop of Southwell.[2] Mary Sumner's anecdote, deployed to illustrate Christian manliness, in which a public school boy is initially 'reviled, mocked, [and] threatened' by his fellows for saying his prayers but eventually by his example 'changed the practice of a whole school', provides an illustration of the topicality of religious revival in public schools.[3]

The 1870 Education Act, that initiated the systematic involvement of government in the provision of mass elementary working class education, codified the state challenge to Anglican dominance in the field of education. The identification by W.E. Forster, the architect of the act, of legislation as a means to reinforce the social order suggests a manoeuvre in the field of power designed to reproduce the status quo. Yet the act also gave women the right to serve on elected school boards, thereby opening up an opportunity for women's access to power in the fields of education and local government.[4] George Sumner's biography of his father and his own writings indicate that the Anglican Church had been anticipating state intervention for some time and had acted with this perceived threat to Church influence in mind. Charles Sumner's 1839 initiation of the Winchester Diocesan Training College for teachers may be seen as a manoeuvre to promote Anglican presence in the field of education.[5] George Sumner was also involved in the

1. Wardle, *English Popular Education, 1780-1970*, 117-124; Mary Sumner, 'Prayer' in *Home Life* (Winchester: Warren and Son, 1895). Thomas Arnold of Rugby School and Edward Thring of Uppingham are noted names in this revival, which was associated with the 'muscular Christianity' movement. George Ridding's predecessor at Winchester College (and his father-in law) George Moberly became Bishop of Salisbury.
2. 'Letters to Lady Chichester, Central President of the Mothers' Union' in *Mothers' Union* (Lambeth Palace Library, 1913-15), April 24th 191?.
3. 'Prayer', 136.
4. Hurt, *Education in Evolution*, 223-224; Jane Martin, *Women and the Politics of Schooling in Victorian and Edwardian England* (London: Leicester University Press, 1998); Patricia Hollis, *Ladies Elect: Women in English Local Government, 1865-1914* (Oxford: Clarendon, 1987).
5. Sumner, *Life of C.R. Sumner*, 261-263. Charles Sumner's biography suggests secularisation of education through government intervention was already a concern. The Diocesan Training College evolved into King Alfred's College and is now the University of Winchester.

College, serving on its management committee from 1860, as treasurer from 1862, and as secretary between 1870 and 1878. In an address to schoolmasters and mistresses delivered in 1862, George Sumner claimed, 'we are now passing through a crisis in the education in this country'. The crisis he perceived was the secularisation of education, and he asked:

> What is the true object of education? In other words, what is the ultimate end of the schoolmaster or school mistress? Now at least, I would observe that, by the schoolmaster I mean the educator, not the mere instructor. What a vast difference there is between them! You may take a young Hindu and teach him reading, writing and arithmetic, together with all the 'ologies' . . . [sic] but if you stop here, I maintain that you have not educated, but only instructed him. You have withheld from him that which is his inalienable right, and which was in your power to have bestowed on him. You have withheld from him the knowledge of the Truth.

His conclusion was that secular education was 'a contradiction in terms and impossibility for the conscientious teacher'.[1] Secularisation of religion was also addressed in the 1868 essay collection, *Principles at Stake,* which George edited. The Rev. Alexander Grant, a former H.M. Inspector of Schools, contributed the chapter 'National Education'. Grant's views accord with the sentiments in George's speech to schoolmasters and mistresses. In the same chapter Grant also commented on the party political dimension of the issue: 'The Liberal Party is making a general crusade against Denominationalism. The crusade is against all religious instruction. Its object is to wrest the office of teaching out of the hands of the Clergy.'[2] George Sumner, speaking at the Diocesan Training College prize giving in 1879, also touched on the antipathy of the Church to the influence of Board Schools:

> It is possible that many of you will be compelled to take work in Board Schools; but, even if your mouths be closed to the utterance of the distinctive Christian doctrine of our Church, yet a firm believer, who has a pure mind and sincere character, will always have great influence.[3]

---

1. Sumner, *Memoir of George Sumner*, 34, 35, 36.
2. Rev. Alexander R. Grant, 'National Education' in *Principles at Stake: Essays on Church Questions of the Day*, ed. George Sumner (London: 1868), 118.
3. Sumner, *Memoir of George Sumner*, 32.

George and Mary Sumner's support for the cultural arbitrary that prioritised Christian doxa was demonstrated in their commitment to religious education as a means of improving individual lives and public conduct. They followed family practice in considering that education and religion were bound together. As noted in a previous chapter, the philanthropy promoted by George and Mary Sumner during their years of parochial ministry was religious but was realised through largely informal educational initiatives. They supported the Christian book hawking scheme and the funding of a village library in 1878, pedagogic action which not only supported an increase in literacy but promoted Christian values by providing 'wholesome', if not exclusively religious, reading.[1] The men's Bible study group led by Mary Sumner was also pedagogic action intended to foster Christian standards of conduct. Her mothers' meeting similarly intended to educate its members in Anglican doctrine and encourage them to become exemplars of Christian behaviour.

George and Mary Sumner also acted to support the Anglican Church in the field of formal education. George extended his sphere of pedagogic action into the village school where he gave religious instruction, as well as taking:

> a great interest in Sunday school work, and was exceedingly careful as to the manner in which the classes were arranged, and the clear and intelligent method of instruction given in Scripture and catechism. He had every week a Sunday School Teachers' meeting at the Rectory. [2]

Some years later, in a substantial act of philanthropy, George and Mary provided £2,000 to fund the building of a new school, All Saints Church of England Primary, which was opened in 1893 in Winchester. The Sumners were amongst a number of influential (and socially distinguished) Anglican supporters of the 'voluntary' movement in the district.[3] The building of voluntary schools (that is those funded

1. Ibid., 16; Rev. George Carew, 'Census Book of Old Alresford' in *Old Alresford* (Hampshire Record Office, 1845). Carew's 1845 record noted a population of 578. 50% of women and 20% of men were communicants. A third of men and a quarter of women could read.
2. Sumner, *Memoir of George Sumner*, 20, 21.
3. Ibid., 107, 101-102, 106. Supporters included the Earl of Northbrook (Lord Lieutenant of the County); W.H. Meyers MP for Winchester; Melville Portal Chairman of the County Quarter Sessions; the Warden of Winchester College; the Master of St Cross (alms house). Also present at the ceremony were 'many

by voluntary subscription such as the Anglican National Schools) had been given impetus by the 'Forster' Elementary Education Act of 1870. It specified that Board Schools were to be established where voluntary provision was insufficient for the local population. The Cowper-Temple amendment (secured by Episcopal pressure) preserved religious teaching in Board Schools, albeit of a non-denominational character, but Anglicans considered this unsatisfactory and favoured specific doctrinal teaching in the curriculum.[1] Ensuring sufficient voluntary places was a manoeuvre designed to prevent the election of the school boards (a political contest in which Anglican supporters might not prevail), which were charged with the establishment of non-denominational Board Schools.

Despite commitment to the Anglican cause, George Sumner was noted for the 'harmonious collaboration' he achieved as Chair amongst the Council of 'Churchmen [meaning Anglicans], Nonconformists, and Roman Catholics' that managed the voluntary school rate in Winchester. In resisting the dilution of denominational teaching represented by the threat of Board Schools, rival denominations found common cause in supporting the denominational influence in the field of elementary education. George commented that 'one of the great advantages of the struggle they had been carrying on in Winchester was that it brought all religious parties together'.[2] Mary Sumner noted the 'Educational triumph' reported by the *Hampshire Chronicle* on the opening of the school. According to the *Chronicle*, Sir William Hart-Dyke MP's opening speech noted: 'In Winchester they had done their best and were determined to have a secure hold over the education – the *religious* education of their children', and George Sumner 'responded that they were determined that the voluntary system should prevail'.[3] Mary Sumner's use of the Mothers' Union to support formal denominational teaching is addressed in the following chapter.

For Mary Sumner, education for both men and women of the lower classes was regarded as a means of individual and collective societal betterment. Literacy was seen as enabling religious education. Yet the dominant social and Anglican interests to which Mary Sumner claimed

---

other clergy and laymen of importance. Mrs Sumner was one of the many ladies present.' The voluntary system relied on the collection of a voluntary rate from subscribers. It was administered by a committee which represented various denominations; George Sumner was chair of the Winchester branch.

1. Murphy, *Church, State and Schools*, 58-60; Hurt, *Education in Evolution*.
2. Sumner, *Memoir of George Sumner*, 106, 104.
3. Ibid., 102, 105.

allegiance considered that access to education and curricula required their mediation to ensure the transmission of their preferred doxa. Whilst intellectual and cultural knowledge was important, it was considered debased without the moral framework and purpose given by religion which, amongst Mary Sumner's network, meant Anglicanism. In the field of (elementary) educational provision, in which voluntarily funded denominational schooling was in contest with non-denominational, state-sponsored provision, George and Mary Sumner sought to ensure a curriculum that included Anglican doctrinal teaching. They also acted to promote Anglicanism through pedagogic action associated directly with the Church, such as religious services or classes, as well as less overtly through the pedagogic work of philanthropic initiatives. These educational initiatives, whether formal or informal, were symbolically violent in that they offered the benefits of literacy (and salvation) in exchange for outward compliance with the Anglican religious (and social) doxa.

The habitus in which Mary Sumner was located and the action of its agents (including Mary herself) were in accord with Anglican views on educational issues that were to be codified in later years by the Lambeth Conference.[1] The 1908 Lambeth resolutions on education summed up the educational agenda that had been pursued for so many decades prior to that date by Mary and George Sumner. Resolution 11 stated: '[I]t is our duty as Christians to make it clear to the world that purely secular systems of education are educationally as well as morally unsound.' Resolution 12 added that 'no teaching can be regarded as adequate religious teaching which limits itself to historical information and moral culture'. It followed that in the words of Resolution 13: 'It is our duty as Christians to be alert to use in all schools every opportunity which the state affords us for training our children in the faith of their parents.' Resolution 19, in particular, endorsed Mary Sumner's MU agenda:

> The Conference desires to lay special stress on the duty of parents in all conditions of social life to take personal part in the religious instruction of their own children, and to show active interest in the religious instruction which the children receive at school.[2]

1. Resolution 17 of the 1908 Lambeth Conference: 'The religious training of teachers should be regarded as a primary duty of the Church.' Charles and George Sumner may be considered pioneers.
2. Anglican Church of Canada Anglican Book Centre, Toronto, 'Lambeth Conferences Resolutions Archive'. By permission, the Secretary General of the Anglican Consultative Council 2006, [http://www.lambethconference.org/resolutions, accessed July 12th 2013].

6.4 Mary Sumner's notions of childhood and childrearing

In founding the MU, Mary Sumner drew on three premises which were underpinned by the permeation of religion into education and the framing of women's roles, notions of approved conduct, and horizons of possibility. The first was that education in religion needed to be upheld because it was being eroded: '[T]he need of religious teaching is daily becoming more pressing in these days of secularism, colourless Board School teaching, irreligion and infidelity.'[1] The second premise was that education in religiously authorised standards of behaviour was the means towards alleviating social problems such as drunkenness, prostitution and poverty that were deemed to have an adverse effect on the wellbeing of the nation.[2] The third was that mothers were the most effective agents for the education of young children into religious faith and moral conduct. Mary Sumner maintained: 'People have tried for long years to do the work of reformation by schools and institutions and agencies of all sorts . . . but they cannot succeed until the parents, and above all the mothers, are awakened to their responsibilities.' She also claimed that 'the character of every child is being formed day by day from the moment of his birth – he sees his mother first . . . he learns *first* from her'.[3]

The assumption that motherhood was the natural province of women was in accord with (Anglican) Christian teaching and was embedded in social practice. In asserting the need for the MU, Mary Sumner acted to increase the symbolic capital accruing to motherhood by claiming that it required pedagogic expertise. In associating motherhood with a divinely ordained role, she also invested children, as well as mothers, with symbolic value. In so doing, she may be considered to be in accord with changing notions of childhood that identified childhood as a stage of development to be respected. Her views reflected ideas of both the Unitarian Harriet Martineau (1802-1876) and the evangelical Anglican Hannah More (1745-1833) in emphasising the role of mothers as moral and religious educators.[4] The view expressed in Hannah More's *Strictures*

1. Mary Sumner, 'When and Why the Mothers' Union Started' (Winchester: Warren and Sons, n.d. surmised 1888).
2. 'Temperance', in *Home Life* (Winchester: Warren and Sons, 1895); 'Mothers' Work Outside'; *Home Life* (Winchester: Warren and Sons, 1895), preface.
3. *Home Life*, 4; 'Obedience', 28.
4. Harriet Martineau, *Household Education* (Smith, Elder & Co., 1870); Hannah More, *Strictures on the Modern System of Female Education: With a View of the Principles and Conduct Prevalent among Women of Rank and Fortune* (printed

on Female Education was that it was desirable for women to be educated in serious matters in order to be competent in the educative role of motherhood. Mary Sumner believed that: 'The Christian Faith should be taught to children first by the Mother in early child life.'[1] She set out her view of the essential tenets of faith that children should know: 'Every baptised child should be taught the Creed, the Lord's Prayer and the Ten Commandments . . . and all other things a Christian ought to know and believe to his soul's health.'[2]

Mary Sumner also expressed her views on the standards of conduct that she felt were appropriate. Children should 'be perfectly and consciously obedient *at three years old*.'[3] To achieve this was not easy: it required 'faith, love, patience, method, self-control and some knowledge of the principles of character training'. She also noted that a mother needed 'some knowledge of the principles of education' and methods for the management of learning.[4] Writing with a Mothers' Union audience in mind, she recalled the birth of her first child as an awe-inspiring charge for which she felt unprepared:

> The child's future depended on my own training and responsibility even more than that of my dear husband because during the first months the mother has special time and opportunity to mould the character of her child. . . . I needed special teaching, motherhood is one of the most important professions and yet there was no profession which has so poor a training, one often entered upon without any sort of preparation hence the failure in character of so many children as they grow up.[5]

If mothering was 'a solemn responsibility', and 'the training of children is a profession', it followed that mothers needed to be 'awakened' to it and equipped for the task.[6] This was the aim of the Mothers' Union. Mary

---

for T. Cadell, Jun. and W. Davies, in the Strand, 1799); Charlotte Mary Yonge, *Hannah More* (London: W.H. Allen & Co., 1888). Mary Sumner's fellow GFS Associate and editor of *Mothers in Council* was a biographer of More.

1. Mary Sumner, 'Letters to Mrs Maude' in *Mothers' Union* (Lambeth Palace Library), June 26th 1917.
2. Porter, Woodward, and Erskine, *Mary Sumner*, 31.
3. Sumner, 'Obedience', 28.
4. Porter, Woodward, and Erskine, *Mary Sumner*, 31; Sumner, 'When and Why the Mothers' Union Started'.
5. 'Account of the Founding of the Mothers' Union and Parochial Work at Old Alresford' in *Mothers' Union* (Lambeth Palace Library).
6. 'When and Why the Mothers' Union Started'; Porter, Woodward, and Erskine, *Mary Sumner*, 31; Sumner, *Home Life*, 10; Object 2 of the Mothers' Union.

Sumner's supporter Bishop Harold Browne recognised the educational potential of the MU for pedagogic work on behalf of the Church and endorsed the pedagogic authority of mothers:

> It is of vital consequence to future generations that education should be conducted on the highest principles of morality, and religion. The women of the nation are its earliest and most effective teachers, and they specially need to be taught.[1]

Mary Sumner prioritised the role of the mother as a home educator but she recognised, and encouraged, the role of the father in parenting and the education of the family in religious habits. Her writings exhorted wives to encourage their participation in family life.[2] She also demonstrated her willingness to assume pedagogic authority over working men by specifically addressing articles to them. In 'To Husbands and Fathers', published in the *MUJ* in 1905, Mary wrote: 'It will not do to say "I leave religion to the missus". Husbands, you must face your responsibilities.'[3] It was the duty of the father 'to see that his children are sent to a school where the Christian religion is taught honestly and faithfully, and where the master and mistress are believers in the Christian faith'. She also considered that men should participate actively in the religious education of their children: 'Sunday is a good day for a Father to give his children religious instruction. He should read the Bible with them and hear them repeat the Catechism.'[4]

The previous chapter noted the significance Mary Sumner attached to the sacrament of baptism, 'the consecration of Child-life' which was to 'remind Mothers that their children are sacred beings' who were 'only lent to their parents to be trained up as His faithful soldiers and servants'. Although Mary Sumner wrote that 'the seeds of evil are born in his [the child's] little heart', her emphasis was not on the eradication of original sin, for 'children are not, as a rule, artful or deceitful unless they are made so by mismanagement or fear', but on the need to protect the child from falling into evil ways by training them for the 'battle of life . . . while they are as yet unsullied by the world' in obedience, truthfulness and self-control, for 'every fallen man or woman . . . was once an innocent child . . . ignorant of sin'.[5] Moreover, she believed: 'There is in every

1. *Memoir of George Sumner*, 60.
2. 'Marriage 2'; 'Purity'; 'Words' in *Home Life* (Winchester: Warren and Son, 1895).
3. 'To Husbands and Fathers', *Mothers' Union Journal*, October 1905.
4. 'Prayer', 153, 154.
5. *Home Life*, 8. This and many of Mary Sumner's views accord with Charlotte

human heart an "impulse towards perfection", a divine yearning for holiness and Heaven, an instinctive straining after God.'[1] Mary Sumner's position reflected not the interpretation of Anglican doctrine upheld by the evangelical Hannah More, which regarded child nature as inherently evil, but rather a 'tabula rasa' which saw the child as having the potential to have character and achievement moulded by experience, example and educational impressions for good or ill.[2]

Mary Sumner's memoir of early life suggests that she had enjoyed a carefree childhood that included adventurous riding and boating escapades with her brother. As an adult she relished 'childish merriment' and took pleasure in the company of children. Cathedral choir boys were regularly entertained for games and tea, and grandchildren, nephews and nieces were welcomed in The Close.[3] Mary Sumner considered the warmth her husband displayed towards children on his school visits worthy of comment: 'He often came in with a smile and a pleasantry ready for some child; usually a laugh was heard before he had been there many minutes – even the youngest child would feel at home with him.'[4] The educational methods advocated by Mary Sumner and mentioned in the pages of MU magazines also suggest that she (and her organisation) were sympathetic to 'child-centred' conceptions of childhood (and contingent educational methods), which sought the happiness of the child and acknowledged the child as a thinking being, rather than an empty vessel to be filled by instruction, ideas exemplified in the work of Friedrich Froebel and Heinrich Pestalozzi.[5]

Maria Shaw Mason, *Home Education: A Course of Lectures to Ladies, Etc* (London: Kegan Paul & Co., 1886). See below for further elaboration; Sumner, 'Obedience', 27; 'Truth', 36; 'Obedience', 34; see also 'Purity' for training in how to resist evil taking hold; 'Words', 53.

1. *To Mothers of the Higher Classes* (Winchester: Warren and Sons, 1888), 2.
2. Wardle, *English Popular Education, 1780-1970*, 81; Sumner, *To Mothers of the Higher Classes*, 2. The Anglican Thirty-Nine Articles (Article IX) expressed the issue thus: 'Original sin stands not in the following of Adam, but it is the fault and corruption of the nature of every man that naturally is engendered of the offspring of Adam whereby man is very far from original righteousness, and is of his own nature inclined to evil.' [http://www.cofec.org/The%2039%20Articles%20of%20Religion, accessed October 24th 2013]. Mary Sumner's interpretation emphasises the first phrase and the word 'inclined'.
3. Porter, Woodward, and Erskine, *Mary Sumner*, 51, 52.
4. Sumner, *Memoir of George Sumner*, 107.
5. Wardle, *English Popular Education, 1780-1970*; Mason, *Home Education*. See Appendix 2 for Charlotte Mason.

Mary Sumner considered that: 'Habits formed at home and in childhood are formed for life.'[1] She appeared to follow (but did not make reference to) the view expressed in Harriet Martineau's *Household Education* that every home is a school.[2] Mary's stated views on childhood and curriculum accord in particular with the ideas put forward by Charlotte Mason (1842-1923), the founder of the Parents' National Education Union (PNEU). Charlotte Mason was, from 1874 to 1878, located in the Winchester diocese as Vice Principal of Bishop Otter Teacher Training College, Chichester. Her book *Home Education*, published in 1886, was recommended reading in the leaflet 'When and Why the Mothers' Union Started'.[3] Although Mary Sumner (as with Harriet Martineau) made no direct references to Charlotte Mason in her writing, many similarities in conceptions of childhood rooted in religious faith, the purpose of education and approaches to learning can be discerned.[4] As an educationalist, Charlotte Mason positioned herself as a practicing Anglican. Her views on childhood and educational methods were informed by faith. She upheld the notion of children as a divine charge. Like Mary Sumner, her interpretation of Anglican doctrine acknowledged the human potential for corruption but emphasised the role of the parent in the preservation of the innocent nature of the child.[5] Charlotte Mason noted that a loving, respectful, and ambitious code of education was to be found in the New Testament in words, 'laid down by Christ himself: OFFEND not – DESPISE not – HINDER not – one of these little ones'.[6] She suggested that this encapsulated 'whatever is included in training up a child in the way he should go', a biblical reference (Proverbs 22.6) that Mary Sumner used in modified form for the motto of the MU. Similarly, the quotation from Wordsworth's *Ode on Intimations of Immortality from Recollections of Early Childhood*, 'trailing clouds of Glory we come

1. Sumner, 'Obedience', 27.
2. Martineau, *Household Education*, 7; Sumner, 'Example', 95. 'Home is the child's first school. The parents are the child's first teachers.'
3. 'When and Why the Mothers' Union Started'; see Margaret A. Coombs, *Charlotte Mason: Hidden Heritage and Educational Influence* (Cambridge: Lutterworth, 2015). Home Education was conceived of either in addition to schooling or as a substitute.
4. A search of the Armitt Library, Ambleside, where Charlotte Mason's archive is housed has not revealed any correspondence with Mary Sumner. The destruction of Mary Sumner's personal papers after her death leaves potential correspondence between them a matter for speculation.
5. Mason, *Home Education*, 330.
6. Ibid., 12.

from God who is our home', which continues, 'Heaven lies about us in our infancy', and which was used by Charlotte Mason, was later used to accompany a cover illustration used on *MIC*.[1]

In *Home Education,* Charlotte Mason asserted her view that children were a public trust rather than the property of their parents and should be nurtured as citizens for the benefit of society. Mary Sumner's views were also in accord with Charlotte Mason's on the mother's educational role and significance. Charlotte Mason reproduced Pestalozzi's assertion that 'the mother is qualified by the Creator Himself to become the principal agent in the development of the child. She also advocated the need for mothers to have an appreciation of educational theory.[2] Charlotte Mason described the curriculum she recommended as 'generous'. Her motto for children, 'I am, I ought, I can, I will', placed emphasis on the moral and spiritual empowerment of the child, and her method of learning and curriculum content fostered enquiry and richness of experience in literature, music, the arts, physical expression and the natural world, in addition to grammar, languages, history and geography.[3]

Mary Sumner's message was voiced according to audiences stratified by class, and her writing reveals her assumption that less socially advantaged homes would have different expectations of curriculum and schooling to the privileged home.[4] Indeed, the term 'educated mothers' was deployed by Mary Sumner to indicate middle and upper-class women in the way that the term 'cottage mother' indicated working-class women and masked their disadvantage in euphemistic language. Her advice on the education of children, although specifying desirable religious knowledge, concentrated on childrearing and the development of character and morals. She echoed Charlotte Mason in asserting that the mother should be 'regular and methodical', for 'babies are law abiding creatures' who should be brought up in 'an atmosphere of love and cheerfulness, of order and obedience to rule'.[5] Mary Sumner considered that the training of children should be undertaken by example, consistent

1. Ibid., 11.
2. Ibid., 2, 3.
3. Stephanie Spencer, '"Knowledge as the Necessary Food of the Mind": Charlotte Mason's Philosophy of Education' in *Women, Education and Agency, 1600-2000*, ed. Jean Spence, Sarah Jane Aiston, and Maureen M. Meikle (London and New York: Routledge, 2010); Mason, *Home Education*.
4. This reflects assumptions in social practice and in government thinking as in the Clarendon and Taunton Commissions and the Forster Act.
5. Sumner, 'Obedience', 28; Mason, *Home Education*, 13. Charlotte Mason notes children as 'law abiding'.

discipline and protection from dangerous influences: 'Children are gifted with two powers during the first seven years, Observation and Imitation. They watch their parents, and must be taught strict obedience and self-control.'[1] Parents should demonstrate the exercise of self-control in disciplining their children:[2] 'The best trained schoolmistresses and masters are taught to rule children by a quiet, self controlled manner, and we advise parents to try the same method at home.'[3] Kindness and consistency were not only appropriate womanly (and manly) virtues but were effective educational measures. Here she echoes Harriet Martineau:[4]

> Remember that obedience is not taught rightly to children by beating, hitting, slapping, rough angry words, and ill usage, but by gentle, loving firmness and self-control. Mr Rarey the great horse tamer has told us that he has known an angry word raise the pulse of a horse ten beats a minute; think then how it must affect a child! The ill usage of children by thoughtless, intemperate and passionate parents is terrible, and they oftentimes satisfy their conscience that they are severe only for the good of their children, while in fact, they are merely giving way to their angry passions. Children are completely at the mercy of those around them; they are often timid, and acutely sensitive.[5]

Nor did Mary Sumner approve of issuing threats: 'Who can tell the misery and terror and nervous excitement such language causes to children.' Her recommendations were to 'speak lovingly, gently but decidedly' and 'think before you give any order and be quite sure your child *can* obey your command'. She advised: '[N]ever give unnecessary orders or more than one at a time, but, when the order is given, see that it is obeyed, even if it costs you time and trouble.'[6] Mary also noted: 'It is by imitation far more than by precept that we learn everything.'[7] The reverent treatment of children should involve treating them with courtesy;[8] it also involved treating them with justice. It was:

1. Sumner, 'Letters to Mrs Maude', June 26th 1917.
2. See 'Parental Discipline', Mason, *Home Education*, 15-16, for similar views on parental example.
3. Sumner, 'Words', 64.
4. Martineau, *Household Education*, 46-48. 'Care of the Powers; Will'.
5. Sumner, 'Obedience', 30.
6. Ibid., 30-35.
7. 'Purity', 50.
8. 'Words', 63.

> a parent's duty to love each child equally and to be fair and just and loving in dealing with each one. . . . It is impossible to overestimate the grief caused to a sensitive child by neglect or indifference, or the bitter feeling of being less appreciated, less loved, less admired and less cared for than the beautiful, clever or fascinating brother or sister. The sorrows of sensitive children are very acute, and very secret, but terribly real.[1]

Whilst (as noted in Chapter 3) conceding authority to men, Mary Sumner felt that the different qualities of the sexes were complementary and should be appreciated and respected. In her 1888 book, *To Mothers of the Higher Classes,* Mary Sumner made a specific comment on the damage to the character of boys by spoiling them at the expense of girls, which also implied recognition of the worth of girls:

> There is one mistake made very commonly in home education, which lies at the root of much evil in men, and that is the preference given by parents (notably by mothers) to their sons. They are more often prized than daughters, especially if there is an ancient name or vast inheritance to be possessed by the eldest son. From his birth he is an object of admiring interest to parents and relations, to friends and servants. They conspire together to spoil him in his childhood: the sisters are put in the shade, and he is the pet and idol of the family. Later on, as a school boy he is indulged in every possible way; and his sisters are expected to submit to his boyish tyranny, to wait upon his whims and wishes until he grows to think that the world in general and his sisters in particular were made for him. This sort of home training of boys *versus* girls, which encourages the tyranny of the boys over the girls, is very general, it is a prodigious wrong done to the children, and it is impossible too strongly to deprecate the short sighted folly of such an education.

If boys were trained to respect women it would lead them to 'purer and nobler lives' and 'prevent the contempt and disrespect for the honour and happiness of women which causes such dark pages to be written concerning the lives of some men'.[2]

1. *To Mothers of the Higher Classes*, 24; Mason, *Home Education*, 17.
2. Sumner, *To Mothers of the Higher Classes*, 22-23.

Parents should set an example of 'truth and honesty'. Children should always be told the truth, even if it was unpalatable. Again, Mary Sumner's view accords with Charlotte Mason's that children's utterances are a window into the child's mind from which those concerned with pedagogy may gain insight.[1] Questions asked by children:

> must be treated, not only truthfully but respectfully, for the child-mind is fresher from God and more unsullied than our travel stained minds, and they teach us marvellous things by their quick-sighted simplicity, and thoughtful, innocent impression of the new world upon which they have entered.[2]

Mary Sumner made references suggestive of a strategy for tackling sex education in remarks made on 'puzzling and perplexing questions'. Parents might postpone answering difficult questions in the case of 'a religious or any other sort of difficulty which it is beyond the capacity of a child to understand'. She suggested saying: 'My child, I will answer this when you are older. Meanwhile do not ask anyone else to explain to you. Always come to me or father when you are puzzled; we will tell you what is the truth, only trust us.'[3] In later years she made reference to sex education in an undated letter to Lady Chichester, her successor as MU Central President. Whilst she endorsed parents as the educators of children in sexual matters:

> I heartily agree [with you] in explaining to children the consecration of body and soul – Holy Baptism and then self reverence and then later on sharing the sacred facts of a child's birth. This every mother is bound to do – It is a mother's duty, it is a father's also (to his sons).

She felt it was 'a mistake to discuss the sex question in public when clergymen and laymen are present'.[4]

The model boy or girl of any class, as envisaged by Mary Sumner, had been taught to pray, to tell the truth, be obedient, to honour parents, to demonstrate self-restraint, and to have a growing understanding of what was forbidden as sinful or impure. Mary Sumner's message that children should be cherished as the handiwork of the Creator was an

1. Mason, *Home Education*, 5.
2. Sumner, 'Truth', 38-39.
3. Ibid.
4. 'Letters to Lady Chichester'; see Lesley Hall, *Sex, Gender and Social Change in Britain since 1880* (Basingstoke: Macmillan, 2000), 33, 44, 88-89, for attitudes to sex education informed by moral, scientific and eugenic viewpoints.

assertion of their worth. She associated them with the religious symbolic capital of innocence; thus its preservation was a source of capital for parents, especially mothers, who were deemed to be divinely ordained as primary carers. In order to uphold their responsibility to God, child and nation (for the right religious education of children represented a capital investment in future citizens), mothers should possess symbolic religious capital as 'good' women. They also needed the pedagogic expertise necessary for moulding character and equipping the child with religious faith. As mothering was a divine charge, it was appropriate that the mother herself should lay the foundations for the future spiritual life of the child. Thus motherhood, identified with the highest authority of religion, was invested with symbolic capital. Sanctifying motherhood may also be interpreted as a strategy for the recruitment of pedagogic workers on behalf of the Church.

6.5 Synopsis: educational habitus and capital values

Mary Sumner's dispositions of habitus recognised educational and cultural capital (frequently symbolic), manifest in attributes such as appreciation of art and music, knowledge of literature and languages, or historical scholarship. Mary Sumner, as the beneficiary of the interest of her antiquarian father, and the services of educational professionals, possessed many attributes which were recognised within her habitus as indices of personal cultural capital. These categories of capital were defined and upheld by the dominant social group (also possessors of economic capital) who had, if male, access as a matter of routine to the elite institutions in the field of education dedicated to the reproduction of this capital. Anglican manoeuvres in the field of education overlapped with those in the field of religion. The dominance it sought to uphold in education and religion was reflected in the high position of individual Churchmen with pedagogic authority across both fields. The Anglican Church also had the power to invest economic and symbolic capital in educational institutions. Educational capital was both authorised and defined by complicity with Anglican doxa and its recognition by the social and religious elite. Mary Sumner and members of her network demonstrated mis/recognition of this cultural arbitrary by accepting that education was inseparable from education in religion. For Mary Sumner and her network, behaviour considered undesirable indicated a deficit in religious capital that could be redressed through education. The dominant group, to which she claimed allegiance, saw themselves, by virtue of their self-defined superior capital (cultural and religious), as authorised to provide education and determine curricula, particularly for those of inferior social status, in an enactment of symbolic violence. This pedagogic action towards upholding the doxa of the dominant group was a means for the acquisition of symbolic capital and pedagogic authority.

Assumptions as to the role and nature of women asserted (and legitimised) by Anglican religious doxa informed notions of desirable educational capital for women. In Mary Sumner's network, the pedagogic role of women conforming to the gendered doxa, as home educators of their children in morality and religion, was recognised and accrued symbolic capital. Women might accumulate pedagogic authority from pedagogic action to perpetuate the doxa beyond the home directed towards social inferiors, both men and women. This could be realised through philanthropy, an overlapping category with education as in the mothers' meeting, Sunday school class, or the men's Bible class run by Mary Sumner. Women in Mary Sumner's network were recognised for their intellectual achievements within the parameters of their discharge of home duties. In her family and wider habitus, women could accrue symbolic capital and achieve pedagogic authority in the public sphere through (intellectual) activity legitimised by complicity with the religious and social doxa, such as in writing on religious themes. In initiating the MU, Mary Sumner drew on existing pedagogic authority accrued from her position in the GFS, educational parish work to men and women, and as a published author on the Holy Land. She claimed the value of maternal educative capital on the grounds that children were a divine charge. Mothers did God's work in protecting the innocent child from corruption through educating the child in religion. In so doing mothers also did pedagogic work for the nation in moulding the character of future citizens. Mary Sumner also asserted the capital of mothering because it required expertise that needed to be acquired through education, thus investing motherhood with pedagogic authority. The value of active mothering was promoted to an upper-class audience and they were encouraged to engage with the principles of childrearing and educational practice. This, whilst not originally innovative, reflected developments in progressive pedagogy and evolving notions of childhood.

Charlotte Yonge

Chapter 7
Spreading the Word: Educating the Populace

7.1 Mary Sumner, a popular educator

Mary Sumner qualifies as a popular educator according to a definition that encompasses informal means intended to modify behaviour, directed towards a wide section of the populace encompassing, but not, (as the chapter will explore in relation to Mary Sumner), exclusively confined to, those of 'lower class'. The emergence of the Mothers' Union can be contextualised not only against the growth of elementary schooling but also against a back ground of increasing literacy and the expansion of the mass production of popular media.[1] As a disseminator of religious knowledge with a 'civilising' intent, her activism fits the definitions offered by David Wardle, as well as John Hurt, who interprets popular educational initiatives in the period contiguous to Mary Sumner's activism as a response to fears of social disorder.[2] Harold Silver's advocacy for attention to religion as contributory to ideas and social movements influential to developments in education affirms her location in this field. Whilst religious educational initiatives may be seen as linked to agendas of social control mediated by both class and gender; conversely, educational religious philanthropy may represent

1. Richard D. Altick, *The English Common Reader: A Social History of the Mass Reading Public, 1800-1900* (Columbus: Ohio State University Press, 1998); Sarah C. Williams, '"Is There a Bible in the House?": Gender Religion and Family Culture' in *Women, Gender and Religious Cultures in Britain, 1800-1940*, ed. Sue Morgan and Jacqueline de Vries (London: Routledge, 2011), 23. Williams notes 'a burgeoning mass market of commercial religious publication'.
2. David Wardle, *English Popular Education, 1780-1970* (London: Cambridge University Press, 1970); John Hurt, *Education in Evolution Church, State, Society and Popular Education 1800-1870* (London: Rupert Hart-Davis, 1971); Harold Silver, 'Knowing and Not Knowing in the History of Education', *History of Education* 21, no. 1 (1992).

opportunity for empowerment. Sarah Jane Aiston has suggested that, by virtue of their exclusion from most formal educational structures, women's educational activism was realised through a range of 'extra institutional' initiatives.[1] Susan Mumm, writing in the context of the GFS, notes that much religiously inspired philanthropy was educational and observes that philanthropic activity reshaped the identities of those engaged in its delivery and thus performed an educative function for patrons as well as the patronised.[2] Sue Morgan sees education as:

> a major vehicle through which nineteenth century religious women could seek to achieve, social moral and political transformation, particularly the achievement of a rational education for women that might better equip them for the vital responsibilities of motherhood.[3]

This chapter focuses on Mary Sumner's negotiation of the obstacles and possibilities presented by a tradition of emphasis on women's education in relation to domesticity and mothering and explores her manoeuvres in the field of education. It begins by noting Mary Sumner's view that mothers of all classes needed to be educated in mothering and her positioning of upper and upper-middle-class 'educated mothers' to act as educators to other mothers via the MU. Mary Sumner's use of the organisation to educate mothers and the wider populace by informal means and her deployment of educational strategies to promote recognition of the MU are examined. The chapter considers the dissemination of religious knowledge through printed materials and contextualises Mary Sumner's views on reading as an educational tool, notes the role of Charlotte Yonge, and discusses education through the Mothers' Union magazines, *Mothers in Council*, and the *Mothers' Union Journal*. The chapter then moves to consider networking with other organisations in relation to the field of education. Mary Sumner's stance on secular schooling is examined and her position and manoeuvres through the MU related to the contest in the field of education between Church and state.

---

1. Sarah Jane Aiston, 'Women, Education and Agency 1600-2000: An Historical Perspective' in *Women, Education and Agency*, ed. Jean Spence, Sarah Jane Aiston, and Maureen Meikle (London and New York: Routledge, 2010), 2-5.
2. Susan Mumm, 'Women and Philanthropic Cultures' in *Women, Gender and Religious Cultures in Britain, 1800-1940*, ed. Sue Morgan and Jacqueline de Vries (London: Routledge, 2010), 56.
3. Sue Morgan, *Women, Religion, and Feminism in Britain, 1750-1900* (Basingstoke: Palgrave Macmillan, 2002), 5.

7.2 Leading by example: education in mothering for all classes

Mary Sumner believed that the Mothers' Union should embrace 'all ranks and classes, for the duty and responsibility of a mother to her child is in principle, identically the same from the highest to the humblest of mothers'. She noted that 'the rules on the [MU] card concern every mother' and asserted the value of all mothers' work in rearing good citizens by claiming 'the future of England depends greatly on the home training of the children of today'.[1] The socially and educationally advantaged mother should lead by example, but moral authority was also needed. Although the 'educated' mother ought to 'know best', Mary Sumner did not assume that social status equated with better parenting and noted: 'There is quite as much need of stirring up the hearts of Mothers in the higher ranks of life to a sense of their responsibility. It is hardly fair to cast all the blame of neglect on one class of Mothers.'[2] Writing directed at middle and upper middle-class mothers repeatedly asserted the importance of active parenting and identified it as a source of symbolic capital. Mothers should be interested in their role, like Charlotte Yonge's exemplary mother Lady Merrifield in her 1885 novel *The Two Sides of the Shield*, who 'preferred the company and training of her children to going into society in her husband's absence'.[3]

Mary Sumner revealed her evangelical emphasis on the need to witness religion in all aspects of life when she chastised the 'worldly' mother, 'busy with society – paying visits, yachting, receiving large shooting parties or going abroad for weeks and months', for allowing her children 'to spend the greater part of their lives with nurses and maid servants, or later with tutors and governesses who even if most excellent and conscientious, as they often are, could never be to the children what the mother if faithful should be'.[4] This was a recurrent theme in her writing and was pursued in the pages of *MIC*. Her concern was that whilst other aspects of education were well attended to, moral and religious education was not. Despite her intention to dignify the capital of motherhood by emphasising it as a religious responsibility, Mary's position also suggested an anxiety, shared amongst upper and upper middle-class mothers who employed staff for childcare, focused on suspicion of the motives, competence and morals of the lower class employee. Charlotte Mason's *Home Education* warned that 'coarseness and rudeness in his nurse does the tender child lasting harm.

1. Mary Sumner, *Home Life* (Winchester: Warren and Son, 1895), 3, 9.
2. *To Mothers of the Higher Classes* (Winchester: Warren and Sons, 1888), 11, 12.
3. Charlotte Mary Yonge, *The Two Sides of the Shield* (London: Macmillan & Co., 1885), 22.
4. Sumner, *To Mothers of the Higher Classes*, 16-17.

Many a child leaves the nursery with his moral sense blunted, and with an alienation from his heavenly Father set up which may last his lifetime'.[1] Charlotte Yonge repeated an anecdote concerned with the subversion of her childhood discipline by a well-meaning but morally misguided maid.[2] Mary Sumner pointed out that French and German governesses were not equipped 'to teach the tenets of our faith' and, consequently, some upper-class children received a worse religious education 'than the children in our National Schools, and are . . . not grounded at all in the doctrines of our Church'. She considered this a 'disgrace' and her suggestion that 'uncertainty in matters of religion, and the growing scepticism of the present day, may be traced . . . to the want of clear and definite religious teaching in our homes' demonstrates her view that good citizenship and social cohesion were related to conformity to religious standards of behaviour.[3] In seeing the remedy for societal ills in parental interventions, Mary Sumner was asserting the value of mothering. She further affirmed the symbolic capital accruing to mothers by associating it with divine authority. Speaking in 1887 at the first MU Diocesan Conference, she said it was 'the duty of every mother with her own lips to teach her child that he is God's child'.[4] To help dispel 'the miasma of doubt and disbelief', mothers should engage with their children in daily Bible reading and prayer.[5]

Mary Sumner acted to motivate and educate upper-class women in her notions of good parenting so that they might act as educators amongst women of their own class, as well as rank and file members. In order to achieve pedagogic authority, these women needed to exemplify religious conduct; they also needed expertise as speakers on educational themes. Speaking on behalf of an organisation authorised by the Church gave them additional pedagogic authority. The messages Mary Sumner directed at the upper-class mother in *To Mothers of the Higher Classes* were the same as those addressed to less socially advantaged mothers, and some passages were reproduced verbatim.[6]

1. Charlotte Maria Shaw Mason, *Home Education: A Course of Lectures to Ladies, Etc* (London: Kegan Paul & Co., 1886), 18.
2. Charlotte Mary Yonge, 'A Real Childhood', *Mothers in Council*, January 1892.
3. Sumner, *To Mothers of the Higher Classes*, 18, 19.
4. Mary Porter, Mary Woodward, and Horatia Erskine, *Mary Sumner: Her Life and Work and a Short History of the Mothers' Union* (Winchester: Warren and Sons, 1921), 31.
5. Sumner, *To Mothers of the Higher Classes*, 20.
6. Ibid., 33, 35; included the same wording as 'Obedience' in *Home Life* (Winchester: Warren and Sons, 1895), 33; 'Truth,' in *Home Life* (Winchester: Warren and Sons, 1895), 39.

When advice differed it concerned the practicalities of supervision. Upper-class mothers were unlikely to allow their daughters out without chaperones, or to send them to the public house. Similarly, the upper-class mother did not have to exercise ingenuity in segregating girls and boys at bed or bath time, but modesty and the avoidance of bad company were advocated for all classes. Mary Sumner emphasised training in obedience, truthfulness and habits of temperance across the social spectrum.[1] Fostering habits of self-restraint were similarly advocated for all mothers, and advice against spoiling children was also a uniting theme. The overriding message was that children should be educated in religion and morality by the example and involvement of mothers and fathers.

The Mothers' Union's local branch meetings (as noted in Chapter 3) included educational content in the form of talks or Bible study.[2] These initiatives required qualified 'lady' speakers. Education for women likely to undertake the role of Associate was addressed in 'Drawing room' meetings. These included the reading of informative papers such as 'The most satisfactory way of promoting Church teaching through the State Schools'; 'The advantage of higher education in women'; 'The desirability of restricting the publication of Police reports in the Press'; or 'The conditions of women at work in factories',[3] which indicate the MU's engagement in matters of topical concern beyond the home. Mary Sumner suggested that 'principles of physical moral and religious education should be studied and reproduced in simple form to the poorer mothers, instruction should be given in sanitary, medical and industrial subjects on cookery and thrift'.[4]

At the Winchester Diocesan Committee meeting of May 1889, Mary Sumner suggested subjects that would be suitable for Associates to initiate for discussion at branch meetings. Later that year, the committee

1. 'Temperance' in *Home Life* (Winchester: Warren and Sons, 1895); *To Mothers of the Higher Classes*, 26, 27.
2. Hearth and Home, 'Leading Societies and Their Work: The Mothers' Union', *Hearth and Home: An Illustrated Weekly Journal for Gentlewomen*, Thursday January 28th 1892.
3. Joyce Coombs, *George and Mary Sumner: Their Life and Times* (Westminster: Sumner Press, 1965), 110.
4. Mary Sumner, 'When and Why the Mothers' Union Started' (Wnchester: Warren and Sons, n.d. surmised 1888); see Meg Gomersall, *Working-Class Girls in Nineteenth-Century England: Life, Work and Schooling* (Basingstoke: Macmillan, 1997) for discussion of the gendered and class stratified influence in informing curricula for working class girls.

resolved 'to form a band of speakers' who could be called upon to address meetings. Later a list of speakers was given in *MIC*.[1] Mary encouraged women to become speakers by asserting the 'wonderful nearness of Christ' that the committed speaker might experience. She also gave practical advice: 'Hints to Associates', also published in *MIC*, offered directions for taking a meeting that sought to diminish an atmosphere of social patronage. Church halls should be made as much like a drawing room as possible, with flowers, a carpet and comfortable chairs not like a hall or a servants' hall.[2] Associates were encouraged to recommend *The Illustrated Catechism* and *Good News Told in Simple Words* as an aid for mothers in Christian Teaching, and were kept up to date with the latest MU publications; in 1899 a lending library for the use of Associates was proposed.[3] Speakers for the MU (as noted in Chapter 3) disseminated information in more public arenas through Diocesan Conferences, Church Conferences and mass meetings. These were educative in affirming the message of the MU amongst its membership and wider audiences, who included clergy and upper and middle-class men. As these occasions were reported in the press, they also served to raise the public profile of the organisation and its identification of mothers as religious educators.

In her efforts to 'stir up' all mothers to exemplify 'the higher life', Mary Sumner exalted the symbolic capital of motherhood by associating with the joy of religious experience and an 'understanding of the value of things eternal'.[4] Through informally educating advantaged women to her notions of religious and educational capital Mary Sumner sought to recruit them to exercise pedagogic action towards their peers and women of lower social status. Through these manoeuvres, the rewards of maternal capital and the pedagogic authority of motherhood could include less socially advantaged women, who, in turn, might act as pedagogic workers in upholding the Christian doxa and notions of childhood and childrearing that Mary Sumner professed.

---

1. Winchester Diocesan Mothers' Union Committee, 'Minute Book 1886-1910' in *Diocese of Winchester Mothers' Union* (Hampshire Record Office), May 28th 1889, November 8th 1889; Anon, 'List of Speakers', *Mothers in Council*, April 1891.
2. Porter, Woodward, and Erskine, *Mary Sumner*, 40; Mary Sumner, 'Hints to Associates', *Mothers in Council*, April 1891, 113. 'Cottage' indicated working class.
3. Winchester Diocesan Mothers' Union Committee, 'Minute Book 1886-1910', November 14th 1894; May 28th 1890; November 2nd 1894.
4. Sumner, *To Mothers of the Higher Classes*, 11, 60, 59.

7.3 The power of reading: education through the Mothers' Union magazines

Expansion in institutional educational provision coincided with a trend towards expansion in the mass production of popular media that reflected the increasing literacy of those lower down (but not at the very bottom of) the social scale.[1] Advisory literature on religious themes in the form of tracts, pamphlets and magazines proliferated, as those seeking to uphold a religious doxa, notably the Religious Tract Society, used publication to promote their views.[2] Disapproval of the 'wrong sort' of literature, as epitomised by the sensational 'penny dreadful' aimed at working class youths, reflected concern amongst upholders of religion, or the social status quo, that reading had the power to corrupt morals and encourage anti-social behaviour.[3]

Mary Sumner used publishing to disseminate her views and to refute ideas or counter material she felt undermined the doxa she upheld. Leaflets, and in particular the quarterly *Mothers' Union Journal* that members were obliged to buy, provided a means to spread educational material to a wider audience.[4] Printed material had the advantage that it might be passed to neighbours, or other family members. Written material also reached members overseas. The distribution of literature was given attention at Winchester Diocesan Committee meetings. Existing Church organisation and other methods were employed to circulate material. In 1888, the Winchester Diocesan Mothers' Union Committee resolved to circulate MU pamphlets to parishes where there was as yet no MU and request their distribution amongst parishioners. Four years later, back numbers of the *MUJ* were distributed to soldiers' wives on troop ships at Portsmouth. Donations of literature were made to poor parishes in the Diocese and to one in East London. Associates were urged to obtain subscriptions from their contacts towards the cost of literature.[5]

1. Altick, *The English Common Reader: A Social History of the Mass Reading Public, 1800-1900*; David Vincent, *Literacy and Popular Culture: England 1750-1914* (Cambridge: Cambridge University Press, 1989). Vincent suggests that there is no direct link between formal schooling and the growth of literacy.
2. The Religious Tract Society (1799) reflected evangelical revival. Sympathetic to Protestant denominations but anti-Roman Catholic, it published from 1879 the *Boys' Own Paper* and the *Girls' Own Paper.*
3. Kelly Mayes, 'The Disease of Reading and Victorian Periodicals' in *Literature in the Marketplace: Nineteenth-Century British Publishing and Reading Practices Cambridge Studies in Nineteenth-Century Literature and Culture Series, No. 5.*, ed. John O. Jordan and Robert L. Patten (Cambridge: Cambridge UP, 1995).
4. Porter, Woodward, and Erskine, *Mary Sumner*, 147.
5. Winchester Diocesan Mothers' Union Committee, 'Minute Book 1886-1910', June 5th 1888; June 8th 1892; November 21st 1890; November 14th 1894.

The rules on the Mothers' Union card encapsulated Mary Sumner's views on the power of reading to influence the reader for good or ill: 'The power of books and general reading in particular in forming character and opinion is well known.'[1] The original card for 'ordinary' members, advocated daily Bible reading in rule 8, and the admonishment, 'Be careful that your children do not read bad books or police reports', came further up the list, as rule 5. Mary's feelings on the subject were unequivocal. In an address to members, she wrote:

> Bad reading is like poison; it injures, it destroys, not the body, but the mind and conscience . . . some of the worse suggestions to break God's laws are taught in print. I dare not speak of the infidel books and papers which are circulated in this country.[2]

Mothers of the 'Higher Classes' had a similar message:

> Unprincipled or trashy novels, whether French or English should be strictly forbidden, because the habit of reading bad novels dissipates and weakens the energies of the mind. . . . But the best literature – poetry, fiction, and history – should be given freely, and in this way a wholesome taste is formed for that which is good and ennobling.[3]

Mary Sumner was not alone in her belief in the power of reading to influence the conduct and character of the reader. She shared the middle and upper-class anxiety about the stability of the social order that was reflected in the belief that sensational literature was an incentive to crime.[4] Mary Sumner's concern that 'bad books' and material on scandalous topics would corrupt the national as well as individual character prompted her to write to *The Times* on two occasions. In 1909 she complained about the circulation of 'improper books' and the following year as a joint signatory with Mothers' Union Vice Presidents Emily Wilberforce and Horatia Erskine 'undesirable literature' was the

1. Sumner, *To Mothers of the Higher Classes*, 25.
2. 'Reading', 84. Police Reports published in newspapers or the sensational Police Gazette might contain details of violent crime, sexual misdemeanours, drunkenness or other examples of immorality. Similar sentiments were expressed on the card for 'educated' mothers.
3. *To Mothers of the Higher Classes*, 25.
4. Patrick A. Dunae, 'Penny Dreadfuls: Late Nineteenth-Century Boys' Literature and Crime', *Victorian Studies* 22, no. 2 (1979); Anon, 'A Youthful Burglar', *The Hampshire Chronicle*, January 6th 1877. The *Chronicle* reported that he was 'inflamed by the study of sensational literature'.

subject of protest.[1] Promoting the 'right' sort of reading was a priority in the Mothers' Union. Literature and plays were selected as subjects for discussion at the London Conference of 1896. Educational materials such as 'Mr Rule's scheme for Bible reading' were discussed and recommended at Diocesan Committee meetings, and in the MU quarterlies, which exemplified the content that the organisation regarded as 'wholesome' and improving.[2]

The magazine *Mothers in Council (MIC)* was initially funded by George Sumner.[3] First published in 1891, it added to a well-established tradition of advisory material aimed at a female readership located in the 'leisured' middle class. *The Mothers' Union Journal (MUJ)*, published as a penny quarterly from 1888, reflected the trend in publications catering to a market broadened by increased mass literacy.[4] The two tier editions, aimed at different classes, followed the pattern adopted previously by the GFS. *Friendly Leaves*, its magazine for members, with its mix of news, stories and notes on Bible study, was similar in format to the *MUJ* and some material appeared in both magazines. There were further links between the MU and GFS publications. Charlotte Yonge, who edited *MIC* from 1890, was also the GFS's Diocesan Literature Correspondent and contributed material to its publications. Her protégée, co-editor and successor as editor of the *Monthly Packet*, Christabel Coleridge, also became the editor of *Friendly Leaves*.[5]

---

1. Mary Sumner, 'Letter to the Editor, *The Times*, "Improper Books"', December 9th 1909; Mary E. Sumner, Horatia E. Erskine, and Emily Wilberforce, 'Letter to the Editor, *The Times*, "Undesirable Literature"', January 13th 1910.
2. Winchester Diocesan Mothers' Union Committee, 'Minute Book 1886-1910', October 4th 1895; November 8th 1893.
3. George Sumner edited *MIC* 1901-8. He contributed a report on the proceedings of the Anglican House of Laymen on the religious education of the middle and upper classes, *MIC*, April 1891, 69-71. Sales of magazines and other literature were a key source of income for the MU. In 1914 an additional magazine *The Workers' Paper* was published.
4. See Deborah Gorham, *The Victorian Girl and the Feminine Ideal* (London: Croom Helm, 1982), 65-80; see also Sally Mitchell, 'The New Heroine: Penny Weekly Magazines of the 1870s' in *The Fallen Angel: Chastity and Women's Reading 1835-1880* (Bowling Green, Ohio: Bowling Green University Popular Press, 1981).
5. Georgina O'Brien Hill, 'Charlotte Yonge's "Goosedom"', *Nineteenth-Century Gender Studies*, no. 8.1, [http://www.ncgsjournal.com/issue81/hill.htm, accessed August 21st 2012]; Elizabeth Lovegrove, '"Dangerous Display": Charlotte Yonge, Christabel Coleridge, and Pseudonyms in the *Monthly Packet*', *Women's History Magazine*, 2013. Christabel R. Coleridge

The Mothers' Union magazines addressed religious themes, including missionary activity, and issues of concern, such as secular schooling, with the intention of informing the views of readers.[1] The theme of educating the readers to be educators was common to both MU magazines, and Mary Sumner was a regular contributor. *MIC* assumed a highly literate readership of middle and upper-class women, who were likely to have received, like Mary Sumner and the magazine's editor Charlotte Yonge, the kind of liberal home education evoked in the latter's novels. The *MUJ* included entertaining fiction that was intended to counter 'the low bad stories sold from a penny to a shilling to the masses of people who crave for exciting literature', the effects of which Mary Sumner (and others) were so fearful.[2] By securing Charlotte Yonge (her fellow Associate in the GFS) as editor of *MIC*, Mary Sumner associated the magazine with a figure invested with considerable symbolic capital as a 'good churchwoman' and with pedagogic authority as a popular educator. Charlotte Yonge was a prolific novelist noted for her morally improving works, which provided models of feminine behaviour in accord with religious principles of self-control, domestic duty and charitable service.[3] She was the author of textbooks, such as *English Church History*, and historical tales for children, also had a reputation as the editor of the highly respectable *Monthly Packet* (1851 to 1890), in which 'appropriate' reading was discussed, a theme that was pursued in *MIC* and in the *MUJ*.[4]

---

and Charlotte Mary Yonge, *Charlotte Mary Yonge: Her Life and Letters* (London; New York: Macmillan & Co., 1903). Through *The Monthly Packet* and the privately circulated *Barnacle*, Charlotte Yonge acted as mentor to young women writers. Christabel Coleridge (1843-1921) was one of these 'Goslings', and Charlotte's first biographer.

1. Rebecca Styler, 'The Contexts of Women's Literary Theology in the Nineteenth Century' in *Literary Theology by Women Writers of the Nineteenth Century* (Farnham: Ashgate, 2010), 3-18. Styler discusses the uses of secular writing to pass on religious doxa and construct women's religious identities.
2. Sumner, 'Reading', 86.
3. Judith Rowbotham, *Good Girls Make Good Wives: Guidance for Girls in Victorian Fiction* (Oxford: Basil Blackwell, 1989).
4. See Charlotte Mary Yonge, *English Church History, Adapted for Use in Schools, Etc* (London: National Society, 1883) for an example of her National Society publications. *Aunt Charlotte's Stories of English History for the Little Ones* (London, 1873) exemplifies her vast output for children. See also Kristine Moruzi, '"Never Read Anything That Can At All Unsettle Your Religious Faith": Reading and Writing in the Monthly Packet,' *Women's Writing* 17, no. 2 (2010).

Charlotte Yonge, like Mary Sumner, had been home educated to a good standard by interested parents and brought up in the expectation that she should participate in the education, particularly the religious education of the 'lower' classes. Her reminiscences of a disciplined and somewhat austere childhood, which featured in *MIC*, note that:

> from seven years old my mother took me to the Sunday-school, first to learn and then to teach, when however I was much too young to be put in authority. I was a more conscientious than a religious child. Except [for] a vehement pleasure in the Sunday-school – which was not so much for religion's sake as for the love of teaching. . . .[1]

Charlotte Yonge sustained a life long association with village schooling, both Sunday and day. Her notes on 'Sunday School Tickets' in the November 1876 *Otterbourne Parish Magazine* illustrate her understanding of children and notions of pedagogy:

> A ticket is the reward for a sacred lesson repeated by heart or writing answers to a question. It ought to be understood that ill repeated lessons do not deserve a ticket, and that it is unfair and unjust to give one not properly earned. Some children can learn more easily but the amount must be proportional to their capacity by the teacher. Tickets are encouragements not so much coin to be purchased by repeating anything however badly as some little girls seem to think.[2]

She provided an appealing portrait of a fictional school and its pupils in the 'Langley' tales, a series which Christabel Coleridge (c. 1903) anticipated would be 'in 1950 or so . . . valuable evidence of what the Church of England did for education and civilization when she still had the village schools in her hand'.[3] Christabel Coleridge also asserted

1. Yonge, 'A Real Childhood'; The childhood memories of another MU and GFS activist can be found in Louise Creighton, *Memoir of a Victorian Woman: Reflections of Louise Creighton 1850-1936* (Bloomington and Indianapolis: Indiana University Press, 1994).
2. Charlotte Yonge, 'Otterbourne Parish Magazine' (Hampshire Record Office); see also Austin Whitaker, 'Winchester Memories 20 Mrs Elliot Talks About Her Old Schoolteacher Charlotte Yonge' in *Winchester Memories: Oral History Recordings* (Hampshire Record Office, 1970).
3. Christabel Coleridge is quoted in Ethel Romaines, *Charlotte Mary Yonge: An Appreciation* (London: Mowbray, 1908), 34.

Charlotte Yonge's influence in encouraging young ladies to act as educational philanthropists, by providing fictional role models who start a school (*The Daisy Chain*) or take GFS classes, as in *The Two Sides of the Shield*, and by making schoolchildren appealing, via the 'Langley School' stories. Just as the 'Langley' tales give a picture of village schooling for the poor, Charlotte Yonge's novels give an insight into the educational experience and aspirations of home educated young ladies, themes that were reflected in the pages of *MIC*.

Charlotte Yonge's childhood reminiscences were not the only articles on the upbringing of children in *MIC*. Following an introduction from Mary Sumner which explained that the purpose of the magazine was to aid its readers in gaining the expertise required in order to accomplish the 'exalted mission' of childrearing in the 'sphere which God has appointed' in the home,[1] the initial editorial announced the intention that:

> Essays will be given in babyhood, childhood, boyhood, girlhood and youth, notices of books likely to be useful . . . in each number some difficult points in training will be propounded and a few pages devoted to mothers' meetings and literature for men.[2]

Mary Sumner's 'Concerning Infants' emphasised the importance of the affectionate maternal attention to young children: 'Do not fail to abundantly caress him and speak kindly.'[3] Articles that signalled the dangers of parental neglect were designed to prick the consciences of upper and upper middle-class women: 'Who Can Prevent It? Physical Dangers', gave anecdotes of illness and accidents attributable to excessive delegation of child care to servants.[4] The following issue also reflected implicit anxiety about class in enumerating the moral perils the child of the neglectful mother might face. The importance of the parental role in moral training was also addressed in articles such as 'Willy's Will', which dealt with moulding the character of the

1. Mary Sumner, 'Introduction', *Mothers in Council*, January 1891, 5, 6.
2. Charlotte Yonge, 'Editorial', ibid., 11-12.
3. Mary Sumner, 'Concerning Infants', ibid., July 1891, 138-145.
4. A Mother, 'Who Can Prevent It? Physical Dangers', ibid., January 1891, 14-20; 'Who Can Prevent It? Moral Dangers', ibid., April 1891, 85-88; see Charlotte Mary Yonge, *The Daisy Chain, or, Aspirations: A Family Chronicle. By the Author of the Heir of Redclyffe, Etc.* (London: John W. Parker & Son, 1856). It includes a cautionary tale of a baby poisoned by laudanum by the ignorant unsupervised nursemaid.

young child. The Reverend E.B. Layard, in 'Boys and Religion', advised mothers to become the confidants of their boys in order to fortify them against the moral perils of school.[1] Authors of *MIC* articles were also interested in developments in pedagogic method. Mary Johnson's 'Bend the Twig and Shape the Tree' advocated the pedagogy of Froebel:

> The system of amusement and instruction formulated by Froebel and his disciples is so valuable and comprehensive I earnestly advise all parents to visit a genuine kindergarten to study the principles as well as to copy the practices there inculcated. For all mothers and indeed fathers it is right to know how to teach their children . . . it is a pity to let them all have to begin at School, when we know and they can learn.[2]

The pages of *MIC* reflected the concern of 'lady mothers' and attitudes to the education of daughters against the context of developments in the provision of formal secondary schooling and higher education for middle and upper-class girls.[3] Whilst *MIC* did not challenge the purpose of girls' education as preparation for motherhood and home duties, it reflected the negotiation and diversity of interpretation as to what means of education were most appropriate. The tone and content of *MIC* locates it as responding to an aspiration amongst women to be better informed and more authoritative. The key issue identified in articles on the choice of educational setting was that the religious faith and moral standing of the girl should not be compromised. Yet the insistence on femininity and respectability emphasised in the curricula and ethos of intellectually aspirational girls' schools and the discouragement of social mixing in elite establishments such as Cheltenham Ladies' College suggests that readers of *MIC* may have also been concerned with preserving their daughters' social capital as young ladies.[4] The article 'High Schools and

---

1. Rev. E.B. Layard, 'Boys and Religion', *Mothers in Council*, January 1891. 'Boys and the Formation of Character', in April 1892, 98-107, addressed similar themes.
2. Mary Johnson, 'Bend the Twig and Shape the Tree', ibid., 33-41.
3. Joan Burstyn, *Victorian Education and the Ideal of Womanhood* (London: Croom Helm, 1980).
4. Joyce F. Goodman, 'Girls' Public Day School Company (Act. 1872-1905)', online edn, Jan 2013 ed., *Oxford Dictionary of National Biography* (Oxford University Press, October 2005), [http://www.oxforddnb.com/view/theme/94164, accessed August 28th 2013]. Girls Public Day School Company schools were more socially inclusive of a broader, predominantly middle-class, spectrum; Sara Delamont, 'The Contradictions in Ladies' Education' in *The Nineteenth-Century Woman: Her Cultural and Physical World*, ed. Sara

Home Education' considered that there were potential drawbacks in both settings. It urged mothers to be vigilant in the choice of school or staff for home teaching so that moral standards might not be compromised.[1] What the article left unvoiced was the concern that schools might be a source of social contamination if girls mixed with those of inferior social status. 'The Modern Education of Girls' and 'Foreign Studies', addressed the recurrent theme of the dangers of foreign governesses, whose religion and moral standards might be misguided and inferior.[2]

In 1892, 'Girls and University Education' gave a cautious welcome to university education for girls as compatible with the development of womanly talents, with the proviso 'never let a girl enter the battlefield of university life whose religious convictions are confused'.[3] Prominent members of the Mothers' Union reflected varying interpretations of appropriate educational provision for girls. Whilst Louise Creighton, Diocesan GFS President for Peterborough and member of the National Union of Women Workers (NUWW), was a keen advocate of university education,[4] Lucy Soulsby, MU delegate at international conferences on morality and Girls Public Day School Company headmistress, opposed the opening of degrees to women. They were united, however, in envisaging a more serious education for women, and arguing for it, as enhancing conventional religiously legitimised notions of womanliness.[5]

Delamont and Lorna Duffin (London: Croom Helm, 1978), 158, 'Schools had to fight to be allowed to teach girls all the subjects boys received'; 'The Domestic Ideology and Women's Education' in *The Nineteenth-Century Woman: Her Cultural and Physical World*, ed. Sara Delamont and Lorna Duffin (London Croom Helm, 1978), 174-177; Gorham, *The Victorian Girl*, 105-109.

1. Mrs Knight, 'High Schools and Home Education', *Mothers in Council*, April 1891, 107-113.
2. Anon, 'The Modern Education of Girls', ibid., January 1892, 43-46; 'Foreign Studies', *Mothers in Council*, April 1892, 108-113.
3. Edith Robson, 'Girls and University Education', ibid., January 1892, 29-32, 32.
4. Two of Creighton's daughters attended university, Lucia (1874-1947) at Newnham and Gemma (1887-1958) at Lady Margaret Hall. Creighton, *Memoir of a Victorian Woman: Reflections of Louise Creighton 1850-1936*, 134; James Thane Covert, *A Victorian Marriage: Mandell and Louise Creighton* (London: Hambledon, 2000), 130, 238.
5. Delamont, 'The Nineteenth Century Woman', 154-160. Delamont identifies 'uncompromising' and 'separatist' views on appropriate higher education. The former favoured existing curricula aimed at males, the latter felt reform was needed to suit women and men. Julia Bush, '"Special Strengths for Their Own Special Duties": Women, Higher Education and Gender Conservatism in Late Victorian Britain,' *History of Education* 34, no. 4 (2005); Kate Flint,

Charlotte Yonge's shifting position on educational provision for girls illustrates the cautious negotiation of women's access to the expanding field of education that was reflected in the pages of *MIC*. Although an advocate of education for women, and sympathetic to the pleasure of intellectual endeavour, she initially (1886) resisted the idea of a college for women, claiming that superior women were formed by home influence and best educated there by their own efforts. Through her writing in the *Monthly Packet* and the privately circulated *Barnacle*, Charlotte Yonge nurtured a generation of women in this category, some of whom went on to be pioneer educators. Amongst other notable educationalists and writers in Charlotte Yonge's circle was Elizabeth Wordsworth, the first principal of the Oxford women's college Lady Margaret Hall (1878), to which Charlotte Yonge gave a guarded welcome, hoping that it would be run on religious principles to raise the standard of womanhood.[1] By 1893, Charlotte Yonge acknowledged public examinations as a means for a girl 'to be useful with your talents', and her reconciliation in old age, to the idea of university life for women was marked by the inauguration of a university scholarship fund in her name in 1899. This was available to girls of the Winchester High School, which had its founder and first headmistress in Charlotte Young's protégé Anna Bramston. Charlotte Yonge was a member of the school's governing body.[2]

MIC offered advice on reading to support parental pedagogic expertise. The article 'Mental Growing Pains' advised on fiction as an aid to discussing character for adolescent girls.[3] In 'Books for the Nursery',

---

'Soulsby, Lucy Helen Muriel (1856-1927),' *Oxford Dictionary of National Biography* (Oxford University Press, 2004), [http://www.oxforddnb.com/view/article/48573, June 21st 2013]. See Appendix 2. At Cambridge Emily Davis established Girton on separatist lines; Jemima Clough at Newnham favoured special women's examinations. At Oxford, Somerville was uncompromising and Lady Margaret Hall separatist.

1. Georgina Battiscombe, *Charlotte Mary Yonge: The Story of an Uneventful Life* (London: Constable & Co., 1943), 146. Letter to Emily Davis; O'Brien Hill, 'Charlotte Yonge's "Goosedom"'; Romaines, *Charlotte Mary Yonge: An Appreciation*, 137-158. For Elizabeth Wordsworth, see Appendix 2.
2. Charlotte Yonge, *The Girl's Little Book*, 1st ed. (London: Skeffington and Son, 1893), 38; Margaret Mare and Alicia Percival, *Victorian Best-Seller: The World of Charlotte M. Yonge* (London: George G. Harrap & Co., 1947), 234-235; Battiscombe, *Charlotte Mary Yonge*, 161-162. For Anna Bramston, see Appendix 2.
3. Charlotte Yonge, 'Mental Growing Pains', *Mothers in Council*, January 1891, 42, 45.

Charlotte Yonge suggested that fairy tales should be an occasional treat. It was her view that reading should be 'above the intellect rather than below'.[1] For older boys and girls, she noted:

> Generally the same books that boys like are pleasant and exciting for girls. But boys after they are scholars do not much care for books about school boys – they know their own world too well – they like real information, if they must have adventure fiction designated as 'books for boys', Ballantyne and Henty provide interest and morality.[2]

There was occasional advice on what adult readers might read on religion in the interest of self-education. Charlotte Yonge disagreed with John Ruskin's assertion that women should avoid theology. In order to teach their children, 'parents should imbibe good doctrine'. Amongst her recommendations were the sermons of Charles Kingsley and 'Bishop Pearson's "On the Creed" . . . strong meat but a really able woman would be all the better for it'.[3] Recommended reading compatible with Anglican Church views was also a regular feature in the *MUJ*. The April 1902 edition recommended a selection of missionary stories for children but regretted (following a reader's complaint) that W.T. Stead's 'Bairns' Bible' was not after all to be recommended.[4] Mary Sumner felt that parents should encourage children to find pleasure and learning through good reading, both religious and secular; advice on appropriate material could be sought from the clergyman or schoolmaster and interest should be shown in what children have read.[5] She thought that good parents should read for their own self education in order to teach their children. Girls were included in her advocacy for education in scientific and technical principles:

---

1. 'Books', *Mothers in Council*, January 1891, 57-60, 57,58.
2. Ibid., 58. John Tosh, *Manliness and Masculinities in Nineteenth-Century Britain: Essays on Gender, Family, and Empire* (Harlow: Pearson Longman, 2005). Henty's and Ballantyne's manly Christian heroes' adventures had an imperial context; Susan Walton, *Imagining Soldiers and Fathers in the Mid-Victorian Era: Charlotte Yonge's Models of Manliness* (Farnham and Burlington: Ashgate, 2010).
3. Charlotte Yonge, 'Church Catechism', *Mothers in Council*, January 1891, 24-29.
4. Anon, 'Recommended Books', *Mothers' Union Journal*, April 1902. The recommendation was regretted on the grounds of the omission of key stories.
5. Sumner, 'Reading', 97.

> Sensible parents will read up certain subjects so as to be able to 'talk well and wisely' for the education of their children. A Father can help his boys and girls to understand a great deal about the moon and stars . . . or if he be a mechanic, he will explain to his children, in simple language the elementary laws of mechanics, and some of the interesting discoveries of modern times.

Mary Sumner elaborated on the theme of reading for self-improvement and gave a list of men of substance, who had made good despite humble origins through 'healthy reading'.[1] Her (implicitly ambivalent) attitude was that 'good' reading might enable social progress and would not lead, if undertaken in the religious home, that accepted the social order as divinely ordained, to challenges to social stratification.[2] The encouragement of reading for self-culture was also promoted in the GFS, which was united with the MU in its stance on morality. Both the GFS and MU saw educational self-culture as an aid to the awareness of, and interest in, public affairs that they considered contributory to good citizenship. Suggestions in *Friendly Leaves* in an article titled, 'How Working Girls May Help Their Sex and Country', for good 'but not highbrow reading', included Ruskin and Carlyle. Mrs Henry Wood's *Danesbury House* 'promoted a warm interest in the Temperance question' and 'on the lighter side', for 'it is quite impossible for working girls to jump on the plane of elevated literature at one bound', George Eliot, Mary Craik, Charles Kingsley, Charlotte M. Yonge, Annie S. Swan, Mary Elizabeth Braddon, Walter Scott, and Louisa M. Alcott were recommended.[3]

There was an expectation that readers might contribute material for publication in *MIC*. In 1899, it was resolved that writers of special articles in *MIC* were to be rewarded with presentation copies of the edition to which they had contributed. *MUJ* readers were also given the opportunity to submit short articles but contributions had to conform to editorial scrutiny in respect of subject and standards of literacy.[4] The *MUJ* encouraged its readers to uphold the religious doxa as encapsulated in the Objects and Rules of the MU through a mixture of advice and

1. Ibid., 89, 92.
2. 'Prayer', 160-161.
3. Priscilla E. Moulder, 'How Working Girls May Help Their Sex and Country by a Working Woman', *Friendly Leaves*, March 1907, 112-114. The GFS had a reading union scheme which required members to answer questions on recommended texts both biblical and secular, as noted in Chapter 4.
4. Winchester Diocesan Mothers' Union Committee, 'Minute Book 1886-1910', February 20th 1899; Lady Jenkyns, 'On Poetry', *Mothers in Council*, April 1903.

exhortation, often via fictional examples. In addition to reading (Rule 5), Mary Sumner wrote on a variety of topics, including marriage and 'Mothers' Work Outside the Home', of which she disapproved on the grounds that working mothers had neither the time nor energy to fulfil their homemaking and educative duties.[1] Parental responsibility for their children's religious education was prioritised. Mary Sumner specified what children should know and how it should be taught in articles that elaborated on the rules on the MU card, these included Bible study (Rule 8), parental example (Rules 6 and 7), purity (Rules 1 and 4), and truth (Rule 1). The *MUJ* gave ideas for teaching children religious knowledge, contributed by other authors. The series, 'Mother's Teaching' (Rule 8), ran over several numbers from April 1902 and took the form of a question and answer dialogue between a mother and her children on religious themes.[2]

Readers were also informed on matters of health, including topics such as vaccination, children's clothing and ventilation. There was an overlap between practical advice and moral exhortation. There was a tendency to conflate moral and physical failings which reflected topical eugenic concerns. It was assumed that both could be passed on to the next generation. According to Mary Sumner maternal neglect 'is one cause of the deterioration of the race in some classes'. The January 1905 edition of the *MUJ* included the article, 'Are We Growing Worse? Gleanings for Mothers from the Report on Physical Degeneration 1904'.[3] Ventilation was linked to temperance in the article 'How Wives are to Blame for their Husbands becoming Drunkards'. In addition to bad food, bad temper and slovenly dress, badly-ventilated bedrooms were suggested as a stimulus to drinking.[4] Temperance (Rule 3) also featured repeatedly in the *MUJ* fiction which took the form of cautionary tales. 'A Dangerous Errand' was typical: it recounted the tragedy of brothers

1. Gerry Holloway, '"Let the Women Be Alive!": The Construction of the Married Working Woman in the Industrial Women's Movement, 1890-1914' in *Radical Femininity; Women's Self Representation in the Public Sphere*, ed. Eileen Janes Yeo (Manchester: Manchester University Press, 1998), 173-177. Yeo gives context for Mary Sumner's views and a working-class perspective on them as out of touch with the realities of working-class life.
2. Anon, 'Mother's Teaching', *Mothers' Union Journal*, January 1902, 15-16. The series continued through the year.
3. Sumner, 'Mothers' Work Outside', 131; Anon, 'Are We Growing Worse? Gleanings for Mothers from the Report on Physical Degeneration 1904', *Mothers' Union Journal*, January 1905, 12-15.
4. Lucy A. Hudson, 'How Wives Are to Blame for Their Husbands Becoming Drunkards', ibid., January 1902, 11-12; Mason, *Home Education*, 29-34.

sent to fetch alcohol from the public house where they taste gin. On the way home the inebriated younger child strays into the traffic, is run over and dies, leaving the elder to vow never to touch strong drink.[1] The virtues of thrift and the perils of gambling were also illustrated in story format.[2]

Articles in the *MUJ* indicate its moral perspective and conservative stance on social issues. 'Girls' Professions', a series that considered the advantages and disadvantages of employment open to girls with Rules 1 and 4 in mind, commenced in January 1904 with advocacy by 'an old grandmother' for domestic service as a morally safe occupation. Rule 3, the avoidance of drink, was reflected in a subsequent article in the October 1904 issue, which condemned bar work as morally dangerous on the grounds that girls would be exposed to the twin evils of drink and rough male company: '[W]e beg parents to forbid girls becoming barmaids.'[3] The *MUJ* did not discuss the choice of occupations for boys but did comment on expectations of their behaviour and training. Mary Sumner and writers for the *MUJ* were keen that working-class men should get the MU message. Wives were encouraged to exert 'influence' over husbands but some articles included passages directed at fathers. However, no such presumption of pedagogic authority over middle or upper-class men occurred in the pages of *MIC*.

The pages of the *MUJ* and *MIC* were a medium for pedagogic action in that they sought to inform and shape opinion towards conforming to, and supporting, the gendered and socially stratified religious doxa with which the MU was identified. Readers were invited to identify themselves with the pedagogic authority of the organisation as pedagogic workers, via the Christian upbringing of their children for Church and country. They could also share by association the pedagogic authority invested in their 'foundress' Mary Sumner and other bearers of symbolic religious and educative capital.

1. 'A Dangerous Errand', *MUJ*, April 1902, 42-43. 'Camomile Tea', January 1902, 4-7 and 'Bobbie's Halfpenny', July 1902, 61-63, provide further examples of the temperance theme. Recipes for non-alcoholic drinks were also a regular feature.
2. Anon, 'Three Scenes in a Woman's Life', *Mothers' Union Journal*, January 1903, 5-7; Holloway, '"Let the Women Be Alive!"', 175-176. Holloway comments on the assumption that working-class women needed the advice and patronage of middle-class women who assumed the right to impart superior moral and practical knowledge to their social inferiors.
3. Old Grandmother, 'Girls' Professions', *Mothers' Union Journal*, January 1904.

7.4 Education matters in the Mothers' Union: networking with other agents and organisations; resistance to secular education

As the Mothers' Union expanded, its educational activity also grew in scope. In 1898, two years after the formal centralisation of the MU, Charlotte Yonge and Mrs (later Lady) Jenkyns were made members of Central Council in acknowledgement of the significance of their editorial role in MU publications. In response to the demand for publications and their significant contribution to the income of the MU, in 1906 the Central Council appointed a literature committee, chaired by Lady Horatia Erskine.[1] The success of the MU as a recognised 'brand' is indicated by Porter, Woodward and Erskine, who noted that an advantage of the legal incorporation of the MU as a Church body was that it would allow redress against publishers, or other societies appropriating the name or publications of the MU.[2]

The Mothers' Union worked to endorse the Anglican doxa by collaboration in educational projects with likeminded groups and individuals in religious and educational and philanthropic fields. MU Council member Lucy Soulsby, noted above for her opposition to girls taking degrees, had secured her reputation as the Headmistress of Oxford High, a Girls Public Day School Company establishment. She produced numerous pamphlets on educational and religious themes including *Stray Thoughts for Mothers and Teachers* (1897) and *Talks to Mothers* (1916). Her 1899 book *Two Aspects of Education: Self Control and Fortitude, Humility and Large Heartedness* advocated notions of good womanly conduct in accord with those asserted in the writings of Mary Sumner, Charlotte Yonge and the publications of the MU and GFS.[3]

Cooperation with the Bishop of London's 'Council for the Home Training of Children in Religion' in 1907 marked the progress of the Mothers' Union in the field of education and is noted by Porter, Woodward and Erskine as the genesis of the society's religious education department. The MU had sustained aspirations to influence school curricula for many years previously. 'How the Mothers' Union May

1. Porter, Woodward, and Erskine, *Mary Sumner*, 10, 113. Lady Jenkyns resigned in 1919 after 31 years at the *Mothers' Union Journal*. The publication of the magazines was passed to the S.P.C.K. By 1921, three sub-committees dealing with publications, libraries and education had been established.
2. Ibid., 124. This was accomplished in 1912 and defined the Mothers' Union as a Church body and gave it legal status in holding property, it required a revised constitution and a single membership card.
3. Lucy Soulsby, *Stray Thoughts for Mothers and Teachers* (London: Longmans, 1897); Soulsby, *Talks to Mothers* (London: Longmans & Co., 1916); Soulsby, *Two Aspects of Education* (London: Longmans, Green and Co, 1899).

Help the Moral and Religious Work of Schools' had been on the Central Conference agenda a decade earlier.[1] However, it was not until 1913 that Mrs George Chitty was appointed Correspondent of the Religious Education Scheme. The scheme sought to advise on a syllabus and to produce and vet material suitable for religious teaching. According to the author of *Fifty Years,* 'No publication is passed until it has been read and passed by several people of responsibility and experience.'[2]

The similarity of the ideas of Charlotte Mason, the founder of the Parents' National Education Union, to those expressed by Mary Sumner has been noted above.[3] There was a crossover of personnel between the PNEU and the Mothers' Union at leadership level. Mrs Emeline Francis Steinthal, who had given evidence to the 1909 Gorell Commission on Divorce on behalf of the MU (as noted in Chapter 3), was a close friend of Charlotte Mason and had been involved as co-founder in the PNEU from 1886. She was noted in the July 1912 edition of the PNEU magazine, *The Parents' Review,* along with future MU President, Emily Wilberforce, amongst PNEU Vice Presidents.[4] The previous year, the appointment of MU representatives to serve on the central council of the PNEU formalised this relationship. At the 1912 PNEU conference in Winchester, MU delegates included religious education Correspondent Mrs George Chitty, and Lady Laura Ridding chaired a lecture session on voluntary work for girls.[5] Two years later, in 1915, the MU held a joint conference with members of the Headmistresses' Association 'with a view to cooperation in the religious training of girls'. It was also sympathetic to the Girl Guides, who in 1917 were considered to be 'providing a wide and sound training for the wives and mothers of tomorrow'.[6]

The Mothers' Union also drew on supporters with an expertise and reputation outside the sphere of schooling to advocate, via printed material, its aims and methods. Noted purity campaigner Jane Ellice Hopkins' *Early Training of Girls and Boys: An Appeal to Working Women,*

---

1. Winchester Diocesan Mothers' Union Committee, 'Minute Book 1886-1910', November 22nd 1897.
2. Porter, Woodward, and Erskine, *Mary Sumner*, 131-132; Mothers' Union, *Fifty Years* (Westminster: The Mothers' Union, 1926), 19-20.
3. Sumner, 'When and Why the Mothers' Union Started'.
4. Charlotte Mason, ed., *The Parents' Review*, July 1912. See also the Armitt Library, Charlotte Mason Collection CM 31 and CM51.
5. Porter, Woodward, and Erskine, *Mary Sumner*, 126, 168-169; Charlotte Mason and Henrietta Franklin, 'Parents' National Education Union Children's Gathering 1912' in *Charlotte Mason* (Armitt Library, 1912).
6. Porter, Woodward, and Erskine, *Mary Sumner*, 135, 143.

first published in 1882, was reissued in 1902 with the subtitle *Especially Intended for Mothers' Unions.* It covered themes that Mary Sumner tackled in very much the same way. Mary Sumner's address 'Purity' from the *MUJ* of October 1888 reproduces Ellice Hopkins' advice on separate bathing, the contrivance of segregated sleeping arrangements for boys via the use of hammocks, preventing girls from mixing with loose company in the streets and not sending children to the public house.[1]

In Mary Sumner's writing the notion of promoting religious education was expanded to encompass resistance to what she perceived as the encroachment of secularisation into educational provision. Although parents should be the foremost religious educators of their children, their responsibility extended to watchfulness over other agents or institutions, involved in the religious education of their children. For Mary Sumner, parental influence could and should be exercised to influence public educational provision. The threat to religious education represented by the provision of non-denominational Board Schools, and legislation on the status of voluntary denominational schools, was the subject of Mothers' Union campaigning. MU magazines and publications were used to encourage parental support to promote the position of the Anglican Church in the field of education and, by implication, to reproduce its position in the wider field of power by associating its doxa with national values and identity. Mary Sumner advised parents to 'select schools . . . where the Christian Religion is taught . . . in the forefront and not the background of education'. In a letter to Lady Chichester, she wrote 'win the parents for God [and] they would demand their children should have Christian schools, schoolmasters and teachers'.[2]

Mary Sumner's 1894 article, 'Secular Education', exemplified her concern with 'the struggle which is going on around us in the educational world'. It raised objections to the limited religious education offered in Local Authority Board Schools, claiming that religion was made meaningless by the avoidance of dogma, and that Christian teachers were inhibited from professing their faith through teaching and thus Board School teaching was drifting towards secularisation. Mary Sumner

1. Ellice Hopkins, *On the Early Training of Girls and Boys: An Appeal to Working Women, Etc* (London: Hatchards, 1882). See Appendix 2, Jane Ellice Hopkins; Sumner, 'Purity'. First published in the *Mothers' Union Journal*, 1888. Mary Sumner (as with her appropriation of Charlotte Mason's ideas) makes no acknowledgement of her source.
2. 'What Is the Mothers' Union?' (London: Gardner, Darton & Co., n.d. surmised after 1896); 'Letters to Lady Chichester, Central President of the Mothers' Union' in *Mothers' Union* (Lambeth Palace Library, 1913-15).

warned that: 'Every effort is apparently being made to advance this [Board School] system and starve out the voluntary and denominational schools.' She urged mothers to recognise and resist the 'dangerous wave of infidelity lying behind the whole question of secular education'.[1]

The political dimension of the anti-secular education campaign was manifest in the use of the *MUJ* as a platform to influence public opinion and mobilise support. Its readers were of the class most directly affected by school provision for the masses. Moreover, since their partial enfranchisement in 1867, working-class men represented a category whose allegiance was sought by political interests. In *MUJ* articles, men were reminded that they could use their votes to influence educational provision. The Mothers' Union welcomed the 1902 Education Act. This legislation secured the funding of voluntary denominational schools (that is, those founded by charitable donations, such as the Anglican National Schools) by providing for the cost of running them from within local authority funds levied from property owners as a 'rate'. In April 1903 an *MUJ* article titled 'The Education Act: A Word to Fathers' sought to justify the financial aid allocated to denominational schools 'on the rates' in the 1902 legislation on the grounds that the 'sacrifice' of volunteers, who provided the initial funding for these schools, represented a substantial gift to the nation. The superiority of denominational religious education was asserted: 'It is only in Voluntary Schools that steps are taken to secure one [a head teacher] who really cares about the religion which he teaches.'[2] The following year, 'Passive Resisters' (a term applied to objectors who withheld local payment of rates for Church, or religiously endowed schools) reiterated the justice of supporting the voluntary school rate.[3] The October 1904 edition of the *MUJ* carried the article 'Fathers Please Read This', in which enfranchised men were asked to 'insist on your MP and your various councillors pledging themselves to a hearty support of the Voluntary Schools'.[4]

1. 'Secular Education,' *Mothers in Council*, October 1894, 193-202.
2. 'A Member of a School Board', 'The Education Act a Word to Fathers', *Mothers' Union Journal*, April 1903, 41-42.
3. Anon, 'Passive Resisters', *Mothers' Union Journal*, July 1904, 61. James Murphy, *Church, State and Schools in Britain 1800-1970* (London: Routledge and Kegan Paul, 1971), 66. Passive resistance was a national movement amongst Nonconformists to withhold payment of rates until the 1902 Education Act, seen by them as preferential to Anglicans (and Catholics), was withdrawn.
4. Mary A. Lewis, 'Fathers Please Read This', *Mothers' Union Journal*, October 1904, 74.

Struggle continued over the religious content of the curriculum. Proposed legislation in 1906, by the Liberal government (which broadly represented Nonconformist and anti-denominational educational opinion), which would transfer voluntary schools in single school areas to Local Education Authority control (and thus end denominational teaching) was resisted by Anglicans and Roman Catholics. Mary Sumner consulted Lady Frederick (Lucy) Cavendish, a Liberal but stalwart Anglican, who had served on the Royal Commission on Education 1894, to discuss raising a petition against it.[1] The bill prompted articles in the *MUJ*: 'The Bible in Our Schools', in the April 1906 edition, suggested that there was a danger of Bible teaching being dropped from the curriculum. Further overage in July featured an extract from Mary Sumner's 'Religion in the School' which suggested that 'parents should openly resist proposals to exclude elementary school religion' because it was 'a cruel injury to the character of the child to have it as a mere extra'. In the same issue her 'Responsibilities of Parents' also made a case for religious teaching along denominational lines.[2]

Political views were also manifest in the concern expressed over Sunday school provision. This highlighted Mary Sumner's suspicion of socialism, which she perceived as not only leading to godlessness but, in its advocacy for class struggle, constituting an incitement to overturn the social order. She feared the 'peril of Anti-Christian Socialist Sunday schools', and the quality of Sunday school provision was the subject of a Lambeth Conference resolution in 1908. Her 1911 leaflet, *A Grave Peril*, which alerted parents to socialist encroachment on religious education, returned to this theme. The strength of concern felt on the issue in the MU is indicated by the reprint of the leaflet in 1921.[3] The position of Mary Sumner and the MU on the quality of Sunday schools and secularisation supported the official stance of the Anglican Church. The

1. Mary Sumner and Lady Frederick Cavendish, 'Correspondence' in *Mothers' Union* (Lambeth Palace Library); see Murphy, *Church, State and Schools*, 96-99. The proposed Liberal bill, which was passed in the Commons but blocked in the Lords, would have ended the public subsidy of schools with a denominational foundation and thus would have reduced denominational teaching.
2. Anon, 'The Bible in Our Schools', *Mothers' Union Journal*, April 1906, 24-27; Mary Sumner, 'Religion in the School', ibid., July 1906, 36; 'Responsibilities of Parents', *Mothers' Union Journal*, July 1906, 57.
3. 'Letter to Dearest Minnie, Lady Addington Anti Christian Sunday Schools' in Mothers' Union (Lambeth Palace Library); 'Letters to Mrs Maude,' in Mothers' Union (Lambeth Palace Library), November 17th 19?; Porter, Woodward, and Erskine, Mary Sumner, 64. [http://www.lambethconference.org/resolutions/1908/1908-14.cfm, accessed July 12th 2013].

resolutions passed at the Lambeth Conference of 1908,[1] which addressed secularisation, teaching of explicit doctrine, and the role of parents, which reflected Mary Sumner's agenda, suggest that her activism had been successful in positioning the MU in the educational work of the Church. This position in the overlapping fields of Anglicanism and education was a vindication of Mary Sumner's conviction that the MU 'could not possibly stand outside a battle for the children's faith'.[2]

7.5 Synopsis: Mary Sumner's manoeuvres in the field of education

In founding the MU, Mary Sumner entered not only the field of religion, but also the field of education.

Her educational manoeuvres were significant towards securing the field position of the Mothers' Union within the Church and the acknowledgement of the capital of women as educators. The genesis of the MU occurred in the context of the acceptance of female engagement in the field of philanthropic work. This allowed Mary Sumner, and women similarly habituated, a means to move, via philanthropy, into the field of education as an organised body. The 1870 school board legislation extended opportunities for women's participation in the field of local political and educational policy, which had hitherto been available only to a few women. This legislation also offered Mary Sumner an opportunity to exploit a contest in the field of education to demonstrate the capital value of women's pedagogic action in support of Anglican doxa.

Mary Sumner's emphasis on the acquisition of intangible symbolic capital through approved conduct, characterised by reputation, piety and good parenting, rather than the alleviation of physical want, gives emphasis to the educational character of the MU. In her aspiration to modify behaviour by educating mothers in childrearing according to religious principles, and the production of material to disseminate its message, the MU can be located in the sub-field of popular education. Its association with Anglican field manoeuvres relative to the provision of schooling and higher education also indicates that the MU should be considered within the field of education.

The initiation of literature and education committees reflects expanding activity in these areas and can be seen as manoeuvres towards advancement in the field of education and the related sub-field of educational publishing. Whereas *MIC*, which reached an audience

1. [http://www.lambethconference.org/resolutions/1908, accessed September 25th 2015].
2. Porter, Woodward, and Erskine, *Mary Sumner*, 64.

from the socially dominant group, advantaged in the field of power and endorsed by the doxa of the Anglican Church, was symbolically violent in its perpetration of a gendered religious arbitrary, the *MUJ*, in its attempt to secure the misrecognition and compliance of the less advantaged to the doxa of the Church, also perpetrated symbolic violence in relation to class. MU magazines made a substantial and sustained contribution to the pedagogic work of the Anglican Church.

The use of printed materials enhanced the pedagogic authority Mary Sumner had accrued by prior public speaking. Pedagogic authority was also enhanced by the widespread circulation of her name in association with organisations (notably the MU and the Church, but also the GFS and CETS) identified with attributes invested with high symbolic capital, including motherhood, purity, temperance and piety. The authority of MU publications was endorsed by drawing on contributors with existing symbolic capital and pedagogic authority, such as Charlotte Yonge, who embodied religious, literary, and educational capital, or Lucy Soulsby, who had achieved distinction in the sub-field of girls' education. Collaboration on educational initiatives with bodies such as the CETS and PNEU also endorsed pedagogic authority in a mutual exchange of capital and pursuit of common goals.

Mary Sumner's most overt engagement with the field of power in relation to education was in the stance she took on the secularisation of education. Through *MIC*, other publications, and in particular through the *MUJ*, which addressed a substantial working-class audience, the MU claimed the necessity of denominational religious instruction in order to be fully educated. It asserted the superiority of Anglican doctrine and thus its superiority over secular or other doctrinal curricula. MU publications, which expressed the views of Mary Sumner, took a stance in support of the Anglican Church in its contest with the state for power in the field of education. Articles sought to mobilise readers' opinions in the choice of schools and in interaction with politicians. Education in Anglicanism was also supported by exhortations to home religious education and through the provision of exemplars of Anglican doctrinal teaching. Whilst it is not possible to evaluate the impact of the MU message on the secularisation of education, the Anglican Church did gain concessions from the legislature on the inclusion of a religious syllabus in Board Schools (1870) and LEA (Local Education Authority) Schools (1902) and secured the denominational integrity of voluntary (Anglican- or other denomination-funded) provision of elementary education. The MU's support for the position of the Anglican Church in the field of education worked to the mutual advantage of both organisations. The resolutions passed by the Lambeth Conference in 1908, which reflected the anti-secularisation agenda that Mary Sumner had pursued for decades, constitute an movement towards recognition of the pedagogic authority of women as individual mothers and also collectively through the MU, and indicate a degree of women's progress in the field of power.

Mary Sumner's view of women as educators was entirely compatible with notions of superior 'womanly' capital recognised within the Anglican Church. In return for their mis/recognition of the superiority of Anglican doxa, MU mothers were offered several symbolic 'gifts'. These included identification with educational expertise and the assurance of doing the best for their children by protecting them from sin, thereby securing their future salvation. Readers of *MIC* and the *MUJ* could identify themselves as 'Churchwomen' who belonged to the moral elite. They might also identify with the 'Foundress' as a celebrity recognised beyond the MU for her pedagogic authority. More tangible rewards offered through the society's publications were education in aspects of childrearing, hints on the religious education of children, advice on appropriate reading and engagement with, and the opportunity to identify with, a body with a 'voice' beyond the home on topical issues such as schooling.

Mary Sumner's activism through the Mothers' Union may be seen to contribute to, and reflect modifications in, horizons of possibility relating to women and education. She was in favour of popular educational self-culture and a vociferous advocate for education for motherhood, but the pages of *MIC* illustrate some ambivalence towards the schooling and higher education of middle- and upper-class women. This ambivalence reflected a diversity of opinion amongst MU activists on appropriate curricula and educational setting but, despite this, the gendered (and socially stratified) doxic notions of womanhood misrecognised as being invested with distinct 'natural' characteristics and contingent roles as helpmeet, carer and exemplar of religious and moral sensibility were not subject to challenge.

Mothers' Union publications may also be seen in the context of the expansion of recognised women's spheres of interest and activity. They articulated a collective women's viewpoint on public affairs and also offered individuals (both professional writers and amateurs) a respectable platform for articulating ideas in a public forum. Whilst Mary Sumner and the MU did not make radical claims for women's education, they may be seen to contribute to some enlargement in the interpretation of esteemed womanly capital and to the familiarisation of women invested with pedagogic authority. Mary Sumner herself achieved unprecedented recognition amongst a mass audience and in the field of religion as a pedagogic authority.

Mary Sumner with a portrait of her husband George c. 1915

Chapter 8
Mary Sumner: Agency and Constraint, Reproduction, Symbolic Violence and Changes in the Doxa

The introduction to the book identified the aim of analysing Mary Sumner's negotiation of constraint and agency and her position in the upholding and transaction of power across domestic, local and global spaces in relation to the fields of religion, mission and education with motherhood as a connecting theme. Agency implies subjective capability and the capacity to act towards self-chosen goals within and across the permeable boundaries of private and public space.[1] As this involves 'the negotiation of social and cultural circumstances and internalising or performing to received stereotypes',[2] agency relates not just to the ability to act but to the claims of value relating to activities and qualities which may be drawn on to validate actions and identities. Whilst it is related to self-realisation, agency may be enacted on behalf of other agents or institutions.

Any attempt to claim to 'know' Mary Sumner's personal feelings in relation to the satisfaction or otherwise of her life must be tentative, especially when working from perspectival sources. However, Bourdieu's analytical 'thinking tools' of habitus, field and capital, provide 'a way of

1. Mary P. Ryan, 'The Public and the Private Good across the Great Divide in Women's History', *Journal of Women's History* 15, no. 1, (2003): 10-27; Simon Morgan, *A Victorian Woman's Place: Public Culture in the Nineteenth Century* (London: Tauris Academic Studies, 2007). See also Sue Morgan 'Theorising Feminist History: A Thirty Year Retrospective', *Women's History Review* 18, no. 3, (2009): 381-407; Linda Kerber, 'Separate Spheres, Female Worlds, Woman's Place; the Rhetoric of Women's History', *Journal of American History* 75, no. 1 (1988); Amanda Vickery, '"Golden Age to Separate Spheres": A Review of the Categories and Chronology of English Women's History' in *Gender and History in Western Europe*, ed. Robert Shoemaker and Mary Vincent (London: Addison-Wesley Longman, 1998).
2. Sarah Jane Aiston, 'Women, Education and Agency 1600-2000: An Historical Perspective' in *Women, Education and Agency*, ed. Jean Spence, Sarah Jane Aiston, and Maureen Meikle (London and New York: Routledge, 2010), 6.

investigating the link between lived lives and the choices in intellectual work with the context, both institutional and social, that structures and shapes those choices'.[1] Bourdieu's approach allows an analysis of Mary Sumner as a historically situated agent negotiating constraint and agency. The categories of habitus, field and capital applied to Mary Sumner locate her values, aims and activism in the context of networks of other agents (such as churchmen and upper and middle-class women) and associations both formal and informal (the GFS for example) in a gendered horizon of possibilities. The theory of reproduction and the concepts of symbolic violence and misrecognition address how arbitrary ascendancies of power such as class and gender are imposed and the knowledge and values favourable to the dominant group legitimised.[2] I draw on these concepts to position Mary Sumner relative to agency and constraint, as dominated and/or dominating. I also position her in relation to the reproduction or negotiation of power with attention to change or modification in relation to the apparently self-evident cultural practice and understanding of social reality encapsulated in the term doxa, which informed gendered horizons of possibility accruing to women.[3]

Mary Sumner's habituation (her acquisition of beliefs and notions of appropriate conduct) as an Anglican 'Churchwoman' and popular educator illustrates the relationship of habitus, field and capital in informing her horizon of possibilities. Bourdieu's understanding of field provides a way to envisage social structures, institutions and spheres of activity such as the Church, religion, mission and education, in which Mary Sumner as an agent made meaning and realised her activism. As

1. Helen M. Gunter, 'Purposes and Positions in the Field of Education Management: Putting Bourdieu to Work', *Educational Management Administration and Leadership* 30, no. 1 (2002): 9.
2. Pierre Bourdieu, Jean-Claude Passeron, and Richard Nice, *Reproduction in Education, Society and Culture* (London: Sage Publications, 1977).
3. Pierre Bourdieu, *Masculine Domination* (Cambridge: Polity Press, 2001); Lisa Adkins and Beverley Skeggs, *Feminism after Bourdieu* (Oxford: Blackwell, 2004); Beate Krais, 'Gender and Symbolic Violence: Female Oppression in the Light of Pierre Bourdieu's Theory of Social Practice' in *Bourdieu: Critical Perspectives*, ed. Craig Calhoun, Edward LiPuma, and Moishe Postone (Cambridge: Cambridge Polity Press, 1993); Terry Lovell, 'Thinking Feminism with and against Bourdieu' in *Reading Bourdieu on Society and Culture*, ed. Bridget Fowler (Oxford: Blackwell, 2000); Toril Moi, *'What is a Woman?' And Other Essays* (Oxford: Oxford University Press, 1999); Joan W. Scott, 'Gender: A Useful Category of Historical Analysis', *American Historical Review* 91, no. 5 (1986).

sites of power, fields inform assumptions of value and belief and are sites where hierarchies of knowledge are contested and meaning established. This is exemplified in Mary Sumner's prioritisation of Anglican capital; her manoeuvres in the field to promote it; her claims to authority drawn from embodying recognised capital attributes and in her association with agents and institutions invested with authority. The capital recognised as of worth by agents whose pedagogic action contributed to her habituation was delineated by the fields (social, religious, educational and philanthropic) in which they were 'players' and to which they claimed allegiance.

Mary Sumner's life illustrates how the possession of capital secured advantage in fields where it was recognised for agents acknowledged as possessing it. Recognised capital could be transacted to secure pedagogic authority, the right to speak in and for the field. Pedagogic work by structures (family, institutions), and pedagogic action by agents, aimed to secure misrecognition of the legitimacy of the capital asserted despite its arbitrary nature. This imposition by dominant groups of preferred values, codes of behaviour and varieties of knowledge favourable to their interests, deemed by Bourdieu the cultural arbitrary, involved the enactment of symbolic violence. Misrecognition of legitimacy required complicity with symbolic violence from the dominated group. Yet the enactment of symbolic violence was also a variety of complicity because the arbitrary nature of the doxa is misrecognised as legitimate by its enacting agents.[1]

Members of Mary Sumner's network, which included religious specialists with high field positions in the Anglican Church, prioritised capital delineated within the field of Anglicanism above that of religious non-believers, other religions and other denominations. Men and women habituated to misrecognise the superiority of Anglicanism as 'owning the goods of salvation' asserted the value of the rewards accruing to complicity with its delineated notions of capital (doctrinal orthodoxy, piety, chastity) and were active (according to gendered parameters) in field manoeuvres to uphold it. This pedagogic action also served to further their own acquisition of symbolic capital as delineated in the religious and social field in which they were located and was thus conducive to self-realisation and transactable into pedagogic authority. Anglicanism was advantageously positioned in the social field and field of power because

1. Frank Poupeau, 'Reasons for Domination: Bourdieu Versus Habermas' in *Reading Bourdieu on Society and Culture*, ed. Bridget Fowler (Oxford Blackwell, 2000); Pierre Bourdieu, *The Logic of Practice* (Cambridge: Polity, 1990), 20, 58, 54.

it was aligned with the interests of the dominant upper and upper-middle classes to which Mary Sumner's network claimed allegiance and was drawn upon to legitimise their arbitrary advantage. For Mary Sumner, 'Church work' was an authorised and accessible sphere for activism in which she could find support from amongst a network of agents with a shared investment in (and possession of) religious and social capital.

Arbitrary notions of gendered difference accruing to women as a category place Mary Sumner as the object of symbolic violence. Mary Sumner's organisational activism commenced against the context of a predominant but contested and defensive Anglican religious doxa that upheld, and misrecognised as legitimate, the advantage of a dominant patriarchy invested with religious authority, educational advantage, economic power, superior legal status, and, ultimately, the means of physical coercion. Anglicanism, in accord with the majority of Christian denominations, asserted divine authority to justify the arbitrary gendered ascription of characteristics to both men and women. This informed notions of desirable capital and legitimised contingent prohibitions and expectations of role. Desirable attributes of Christian womanhood accrued around the conflation of woman with motherhood and prioritised domestic responsibility, sexual continence, and submission to patriarchal authority. The authoritative and dominant positions ascribed to men were euphemised by the notions of protectiveness and chivalry, gendered capital attributes that appear, according to the perspectival sources, to have been upheld by the men in Mary Sumner's life.

Mary Sumner's simultaneous positioning as object of, and agent of, symbolic violence is demonstrated in her advocacy for chastity and the sacrament of marriage and in her apparent complicity with patriarchal authority in family and the Church. However, 'woman' as a category was mediated by class, a significant factor in Mary Sumner's horizon of possibilities.[1] Pedagogic action by agents and the pedagogic work of structures informed dispositions of habitus complicit with the advantage of the dominant group. As in the case of arbitrary understanding of gender, Mary Sumner accepted social stratification as 'the natural order'. Social stratification was also mis/recognised as legitimate by those in the Mothers' Union who were its objects and Mary enacted symbolic violence in her assumption of authority over men and women of lesser social status. Yet, her insistence on the distance between the 'good' women of the MU and GFS from the deficit model of sexually incontinent women,

1. Joan Wallach Scott, *Gender and the Politics of History* (New York: Columbia University Press, 1999); Sue Morgan, ed. *The Feminist History Reader* (London: Routledge, 2006); Moi, *What Is a Woman?*, 291, 293.

and her avowal of the distinctive contribution of women in the moral and educative sphere of home life, may be interpreted as advocacy for an increased recognition of the capital worth of activity assigned to women. In the context of the struggle for ascendancy by interest groups, factions or denominations played out within fields, this may be seen as a manoeuvre towards increasing, although within gendered parameters, the pedagogic authority of woman as a category that would advance women in the religious field. By founding an Anglican organisation, run by and for women, Mary Sumner advanced the field position of women in the Anglican Church. Through the MU, pedagogic action to support Anglicanism in its contest with other denominations for 'the goods of salvation' was exercised.[1]

Religion may be seen as the decisive element in Mary Sumner's habitus and the advancement of preferred religious doxa informed and responded to manoeuvres in the related fields of mission and education that, like habitus, field and capital, may be visualised as overlapping. Shared notions of capital served to inform mutually advantageous activities or manoeuvres within and across the fields and sub-fields.[2] Mary Sumner's preferred religious doctrine identified the symbolic capital to be gained from evangelical outreach with the aim of winning converts through 'mission', domestically, locally and in more distant spaces. The use of 'mission' is an example of the appropriation of language associated with institutions or agents of distinction that is recognised as invested with capital. By using such authorised language, Mary Sumner and others in her network claimed to speak for and assumed the authority accruing to religion and to agents invested, by virtue of the recognition of their capital, with distinction in the field.[3] Drawing on the distinction attributed to missionaries, the religious terminology of mission was applied by Mary Sumner, those in her networks, and others

1. Pierre Bourdieu, 'Genesis and Structure of the Religious Field', *Comparative Social Research* 13, no. 1 (1991); *Practical Reason: On the Theory of Action* (Cambridge: Polity Press, 1998), Appendix; Remarks on the Economy of the Church, 124-126; Terry Rey, 'Marketing the Goods of Salvation: Bourdieu on Religion', *Religion* 34, no. 4 (2004).
2. Margaret Keck and Kathryn A. Sikkink, *Advocacy Networks in International Politics Activists Beyond Borders* (Ithaca and London: Cornell University Press, 1998); see also Eckhardt Fuchs, 'Networks and the History of Education', *Paedagogica Historica* 42, no. 2 (2007) for a discussion of the concept of exchange theory.
3. Pierre Bourdieu, 'Authorised Language: The Social Conditions for the Effectiveness of Ritual Discourse' in *Language and Symbolic Power* (Cambridge: Polity Press, 1991); Terry Rey, *Bourdieu on Religion: Imposing Faith and Legitimacy* (London: Equinox Publishing, 2007).

of similar habitus, to legitimise the prescribed domestic role of women as maternal 'angels' in the house, a position of complicity with the symbolic violence perpetrated by the dominant patriarchal interest served by the doxa of Anglicanism. The conflation of women with mothers in a dominant discourse of motherhood allocated symbolic 'maternal' capital to the respectable unmarried woman.[1] The appropriation of authorised language also 'sanctified' this maternal capital so that it could be transacted as pedagogic authority for women invested with it. Similarly, the term mission was applied to the symbolically violent imposition of doxa through philanthropic endeavour, activity complicit with doxically framed notions of the 'maternal' character of women. This appropriation of the religious terminology of mission served to enhance the capital accruing to participation in philanthropic activity that could be drawn on as a source of pedagogic authority.[2]

Mary Sumner's association of the Mothers' Union with Church work overseas supported Christianity and specifically Anglicanism, in the competitive transnational religious field. The sponsorship of women missionary workers (who exemplified gendered notions of desirable capital as self-sacrificing, valorous workers for Christianity) by the MU, initiated by Mary Sumner, was instrumental towards securing their position in the religious sub-field of missionary work. This also served to secure the field position of the MU as a body within the Church, recognised for its pedagogic action in support of overseas mission. Mary Sumner's field manoeuvre of associating with women missionary workers as religious specialists invested with high religious capital and contingent pedagogic authority enabled capital by association to be claimed for the women of the MU. Exemplars of 'English Christian womanhood', capital attributes delineated within the Anglican field, could claim pedagogic authority from upholding its doxa whether they were colonial settlers, transnational expatriates or women 'at home'. This also served to advance the field position of the MU by indicating the capital that members could share in by association, so enhancing the desirability of membership. Overseas manoeuvres (like those 'at home') also served to reinforce Mary Sumner's pedagogic authority by identifying her as the personification of 'her' religious organisation and the capital invested in it.

1. Eileen Janes Yeo, 'Some Contradictions of Social Motherhood' in *Mary Wollstonecraft: 200 Years of Feminisms*, ed. Eileen Janes Yeo (London and New York: Rivers Oram Press, 1997).
2. Alison Twells, *The Civilising Mission and the English Middle Class, 1792-1850: The 'Heathen' at Home and Overseas* (Basingstoke: Palgrave Macmillan, 2009).

Engagement in the religious field overseas intersected with manoeuvres within the wider field of power. The Anglican Church sought to reproduce its advantaged position in the wider field of power in the context of British intervention overseas. Just as imperialists, who included Mary Sumner and members of her network, notably Laura Ridding and Ellen Joyce, saw the propagation of what they regarded as a superior religious doxa as a legitimising rationale for the imposition of a political arbitrary, the Anglican Church was reciprocally complicit with the symbolic violence enacted through imperial rule. Through drawing on notions of patriotism and imperial destiny, the Anglican Church sought to claim capital by association and so to reinforce the legitimacy of the religious arbitrary and thus revitalise the Church 'at home'.[1] Likewise, Mary Sumner and other speakers and writers for the MU (and also the GFS) laid claim to the capital associated with overseas endeavour. The rhetoric of patriotism and empire was combined with a discourse of motherhood to assert the capital of women as, in the case of the GFS, 'civilising' pioneer colonists or, as emphasised by Mary Sumner, the maternal educators of imperial citizens possessing superior moral capital and 'race' attributes.[2] Whilst this manoeuvre was pedagogic work towards upholding and legitimising national pre-eminence in the imperial field of power, it also served to advance the field position of the MU.

Through the Mothers' Union, Mary Sumner offered symbolic gifts (membership of an 'elite' category and 'the goods of salvation') to 'different' ethnicities complicit with the Christian/Anglican doxa.[3] This perceived inclusiveness was celebrated as an indicator of MU success. Yet Mary Sumner also enacted an implicit embedded racialisation by conflating ethnicity and religious and cultural difference into the category of 'race'.[4] She and members of her network were agents of symbolic violence in imposing a doxa which prioritised capital attributes that were predominantly located in persons also embodying 'whiteness'. However, colour was not the single arbiter of the ascription of racial stereotypes, as Mary also made categorical judgements about European peoples.

---

1. A.N. Porter, *The Imperial Horizons of British Protestant Missions, 1880-1914* (Grand Rapids, Michigan: Wm. B. Eerdmans, 2003).
2. Julia Bush, *Edwardian Ladies and Imperial Power* (London: Leicester University Press, 2000).
3. Rey, 'Marketing the Goods of Salvation: Bourdieu on Religion'.
4. Julia Bush, 'Edwardian Ladies and the "Race" Dimensions of British Imperialism', *Women's Studies International Forum* 21, no. 3 May-June (1998).

Symbolic violence was not only 'perpetrated' on 'other' religions, cultures and 'races'. Contrast with the religious, social and cultural 'oppression' of indigenous women was drawn on to affirm the capital of the Christian woman and served to disguise her own constraint by gender and class. Women 'at home' could draw, by implication, symbolic capital from association with the superior attributes of 'civilised', 'white', Christian and 'English'.[1] For the upper and middle classes, as exemplified by members of Mary Sumner's network, the assertion of symbolic maternal capital in the context of an empire, with the matriarchal Queen Victoria as its figurehead, opened a space in the wider field of power in which they could be active and manoeuvre to advance their personal capital.[2]

Mary Sumner upheld religious (specifically Anglican) doxa in prioritising religious knowledge and in considering educational capital of limited worth unless it included a Christian religious dimension: the MU was educational in intent and practice. Mary Sumner was an agent of symbolic violence in seeking to impose on others conformity to the cultural arbitrary to which she (and others of similar habitus) claimed allegiance and misrecognised as legitimate;[3] yet, in her insistence on the recognition of mothers as educators, and the strategies she deployed to enhance maternal pedagogic authority, sources of empowerment for them may be discerned.

Capital delineated in the religious field was transacted to authorise mothers as participants in the educational field. If the habituation of children, claimed by Mary Sumner to be invested with the symbolic capital of the highest order 'as gifts from God', into religion was important, it followed that mothers needed to be educated in order to accomplish this role. The notion that Christian capital was an essential attribute for compliant citizenship (which transacted religious capital into the social field and the wider field of power) was also used to validate the significance of mothers as educators. Mothers should be recognised for the significance of their pedagogic action in upholding Church and nation. Maternal educative capital, as envisaged by Mary Sumner, was vested in

1. Jane Rendall, 'The Condition of Women, Women's Writing and the Empire in Nineteenth Century Britain' in *At Home with the Empire Metropolitan Culture and the Imperial World*, ed. Catherine Hall and Sonia O. Rose (Cambridge: Cambridge University Press, 2006).
2. Bush, *Edwardian Ladies and Imperial Power*; Lisa Chilton, *Agents of Empire: British Female Migration to Canada and Australia, 1860s-1930* (Toronto; Buffalo: University of Toronto Press, 2007).
3. John Hurt, *Education in Evolution Church, State, Society and Popular Education 1800-1870* (London: Rupert Hart-Davis, 1971).

the possession of the moral attributes and Biblical knowledge of Christian womanhood, delineated within the field of religion. Maternal educative capital was also vested in the possession of the pedagogic expertise in childrearing. Both aspects were asserted as sources of pedagogic authority. The pedagogic work and field manoeuvres of Mary Sumner were dedicated to substantiating and securing recognition of these claims, firstly, amongst mothers themselves. A further dimension of pedagogic action pursued through personal lobbying, public speaking, correspondence, and publications was the education of the clergy, fathers, and agents with power in the wider field to recognise the worth of maternal educative capital.

Mary Sumner valued literacy, varieties of 'culture' and intellectual achievement. She used educational capital to validate maternal/womanly pedagogic authority. Mary Sumner and the women activists she recruited to forward the Mothers' Union classified themselves as 'educated' and therefore authorised to speak both for themselves and on behalf of the 'less educated' (a category which translated into working-class or indigenous women overseas). MU publications drew on contributors likewise invested with pedagogic authority. They included 'experts' in fields where women were gaining access, such as educationalist Lucy Soulsby, moral campaigner Ellice Hopkins and writer Charlotte Yonge. Contemporary developments in pedagogic theory received a positive response. Mary Sumner's emphasis on the capital worth of children informed an attitude sympathetic to pedagogy which envisaged the child as a person and used positive strategies for reinforcing behaviour and fostering learning. Through the pages of MU publications, mothers across social classes were offered not only the affirmation of their possession of symbolic religious capital but fellowship in a community of mothers. MU magazines kept the attention of readers focused on missionary and MU activity in distant places.[1] Mothers could also gain practical pedagogic advice and draw symbolic capital from the notion that childrearing was expert work.

The use of printed media that educated informally through news, stories and informative articles to a mass audience, locates Mary Sumner as a popular educator.[2] She exploited increasing literacy to promote her

1. Susan Thorne, 'Religion and Empire at Home' in *At Home with the Empire Metropolitan Culture and the Imperial World*, ed. Catherine Hall and Sonia O. Rose (Cambridge: Cambridge University Press, 2006); Ruth Watts, 'Education, Empire and Social Change in Nineteenth Century England', *Paedagogica Historica* 45, no. 6 (2009).
2. David Wardle, *English Popular Education, 1780-1970* (London: Cambridge University Press, 1970).

notions of desirable capital and as a means to counter the perceived corrupting influence of material considered 'undesirable'. The scope of MU publications in circulation and spatial distribution, and as representative of the voice of a women's organisation, may be considered as indicative of a substantial presence in the sub-field of educational publishing. The *MUJ* in particular was innovative as a special interest 'quality' publication devoted to the interest of working-class mothers.

Mary Sumner's prioritisation of maternal home education and informal education may be seen as a manoeuvre to secure the transmission of Anglican religious doxa against institutional encroachment, where religious doxa (if any) might not meet preferred standards. An overt example of this can be seen in Mary Sumner's canvassing the support of mothers and enfranchised fathers, through the pages of the *MUJ*, for the place of the Anglican Church in formal education. For Mary Sumner, the provision of state elementary schooling was a threat not only to Anglicanism but also to the recognition of religious capital in the field of education and the wider field of power.

Prioritising Anglican religious doxa also informed Mary Sumner's attitude and the stance adopted in MU publications to the expansion of curricula for middle and upper-class girls in school and the emergence of institutional higher education for women.[1] Formal education was largely approved (although with some diversity of interpretation on appropriate curricula) if moral and religious 'womanly' attributes were not compromised. Whilst assuming the destiny of women was as wives and mothers, in line with the dominant gendered arbitraries of Church and social practice, education was agreed as desirable capital for the successful accomplishment of this role and the participation of women in related 'caring' or 'educative' spheres was considered legitimate.

An understanding of agency as the ability to act (notwithstanding a degree of circumstantial constraint) towards the realisation of (self-defined) goals[2] can be applied to Mary Sumner and to other women within her network, whose gendered horizons of possibility accommodated, albeit within gendered parameters, opportunities for the acquisition of symbolic capital and the exercise of a degree of authority. Mary Sumner was richly rewarded with symbolic capital for conformity with arbitrary, but doxically approved, notions of gendered religious and social 'womanly' conduct informed by and misrecognised as legitimate

1. Joan Burstyn, *Victorian Education and the Ideal of Womanhood* (London: Croom Helm, 1980).
2. Aiston, 'Women, Education and Agency 1600-2000, An Historical Perspective', 1-8.

in her habitus. This symbolic capital gave opportunities for further capital acquisition and delineated and authorised a space for 'useful' action and agency that allowed Mary Sumner to move into the field of the Anglican Church and the field of popular education. By working within notions of gendered capital delineated within Anglicanism and transacting pedagogic authority from it, she was able to move from the limited localised authority of the helpmeet to a clergyman to become the iconic leader of a worldwide women's organisation, which achieved an acknowledged voice in the Church, a position in the field of popular education and a distinctive presence in the social fabric of the nation, with reach into settler colonies and empire. Mary Sumner achieved recognition for embodying the religiously sanctioned notions of capital she promoted through the MU. She appeared to personify the rewards it promised for complicity with these notions of good womanhood.

Mary Sumner's activism was strongly facilitated by her network location in relation to the field of the Anglican Church and agents with positions of advantage within it (including her supportive husband George). Contextual circumstances, such as the recognition of women's role in philanthropy, aspirations for education and towards citizenship and the expansion of empire also framed her activism.[1] However, Mary Sumner's role in the rapid growth and extensive spread of the MU should not be overlooked. An agent located between other agents and structures, she was highly effective in her negotiation of horizons of possibility towards realising her aims. In her ability to mobilise those of similar habitus by drawing on, transacting and accumulating recognised notions of capital towards pedagogic authority and field position, she operated as a successful 'player' in the gendered fields of religion, mission and education in which her activism was realised.[2] Mary Sumner also sustained her trajectory of activism over a considerable period of time and the sources consulted assert not only her tenacity in publicising the MU message but her persuasiveness as a speaker and writer and ability to suggest the personal inclusiveness of her message.

The degree of agency Mary Sumner achieved on behalf of other women raises questions about working-class and indigenous women, whose voices are elusive in early Mothers' Union records and Mary Sumner's archive. This limitation in evidence deserves further investigation. The absence of the voices of working class and indigenous women reflects

1. Sean Gill, *Women and the Church of England: From the Eighteenth Century to the Present* (London: Society for Promoting Christian Knowledge, 1994), 63, 84, 91, 104.
2. Bourdieu and Wacquant, *An Invitation*, 120; Bourdieu, *Logic of Practice*, 66.

Mary Sumner's assumption of authority over, and right to speak for, those of assumed lesser status. Not only were working-class and indigenous women objects of a symbolically violent imposition of doxa but their complicity with it accrued capital that was largely symbolic. However, the discourse of motherhood offered by Mary Sumner to women whose horizons of possibility were framed by gendered assumptions and circumstances that allocated them a domestic role was an assertion of its value.[1] The MU also represented mothers collectively in an authoritative Church organisation, personified by a woman of distinction, which amplified women's voices in the wider field of power. Membership numbers confirm that Mary Sumner's MU did appeal to large numbers of women.

Mary Sumner's activism was located in a context of imperial expansion, educational development, the contested orthodoxies of (religious) belief and the negotiating of access to citizenship, mediated by gender and class. In respect of women advantaged by class, the MU offered a field of action that built on the accommodation of women as philanthropic and educational activists. It opened a sub-field for women with aspirations towards leadership and 'influence' on religious, social and national life, which despite diverse positions held on the franchise, translates as an appetite for power. Through the MU, such women were offered an organised network of likeminded contacts and a platform for their views. As speakers for the Church, they were invested with pedagogic authority. Access, via an organised body, into the field of Anglicanism represented a significant expansion of women's authority and could be drawn on to legitimise engagement in other fields, notably in relation to empire.

Thinking with Bourdieu locates Mary Sumner as an agent temporally and spatially located in a network of other agents and structures and demonstrates that she was simultaneously an object of, and an agent of, domination. As a woman she was categorically disadvantaged by the religious and social doxa; yet through her misrecognition of its legitimacy and her complicity with this arbitrary imposition of notions of gendered capital, she was able to accrue symbolic capital and transact it towards considerable pedagogic authority and distinction in her field. Her position amongst the socially dominant group alleviated, to an extent, the disadvantage of gender. In her pedagogic work on behalf of reproducing the power vested in Church, class and country, she was an agent of symbolic violence.

1. Cordelia Moyse, *A History of the Mothers' Union: Women, Anglicanism and Globalisation, 1876-2008* (Woodbridge: Boydell Press, 2009). Moyse asserts the spiritual sustenance offered by the MU.

Mary Sumner's life trajectory illustrates how pedagogic action, by agents and institutions (family and Church), informs habitus. For Mary Sumner, received pedagogic action gave her an internalised unquestioning conviction (that is, misrecognition) of the legitimacy of the gendered cultural arbitraries of Church, class, nation and empire that she sought to uphold through her own pedagogic action. For Mary Sumner, there was a close accord with internalised, misrecognised cultural arbitraries and opportunities for agency and self-realisation through the acquisition and transaction of capital. Her initial horizon of possibility allowed for the acquisition of capital transactable for pedagogic authority and thus the enlargement of her horizons of possibility. The opportunity thus allowed her suggests that her experience may indeed have been 'a wonderful life'.

In relation to agency, change, and constraint, Mary Sumner simultaneously occupies diverse positions. In securing the recognition of women as an organised body representing the perspective of Christian women, Sumner opened the way for further enlargement of women's horizons of possibility and the engagement with public affairs, so evident in the issues engaged in by the contemporary MU.[1] In so doing she may also be perceived as agent of change. Conversely, the field position conceded to the MU by the Church may be regarded as constraining in that the women's voice it articulated was subject to upholding a religious doxa that was fearful of women's sexuality and theological authority.[2] In upholding religiously framed notions of womanhood that reflected patriarchal domination and class differentiation, Mary Sumner was an agent of symbolic violence and constraint but also subject to it. Yet as an activist recognised worldwide who exercised control towards the achievement of self-defined goals, she was an empowered individual agent. Mary Sumner was, according to Bourdieu's analogy, a highly effective 'player' in the field of religion who accrued and transacted her capital to be highly innovative in achieving lasting global personal distinction in the Anglican religious field. She exemplifies what Gail Malmgreen has identified as 'the central paradox of religion as opiate and embodiment of institutional sexism and religion as transcendent and liberating force'.[3]

1. Moyse, *History of the Mothers' Union*, 252.
2. Lucy Bland, 'Purifying the Public World: Feminist Vigilantes in Late Victorian England', *Women's History Review* 1, no. 3 (1992): 377-412.
3. Gail Malmgreen, *Religion in the Lives of English Women, 1760-1930* (London: Croom Helm, 1986), 7.

Tables

Table 1: Activists in the GFS and Mothers' Union

Activist	Mothers' Union (MU)	Girls' Friendly Society (GFS)	Bishop as Spouse
Mrs Mary Sumner	Foundress Diocesan President 1885-1915 Central President 1896-1909	GFS Founding Associate Winchester 1875 Diocesan Vice President 1885 Diocesan President 1887	**Archdeacon George Sumner,* Suffragan Bishop of Guildford from 1888**
Mrs Louisa Barrington Gore Browne (daughter of Mary Sumner)	MU Associate Botley c. 1882 Speaks to central council re: Mary Sumner's views on divorce	Assists with Old Alresford GFS branch between 1875-1882	
Miss Dorothy Gore Browne (daughter of Louisa Barrington Gore Browne)		Winchester Diocesan President 1911	
Miss Charlotte Yonge	Winchester Diocesan Committee member 1886. Editor *MIC* 1890-1901	Founding Associate 1875 GFS Literature Correspondent Her 1886 novel *The Two Sides of the Shield* features the GFS	

The Hon. Ellen Joyce	Original Winchester Diocesan Committee member 1885	GFS Founding Associate 1875 GFS Emigration Correspondent 1883 Founder of Winchester Emigration Society 1882, which by affiliation became British Women's Emigration Association 1888 Sister-in-law to Lady Dynevor, GFS Diocesan President, St David's, 1881, 1920	
Mrs Emily Wilberforce	MU Central President 1916-20 Started Newcastle MU after Portsmouth Church Congress 1885 Her daughter Mrs Russell became MU Temperance Correspondent in 1917	Chichester Diocesan President 1897	Ernest Wilberforce,* Bishop of Newcastle 1882, Bishop of Chichester 1896-1907
Mrs Elizabeth Harold Browne	Winchester Diocesan Committee 1885	Winchester Diocesan President 1879	Edward Harold Browne,* Bishop of Ely 1864, Bishop of Winchester 1873-1891

The Hon. Mrs Augusta Maclagan	Central Vice President 1903 Friend of Mary Sumner, organised mothers' meetings Lichfield 1873/4	Lichfield Diocesan President 1880 York Diocesan President 1892	William Maclagan, Bishop of Lichfield 1878, Archbishop of York* 1891-1908
Mrs Frances Atlay	Started MU in Hereford after Portsmouth Church Conference 1885	First Hereford Diocesan President 1880	James Atlay, Bishop of Hereford, 1868-1894
Mrs Ellen Bickersteth	Inaugurated Exeter MU after Portsmouth Church Congress 1885 Friend of Mary Sumner	Ripon Diocesan President 1881	Edward Bickersteth, Bishop of Exeter, 1885-1900
Emily Dowager Marchioness of Hertford	Associate from 1888 Started MU Diocese of London 1890 with her daughter	Worcester Diocesan President 1881	
Lady Horatia Erskine (daughter of Dowager Marchioness of Hertford)	Central Life Vice President Sisters supported MU as diocesan presidents or leaders	Winchester Diocesan Council 1887	
Mrs Sophia Wickham Her daughter Lucy Ogilvy was also a member of the MU	Winchester member c. 1894, district speaker 1896 Friend of Mary Sumner	Associate c. 1894	

Mrs Louise Creighton	Peterborough Diocesan President 1891 and Central Council member 1896 1908 Pan Anglican Congress Women's Committee	Newcastle Diocesan President 1883	Mandell Creighton, Bishop of Peterborough, 1891, Bishop of London, 1897-1901
Lady Laura Ridding (close friend of L.C.)	Instigator of MU Watch Committee 1912 Instigated Women's League Southwell Used MU prayer 1884	Winchester Diocesan Council Southwell diocesan GFS instigated 1884, attempted to combine into Women's League 1886 Her mother Lady Selborne was at the GFS Conference Winchester 1887	George Ridding,* Bishop of Southwell, 1884-1904
Mrs Eleanor Chaloner Chute	Winchester Diocesan Committee 1888	Winchester Diocesan President 1889 President Central Council 1901 onwards	
Mrs Beatrice Temple	Supported Laura Ridding's Women's League 1886. Hosted meeting to discuss London Diocesan MU	First Exeter Diocesan President 1880	Frederick Temple Exeter 1869, Bishop of London 1885, Archbishop of Canterbury 1896-1902

Mrs Mary Benson	Speaker at Winchester Diocesan Conference 1887 and first central meeting Supported Laura Ridding's Women's League	Central President 1893-1885	Edward Benson, Archbishop of Canterbury, 1883-1896
Mrs Edith Randall Davidson	Winchester Diocesan Vice President 1898 Central Vice President		Randall Davidson, Bishop of Winchester, 1895, Archbishop of Canterbury, 1903-1928
Barbarina The Hon. Lady Grey	Speaker at Winchester Diocesan Conference 1887 Diocesan Council Member 1891	Member of Council 1877 President of Central Council 1883-1899	
Mrs Emeline Francis Steinthal	Hon. Sec. Ripon MU 1909 Gave evidence on behalf of MU to Gorell commission on divorce 1909	Ripon Diocesan President 1914	

Table 2: Episcopal Contacts of George and Mary Sumner

Kin, including by marriage, are represented by bold type
Friends and associates in italics
Connection to the MU or GFS is marked with * and § indicates marriage to a woman active in the Mothers' Union.
(GHSDD) indicates Mary Sumner's memoir, *George Henry Sumner D.D., Bishop of Guildford.*

Bishop	Nature of relationship	Remarks
John Bird Sumner, Archbishop of Canterbury, 1848-1862	George Sumner's uncle	Evangelical George (abbreviated as GHS) is his chaplain
Charles Richard Sumner, Winchester, 1827-1869 (abbreviated as CRS)	George's father	Evangelical George is his chaplain Appoints to George to Old Alresford 1851
Samuel Wilberforce, Winchester, 1869-1873 (abbreviated as SW)*	Distant cousin Friend Patron	Son of William Wilberforce CRS patron to SW patron to GHS, 1873. Broad churchman Son Ernest see below
Edward Harold Browne, Winchester, 1873-1891 (abbreviated as EHB)*§	Second son Barrington Gore Browne married Louisa, daughter of Mary Sumner, in 1882	MU supporter Mrs HB GFS and MU supporter Moderate high churchman Appointed George Archdeacon 1886, Bishop of Guildford 1888
Richard Trench, Archbishop of Dublin, 1864-1907 (formerly Dean Trench)	Rector of Itchenstoke Friend and advisor to George prior to 1864	Friend to Mary's father Thomas Heywood High Church

Ernest Wilberforce, Newcastle, 1882-1896, Chichester, 1896-1907*§	Son of Samuel Wilberforce Friend	Prompts Mary to speak Mrs Emily Wilberforce an MU activist and London MU President, Central President 1916 Temperance enthusiast
William Maclagan, Lichfield 1878, Archbishop of York 1891-1908§*	Friend	High Church MU supporter Mrs Maclagan initiated early version of MU MU mass meeting speaker
Lord Alwyne Compton, Ely 1886-1904, succeeds EHB	Friend Colleague in Convocation	High Church Early MU branches in diocese
Edward Bickersteth, Exeter, 1885-1900§	Friend	Early MU branches in diocese Evangelical
George Ridding, Southwell, Nottinghamshire, 1884-1904§*	Friend Former Headmaster of Winchester College in Moberly and Yonge circle	Husband of Laura Ridding
*Cosmo Gordon Lang, Stepney, 1901, Archbishop of York, 1909-1928**	Inducted to living of Portsea by George Sumner in early 1890s	Invites MU conference to York Offers advice on MU divorce petition Mass Meeting speaker
Edgar Charles Sumner Gibson, Gloucester, 1905-1924	Nephew Son of George's elder sister, Louisanna (d. 1899), second wife of William Gibson, Rector of Fawley.	Read prayer at George's funeral

Alan George Sumner Gibson, Coadjutor Bishop of Capetown, 1894-1906	Nephew As above	
Edward Benson, Archbishop of Canterbury, 1883-1896§	Hosts to George and Mary at times of Convocation.	'Death of Benson a great sorrow, a true friend and advisor' (GHSDD 70)
Frederick Temple, Archbishop of Canterbury, 1896-1902§	Mrs Beatrice Temple, London MU Diocesan President	'Archbishop and Mrs Temple carried on the kind hospitality and friendship' (GHSDD 70)
Anthony Thorold, Winchester, 1891-1895	Served by George as Suffragan Bishop	
Randall Davidson, Winchester 1895-1903, Archbishop of Canterbury, 1903-1928*§	Served by George as Suffragan Bishop	Davidson advisor to MU central committee Mrs Edith Davidson MU Central President for London and MU Vice President (GHSDD 147)
George Augustus Selwyn 1st Bishop of New Zealand, 1841, Bishop of Lichfield, 1867-1878	Tutor to George at Eton	

Table 3: Mothers' Union Cards Original Wording

Members' card as used at Old Alresford from 1876	Subscribing members' card original wording as used from 1886
1. Try, by God's help, to make them truthful, obedient and pure. 2. Never allow coarse jests, bad, angry words, or low talk in your house. Speak gently. 3. You are strongly advised never to give your children beer, wine or spirits, without the Doctor's orders, or to send young people to the public house. 4. Do not allow your girls to go about the streets at night, and keep them from unsafe companions and from dangerous amusements. 5. Be careful that your children do not read bad books or police reports. 6. Set them a good example in word and deed. 7. Kneel down and pray to God morning and evening, and teach your children to pray. 8. Try to read a few verses of the Bible daily, and come to Church as regularly as possible. (Reproduced in Sumner, *Home Life*, 1895, 6.)	1. I desire, by God's help, to make them truthful, obedient and pure. 2. To watch over their words and to prevent to the utmost of my power, evil speaking, slander and gossip in my home. 3. To guard my Children, as far as I can from frivolous bad, or doubtful companions, influences or amusements. 4. To be very careful as to the books and newspapers that they read or which are seen in the house. 5. To teach them habits of moderation and self control, and if possible avoid giving them beer wine or spirits without the doctor's orders. 6. To set them a good example in word and deed. 7. Pray with them daily 8. To read and explain the Bible and instruct them in our Holy Christian Faith. 9. To hallow God's Day and to worship Him regularly in His House of Prayer. (This example from Wickham of Binsted HRO 38M49/E7/104. Card retained by Sophia Wickham, a MU Associate c. 1894.)

Table 4: Royal Patronage of the Mothers' Union and Girls' Friendly Society

Royal Patron	**MU**	**GFS**
Queen Victoria	1897	1880-1901
Queen Alexandra*	1899 as Princess of Wales 1901 as Queen Meets Mary Sumner	1901
Princess Louise, daughter of Queen Alexandra		Mass meeting patron 1920
Queen Mary	1899 as Duchess of York then as Queen 1910 Visitor to Mary Sumner House 1919	
HRH Duchess of Albany Princess Helen* of Waldbeck m. Leopold, Victoria's 8th child, who was a haemophiliac and d. before the birth of their second child	Addressed MU 1911 Winchester Guildhall on the Duty of Mothers Profile in early *MUJ* Patron of Winchester 1898[1]	
Princess Beatrice* ('Baby' – the Queen's 9th child and 'home daughter') m. Henry of Battenberg	Patron of Isle of Wight 1898 Guest of Honour at opening days of Mary Sumner House 1925	
Princess Christian* Helena, 5th child of Queen Victoria, married Christian of Schleswig-Holstein in 1866, founder member of the Red Cross Her daughter Princess Helena Victoria founded the YWCA women's auxiliary	1908 Patroness of MU for London Opened the first Mary Sumner House in 1917	'Working Associate' of Old Windsor Branch. Patron of GFS mass meeting 1920

1. Coombs, *George and Mary Sumner*, 96, 97.

Princess Frederica* of Hanover	Interested by Helen Duchess of Albany 1912 Patroness for the continent Started Biarritz branch of MU	
Duchess of Connaught, Louise Margaret, m. to Arthur, 7th child of Queen Victoria	Patron of the MU army branch from 1895 Opened Connaught House in Winchester, a home for ex-workhouse girls	
Princess Mary (Vicountess Lascelles) d. of Queen Mary	1919 visited Mary Sumner House with Queen Mary 1925 opened new Mary Sumner House	1902 Vice Patron as Princess of Wales

Appendix 1
Mary Sumner's Speech at the Portsmouth Church Congress[1]

Will you help me for a moment by offering up a heart-felt prayer to God so he may help me address you aright, for I feel so strongly my great responsibility and also my great weakness? 'O Lord, give me Thy Holy Spirit. For Jesus Christ's sake. Amen.'

My dear friends, at the present moment the eyes of England are in a very special manner upon the women. It is said that there is a very terrible want of purity and high tone amongst the women of this country, and the question is, 'What can be done to raise that tone?' The answer is, 'Let us appeal to the mothers of England.' It is the mothers that can work the reformation of the country. 'Those who rock the cradle rule the world.' How so? Because the mother has charge of the child for the first ten years of its life; those years so all-important to the future of each child; and may I tell you why the tone of the women is not so high as it should be? One reason is the neglect of the mothers. Forgive me for speaking plainly, but I feel that if you only knew your power, you would use it; and if you knew your duty you would arise and do it. Believe me, the neglect of the mothers is the reason why so many young lives around us are failures. When God gives you a little infant, do you remember that it is an immortal soul? You carry your little one to Holy Baptism, and place it in the arms of the Lord Jesus, to be his soldier and servant; and as you carry it home again, God whispers in your heart, 'Take this child and nurse it for Me' – for me – not Satan. You should look solemnly at your child and say to yourself, 'This is God's child; I have to nurse it for Him and for heaven.' But how many mothers think that if they feed and clothe their children, it is all that is required of them? My sisters, God will ask you at the last great day, 'What have you done with that child – those children – I gave you to train for Me?' Each child is a gift

1. Charles Dunkley, *The Official Report of the Church Congress, Held at Portsmouth: On October 6th, 7th, 8th, and 9th, 1885* (London: Bemrose & Sons, 1885), 448-449.

from God. We who are Associates of the Girls' Friendly Society have started a society to help the girls and to try to keep them pure; but we are not the mothers of the children. And it is impossible for us to succeed in our work unless the mothers help us, and without them our efforts must be useless. The country can only be leavened through the mothers. But look how mothers bring up their girls. How thoughtlessly and carelessly. See what liberty they allow them; see how little they watch over them. A lady friend of mine in a northern town noticed two handsome girls going about the streets at night. She went to the mother and warned her of the evil it might bring into their young lives. The mother only tossed her head and said, 'I have not much to give them so I give them their liberty.' Was that a true mother? Was that a Christian mother? Watch over your girls. Keep them from going out in the evening unless under careful protection. Believe me, this is the duty of every mother; and set them an example yourself of purity in word and deed. Be yourself what you wish your children to be. May I now tell you another reason why the tone of the women of England is not so high as it should be? The reason is intemperance; so many girls are lost through drink. The wide spread ruin of young lives is simply appalling. Would that I could persuade everyone in this hall to be a total abstainer. Example is far more powerful than precept. Once more let me say 'Be yourself what you wish your children to be.' A poor woman once came to me about her son, who was living a very wicked life and who was a confirmed drunkard. She had prayed for him very earnestly but it seemed all in vain. I asked if she was a total abstainer, but she said. 'No; I am a hard working woman and I am obliged to have some beer to keep my strength up. I cannot do without it.' 'Not even to help your son? My good woman; you must give it up yourself – your example will be all-powerful.' 'No,' she said, 'I cannot do that; I could not do my heavy washing without a glass of beer.' 'Then,' I replied, 'you will not give up your glass of beer for the sake of your child?' She went away sadly. Some weeks afterwards I called upon her and she said, 'I have given up my beer but my son is just as bad as ever.' 'Never despair,' I answered; 'keep on praying to God for him and set him an example of total abstinence, and the answer will come.' A week later she came to the temperance meeting to take the pledge, and, as she stood up to give her solemn promise, the door opened; her son crept in and stood behind her, and his voice joined with hers in taking the pledge. The poor woman could hardly believe it was true until she looked round and saw him. She burst into tears and said, 'There is my prayer answered.' That son took the pledge and became a reformed character. He married a teetotal wife, and has continued faithful to his pledge ever since. My friends, you have a great work to do. You have to train your children to love God, and to pray to him, to consecrate body and soul to His blessed service, to live as His faithful soldiers and servants until their lives end; and no one can do this work like a mother. I know how hard your lives are, and what bodily pain and secret sorrows you have to suffer in your busy hard working lives. No one but a mother knows all a mother has to bear, and many of you endure these trials and troubles so patiently and nobly, that my whole heart loves, and respects, and reverences you. I learn many a lesson from the poor working woman which can never be forgotten. But, dear sisters, let me cheer you by pointing you to the one source of all strength and comfort – the Lord Jesus Christ. Make Him your friend; tell Him everything. He loves you so dearly, so tenderly. His heart is so large that it can take every grief and every sigh of his poor toiling children, and then he knows what pain and anguish mean. We can never suffer as our Lord Jesus suffered; we can never weep as He wept, and we can never be as forsaken and lonely as He was. Look at his sorrow in the Garden of Gethsemane, when He sweated great drops of blood. Look at His sufferings when they nailed his sacred hands and feet to the cross, Look at Him hanging upon that cross for six hours, lonely, faint, bleeding, broken-hearted, and all because He loved us so dearly because He yearned to save us, because He wants us all to live with Him for evermore. Oh! What a mighty friend we have our Lord Jesus! My sisters come to Him; spread out all you cares before Him; tell Him about your children, your anxieties, your troubles, you pains, your disappointments – tell Him everything. He will listen to you so patiently and tenderly. Hear His own words; 'Come unto Me all ye that labour and are heavy laden, and I will give you rest.' Rest that is what you want, you poor suffering, toiling, hard working mothers! Come to Him, not only in Holy communion, though that is the most blessed of all ways to draw near the Him, but daily and hourly pour out your hearts at His sacred feet. Look up into His loving face, He will not send you empty away. He will bless you, and help you, and comfort you. He will make you holy and heavenly minded. He will make you a good wife and mother. He will bless your homes, your husbands, your children. Oh, that you may meet at last before the throne of God, one happy, united family, to be forever with the Lord! God bless you all.

Appendix 2
Biographical Notes on Women Activists

Anna Bramston (1847-1931)

Anna Bramston, the daughter of John Bramston Dean of Winchester Cathedral (1872-1883), was active in the GFS. A friend of Charlotte Yonge, she became the first Headmistress of Winchester High School for girls. Her sister **Mary Elizabeth Bramston** (1841-1912), also a Yonge protégé, was a novelist on religious and moral themes who wrote for MU and GFS magazines. She took positions supervising school boarding houses between 1875 and 1896 when she moved back to Winchester.[1]

Isabella Bird Bishop (1831-1904)

Isabella Bird Bishop was the daughter of an evangelical Anglican vicar. She travelled to New Zealand and Australia in 1872. She also travelled to Hawaii and published an account of her travels in the Rocky Mountains in 1879. After the death of her husband, the doctor John Bishop, in 1876, Isabella studied practical medicine and during the 1880s and 90s travelled to Japan, India, Korea, Persia, and Tibet, where she was involved in medical missions. She was made a Fellow of the Royal Geographical Society in 1892.[2]

Lucy, Lady Frederick Cavendish (1841-1925)

Lucy, Lady Frederick Cavendish, wife of Lord Frederick Cavendish, was a supporter of education for women via the Girls' Public Day School

1. Georgina Battiscombe, *Charlotte Mary Yonge: The Story of an Uneventful Life* (London: Constable & Co., 1943); Georgina O'Brien Hill, 'Charlotte Yonge's "Goosedom"', *Nineteenth-Century Gender Studies*, no. 8.1. [http://www.ncgsjournal.com/issue81/hill.htm, accessed August 21st 2012].
2. Dorothy Middleton, 'Bishop [Bird], Isabella Lucy (1831-1904)', *Oxford Dictionary of National Biography* (Oxford University Press, 2005). [http://www.oxforddnb.com/view/article/31904, accessed January 3rd 2014].

Trust and served on the Royal Commission on Education in 1894. She is commemorated in Lucy Cavendish College Cambridge.[1]

Christabel Coleridge (1843-1921)

Christabel Coleridge (1843-1921), the daughter of Derwent Coleridge and granddaughter of the poet Samuel Taylor Coleridge, was a journalist and novelist. Mentored by Charlotte Yonge, she was one of the 'Goslings' and was Yonge's first biographer. Christabel Coleridge succeeded Charlotte Yonge as editor of the *Monthly Packet* from 1890 and edited the GFS magazine *Friendly Leaves*.[2]

Louise Creighton (1850-1936)

Louise Creighton was the wife of Bishop Mandell Creighton (Peterborough 1891, London 1897). She was friends with Laura Ridding and Mary Ward and was initially anti-suffrage. Creighton was the first president of the National Union of Women Workers (NUWW) (1895), was active in the MU and GFS and addressed women's sessions at Church congresses. In 1901 she initiated the Girls' Diocesan Association, her daughter Beatrice serving as its first president. She was a prolific author, most notably of biographies and as editor of her husband's letters. In 1908, she chaired the women's meetings at the Pan-Anglican Congress. She was involved in the Society for the Propagation of the Gospel, and participated in the Edinburgh World Missionary Conference in 1910.[3] Creighton later served on the Venereal Disease Commission of 1913.

Jane Ellice Hopkins (1836-1904)

Ellice Hopkins was an evangelical purity campaigner noted for her 'rescue' work for 'fallen' women and her attempts to reform male morals through the White Cross Army.[4] She was a prolific pamphleteer and

1. G.C. Boase and H.C.G. Matthew, 'Cavendish, Lord Frederick Charles 1836-1882', *Oxford Dictionary of National Biography* (Oxford: Oxford University Press, 2004). [http://www.oxforddnb.com/view/article/4932, accessed August 28th 2013].
2. Battiscombe, *Charlotte Mary Yonge: The Story of an Uneventful Life.*
3. James Thayne Covert, 'Creighton, Louise Hume (1850-1936)', *Oxford Dictionary of National Biography* (Oxford: Oxford University Press, 2004).
4. Sue Morgan, *A Passion for Purity: Ellice Hopkins and the Politics of Gender in the Late-Victorian Church* (Bristol: Centre for Comparative Studies in Religion and Gender, University of Bristol, 1999).

her *Early Training of Girls and Boys: An Appeal to Working Women*, first published in 1882, was reissued in 1902 with the subtitle *Especially Intended for Mothers' Unions.*[1]

Ellen Joyce (1832-1924)

The Hon. Ellen Joyce was the daughter of Baron Dynevor. Her son was the incumbent of St Martin's Winchester, where she lived from 1887. She was a Founding Associate of the GFS and active in the Mothers' Union. An exponent of women's emigration, she initiated the GFS Emigration Department in 1885. She also founded the Winchester Women's Emigration Society which later amalgamated with other societies to become the British Women's Emigration Association (BWEA) in 1888. A keen imperialist, she supported the Conservative Primrose League and the campaign for a 'White Australia'.[2]

Gertrude King (1867-1954)

A social worker and missionary, Gertrude King, whose religious beliefs were evangelical and High Church, acted as the helpmeet to her clerical brother in his parochial work between 1885 and 1899. In 1900 Gertrude followed her brother to the French colony of Madagascar where he had been appointed as Bishop of this missionary Diocese. Here, working through the women's section of the Society for the Propagation of the Gospel (SPG), she started the first branch of the Mothers' Union for indigenous members in Africa. By 1910 there were seventeen branches with 1000 members. She corresponded with Mary Sumner and pioneered the practice of linking overseas branches of the MU with 'home' branches, thus helping to promote the MU as a worldwide organisation and to shape its missionary stance. On her return from Madagascar in 1919 she served as MU overseas secretary and was influential in setting up the first overseas MU conference.[3]

Lady Knightly of Fawsley (1842-1914)

Lady Knightly of Fawsley, like Ellen Joyce, a keen imperialist, was a prominent figure both in the GFS (Diocesan President for Peterborough

1. Ellice Hopkins, *On the Early Training of Girls and Boys: An Appeal to Working Women, Etc* (London: Hatchards, 1882).
2. Julia Bush, 'Joyce, Ellen (1832-1924)', *Oxford Dictionary of National Biography* (Oxford University Press, 2006). [http://www.oxforddnb.com/view/article/74348, accessed November 26th 2012]
3. Elizabeth Prevost, 'King, Gertrude May (1867-1954)', *Oxford Dictionary of National Biography* (Oxford: Oxford University Press, 2012). [http://www.oxforddnb.com/view/article/103386, accessed January 3rd 2014].

1887-1905) and in the Conservative pro-imperial Primrose League (1885). She edited *The Imperial Colonist,* the journal of the British Women's Emigration Society (1902).[1] Lady Knightly also served as the president of the South African Colonisation Society (SACS), an offshoot of the BWEA which was instigated in anticipation of increased emigration after the Boer War in 1903.[2] The GFS sent Lady Knightly on a visit to South Africa in 1905.[3]

Charlotte Mason (1842-1923)

Charlotte Mason was the founder of the Parents' National Education Union (PNEU). A practicing Anglican and advocate of female suffrage, she was from 1874 to 1878 located in the Winchester Diocese as Vice Principal at Bishop Otter Teacher Training College, Chichester. Her book *Home Education* was published in 1886.[4] *Home Education* (which ran to repeated editions) was followed by further volumes, *Parents and Children, School Education, Ourselves, Formation of Character,* and *A Philosophy of Education.* In 1891 she established her own training college, The House of Education, in Ambleside, Cumbria.[5]

Charlotte Annie Moberly (1846-1937)

Charlotte Annie Moberly was the daughter of George Moberly, head master of Winchester College and later Bishop of Salisbury. She wrote under the alias of Elisabeth Morrison and served as the first principal of St Hugh's College Oxford (1886-1915). She recorded a memoir of her father

1. Julia Bush, '"The Right Sort of Woman": Female Emigrators and Emigration to the British Empire, 1890-1910', *Women's History Review* 3, no. 3 (1994); *Edwardian Ladies and Imperial Power* (London: Leicester University Press, 2000), 68, 79, 194.
2. Cecillie Swaisland, *Servants and Gentlewomen to the Golden Land: The Emigration of Single Women from Britain to Southern Africa, 1820-1939* (Oxford; Providence: Berg; Pietermaritzburg, South Africa: University of Natal Press, 1993).
3. Mary Heath-Stubbs, *Friendship's Highway: Being the History of the Girls' Friendly Society* (London: Girls' Friendly Society, 1926), 160; Bush, *Edwardian Ladies and Imperial Power.*
4. Margaret A. Coombs, *Charlotte Mason: Hidden Heritage and Educational Influence* (Cambridge: Lutterworth, 2015). Home Education advocated parental responsibility for education whether at home or in school.
5. David Wardle, *English Popular Education, 1780-1970* (London: Cambridge University Press, 1970), 92-94.

and family.[1] Charlotte's sister, Edith, started the GFS in Salisbury when her father became Bishop there. George Ridding, the next Headmaster of Winchester College, had been married to another Moberly sister, Mary, who died after a year of marriage in 1859. He married Lady Laura Palmer in 1876. The Moberly family were close friends with Charlotte Yonge.[2]

Lady Laura Ridding (1839-1949)

Laura Ridding was the daughter of Roundell Palmer, 1st Lord Selborne, and a supporter of philanthropic projects. In 1876 she married George Ridding, Headmaster of Winchester College and the successor to George Moberly, who became Bishop of Southwell in 1884. She was an early GFS committee member and instigator of the MU Watch Committee (1912). Ridding, a prolific diarist, became president of the NUWW and gave frequent addresses to Church congresses. Pro-suffrage and a keen imperialist, she was friends with Louise Creighton and Ellen Joyce. Laura Ridding's brother, Lord Selborne, served as Governor-General of South Africa (1905-1910) and his wife, Maud, was an activist in the Primrose League, the South African Colonial Society and the Victoria League. As their guest, Laura Ridding undertook an extended tour of South Africa in 1908. Whilst there, she kept a notebook which included reflections on social and educational issues and 'the native problem'.[3]

Lucy Soulsby (1856-1927)

MU Council member Lucy Soulsby, noted above for her opposition to girls taking degrees, secured her reputation as the Headmistress of Oxford High School, a Girls' Public Day School Company establishment.[4] She sat on the council of Lady Margaret Hall and opposed girls' access to the Oxford degree in 1895, the only Girls' Public Day School Company Head to do so. Soulsby also signed Mrs Humphrey Ward's anti-suffrage

1. C.A.E. Moberly, *Dulce Domum: George Moberly, His Family and Friends* (London: John Murray, 1911).
2. See Georgina Battiscombe, *Charlotte Mary Yonge: The Story of an Uneventful Life* (London: Constable and Co., 1943).
3. Lady Laura Ridding, *South African Note Book*, Selborne Papers, Hampshire Record Office 9M68/61, December 1908; Serena Kelly, 'Ridding, Lady Laura Elizabeth (1849-1939)' in *Oxford Dictionary of National Biography* (Oxford: Oxford University Press, 2004).
4. Kate Flint, 'Soulsby, Lucy Helen Muriel (1856-1927)', *Oxford Dictionary of National Biography* (Oxford University Press, 2004). [http://www.oxforddnb.com/view/article/48573, accessed June 21st 2013]. An obituary by Mrs Hubert Barclay appeared in *MIC*, July 1927, 160-2.

petition in 1889. Lucy Soulsby produced numerous pamphlets on educational and religious themes including *Stray Thoughts for Mothers and Teachers* (1897) and *Talks to Mothers* (1916).[1] Her *Two Aspects of Education* (1899), *I Self Control* and *II Fortitude, Humility and Large Heartedness*, advocated notions of good womanly conduct in accordance with those asserted in the writings of Mary Sumner and Charlotte Yonge and the publications of the MU and GFS.

Mary Townsend (1841-1918)

Mary Townsend, the 'Foundress' of the GFS, was the wife of a landed gentleman. Her friendship with Bishop Samuel Wilberforce was the catalyst for the initiation of the GFS, which aimed to protect the chastity of working women, in the Winchester diocese in 1874. She recruited Mary Sumner, Charlotte Yonge and Ellen Joyce as Founding Associates.[2]

Elizabeth Wordsworth (1840-1932)

Elizabeth Wordsworth, the daughter of Christopher Wordsworth, the Headmaster of Harrow School and Bishop of Lincoln (1868), was the first principal of the Oxford women's college Lady Margaret Hall from 1878 to 1909. Her commitment to women's education was based on the assumption that educated women would be better wives, mothers and churchwomen. In 1870 she met Charlotte Yonge and they became lifelong friends.[3]

Charlotte Yonge (1823-1901)

Charlotte Yonge was a prolific novelist, author of religious and historical text books, and editor of *The Monthly Packet* (until 1890). She served the GFS as Winchester Diocesan Head of Literature until 1900 and

1. Lucy Soulsby, *Stray Thoughts for Mothers and Teachers* (London: Longmans, 1897). Lucy Helen Muriel Soulsby, *Talks to Mothers* (London: Longmans & Co., 1916).
2. G.M. Harris, 'Townsend, Mary Elizabeth (1841-1918)', *Oxford Dictionary of National Biography* (Oxford: Oxford University Press, 2004); Brian Harrison, 'For Church, Queen and Family: The Girls' Friendly Society 1874-1920', *Past and Present* 61 (1973).
3. Frances Lannon, 'Wordsworth, Dame Elizabeth (1840-1932)', *Oxford Dictionary of National Biography* (Oxford: Oxford University Press, 2004). [http://www.oxforddnb.com/view/article/37024, accessed January 3rd 2014]; Ethel Romaines, *Charlotte Mary Yonge: An Appreciation* (London: Mowbray, 1908).

contributed to GFS publications. Charlotte Yonge edited the MU's *Mothers in Council* from 1891-1901.[1] Her novels, which she conceived of 'as a sort of instrument for popularising Church Views', reflect her religious motivation and can be interpreted as evangelical in intent. Her spiritual mentor was John Keble, a founder of the 1833 Tractarian Movement.[2] Charlotte Yonge's enthusiasm for foreign missions was exemplified by her financial support for the missionary ship *Southern Cross* in 1854, and her 1875 biography of her relative, the martyred missionary Bishop John Coleridge Patteson of Melanesia.[3] Charlotte Yonge also included missionary themes in her fiction, where she gives a role to women as helpmeets and teachers in the missionary enterprise. *New Ground* (1868) also made distinct the superiority of Christian (as opposed to white or English) treatment of the 'native Kaffirs'.[4] Her 1856 novel *The Daisy Chain* affirmed the spiritual status of the character Norman May by awarding him a missionary vocation in which he is to be supported by his loyal bride, Meta. Ethel May, the central character of the book, observes that together 'they will make a noble missionary!'[5] The book also exemplifies a higher life of service, one open to Ethel, who has relinquished aspirations for wider horizons due to the claims of home duty, yet gains fulfilment through teaching and fundraising for the establishment of a church, a 'missionary' venture in a local industrial area. Through *The Monthly Packet* and the more select privately circulated *Barnacle*, Charlotte Yonge acted as mentor to young women aspiring to write, including Christabel Coleridge and Anna and Mary Bramston. She was friends with Elizabeth Wordsworth and the Moberly family.

1. Heath-Stubbs, *Friendship's Highway*, 6.
2. Battiscombe, *Charlotte Mary Yonge: The Story of an Uneventful Life*, 15. Charlotte Yonge quoted in the Introduction by E.M. Delafield; Elisabeth Jay, 'Yonge, Charlotte Mary (1823-1901)', *Oxford Dictionary of National Biography* (Oxford: Oxford University Press, 2004).
3. Battiscombe, *Charlotte Mary Yonge: The Story of an Uneventful Life*, 90-91; Romaines, *Charlotte Mary Yonge: An Appreciation*, 115-127. Romaines notes Charlotte Yonge's 1871 study of missionary lives, 'Pioneers and Founders'; Charlotte Mary Yonge, *Life of John Coleridge Patteson: Missionary Bishop of the Melanesian Islands* (London: Macmillan, 1875).
4. Charlotte Mary Yonge, *New Ground* (London: J. & C. Mozeley, 1868).
5. Charlotte Mary Yonge, *The Daisy Chain; or, Aspirations. A Family Chronicle. By the Author of the Heir of Redclyffe, Etc.* (London: John W. Parker & Son, 1856), 566.

Primary Sources

Archival Sources

Lambeth Palace Library Mothers' Union Collection
Presidential correspondence MU/CO/PRES
Miscellaneous correspondence BOX 452
Printed materials MU/CO/PM
Manuscripts MU/MSS
Central Council MU/CC
Overseas MU/OS

Church of England Record Centre
Mothers' Union Journal (from 1888)
Mothers in Council (from 1890)

Hampshire Record Office
Diocese of Winchester Mothers' Union
Winchester Diocesan Girls' Friendly Society
Selborne Papers
Wickham of Binsted Collection
Old Alresford
Otterbourne
Winchester Memories Oral History Audio Visual Collection

Armitt Library, Ambleside, Cumbria
Charlotte Mason Collection

King's College London Maughan Library
Official Reports of the Church Congress

Works by Mary Sumner

Sumner, Mary Elizabeth. *Our Holiday in the East*. London: Hurst & Blackett, 1881.
Sumner, Mary. *To Mothers of the Higher Classes*. Winchester: Warren and Sons, 1888.
Sumner, Mary. 'A Mother's Greatest Duty.' London: Mothers' Union, n.d.

Sumner, Mary. 'The Home.' Winchester: Warren and Sons, n.d.
Sumner, Mary. *Home Life*. Winchester: Warren and Son, 1895.
Sumner, Mary. *Memoir of George Henry Sumner, D.D., Bishop of Guildford: Published for His Friends by Special Request*. Winchester: Warren and Sons, 1910.
Sumner, Mary. *What is the Mothers' Union?* London: Gardner Darton and Co, n.d. surmised after 1896.
Sumner, Mary. 'When and Why the Mothers' Union Started.' Winchester: Warren and Son, n.d. surmised 1888.

Organisational Histories of the MU

Hill, Florence. *Mission Unlimited*. Mothers' Union, 1988.
Lancaster, Violet. *A Short History of the Mothers' Union*. London: Mothers' Union, 1958.
Mothers' Union. *Fifty Years*. Westminster: The Mothers' Union, 1926.
Parker, Olive. *For the Family's Sake: A History of the Mothers' Union, 1876-1976*. Folkestone: Bailey and Swinfen, 1975.
Porter, Mary, Mary Woodward, and Horatia Erskine. *Mary Sumner: Her Life and Work and A Short History of the Mothers' Union*. Winchester: Warren and Sons, 1921.

Newspapers and Periodicals

Friendly Leaves
Girls' Friendly Society Associates Journal
English Woman's Review
Hampshire Chronicle
Hearth and Home: An Illustrated Weekly Journal for Gentlewomen
Hereford Journal
The Monthly Packet of Evening Readings for Younger Members of the Church of England
The Times
The Parents' Review

Additional Primary Sources

Anglican Book Centre, Anglican Church of Canada, Toronto. 'Lambeth Conferences Resolutions Archive.' By permission, the Secretary General of the Anglican Consultative Council 2006, [http://www.lambethconference.org/resolutions, accessed July 12th 2013].
Ashwell, Arthur Rawson, and Reginald Garton Wilberforce. *Life of the Right Reverend Samuel Wilberforce, D.D.: Lord Bishop of Oxford and Afterwards of Winchester, with Selections from His Diaries and Correspondence* [in English]. London: John Murray, 1880.

Bishop of Willesden. *New Dimensions: The Report of the Bishop of Willesden's Commission on the Objects and Policy of the Mothers' Union*. London: S.P.C.K., 1972.

Burdett-Coutts, Angela Georgina. *Woman's Mission: A Series of Congress Papers on the Philanthropic Work of Women by Eminent Writers*. London: Sampson Low, Marston and Company, 1893. Facsimile reprint, Portrayer Publishers 2002 ed.

Coleridge, Christabel R., and Charlotte Mary Yonge. *Charlotte Mary Yonge: Her Life and Letters*. pp. xiii. 391. Macmillan & Co.: London, New York, 1903.

Creighton, Louise. *Memoir of a Victorian Woman: Reflections of Louise Creighton 1850-1936*. Bloomington and Indianapolis: Indiana University Press, 1994.

De Bunsen, Henry George. 'The Bookhawker: His Work and His Day: Being a Paper Read at the Conference of the Church of England Bookhawking Union, Held at Derby, Sept. 21, 1859.' Published for the Church of England Bookhawking Union, Aylott and Sons, 1859.

Evans, M.G, and Austin Whitaker. *Winchester Life Histories No. 31 Mrs M.G. Evans*. October 2nd 1971. Hampshire Record Office Winchester Memories AV12/31/S1.

Grant, Rev. Alexander R. 'National Education.' In *Principles at Stake: Essays on Church Questions of the Day*, edited by George Sumner. London, 1868. 109-132.

Heath-Stubbs, Mary. *Friendship's Highway: Being the History of the Girls' Friendly Society*. London: Girls' Friendly Society, 1926.

Heywood F.S.A., Thomas, Sir Benjamin Heywood Bart, and George Henry Sumner Bishop of Guildford. *A Memoir of Sir Benjamin Heywood . . . By His Brother, T.H. [Completed by G.H. Sumner.] with Two Chapters of Domestic Life, and Letters, 1840-1865*. pp. vi. 339. Printed for private circulation: Manchester, 1888.

Heywood, Isabel Mary, and Sir Thomas Percival Heywood. *Reminiscences, Letters and Journals of Thomas Percival Heywood, Baronet. Arranged by His Eldest Daughter (Isabel Mary). With a Preface by the Rev. George Body*. Printed for private circulation: Manchester, 1899.

Hopkins, Ellice. *On the Early Training of Girls and Boys. An Appeal to Working Women, Etc*. London: Hatchards, 1882.

Mason, Charlotte Maria Shaw. *Home Education: A Course of Lectures to Ladies, Etc*. London: Kegan Paul & Co., 1886.

--- 'Home Education Series.' [http://www.amblesideonline.org/CM/vol1complete.html#1_1, accessed November 20th 2013]

Martineau, Harriet. *Household Education*. Smith, Elder & Co., 1870.

Maude, Mrs. 'Leaflet Number 4 for Subscribing Members.' Edited by Diocese of London Mothers' Union, n.d.

Moberly, C.A.E. *Dulce Domum: George Moberly, His Family and Friends*. London: John Murray, 1911.

Money, Agnes L. *History of the Girls' Friendly Society*. London: Wells Gardner, Darton, 1902.

--- *History of the Girls' Friendly Society*. New and rev. ed. London: Wells Gardner, Darton, 1905.
More, Hannah. *Strictures on the Modern System of Female Education: With a View of the Principles and Conduct Prevalent among Women of Rank and Fortune*. Printed for T. Cadell, Jun. and W. Davies, in the Strand., 1799
Mothers' Union. 'Brave Women.' London: Mothers' Union, 1914.
--- 'To British Mothers: How They Can Help Enlistment.' London: Mothers' Union, 1914.
Pitman, Emma Raymond. *Missionary Heroines in Eastern Lands: Woman's Work in Mission Fields*. London: S.W. Partridge & Co., 1895.
Randall, James. *Book-Hawking: A Means of Counteracting the Evils of the Day*. 1862.
Romaines, Ethel. *Charlotte Mary Yonge: An Appreciation*. London: Mowbray, 1908.
Ruskin, John. *Sesame and Lilies*. Nelson: Hendon, 2000 (1865).
Soulsby, Lucy. *Stray Thoughts for Mothers and Teachers*. London: Longmans, 1897.
--- *Two Aspects of Education*. London: Longmans, Green and Co, 1899.
Soulsby, Lucy Helen Muriel. *Talks to Mothers*. London: Longmans & Co., 1916.
Sumner, George Henry. *Book Hawking; as Conducted in Hampshire*. London: Wertheim and Macintosh, 1855.
--- *Life of C.R. Sumner, D.D., Bishop of Winchester, During a Forty Years' Episcopate*. London, 1876.
Sumner, George Henry, ed. *Principles at Stake: Essays on Church Questions of the Day*: London, 1868.
Sumner, Heywood. 'Memorials of the Family of Sumner from the Sixteenth Century to 1904.' Southampton, 1904.
Vaughan, John, and Mary Elizabeth Sumner. *A Short Memoir of Mary Sumner, Founder of the Mothers' Union. [with Portrait]*. pp. 16. Warren and Sons: Winchester, 1921.
Yonge, Charlotte Mary. *The Two Sides of the Shield*. London: Macmillan & Co., 1885.
--- *The Girl's Little Book*. London: Skeffington & Son, 1893.
--- *Womankind*. 2nd ed. London and New York: Macmillan, 1890, first published 1876.
--- *Aunt Charlotte's Stories of English History for the Little Ones*. London, 1873.
--- *The Daisy Chain, or, Aspirations: A Family Chronicle*. London: Virago, 1988 [1856].
--- *English Church History, Adapted for Use in Schools, Etc*. London: National Society, 1883.
--- *Hannah More*. London: W.H. Allen & Co., 1888.
--- *Lads and Lasses of Langley*. London: Walter Smith, 1881.
--- *Langley Adventures*. London: Walter Smith, 1884 [1883].
--- *Langley Little Ones. Six Stories*. London: Walter Smith, 1882.

Bibliography

Adkins, Lisa, and Beverley Skeggs. *Feminism after Bourdieu*. Oxford: Blackwell, 2004.

Aiston, Sarah Jane. 'Women, Education and Agency 1600-2000, an Historical Perspective.' In *Women, Education and Agency*, edited by Jean Spence, Sarah Jane Aiston and Maureen Meikle. London and New York: Routledge, 2010. 1-8.

Altick, Richard D. *The English Common Reader: A Social History of the Mass Reading Public, 1800-1900*. 2nd ed. With a foreword by Jonathan Rose, ed. Columbus: Ohio State University Press, 1998.

Anderson-Faithful, Sue. 'Mary Sumner and Maternal Authority: From the Drawing Room to the Homes of the Nation.' *History of Education Researcher Special Issue Educated Women: Finding Place, Claiming Space* 89 (2012): 18-26.

--- 'A "Mission to Civilise": The Popular Educational Vision of the Anglican Mothers' Union and Girls Friendly Society 1886-1926'. *Revista Brasileira de História da Educação* 11, no. 1 [28] (2012): 15-43.

Armitt Library. *Charlotte Mason*. [http://armitt.com/armitt_website/charlotte-mason-armitt-museum-art-gallery-and-library/, accessed September 1st 2013].

Barbour, Jane. 'Sumner, (George) Heywood Maunoir (1853-1940).' *Oxford Dictionary of National Biography*: Oxford University Press, 2004. [http://www.oxforddnb.com/view/article/38033, accessed November 26th 2012].

Battiscombe, Georgina. *Charlotte Mary Yonge the Story of an Uneventful Life*. London: Constable & Co., 1943.

Beaumont, Catriona. *Housewives and Citizens: Domesticity and the Women's Movement in England, 1928-64*. Gender in History. Manchester: Manchester University Press, 2013

Bebbington, D.W. *Evangelicalism in Modern Britain: A History from the 1730s to the 1980s* London: Routledge, 1988.

--- 'Atonement, Sin and Empire 1880-1914.' In *The Imperial Horizons of British Protestant Missions, 1880-1914*, edited by Andrew Porter. Michigan: Wm. B. Eerdmans, 2003.

--- 'Unitarian Members of Parliament in the Nineteenth Century.' (2009). [http://hdl.handle.net/1893/1647, accessed May 17th 2017]

Bland, Lucy. 'Purifying the Public World: Feminist Vigilantes in Late Victorian England.' *Women's History Review* 1, no. 3 (1992): 377-412.

Bourdieu, Pierre. 'Authorised Language: The Social Conditions for the Effectiveness of Ritual Discourse.' In *Language and Symbolic Power*. Cambridge: Polity Press, 1991. 107-16.

--- 'The Biographical Illusion.' In *Identity: A Reader*, edited by Paul Du Gay, Jessica Evans and Peter Redman. London: Sage, 2000. 299-305.

--- *Distinction: A Social Critique of the Judgement of Taste* [translation of *La distinction*]. London: Routledge & Kegan Paul, 1984.

--- *The Field of Cultural Production: Essays on Art and Literature*. Cambridge: Polity Press, 1993.

--- 'Genesis and Structure of the Religious Field.' *Comparative Social Research* 13, no. 1 (1991): 1-44.

--- *Language and Symbolic Power* [translated from French]. Cambridge: Polity Press, 1991.

--- 'Legitimation and Structured Interest in Weber's Sociology of Religion.' In *Max Weber, Rationality, and Modernity*, edited by Scott Lash and Sam Whimster. London: Allen and Unwin, 1987. 119-36.

--- *The Logic of Practice* [translation of *Le sens pratique*]. Cambridge: Polity, 1990.

--- *Masculine Domination* [translation of *La domination masculine*]. Cambridge: Polity Press, 2001.

--- *Outline of a Theory of Practice*. Cambridge University Press, 1979.

--- *Practical Reason: On the Theory of Action* [translated from French]. Cambridge: Polity Press, 1998.

Bourdieu, Pierre, and Jean-Claude Passeron. *Reproduction in Education, Society and Culture* [in Translation of: La reproduction.]. Rev. ed. Preface to the 1990 edition by Pierre Bourdieu, ed. London: Sage, 1990.

Bourdieu, Pierre, and Loic J.D. Wacquant. *An Invitation to Reflexive Sociology*. Cambridge: Polity Press, 1992.

Bradley, Ian. *The Call to Seriousness; the Evangelical Impact on the Victorians*. London: Jonathan Cape, 1976.

Braster, Sjaak. 'The People, the Poor, and the Oppressed: The Concept of Popular Education through Time.' *Paedagogica Historica* 47, no. Nos. 1-2 (2011): 1-14.

Brewis, Georgina. 'From Working Parties to Social Work: Middle Class Girls' Education and Social Service 1890-1914.' *History of Education* 38, no. 6 (2009): 761-77.

Buettner, Elizabeth. '"Not Quite Pukka": Schooling in India and the Acquisition of Racial Status.' In *Empire Families: Britons and Late Imperial India*. Oxford: Oxford University Press, 2004. 72-109

Burstyn, Joan. *Victorian Education and the Ideal of Womanhood*. London: Croom Helm, 1980.

Bush, Julia. *Edwardian Ladies and Imperial Power*. Leicester: Leicester University Press, 2000.

--- 'Edwardian Ladies and the "Race" Dimensions of British Imperialism.' *Women's Studies International Forum* 21, no. 3 May-June (1998): 277-89.
--- '"The Right Sort of Woman": Female Emigrators and Emigration to the British Empire,1890-1910.' *Women's History Review* 3, no. 3 (1994): 385-40.
--- '"Special Strengths for Their Own Special Duties": Women, Higher Education and Gender Conservatism in Late Victorian Britain.' *History of Education* 34, no. 4 (2005): 387-405.
Caine, Barbara. 'Feminist Biography and Feminist History.' *Women's History Review* 3, no. 2 (1992): 247-60.
Calhoun, Craig J., Edward LiPuma, and Moishe Postone, eds. *Bourdieu: Critical Perspectives*. Cambridge: Polity Press, 1993.
Cannadine, David. *Class in Britain*. New Haven; London: Yale University Press, 1998.
Chadwick, Owen. *The Victorian Church Part I, 1827-1859*. London: A&C Black, 1966.
--- *The Victorian Church Part 2, 1860-1901*. London: A&C Black, 1972.
Chandler, Michael. *An Introduction to the Oxford Movement*. New York: Church Publishing, 2003.
Chilton, Lisa. *Agents of Empire: British Female Migration to Canada and Australia, 1860s-1930*. Toronto; Buffalo: University of Toronto Press, 2007.
Colón, Susan E. 'Realism and Reserve: Charlotte Yonge and Tractarian Aesthetics.' *Women's Writing* 17, no. 2 (2010): 221-35
Copley, Terence. *Spiritual Development in the State School: A Perspective on Worship and Spirituality in the Education System of England and Wales*. Exeter: University of Exeter Press, 2000.
Coombs, Joyce. *George and Mary Sumner: Their Life and Times*. Westminster: Sumner Press, 1965.
Coombs, Margaret A. *Charlotte Mason: Hidden Heritage and Educational Influence*. Cambridge: Lutterworth, 2015
Cooper, Frederick, and Ann Laura Stoler. *Tensions of Empire: Colonial Cultures in a Bourgeois World*. Berkeley: University of California Press, 1997.
Covert, James Thane. *A Victorian Marriage: Mandell and Louise Creighton*. London: Hambledon, 2000.
Cunningham, Peter. 'Innovators, Networks and Structures: Towards a Prosopography of Progressivism.' *History of Education* 30, no. 5 (2001): 433-51.
Curthoys, M.C. 'Heywood, James (1810-1897).' In *Oxford Dictionary of National Biography* [online edn]. Oxford: Oxford University Press, 2009. [http://www.oxforddnb.com/view/article/56315, accessed August 28th 2013].
Daggers, Jenny. 'The Victorian Female Civilising Mission and Women's Aspirations Towards Priesthood in the Church of England.' *Women's History Review* 10, no. 4 (2001): 651-70.
Daggers, Jenny, and Diana Neal. *Sex, Gender and Religion: Josephine Butler Revisited*. Frankfurt am Main; New York: Peter Lang, 2006.
Davin, Anna. 'Imperialism and Motherhood.' *History Workshop* 5 (1978): 9-65.

Delamont, Sara. 'The Contradictions in Ladies' Education.' In *The Nineteenth-Century Woman: Her Cultural and Physical World*, edited by Sara Delamont and Lorna Duffin. London: Croom Helm, 1978. 134-163.

Delamont, Sara. 'The Domestic Ideology and Women's Education.' In *The Nineteenth-Century Woman: Her Cultural and Physical World*, edited by Sara Delamont and Lorna Duffin. London: Croom Helm, 1978. 164-187.

Dennis, Barbara. *Charlotte Yonge (1823-1901): Novelist of the Oxford Movement: A Literature of Victorian Culture and Society*. Lewiston: Mellen, 1992.

Dickey, Brian 'Evangelicals and Poverty.' In *Evangelical Faith and Public Zeal: Evangelicals and Society 1780-1980*, edited by John Wolffe. London: SPCK, 1995. 38-59.

Dunae, Patrick A. 'Penny Dreadfuls: Late Nineteenth-Century Boys' Literature and Crime.' *Victorian Studies* 22, no. 2 (1979): 133-150.

Dyhouse, Carol. *Girls Growing up in Late Victorian and Edwardian London* London: Routledge, 1981.

Elkins, Caroline, and Susan Pedersen. 'Introduction. Settler Colonialism: A Concept and Its Uses.' In *Settler Colonialism in the Twentieth Century; Projects, Practices, Legacies*. New York, N.Y.; London: Routledge, 2005.

Fitzgerald, Tanya. 'Cartographies of Friendship: Mapping Missionary Women's Educational Networks in Aotearoa/New Zealand, 1823-40.' *History of Education* 32, no. 5 (2003): 515-27.

Francis-Dehquani, Guli. 'Women Missionaries in Persia: Perceptions of Muslim Women and Islam, 1884-1934.' In *The Church Mission Society and World Christianity, 1799-1999*, edited by Kevin Ward and Brian Stanley. Grand Rapids and Cambridge: Wm. B. Eerdmans, 2000.

Fuchs, Eckhardt. 'Networks and the History of Education.' *Paedagogica Historica* 42, no. 2 (2007): 185-97.

Gerard, Jessica. 'Lady Bountiful Women of the Landed Classes and Rural Philanthropy.' *Victorian Studies* 30, no. 2 (1987): 183-210.

Gill, Sean. *Women and the Church of England: From the Eighteenth Century to the Present*. London: Society for Promoting Christian Knowledge, 1994.

Gleadle, Kathryn. *The Early Feminists: Radical Unitarians and the Emergence of the Women's Rights Movements, 1831-51*. Macmillan, 1995.

Godden, Judith. 'Containment and Control: Presbyterian Women and the Missionary Impulse in New South Wales, 1891-1914.' *Women's History Review* 6, no. 1 (1997): 75-93.

Gomersall, Meg. *Working-Class Girls in Nineteenth-Century England: Life, Work and Schooling*. Basingstoke: Macmillan, 1997.

Goodman, Joyce F. 'Girls' Public Day School Company (Act. 1872-1905).' *Oxford Dictionary of National Biography*: Oxford University Press, 2005. [http://www.oxforddnb.com/view/theme/94164, accessed August 28th 2013].

--- 'The Gendered Politics of Historical Writing in History of Education.' *History of Education* 41, no. 1 (2012): 9-24.

Goodman, Joyce, and Jane Martin. 'Networks after Bourdieu: Women, Education and Politics from the 1980s to the 1920s.' *History of Education Researcher* 80, no. November (2007): 65-75.
Gorham, Deborah. *The Victorian Girl and the Feminine Ideal*. London: Croom Helm, 1982.
Grenfell, Michael, and Cheryl Hardy. *Art Rules: Pierre Bourdieu and the Visual Arts*. Oxford: Berg, 2007.
Grenfell, Michael, and David James. *Bourdieu and Education: Acts of Practical Theory*. London: Falmer Press, 1998.
Grierson, Janet. *The Deaconess*. London: CIO, 1981.
Griffiths, Morwenna. *Feminisms and the Self: The Web of Identity*. London: Routledge, 1995.
Grimshaw, Patricia. 'In Pursuit of True Anglican Womanhood in Victoria, 1880-1914.' *Women's History Review* 2, no. 3 (1993): 331-47.
Gunter, Helen M. 'Purposes and Positions in the Field of Education Management: Putting Bourdieu to Work.' *Educational Management Administration and Leadership* 30, no. 1 (2002): 7-29
Haggis, Jane. '"A Heart That Has Felt the Love of God and Longs for Others to Know It": Conventions of Gender, Tensions of Self and Constructions of Difference in Offering to Be a Lady Missionary.' *Women's History Review* 2 (1998): 171-93.
Hall, Catherine. *Cultures of Empire: A Reader: Colonisers in Britain and the Empire in Nineteenth and Twentieth Centuries*. Manchester: Manchester University Press, 2000.
--- *Civilising Subjects: Metropole and Colony in the English Imagination, 1830-1867*. Cambridge: Polity Press, 2002.
Hall, Catherine, and Sonia O. Rose, eds. *At Home with the Empire: Metropolitan Culture and the Imperial World*. Cambridge: Cambridge University Press, 2006.
Hall, Lesley. *Sex, Gender and Social Change in Britain since 1880*. Basingstoke: Macmillan, 2000.
Harrison, Brian. *Drink and the Victorians: The Temperance Question in England, 1815-1872*. London: Faber and Faber Ltd, 1971.
--- 'For Church, Queen and Family; the Girls' Friendly Society, 1874-1920.' *Past and Present* 61 (1973): 107-38.
Heeney, Brian. *Mission to the Middle Classes: The Woodard Schools, 1848-1891*. London: S.P.C.K., 1969.
--- *The Women's Movement in the Church of England, 1850-1930*. Oxford: Clarendon, 1988.
Herring, George. 'Wilberforce, Ernest Roland (1840-1907).' *Oxford Dictionary of National Biography*. Oxford University Press, 2006. [http://www.oxforddnb.com/view/article/36892, accessed November 26th 2012].
Hollis, Patricia. *Ladies Elect: Women in English Local Government, 1865-1914*. Oxford: Clarendon, 1987.

Holloway, Gerry. '"Let the Women Be Alive!": The Construction of the Married Working Woman in the Industrial Women's Movement, 1890-1914.' In *Radical Femininity; Womens' Self Representation in the Public Sphere*, edited by Eileen Janes Yeo. Manchester: Manchester University Press, 1998. 173-195.

Huffman Traver, Teresa. 'The Ship That Bears through the Waves.' *Women's Writing* 17, no. 2 (2010): 255-67.

Hurt, John. *Education in Evolution: Church, State, Society and Popular Education 1800-1870*. London: Rupert Hart-Davis, 1971.

Hylson-Smith, Kenneth. *Evangelicals in the Church of England, 1734-1984*. London: T&T Clark, 1988.

Jacobs, Andrea. 'Examinations as Cultural Capital for the Victorian School Girl; Thinking with Bourdieu.' *Women's History Review* 16, no. 2 (2001): 245-61.

Jenkins, Richard. *Pierre Bourdieu*. London: Routledge, 1992.

Jordan, Jane. *Josephine Butler*. London: John Murray, 2001.

Keck, Margaret, and Kathryn A. Sikkink. *Advocacy Networks in International Politics, Activists Beyond Borders*. Ithaca; London: Cornell University Press, 1998.

Kelly, Serena. 'A Sisterhood of Service: The Records and Early History of the National Union of Women Workers.' *Journal of the Society of Archivists* 14, no. 2 (1993): 167-74.

Kendall, Diana. *The Power of Good Deeds: Privileged Women and the Social Reproduction of the Upper Class*. Boston: Rawman Littlefield, 2002.

Kerber, Linda. 'Separate Spheres, Female Worlds, Woman's Place; the Rhetoric of Women's History.' *Journal of American History* 75, no. 1 (1988): 9-39.

Kidd, Alan J., and K.W. Roberts. *City, Class and Culture: Studies of Social Policy and Cultural Production in Victorian Manchester*. Manchester: Manchester University Press, 1985.

Knight, Frances. *The Nineteenth-Century Church and English Society*. Cambridge: Cambridge University Press, 1995.

Krais, Beate. 'Gender and Symbolic Violence: Female Oppression in the Light of Pierre Bourdieu's Theory of Social Practice.' In *Bourdieu: Critical Perspectives*, edited by Craig Calhoun, Edward LiPuma and Moishe Postone. Cambridge: Cambridge Polity Press, 1993.

Lane, Jeremy F. *Pierre Bourdieu: A Critical Introduction*. London: Pluto, 2000.

Lake, Marilyn, and Henry Reynolds. ' White Australia Points the Way.' In *Drawing the Global Colour Line: White Men's Countries and the International Challenge of Racial Equality*. Cambridge: Cambridge University Press, 2008. 137-165.

Lawson, John, and Harold Silver. *A Social History of Education in England*. Reprinted ed. London: Methuen, 1978.

Lentin, Anthony. 'Anglicanism, Parliament and the Courts.' In *Religion in Victorian Britain Volume II Controversies*, edited by Gerald Parsons. Manchester: Manchester University Press, 1988.

Lovegrove, Elizabeth. '"Dangerous Display": Charlotte Yonge, Christabel Coleridge, and Pseudonyms in the *Monthly Packet*.' *Women's History Magazine*, 2013, 12-18.

Lovell, Terry. 'Thinking Feminism with and against Bourdieu.' In *Reading Bourdieu on Society and Culture*, edited by Bridget Fowler. Oxford: Blackwell, 2000. 27-48.

Mackarill, D.R. 'Book-Hawking-a Moral Enterprise.' *Antiquarian Book Monthly* 27, no. 7(2000): 35-39.

Malmgreen, Gail. *Religion in the Lives of English Women, 1760-1930*. London: Croom Helm, 1986.

Mangion, Carmen M. 'Women and Female Institution Building.' In *Women, Gender and Religious Cultures in Britain, 1800-1940*, edited by Sue Morgan and Jacqueline de Vries. London: Routledge, 2011. 72-93.

Mare, Margaret Laura,and Alicia Constance Percival. *Victorian Best-Seller: The World of Charlotte M. Yonge*. London: George G. Harrap & Co., 1947.

Martin, Jane. *Women and the Politics of Schooling in Victorian and Edwardian England*. London: Leicester University Press, 1998.

Martin, Jane, and Joyce Goodman. *Women and Education, 1800-1980*. Basingstoke: Palgrave Macmillan, 2004.

Maughan, Steven. 'Imperial Christianity? Bishop Montgomery and the Foreign Missions of the Church of England, 1895-1915.' In *The Imperial Horizons of British Protestant Missions 1880-1914*, edited by A. N. Porter. Grand Rapids, Michigan: Wm. B. Eerdmans, 2003. 32-57.

Mayes, Kelly. 'The Disease of Reading and Victorian Periodicals.' In *Literature in the Marketplace: Nineteenth-Century British Publishing and Reading.* Practices Cambridge Studies in Nineteenth-Century Literature and Culture Series, No. 5., edited by John O. Jordan and Robert L. Patten. Cambridge: Cambridge UP, 1995. 165-194.

McConnell, Anita. 'Heywood, Sir Benjamin, First Baronet (1793-1865).' In *Oxford Dictionary of National Biography.* Oxford: Oxford University Press, 2004. [http://www.oxforddnb.com/view/article/1317911, accessed November 30th 2012].

Mehrotra, S.R. 'On the Use of the Term "Commonwealth".' *Journal of Commonwealth Political Studies* 2, no. 1 (1963): 1-16.

Melman, Billie. *Women's Orients: English Women and the Middle East, 1718-1918: Sexuality, Religion and Work.* 2nd ed. Basingstoke: Macmillan, 1995.

Midgley, Clare. 'Women, Religion and Reform.' In *Women, Gender and Religious Cultures in Britain, 1800-1940*, edited by Sue Morgan and Jacqueline de Vries. London: Routledge, 2010. 138-58.

Mitchell, Sally. 'The New Heroine: Penny Weekly Magazines of the 1870s.' In *The Fallen Angel: Chastity, and Women's Reading 1835-1880*. Bowling Green, Ohio: Bowling Green University Popular Press, 1981. 145-162.

Moi, Toril. *'What is a Woman?' And Other Essays*. Oxford: Oxford University Press, 1999.

Morgan, Simon. *A Victorian Woman's Place: Public Culture in the Nineteenth Century*. London: Tauris Academic Studies, 2007.

Morgan, Sue. *A Passion for Purity: Ellice Hopkins and the Politics of Gender in the Late-Victorian Church*. Bristol: Centre for Comparative Studies in Religion and Gender, University of Bristol, 1999.

--- 'Theorising Feminist History: A Thirty Year Retrospective.' *Women's History Review* 18, no. 3 (2009): 381-407.

--- *Women, Religion, and Feminism in Britain, 1750-1900*. Basingstoke: Palgrave Macmillan, 2002.

Morgan, Sue, and Jacqueline de Vries. *Women, Gender and Religious Cultures in Britain, 1800-1940*. 1st ed. London: Routledge, 2010.

Morgan, Susan, ed. *The Feminist History Reader*. London: Routledge, 2006.

Moruzi, Kristine. '"Never Read Anything That Can at All Unsettle Your Religious Faith": Reading and Writing in the Monthly Packet.' *Women's Writing* 17, no. 2 (2010): 288-304.

Moyse, Cordelia. *A History of the Mothers' Union: Women Anglicanism and Globalisation, 1876-2008*. Woodbridge: Boydell Press, 2009.

--- *The Mothers' Union, 1876-2001: 125 Years Caring for the Family*. London: Mothers' Union, 2001.

Mumm, Susan. 'Women and Philanthropic Cultures.' In *Women, Gender and Religious Cultures in Britain, 1800-1940*, edited by Sue Morgan and Jacqueline de Vries. London: Routledge, 2010. 54-71.

Murphy, James. *Church State and Schools in Britain 1800-1970*. London: Routledge and Kegan Paul, 1971.

Nardin, Jane. 'Hannah More and the Rhetoric of Educational Reform.' *Women's History Review* 10, no. 2 (2001): 211-28.

Newsome, D. *The Parting of Friends: A Study of the Wilberforces and Henry Manning*. London: Murray, 1966.

Norman, E.R. *Church and Society in England, 1770-1970: A Historical Study*. Oxford: Clarendon Press, 1976.

O'Brien, Anne. 'Militant Mothers: Faith Power and Identity in the Mothers' Union in Sydney 1896-1950'. *Women's History Review* 9, no. 1 (2000): 35-53.

O'Brien Hill, Georgina. 'Charlotte Yonge's "Goosedom".' *Nineteenth-Century Gender Studies* no. 8.1. Published electronically, Spring 2012. [http://www.ncgsjournal.com/issue81/hill.htm, accessed August 21st 2012].

Olsen, Stephanie. 'The Authority of Motherhood in Question: Fatherhood and the Moral Education of Children in England, C. 1870-1900.' *Women's History Review* 18, no. 5 (2009): 765-80.

Parsons, Gerald. *Religion in Victorian Britain. Vol.1, Traditions*. Manchester University Press in association with the Open University, 1988.

Plant, Helen. '"Ye Are All One in Christ Jesus": Aspects of Unitarianism and Feminism in Birmingham, c. 1869-90.' *Women's History Review* 9, no. 4 (2000): 721-42.

Pickles, Katie. *Female Imperialism and National Identity: Imperial Order Daughters of the Empire*. Manchester: Manchester University Press, 2002.

Porter, A.N. *The Imperial Horizons of British Protestant Missions, 1880-1914.* Grand Rapids, Michigan: Wm. B. Eerdmans, 2003.
Postone, Moishe, Edward LiPuma, and Craig J. Calhoun. 'Introduction.' In *Bourdieu: Critical Perspectives*, edited by Craig J. Calhoun, Edward LiPuma and Moishe Postone. Cambridge: Polity Press, 1993.
Poupeau, Frank 'Reasons for Domination: Bourdieu Versus Habermas.' In *Reading Bourdieu on Society and Culture*, edited by Bridget Fowler. Oxford: Blackwell, 2000.
Pratt, Mary Louise. *Imperial Eyes: Travel Writing and Transculturation.* London: Routledge, 1992.
Prevost, Elizabeth E. *The Communion of Women: Missions and Gender in Colonial Africa and the British Metropole.* Oxford: Oxford University Press, 2010.
Prochaska, F.K. *Women and Philanthropy in Nineteenth Century England.* Oxford: Clarendon Press, 1980.
--- *The Angel out of the House: Philanthropy and Gender in Nineteenth-Century England.* Charlottesville and London: University of Virginia Press, 2002.
Pugh, R.K. *The Letter Books of Samuel Wilberforce, 1843-1868.* Oxford: Oxford Record Society, 1969.
Purvis, June. *A History of Women's Education in England.* Milton Keynes: Open University Press, 1991.
--- 'Using Primary Sources When Researching Women's History from a Feminist Perspective.' *Women's History Review* 1, no. 2 (1992): 273-306.
Rendall, Jane. 'Uneven Developments: Women's History, Feminist History and Gender History in Great Britain.' In *Writing Women's History: International Perspectives*, edited by Karen R. Offen, Ruth Roach Pierson and Jane Rendall. London: Macmillan, 1991.
--- 'The Condition of Women, Women's Writing and the Empire in Nineteenth Century Britain.' In *At Home with the Empire: Metropolitan Culture and the Imperial World*, edited by Catherine Hall and Sonia O. Rose. Cambridge: Cambridge University Press, 2006. 101-21.
Rey, Terry. *Bourdieu on Religion: Imposing Faith and Legitimacy*. London: Equinox Pub., 2007.
--- 'Marketing the Goods of Salvation: Bourdieu on Religion.' *Religion* 34, no. 4 (2004): 331-43.
Ross, Andrew. 'Christian Missions and the Mid-Nineteenth Century Change in Attitudes to Race: The African Experience.' In *The Imperial Horizons of British Protestant Missions*, edited by Andrew Porter. Grand Rapids, Michigan; Cambridge: Wm. B. Eerdmans, 2003. 85-103.
Rowbotham, Judith. *Good Girls Make Good Wives: Guidance for Girls in Victorian Fiction*. Oxford: Basil Blackwell, 1989.
--- 'Ministering Angels, Not Ministers: Women's Involvement in the Foreign Missionary Movement, c. 1860-1910.' In *Women, Religion and Feminism in Britain, 1750-1900*, edited by Sue Morgan. Basingstoke: Palgrave Macmillan, 2002. 179-195.

Rowbotham, Sheila. 'The Trouble with Patriarchy.' In *The Feminist History Reader*, edited by Sue Morgan. London: New York: Routledge, 2007. 51-56.

Ryan, Mary P. 'The Public and the Private Good across the Great Divide in Women's History.' *Journal of Women's History* 15, no. 1 (2003): 10-27.

Said, Edward W. *Orientalism*. Harmondsworth: Penguin, 1985.

Schaffer, Talia. 'Taming the Tropics: Charlotte Yonge Takes on Melanesia.' *Victorian Studies* 47 (2005): 204-14.

Scotland, Nigel. *John Bird Sumner: Evangelical Archbishop*. Leominster: Gracewing, 1995.

--- *Squires in the Slums: Settlements and Missions in Late Victorian Britain*. London: I. B. Tauris, 2007.

Scott, Joan. *Feminism and History*. Oxford: Oxford University Press, 1996.

--- 'Gender: A Useful Category of Historical Analysis.' *American Historical Review* 91, no. 5 (1986): 1073-75.

--- *Gender and the Politics of History*. New York: Columbia University Press, 1999.

--- 'Gender: Still a Useful Category of Analysis?' *Diogenes* (2010). [http://dio.sagepub.com/content/57/1/7.refs.html, accessed October 10th 2010].

Silver, Harold. 'Knowing and Not Knowing in the History of Education.' *History of Education* 21, no. 1 (1992): 97-108.

Skeggs, Beverly. 'Exchange, Value and Affect: Bourdieu and "the Self".' In *Feminism after Bourdieu*, edited by Linda Adkins and Beverly Skeggs. Blackwell, 2004. 75-96.

--- 'Context and Background: Pierre Bourdieu's Analysis of Class, Gender and Sexuality.' *The Sociological Review* 52 (2004): 19-33.

Spencer, Stephanie. '"Knowledge as the Necessary Food of the Mind": Charlotte Mason's Philosophy of Education.' In *Women, Education and Agency,1600-2000*, edited by Jean Spence, Sarah Jane Aiston and Maureen M. Meikle. London and New York: Routledge, 2010. 105-25.

Spender, Dale. *The Education Papers: Women's Quest for Equality in Britain 1850-1912*. London: Routledge and Kegan Paul, 1987.

Spring, David. 'The Clapham Sect: Some Social and Political Aspects.' *Victorian Studies* 5, no. 1 (1961): 35-48.

Stanley, Brian. *The Bible and the Flag: Protestant Missions and British Imperialism in the Nineteenth and Twentieth Centuries*. Leicester: Apollos, 1990.

--- 'Church State and the Hierarchy of "Civilization": The Making of the World Missionary Conference, Edinburgh 1910.' In *The Imperial Horizons of British Protestant Missions, 1880-1914*, edited by A.N. Porter. Grand Rapids, Michigan; Wm. B. Eerdmans, 2002. 58-84.

Stephens, W. B. *Education in Britain, 1750-1914*. Basingstoke: Macmillan, 1998.

Stott, Anne. '"A Singular Injustice Towards Women": Hannah More, Evangelicalism and Female Education.' In *Women, Religion and Feminism in Britain, 1750-1900*, edited by Sue Morgan. Basingstoke: Palgrave Macmillan, 2002. 23-38.

Styler, Rebecca. *Literary Theology by Women Writers of the Nineteenth Century*. Farnham: Ashgate, 2010.

Sutton, C.W., and Alan G. Crosby. 'Thomas Heywood (1797-1866).' *Oxford Dictionary of National Biography*: Oxford University Press, 2010. [http://www.oxforddnb.com/view/article/13191, accessed November 27th 2012].

Swaisland, Cecillie. *Servants and Gentlewomen to the Golden Land: The Emigration of Single Women from Britain to Southern Africa, 1820-1939*. Oxford; Providence: Berg; Pietermaritzburg, South Africa: University of Natal Press, 1993.

Tamboukou, Maria. *Sewing, Fighting and Writing: Radical Practices in Work, Politics and Culture*. Lanham: Rowman Littlefield International, 2015.

Thompson, David M. *Nonconformity in the Nineteenth Century*. London: Routledge and Kegan Paul, 1972.

Thorne, Susan. 'Religion and Empire at Home.' In *At Home with the Empire: Metropolitan Culture and the Imperial World*, edited by Catherine Hall and Sonia O. Rose. Cambridge: Cambridge University Press, 2006. 143-65.

Tiana Ferrer, Alejandro. 'The Concept of Popular Education Revisited – or What Do We Talk About When We Speak of Popular Education.' *Paedagogica Historica* 47, no. Nos. 1-2 (2011): 15-31.

Tosh, John. *A Man's Place: Masculinity and the Middle-Class Home in Victorian England*. New Haven, Connecticut; London: Yale University Press, 2007.

––– *Manliness and Masculinities in Nineteenth-Century Britain: Essays on Gender, Family, and Empire*. Harlow: Pearson Longman, 2005.

Turner, Frank. 'The Victorian Crisis of Faith and the Faith That Was Lost.' In *Victorian Faith in Crisis*, edited by Richard J. Helmstadter and Bernard Lightman. California: Stanford, 1991. 9-38.

Twells, Alison. *The Civilising Mission and the English Middle Class, 1792-1850: The 'Heathen' at Home and Overseas*. Basingstoke: Palgrave Macmillan, 2009.

Vaughan-Pow, Catherine J. 'A One-Way Ticket? Emigration and the Colonies in the Works of Charlotte M. Yonge.' In *Imperial Objects: Victorian Women's Emigration and the Unauthorized Imperial Experience*, edited by Rita Krandidis. New York: Twayne, 1998. 248-264.

Vicinus, Martha. *Independent Women: Work and Community for Single Women: 1850-1920*. London: Virago, 1985.

Vickery, Amanda. '"Golden Age to Separate Spheres": A Review of the Categories and Chronology of English Women's History.' In *Gender and History in Western Europe*, edited by Robert Shoemaker and Mary Vincent. London: Addison-Wesley Longman, 1998. 197-225.

Vincent, David. *Literacy and Popular Culture: England 1750-1914*. Cambridge: Cambridge University Press, 1989.

Walton, Susan. 'Charlotte Yonge: Marketing the Missionary Story.' *Women's Writing* 17, no. 2 (2010): 236-54.

––– *Imagining Soldiers and Fathers in the Mid-Victorian Era: Charlotte Yonge's Models of Manliness*. Farnham and Burlington: Ashgate, 2010.

Wardle, David. *English Popular Education, 1780-1970*. London: Cambridge University Press, 1970.
Watts, Ruth. 'Gendering the Story: Change in the History of Education.' *History of Education* 34, no. 3 (2005): 225-241.
--- 'Education, Empire and Social Change in Nineteenth Century England.' *Paedagogica Historica* 45, no. 6 (2009): 773-86.
--- *Gender, Power and the Unitarians in England, 1760-1860*. London: Longman, 1998.
Williams, Sarah C. '"Is There a Bible in the House?" Gender Religion and Family Culture.' In *Women, Gender and Religious Cultures in Britain, 1800-1940*, edited by Sue Morgan and Jacqueline de Vries. London: Routledge, 2011. 11-31.
Yamaguchi, Midori. *Daughters of the Anglican Clergy: Religion, Gender and Identity in Victorian England*. Basingstoke and NY: Palgrave, 2014.
Yeo, Eileen Janes. 'The Creation of "Motherhood" and Women's Responses in Britain and France 1750-1914.' *Women's History Review* 8, no. 1 (1999): 201-21.
--- 'Protestant Feminists and Catholic Saints.' In *Radical Femininity: Women's Self Representation in the Public Sphere*, edited by Eileen Janes Yeo. Manchester: Manchester University Press, 1998. 125-4564.
--- 'Some Contradictions of Social Motherhood.' In *Mary Wollstonecraft 200 Years of Feminisms*, edited by Eileen Janes Yeo. London and New York: Rivers Oram Press, 1997. 121-27.
--- 'Some Paradoxes of Empowerment.' In *Radical Femininity: Women's Self Representation in the Public Sphere*, edited by Eileen Janes Yeo. Manchester: Manchester University Press, 1998. 9-17.

Index

A Dangerous Errand (article in *MUJ*), 191
A Grave Peril (pamphlet), 196
A Practical View of the Prevailing Religious System of Professed Christians in The Higher and Middle Classes of this Country Contrasted with Real Christianity (William Wilberforce publication), 41
Account of Early Life at Hope End (by Mary Sumner), 150
Addington, Lady Minnie, 58
advocacy network, 9, 129
Africa, 91, 103, 112, 130, 136, 228
Alcott, Louisa M., 189
Algeria, 106, 107, 133
All Saints Church of England Primary School, Winchester, 158
Anglican Church/Anglicanism, 5, 15, 27, 336, 45, 46, 47, 52, 53, 54, 55, 60, 62, 63, 64, 70, 78, 79, 83, 84, 85, 94, 100, 109, 123, 141, 143, 144, 146, 150, 158, 160, 164, 170, 188, 194, 196, 198, 199, 203, 205, 207, 210, 211
  and cultural arbitrary, 82, 83, 84, 117
  and divine authority, 74
  and doctrinal teaching, 158, 159
  and doxa/Anglican/religious, 82, 118, 170, 171, 179, 204, 207, 210 (see also GFS, MU and Sumner, Mary)
  and doxic values/gendered doxic values, 83, 160
  and elementary education, 154, 155, 158-159
  and field of education, 7, 156, 170, 194, 198
  and field manoeuvres, 48, 52, 65, 23, 154, 197, 203
  and field of power, 155, 194, 198, 207, 210
  and goods of salvation, 203, 205, 207, 210
  and imperialist sentiment, 122
  and patriarchy, 204
  and patriotism, 207
  and pedagogic action, 65, 117/118, 154, 155, 158, 171, 203
  and power in political and religious field, 27-28
  and religious capital, 100 (see also GFS, MU and Sumner, Mary)
  and symbolic capital, 170
  and symbolic violence, 100, 118, 143, 198, 206, 207
  and Tractarianism, 47-49
'Are We Growing Worse? Gleanings for Mothers from the Report on Physical Degeneration, 1904' (article in *MUJ*), 190
Australia, 115
  and White Australia project, 115-116

Bachelard, Gaston, 12
Barclay, Mrs Hubert, 81
Barnacle (periodical), 187, 232
Barrett-Browning, Elizabeth, 33
Barrett, Edward Moulton, later Browning, 33
Barton, John, 31
Barton, Mary Elizabeth, 31
Basdell, Marion, 75
Bishop Otter Teacher Training College, Chichester, 161, 165
Board School(s), 150, 154, 157, 159, 161, 194-195
Boer War (South African war of 1899-1902), 130, 139, 229
book hawking, 98, 158
Bourdieu, Pierre
  and capital, 4, 13
    cultural capital, 16, 17
    embodied cultural capital, 17
    institutionalised cultural capital, 17
    objectified cultural capital, 17
    economic capital, 16-17
    linguistic capital, 20
    social capital, 16-17
    symbolic capital, 16-17 (see also MU and Sumner, Mary)
  and cultural arbitrary, 17, 18, 19, 20, 203
  and doxa, 14, 15
  and doxic relations, 14
  and field, 4, 13, 15, 16, 17
  and field of power, 27
  and gender, 22-24
  and goods of salvation, 21
  and habitus, 4, 13-14, 20, 24-25, 27
    linguistic habitus, 20
  and horizons of possibility, 14, 27
  and misrecognition, 19-21, 202
  and networks, 17, 24, 25
  and pedagogic action, 13, 18, 19
  and pedagogic authority, 18, 19, 20
  and pedagogic work, 19
  and philosophy of action, 13
  and players, 13, 15, 16
  and practice, 13
  and race, 17, 22, 23
  and reproduction, 20, 27
  and symbolic violence, 18, 19, 20, 27
  influences of:
    Gaston Bachelard, 12
    Émile Durkheim, 12
    Ervin Goffman, 12
    Claude Lévi-Strauss, 12
    Karl Marx, 12
    Maurice Merleau Ponty, 12
    Max Weber, 12
Bowen Thompson, Mrs, 107
Braddon, Mary Elizabeth, 189
Bramston, Anna, 187, 226, 228
Bramston, Mary, 232
British and Foreign Schools Society, 155
British Syrian Schools, 107
British Women's Emigration Society (BWEA), 114-116
Burdett-Coutts, Baroness Angela, 128
Butler, Josephine, 69, 90
buttress fund, 133
Buxton, Lady Victoria, 139

Cairo, 130
Canada, 114, 130
Carlyle, Thomas, 152, 189
capital, see Bourdieu, Pierre, Christian capital, cultural capital, economic capital, educational capital, linguistic capital, maternal educative capital, religious capital, social capital, symbolic capital, womanly capital
Cavendish, Lady Lucy, 196, 226, 228-229
census 1851, 45
Ceylon, 130
chastity, 54, 67, 68, 69, 70, 82, 111, 144, 203, 204

Cheltenham Ladies' College, 185
Chetham's Society, The, 34
Chichester, Lady Alice, 58, 76, 127, 141, 169, 194
Chitty, Mrs George, 193
chivalry, 76, 105, 126, 204
Christian capital, 208
Christian chivalry, 61, 72
Christian manliness, 73, 156
Church Congress Exeter (1894), 76
Church Congress Wolverhampton (1887), 76
Church Congress, Hull (1890), 57, 63, 74
Church Congress, Liverpool (1904), 57
Church Congress, Newcastle upon Tyne (1881), 59
Church Congress, Nottingham (1897), 61
Church Congress, Portsmouth (1885), 1, 55, 57, 61, 124
Church Congress, Southampton (1913), 57
Church Congress, Weymouth (1905), 57
Church Congresses and women's role, 60-63
Church Family Newspaper, 127
church halls, 178
Church Mission Society (CMS), 96, 97, 112, 134, 143
Church of England Temperance Society (CETS), 15, 16, 118, 121, 127, 198,
Church of England Zenana Mission Society (CEZMS), 112, 134
'churchwomen', 8, 199, 231
Chute, Mrs Eleanor Chaloner, 130, 134
civilising mission, 7, 10, 89
Clapham Sect, The, 36
Coleridge, Christabel, 181, 183, 229
colonial expansion, 144
Concerning Infants (by Mary Sumner), 184
Conference of Overseas Workers (1920), 135
Contagious Diseases Acts, 69
contested authority, 31, 44, 149
Coombs, Joyce, 3, 33
Cottage Garden Society, 44, 99
Council for the Home Training of Children in Religion (1907), 192
Countess of Airlie, 80
Cowper-Temple amendment (to the Forster Act), 159
Craik, Mary, 189
Crawford, Mrs, 135
Crawley (near Winchester), 35
Creighton, Louise, 56, 60, 129, 141, 186, 227, 230
Cross Street Chapel, 32, 93
cultural arbitrary, see Anglican Church/Anglicanism, Bourdieu, Pierre, MU, Sumner, Mary
cultural capital (see Bourdieu, Pierre)
Cunard Line, 130
curriculum, 154, 155, 159, 160, 165, 166, 196

Davidson, Dr Randall, Bishop of London and Archbishop of Canterbury, 1, 81
Davis, Miss, 134
Denstone School, 152
diamond wedding anniversary (George and Mary Sumner), 65
Diocese of Winchester, 1, 54, 119, 143
divorce, 58, 82, 128
Divorce Act, 1857 70
domesticity, 41, 71, 174
doxa, see Anglican Church/Anglicanism, Bourdieu, Pierre
doxic notions of womanhood, 199
doxic values, see Anglican Church/Anglicanism
Durkheim, Émile, 12

Early Life at Hope End and Account of the Founding of the Mothers' Union (by Mary Sumner), 38
Early Training of Girls and Boys: An Appeal to Working Women (1882) (by Jane Ellice Hopkins), 193
economic capital, see Bourdieu, Pierre
Education Act (1870), 150, 156, 159
Education Act (1902), 195
educational capital for women, 150, 154, 170, 171, 178, 208, 209
educational philanthropy, see Sumner, Mary
Edward VII, 139
Egypt, 100, 104, 106, 107
elementary education, 7, 11, 150, 198 (see also Anglican Church/Anglicanism)
Eliot, George, 189
Ely, Diocese of, 62
Emery, Archdeacon, 63
emigration, 114/115, 122 (see also GFS and Joyce, Ellen)
empire, 6, 91, 112, 122, 129, 134, 144, 207, 208, 211, 212 (see also BWEA, GFS, MU, Ridding Laura, Sumner, Mary)
enfranchisement, 195
English Christian womanhood, 206
Erskine, Lady Horatia, 61, 76, 80, 134, 135, 137, 138, 180, 192
Etheridge, Edward Harold, 97
Eton College, 53, 151, 153, 154
eugenic concerns, 190
evangelical outreach, 205
exchange theory, 9
exemplar of religious and moral sensibility, 199

Farnham Castle, 35, 38, 42
fathers (in home life), 41, 54, 62, 63, 72, 73, 139, 177, 185, 191, 195, 209, 210
'Fathers Please Read This' (article in *MUJ*), 195
femininity, 185
feminist history, 25
field(s), Bourdieu, Pierre
  field of education, see Anglican Church/Anglicanism, MU, Sumner, Mary, Yonge, Charlotte
  field of philanthropy, see GFS and Sumner, Mary
  field of power, 144, 155, 156, 194, 198, 207, 208, 210, 212, (see also Anglican Church/Anglicanism, Bourdieu, Pierre, imperial field of power and Sumner, Mary)
  field of religion, 5, 31, 51, 54, 144, 170, see also Sumner, Mary
field manoeuvres, see Anglican Church/Anglicanism, GFS, MU, Sumner, Mary
Forster Act, The, 1870 Education Act, see Education Act (1870)
Forster, William E., 156
France, 102, 151
Friendly Leaves, 113, 114, 181, 189
Friendship's Highway, 3, 109
Froebel, Friedrich, 149, 164, 185
Froude, Richard Hurrell, 45

Gaskell, William, 32
gender, 4, 17, 26, 84, 133, 204 (see also Bourdieu, Pierre)
  and class, 27, 82, 83, 123, 149, 173, 202, 208, 212
gender history, 25
gender identities, 92
gender relations, 143
gender roles, 84
gender stratification, 117
gendered parameters, 84, 203, 205, 210,
Geneva, 38
George and Mary Sumner: Their Life and Times (by Joyce Coombs), 3

Germany, 151
Gibson, Alan George Sumner, 97
Gibson, Miss, 134
Girl Guides, 193
girls and university education, 186
Girls' Friendly Society (GFS)
  and Associates, 55, 108, 109, 111, 114, 116, 117, 226
  and Elementary Reading Union course, 113
  and empire, 114, 139
  and emigration, 109, 114, 115, 117, 145
  and field of philanthropy, 110
  and field manoeuvres, 109, 130
  and gendered doxa of Anglicanism, 116
  and misrecognition, 116-117
  and mission/women's mission, 108 111, 116, 118 (See also MU and Sumner, Mary)
  and 'Mission of Women to Women', 109
  and missionary
    activity, 144
    philanthropy, 116, 143
    work(ers) overseas, 109, 112, 113, 122, 143, 206
  and 'Objects', 55, 74
  and pedagogic authority, 116, 117
  and reading for self-culture, 189
  and religious capital, 70, 117 (see also Anglican church/ Anglicanism, MU and Sumner, Mary)
  and settler colonies, 112, 116 (see also MU and Sumner, Mary)
  and shared (group) habitus, 109
  and symbolic violence, 116
'Girls' professions' (article in *MUJ*), 191
Girls' Public Day School Company, 186, 192
Goffman, Ervin, 12
golden wedding anniversary (George and Mary Sumner), 65, 138
goods of salvation, see Anglican Church/Anglicanism, Bourdieu, Pierre, Sumner, Mary
good parenting, 176, 197
Gore Browne, Louisa Barrington (see Sumner, Louisa)
Gore Browne, Margaret, 109
Gore Browne, The Reverend Barrington, 39, 99
Gorham, Reverend and The Gorham Case, 47
Grant, Reverend Alexander, 157

habitus, see Bourdieu, Pierre, GFS and Sumner, Mary
Hampshire Chronicle (newspaper), 56, 99, 159
'handmaids of the church', 62
harems, 103, 133
Harold Browne, Edward, 50, 163
Harold Browne, Elizabeth, 39, 54
Harrow School, 153
Hart-Dyke, Sir William MP, 159
Headmistresses' Association, 193
Heir of Redclyffe (by Charlotte Yonge), 131
'helpmeet', 42-44, 51, 61, 66, 83, 100, 118, 153, 198, 211
Heywood, Arthur Percival, 38
Heywood, Isabel, 37, 48
Heywood, James, 33
Heywood, Margaret, 34, 38
  and conversion to Catholicism, 48
Heywood, Nathaniel, 32
Heywood, Oliver, 94
Heywood, Sir Benjamin, 32-33, 34, 37, 38, 39, 94 152
Heywood, Thomas, 32-33, 34, 37, 39, 49, 94, 151
Heywood, Thomas Percival, 38, 39, 49-50, 94, 152

higher education for middle and upper-class women and girls, 7, 11, 177, 185, 199, 210
History of Mothers' Union's Fifty Years, 3, 81-82
Holy Land, the, 93, 101, 105, 121
'home above', 40, 71
Home Education (by Charlotte Mason), 165-166, 175-176
Home Life (by Mary Sumner), 2, 69
Hong Kong, 130
'hop Sunday', 95
Hope End, Ledbury, 33-34, 38, 94-95
Hopkins, Jane Ellice, 90, 193-194, 209, 229-230
horizons of possibility, see Bourdieu, Pierre, MU and Sumner, Mary
'How Wives are to Blame for their Husbands becoming Drunkards' (article for *MUJ*), 190
'How Working Girls May Help their Sex and Country' (in *Friendly Leaves*), 189

Imperial Colonist (periodical), 114
imperial expansion, 212
imperial field (of power), 145, 207
imperial rule, 6, 89, 92, 117, 122, 138, 139, 143, 144
India, 112, 113, 114, 130, 131, 132, 133, 134, 136
International Federation for the Abolition of State Regulation of Vice, 127-128
Ireland, 128

Japan, 112
Jenkyns, Mrs, 192
Joyce, Ellen, 114, 116, 131, 230
Jubilee Pageant, 111

Keble, John, 46-47, 48
King George V, 78
King, Gertrude, 132, 134, 230
Kingsley, Charles, 188
Kroff, Herr, 151

Lady Margaret Hall, Oxford, 187
Lambeth Conference, the, 135, 196, 197, 199
Lambeth Palace, 54
Lancaster, Joseph, 155
Landseer, Sir Edwin, 152
Lang, Cosmo, Archbishop of York, 81
Layard, Reverend E.B., 185
Leighton, Sir Frederick, 152
Lévi-Strauss, Claude, 12
Liberal party, 79, 157
linguistic capital, see Bourdieu, Pierre
literacy, 8, 158, 159, 160, 173, 179, 181, 189, 209
Loader, Miss, 134
Local Education Authority (LEA) and Schools, 198
London Diocesan Mothers' Union, 3

Macintosh, Mr, 107
Madagascar, 134, 136-137
Malta, 130
Manchester Grammar School, 32
Manning, Cardinal Henry, 46
marriage, 41, 44, 45, 154, (see also MU and Sumner Mary)
Martineau, Harriet, 161, 165, 167
Marval, Dr Alice, 112
Marx, Karl, 12, 16
Mary Sumner: Her Life and Work, 3, 33
Mason, Charlotte, 9, 165-166, 193, 231
maternal educative capital, 171, 208-209
Maude, Mrs (Mothers' Union Central Secretary), 58, 59, 72, 127, 131
Mechanics' Institute, 34, 152
Merleau-Ponty, Maurice, 12

Methodists, 36
metropole, the, 6, 11, 89, 92, 129, 136, 142, 143, 145
Miles Platting Affair, 50
misrecognition, see Bourdieu Pierre, GFS, MU and Sumner, Mary
mission/women's mission, see MU and Sumner, Mary
Mission of Women to Women, 109
Missionary
    and activity, 113 (see also GFS and MU)
    and endeavour, 123 (see also MU and Sumner, Mary)
    and enterprise(s), 97 (see also MU and Sumner, Mary)
    and exploits, see MU
    and identity, see MU
    and intelligence, 91
    and intervention, 106
    and martyr, see Marval, Dr Alice
    and mothers, 10
    and news, see MU
    and organisations/societies, 6, 89, 93 (see also MU)
    and philanthropy, see GFS and MU
    and role, see Sumner, Mary
    and schools, 107
    and stories, see *MIC* and *MUJ*
    and valour, 95, 145-146
    and worker(s), 113, 115, 141 (see also GFS and MU)
Moberly, Charlotte, 46, 231-232
Moberly, Edith, 110
Moberly, George, 47
Money, Agnes, 68, 113
Montgomery, Henry, 141
Montgomery, Maud, 141
Monthly Packet, The (periodical), 110, 182, 187
morality, 1, 26, 55, 58, 66, 69, 108, 116, 126, 163, 171, 186, 188, 189
More, Hannah, 161-162, 164
Mormonism, 48
'mother country', 122, 135, 136, 139
motherhood and spiritual educative vocation, 66
mothering, 66, 122, 124, 162, 170, 171, 174, 175, 176
mothers as home educators, 171
Mothers in Australia, 131
Mothers in Council (*MIC*) (periodical), 132, 166, 175, 178, 181, 182, 183, 184, 185, 187, 189, 191, 197, 199
    and missionary stories, 132-133
    and pedagogic action, 191
'mother in Israel', 43
Mothers' Union (MU)
    and Anglican (Christian) doxa, 192, 207
    and anti-secular education movement, 58, 182, 195, 199, see also secular education
    and Army branches, 78
    and Associates, 121, 130, 132, 133, 177, 178, 179
    and brooch, 57
    and Committee of Presidents, 58
    and cultural arbitrary, 123, 145
    and denominational religious instruction, 198
    and divorce, 58, 77, 80, 81, 82, 128, 193
    and 'Drawing room' meetings, 56, 177, 178
    and education through magazines, 174, 179-182
    and empire, 121, 123, 129, 139, 141
    and field of education, 192, 197
    and field manoeuvres, 65, 109, 123,130,197
    and horizons of possibility, 161, 199, 213 (see also Bourdieu, Pierre and Sumner, Mary)
    and imperial identity, 139, 141
    and legislation on moral issues, 90

and logo, 57
and marriage, 67, 80, 81-82, 109, 128 (see also Sumner, Mary)
and membership cards, 1, 100
and misrecognition, 64, 198
and mission/women's mission, 20, 121, 123, 128, 130, 134, 139, 184 (see also GFS and Sumner, Mary)
and missionary
activity, 131, 144, 182, 209 (see also GFS)
endeavour, 130 (see also Sumner, Mary)
enterprise(s), 121, 123, 133
exploits, 132
identity, 123, 126, 132
news, 134
organisations/societies, 132, 142
philanthropy, 143 (see also GFS and Sumner, Mary)
missionary work(ers), 122, 143, 157, 195, 206 (see also GFS)
and Mormonism, 80
and Navy branches, 78
and 'Objects', 47, 124
and Overseas Committee, 130, 137
and patriarchal authority, 65
and patriotism, 78-79, 207
and pedagogic action, 109, 146, 178, 191, 205, 206 (see also pedagogic action, separate entry Anglican Church/Anglicanism, Bourdieu, Pierre and Sumner, Mary)
and pedagogic authority, 163, 176, 178, 182, 191, 199, 208, 209, 211,212
and pedagogic work(ers), 84, 85, 100, 142, 145, 163, 172, 178, 198, 207
and philanthropic patronage, 56
and positive eugenics, 122
and race, 145
and reading for self-culture, 189
and religious capital, 70, 83, 129, 145 209 (see also Anglican church/Anglicanism, GFS and Sumner, Mary)
and religious doxa, 85, 142, 144, 189
and religious education, 1, 38, 151, 190, 192, 193, 199
and settler colonies, 130 (see also GFS and Sumner, Mary)
and sub field of educational publishing, 197, 210
and symbolic capital, 70, 84, 143, 145, 161, 182, 198, 209
and symbolic gifts, 207
and symbolic violence, 145, 207, 208 (see also Anglican church/ Anglicanism, Bourdieu, Pierre, GFS and Sumner, Mary)
and transnational expansion, 1, 89, 93, 122, 129, 206
and women's citizenship, 73, 79
as a brand, 192
Mothers' Union Journal (*MUJ*), 131, 181, 182, 188, 189, 190, 191, 194, 195, 196, 198, 199
and missionary stories, 188
and pedagogic action/work, 191
Mrs Wilberforce's Narrative, 123

National Society for Promoting the Education of the Poor in the Principles of the Church of England (The National Society), 155
National Union of Women Workers (NUWW), 129, 186
networks, see Bourdieu, Pierre and Sumner, Mary
networking, 54, 123, 130, 131, 135, 174, 192
New Zealand, 112, 130, 131,132, 135
Newman, John Henry, 45

non-conformists, 150
North, Brownlow, 44
North, Francis, 44

Old Alresford, 2, 37, 38, 44, 50, 54, 97, 98, 108, 152
Oluwole, Mrs, 142
Otterbourne Parish Magazine, 183
Our Holiday in the East (by Mary Sumner), 2, 93, 100, 133

Palmer, William, 45
parental example, 190
Parents' National Education Union (PNEU), 165, 193, 198
Parker, Miss (governess), 151
passive resisters, 195
patriarchal authority, see MU and Sumner, Mary
patriarchal domination, 51, 82, 213
patriarchal hegemony, 149
patriarchy, see Anglican Church/Anglicanism
patriotism, 78, 79, 207
Patteson, John Coleridge, Bishop of Melanesia, 131
pedagogic action, 171, 197 (see also Anglican Church/Anglicanism, Bourdieu, Pierre, *MIC*, MU, *MUJ* and Sumner, Mary)
pedagogic authority, see Bourdieu, Pierre, GFS, MU, Sumner, Mary, Yonge, Charlotte
pedagogic work(ers), 170, 178 (see also Bourdieu, Pierre, MU and Sumner, Mary)
'penny dreadful', 179
Pestalozzi, Heinrich (1746-1827), 149, 164, 166
philanthropy, 2, 5, 8, 10, 15, 24, 33, 51, 60, 62, 83, 90, 91, 92, 93, 94, 95, 97, 100, 109, 110, 116, 117, 118, 121, 122, 123, 133, 143, 146, 152, 158, 171, 173, 174, 197, 211
philanthropic activity, 6, 36, 89, 90, 91, 94, 95, 121, 174, 206
philosophy of action, see Bourdieu, Pierre
Philpotts, Bishop Henry, 47
piety, 17, 33, 47, 51, 66, 60, 85, 95, 112, 197, 198, 203,
popular media, 179
Porter, Mary, 134
Primrose League, 79, 114
Prince Albert, 77
Princess Christian, see Princess Helena
Princess Helena, 77, 127
Principles at Stake (anti-Tractarian essays), 49, 50
Pugin, Augustus, 45

Queen Alexandra, 77
Queen Mary, 77
Queen Victoria, 47, 77
  and as empress, 122, 132, 134, 138
  and as maternal icon, 122, 138, 208

race, see Bourdieu, Pierre, Joyce, Ellen, MU, Oluwole, Mrs, Ridding, Laura, Sumner, Mary
racial coexistence, 139
radicals, 155
Religion in the School (article in *MUJ*), 196
religious capital, see Bourdieu, Pierre, GFS
religious doxa, see Anglican Church/Anglicanism, MU and Sumner, Mary
religious education, see MU
religious observance, 53
Religious Tract Society, 179
respectability, 61, 74, 185
'Responsibilities of Mothers' (paper by Mary Sumner), 128
'Responsibilities of Parents' (article by Mary Sumner in *MUJ*), 196

Ridding, Lady Laura Elizabeth (formerly Palmer), 79, 80, 109, 130, 193, 207, 232
and attitude to Empire, 129, 140
Rix, Miss, 134, 136
Roman Catholic Church and Tractarianism, 47-49
Roman Catholic(ism), 36, 46, 48, 60, 97, 104, 159, 196
Rome, 34, 38, 151
Royal Commission on Education (1894), 196
Ruskin, John, 152, 188, 189
Russell, Mrs, 80

Scott, Sir Walter, 189
secondary schooling for middle and upper-class girls, 185
Secular Education (by Mary Sumner), 79, 194,
secular education, 58, 195
and resistance to secularisation, 157, 195 (see also MU)
Senior, Jeanie Elizabeth Nassau, 54
Seville, 38
Short History of the Mothers' Union, A, 1, 3, 33
Short, Norah, 134
social capital, see Bourdieu, Pierre
social control, 173
social stratification, 26, 53, 74, 83, 91, 117, 189, 204
socialist Sunday Schools, 196
socialists/socialism, 196
Soulsby, Lucy, 129, 186, 192, 198, 209, 232-233
South Africa, 114, 130, 131, 137, 139, 140, 229, 230
South African Colonisation Society (SACS), 140
South America, 130
Southwell Women's League, 127
spiritual inclusiveness, 74, 140
St Cross, Winchester, alms-houses, 44
St Mary's, Southampton, 44
St Monica, 125
Stanhope, Reverend, later Archdeacon, 100
Stead, W.T. and Bairn's Bible, 188
Steinthal, Emeline Francis, 193
Stray Thoughts for Mothers and Teachers (1897 pamphlet), 192
Sumner, Charles Richard, Bishop of Winchester, 3, 34, 36, 39, 42, 44, 45, 46, 47, 49, 50, 95-96
and tour to Ireland, 97
and visit to the Channel Islands, 96
(see also Winchester Diocesan Training School)
Sumner, George Henry (1824-1909), 34, 38, 40, 47, 49, 78, 79, 98, 156-157, 159
Sumner, Hannah Bird, 37, 42
Sumner, (George) Heywood, 57, 153
Sumner, Jennie, 40, 42, 43, 96
Sumner, John Bird, Archbishop of Canterbury, 3, 34, 36, 37, 44, 45, 46, 47, 60
Sumner, Louisa Mary Alice (Loulie), 39, 81
Sumner, Louisanna, 39
Sumner, Mary
and activism, 5, 6, 7, 8, 9, 10, 11, 15, 17, 22, 25, 26, 31, 34, 52, 59, 85, 89, 149, 154, 173, 174, 197, 199, 202, 204, 211, 212
and agency, 5, 9, 10, 11, 22, 25, 201, 202, 211, 213
and Anglican faith/Anglican doxa, 10, 118, 197
and anti-secular education movement, see MU and secular education
and childhood and child rearing notions of, 161-164
and Christian Science, 48
and civilising mission, 7, 10, 115
and cookery, 177

and constraint, 5, 10, 13, 22, 201, 202, 208, 213
and cultural arbitrary, 20, 51, 8.2, 84, 118, 145, 158, 170, 208
and death of, 1, 2, 3, 40
and denominational religious instruction, 198
and divorce (attitude to), 58, 70, 77, 80, 81
and divine authority, 204
and educational capital, 151, 154, 170, 171, 178, 208, 209
and educational habitus, 150
and educational philanthropy, 152
and empire, 6, 11, 109, 115, 123, 135, 138, 142, 145, 146, 211, 213
and empowerment, 4, 25, 174, 208
and experience of childhood, see Hope End, Ledbury
and family life, see Old Alresford
and field of education, 15, 149, 150, 154, 174, 197
and field of philanthropy, 100
and field of power, 198-199
and field of religion, 15, 84, 146, 197, 199, 209, 213
and field manoeuvres, 27, 59, 83, 209
and forced marriage (attitude to), 106
and gendered conduct, 82
and gendered religious doxa, 84
and gift language of the child races, 137, 138
and goods of salvation, 51, 207
and Greek Orthodox Church, 104
and habitus/group habitus, 15, 51, 52, 59, 90, 93, 100, 109, 117, 118, 121, 146, 149, 154, 160, 170, 204, 205, 211
and higher education, 11, 185, 197, 199, 210
and 'the higher life', 178
and home life, see separate entries, Hope End, Ledbury and Old Alresford
and Hope End, see separate entry
and horizon/gendered horizons of possibility, 4, 9, 14, 26, 27, 31, 154,161, 199, 202, 210, 211, 213 (see also Bourdieu, Pierre and Mothers' Union)
and indigenous women, 113, 134, 208, 209, 211-212
and Jews, 104
and kinship network(s), 31, 45, 51, 93, 117
and marriage (to George Sumner), 31, 51, 56 (see also golden and diamond wedding anniversaries)
and marriage, views on, 54, 66, 69-71, 82, 190, 204
and maternal exemplars, 51
and men's Bible Study group, 98, 158
and misrecognition, 27, 70, 82, 85, 100, 136, 145, 203, 211, 213
and mission/women's mission, 6-7, 10, 20, 22, 27, 89-91, 93, 95, 100, 108-111, 138, 149, 201, 202, 205, 206, 211 (see also GFS and MU)
and Mormonism, 48
and Muslims, 104
and networking, 130, 135 (see also networking separate entry)
and networks, 3, 4, 9, 15, 202 (see also kinship networks and Bourdieu, Pierre)
and non-Christian religions, 118
and organisational activism, 204
and parental authority, 137
and patriarchal authority, 204
and patriarchal domination, 51, 82, 213

and patriotism, 207
and pedagogic action, 18, 20, 51, 65, 82, 84, 90, 146, 160, 178, 203, 204, 208, 209, 213 (see also pedagogic action, separate entry, Anglican Church/ Anglicanism, Bourdieu, Pierre and MU)
and pedagogic authority, 20, 54, 59, 63, 119-120, 121, 143, 145, 151, 163, 171, 198, 203, 206, 209, 213
and pedagogic work(ers), 18, 118, 160, 170, 178, 203, 204, 209, 210,
and popular educator, as 8, 150, 173, 202
and the power of books, 180
and the power of reading, 180
and public speaking, 124, 198, 209
and race, 4, 6, 93, 109, 123, 136, 139, 145 (see also race, separate entry, Australia, Bourdieu, Pierre and MU)
and religious capital, 31, 51, 52, 53, 59, 65, 70, 83, 108, 109, 129, 170, 206, 208, 210 (see also Anglican church/Anglicanism, GFS and MU)
and religious doxa, 70, 83
and religious education, 7, 135, 158, 159, 163, 170, 173, 175, 176, 177, 183, 190, 194, 195, 196, 198
and role of women, 10, 60, 123, 171, 206
and self-restraint, 66, 169, 177
and settler colonies, 130, 144, 211 (see also GFS and MU)
and Socialist Sunday schools, 196
and symbolic capital, 51, 72, 108, 117, 118, 121, 143, 154, 161, 170, 171, 172, 176, 178, 197, 205, 208, 210, 211, 212
and symbolic violence, 51, 82, 84, 145, 203, 204, 207, 208, 213
and thrift, 177
and undesirable literature, 180
Sunday School(s), 95, 152, 155, 158, 171, 196
Swan, Annie S., 189
symbolic capital, see Bourdieu, Pierre, Sumner, Mary
symbolic gifts, see MU
symbolic violence, see Anglican Church/Anglicanism, Bourdieu, Pierre, GFS, MU and Sumner, Mary

'tabula rasa', 164
Talks to Mothers (pamphlet), 192
Tasmania, 130, 141
temperance, 44, 58, 80, 99, 111, 124, 125, 177, 189, 190, 198
Temple, Beatrice, 133
Temple, Archbishop William, 51
Thackeray, William M., 152
'The Bible in Our Schools' (article in *MUJ*), 196
'The Call of the Empire' (1909 paper by Laura Ridding), 140
'The Education Act: A Word to Fathers' (article in *MUJ*), 195
The English Women's Review (periodical), 63
The Illustrated Catechism, 178
'The Modern Education of Girls' (article in *MIC*), 186
'The Mothers' Union in Many Lands' (lantern show), 131
The Parents' Review (periodical), 193
The Times (newspaper), 180
Thorold, Bishop Anthony, 66
'To Husbands' (article in *MUJ*), 72
'To Husbands and Fathers' (article in *MUJ*), 72, 164
To Mothers of the Higher Classes (publication by Mary Sumner), 56, 176

Tory party, 79
Townend, Kathleen, 114
Townsend Mary, 55, 61, 74, 233
Tractarians, 45, 49
Tracts for the Times, 45
Transnational expansion, see MU
Trollope, Anthony, 44
Two Aspects of Education: Self Control and Fortitude, Humility and Large Heartedness (by Lucy Soulsby), 192

Unitarianism, 31-34, 39, 46, 93, 151-152
  and the Heywood family, 39

vaccination, 190
ventilation, 190
voluntary denominational schools, 194, 195

Watch Committee, 80
Weber, Max, 12
Wellington Heath, 34, 35, 49, 94, 95
Wesley, John, 36
West Indies, 130, 131, 142
Western Equatorial Africa, 142
What is the Mothers' Union? 126
Whatley, Mary Louisa, 107
Whigs, see Liberal party
White Crusade, The, 111
White Horse Project, The, 111
White Star Line, 130
Wilberforce, Emily, 61, 180, 193
Wilberforce, Ernest, 55, 61, 80
Wilberforce, Samuel, 3, 46, 50, 55
Wilberforce, William, 37, 41
Winchester Cathedral (and Close), 2, 69, 133, 135
Winchester Diocesan Committee, 57, 127, 177, 179
Winchester Diocesan Training College, 156
Winchester Emigration Society, 114
Winchester High School, 186
Winchester Juvenile Union of The Church of England Temperance Society, 99
Wolvesey Palace, Winchester, 65
womanly capital, 70, 83, 199
'womanly sphere', 153
women as educators, 150, 199
Woodward, Mary, 61, 131, 134, 135, 137, 192
Wordsworth, Elizabeth, 187, 233
Wordsworth, Mrs (wife of the Bishop of Salisbury), 125
Wordsworth, William, 165
World's Purity Federation Congress, 129

Yonge, Charlotte, 56, 62, 75, 182, 183, 184, 187, 188, 192, 233-234
  and *Books for the Nursery,* 187
  and *Daisy Chain, The,* 184
  and field of education, 187
  and *Langley Tales,* 184
  and pedagogic authority, 176
  and *Two Sides of the Shield,* 184
York, 59
Young Men's Association, 98

Zenana, 92, 93, 106

If you liked this book, why not try some of our other titles?

Charlotte Mason

Hidden Heritage and Educational Influence

Margaret A. Coombs

ISBN: 9780718894023
ePub ISBN: 9780718844066
Kindle ISBN: 9780718844080
PDF ISBN: 9780718844073

As the acknowledged founder and philosopher of the Parents' National Educational Union (PNEU), Charlotte Mason was revered by her followers as a saintly Madonna figure. She died in 1923 at the peak of her fame, having achieved mythic status as the Principal of her House of Education and wide recognition after the introduction of her liberal educational programmes into state schools. Yet her early life and heritage remained shrouded in mystery. Drawing upon insubstantiated sources, the official biography released in 1960 confused rather than illuminated Charlotte's background, contributing to several enduring misapprehensions.

In her new and definitive biography, Margaret Coombs draws on years of research to reveal for the first time the hidden backdrop to Charlotte Mason's life, tracing the lives of her previously undiscovered Quaker ancestors to offer a better understanding of the roots of her personality and ideas. Coombs charts her rise from humble beginnings as an orphaned pupil-teacher to great heights as a lady of culture venerated within prestigious PNEU circles, illustrating how with determination she surmounted the Victorian age's rigid class divisions to achieve her educational vision. A thorough analysis of Charlotte Mason's educational influences and key friendships challenges longstanding notions about the roots of her philosophy, offering a more realistic picture of her life and work than ever accomplished before.

With a growing following in the USA and Australia, Charlotte Mason's ideas have a clear relevance to the continuing educational debate today. Admirers of her philosophy and scholars of the history of education will find much to enthral and instruct them in these pages.

Mere Education

C.S. Lewis as Teacher for our Time

Mark A. Pike

ISBN: 9780718893255
ePub ISBN: 9780718841874
Kindle ISBN: 9780718841881
PDF ISBN: 9780718841867

Drawing upon a wide range of C.S. Lewis's fiction and non-fiction, both well known and relatively unknown, Mark A. Pike applies this remarkable author's educational vision to current issues of critical importance for parents, students, teachers and school leaders. *Mere Education* clearly describes the boundaries Lewis perceived that will protect schooling from an incoming tide of ideological assumptions that threaten to erode and undermine excellence.

C.S. Lewis was an inspirational teacher and took a keen interest in secondary schooling. Yet the contribution of C.S. Lewis to the field of education goes far beyond this. During the Second World War, Lewis taught the people of a whole country through his radio broadcasts and criss-crossed Great Britain giving talks and answering questions on military bases about the purpose of life. He also showed how schooling could be undertaken in the light of that purpose.

As parents, teachers and school leaders we know we are responsible for helping our children and young people to acquire knowledge and skills, but also virtue and good character. C.S. Lewis believed educational excellence concerned the cultivation of both. *Mere Education* shows how excellence should be nurtured in school leadership, teaching and learning by evaluating a range of current policies and practices in schooling in the light of the thought of C.S. Lewis. The result is a much-needed and controversial appraisal of modern education.

Doors of Possibility

The Life of Emmeline Tanner 1876-1955

Susan Major

ISBN: 9780718829223

Emmeline Tanner's story spans a period of intense change in girls' secondary education, and tells of a professional career which is in many respects unique. She started to teach at the age of thirteen, struggling to educate herself within the confines of the late Victorian, provincial, chapel-going society into which she had been born. By the time she became Headmistress of Roedean School in 1924, she was recognised as an influential leader of headmistresses and a champion of broadening the path. Driven by the First World War to stalwart support for the League of Nations and internationalism, from the 1920s she engaged in far-reaching educational controversies, acted as a spokesperson for headmistresses, was never daunted by frequent frustration of reforming ideas, and was still striving to widen opportunity throughout the Second World War as Chairman of the Joint Committee of the Four Secondary Associations, and later as a member of the Fleming Committee.

Emmeline Tanner evinced immense enjoyment in seeking out new experience and new people. It was this gusto, enthusiasm and humanity which marked her out as an exceptional educationist, campaigner and visionary: 'In dealing with young minds,' she believed, 'there must be open doors of possibility, even while we recognise that different minds find joy in different materials.'

Relying chiefly on unpublished material, *Doors of Possibility* examines the evolution of girls' secondary education between the 1880s and the 1940s. This book will appeal to both the general and professional educationalist, and the detailed biographical detail gives a glimpse into women's educational history during the late and post-Victorian eras.

Mary Slessor – Everybody's Mother

The Era and Impact of a Victorian Missionary

Jeanette Hardage

ISBN: 9780718891855
PDF ISBN: 9780718842024

This is a story of Mary Slessor, a petite redhead from the slums of Dundee who became one of the most influential people in a land known to her compatriots as 'the white man's grave'.

Despite her eccentricities, this woman truly understood and connected with the Africans among whom she lived, so much so that the British government appointed her their first woman magistrate anywhere in the world and later awarded her the highest honour then bestowed on a woman commoner.

Mary Slessor – Everybody's Mother examines the era and influence of this extraordinary woman, who spent thirty-eight years serving as a Presbyterian missionary in Calabar. This work not only answers questions about the public Mary Slessor, it also reveals aspects of her private life that the author has gathered from her own writings and those of others of her era, reminiscences of her adopted Nigerian son, and assessments from contemporary sources.

Slessor's audacity in remote areas of Nigeria contrasted with her timidity in public meetings in Scotland. She shunned the limelight and wondered why anyone would want to know about her. Her fame continues, especially in Nigeria and Scotland. She was certain God called her to serve in Calabar, the home she claimed as her own, where she became *eka kpukpru owo* – everybody's mother.

Available now with more excellent titles in Paperback, Hardback, PDF and Epub formats from the Lutterworth Press.

(L)